From Empiricism to Expressivism

From Empiricism to Expressivism

BRANDOM READS SELLARS

Robert B. Brandom

Harvard University Press

Cambridge, Massachusetts, and London, England • 2015

Copyright © 2015 by the President and Fellows of Harvard College
All rights reserved

Library of Congress Cataloging-in-Publication Data
Brandom, Robert.
　From empiricism to expressivism : Brandom reads Sellars / Robert B. Brandom.
　　pages cm
　Includes bibliographical references and index.
　ISBN 978-0-674-18728-3 (alk. paper)
　1. Sellars, Wilfrid. 2. Empiricism. 3. Pragmatism. 4. Expressivism (Ethics) I. Title.
　B945.S444B73 2014
　170'.42—dc23　　2014008332

Even without this explicit dedication,
it would be clear that this one is for Wilfrid

Contents

Title Abbreviations ... ix

Introduction ... 1

1 Categories and Noumena: Two Kantian Axes of Sellars's Thought ... 30

2 The Centrality of Sellars's Two-Ply Account of Observation to the Arguments of *Empiricism and the Philosophy of Mind* ... 99

3 Pragmatism, Inferentialism, and Modality in Sellars's Arguments against Empiricism ... 120

4 Modality and Normativity: From Hume and Quine to Kant and Sellars ... 145

5 Modal Expressivism and Modal Realism: Together Again ... 174

6 Sortals, Identity, and Modality: The Metaphysical Significance of the Modal Kant-Sellars Thesis ... 216

7 Sellars's Metalinguistic Expressivist Nominalism ... 236

Credits ... 273

Index ... 275

Title Abbreviations

EPM	*Empiricism and the Philosophy of Mind*
PPPW	*Pure Pragmatics and Possible Worlds: The Early Essays of Wilfrid Sellars*
CDCM	"Counterfactuals, Dispositions, and the Causal Modalities"
TTC	"Toward a Theory of the Categories"
RNWW	"Realism and the New Way of Words"
GE	"Grammar and Existence: A Preface to Ontology"
NS	"Naming and Saying"
AE	"Abstract Entities"
BSD	*Between Saying and Doing*

From Empiricism to Expressivism

Introduction

1. Kant, Pragmatism, and the "New Way of Words"

Wilfrid Stalker Sellars (1912–1989) was the greatest American philosopher of the middle years of the twentieth century. The depth, originality, and range of his philosophical thought earn him a place alongside Charles Sanders Peirce, the greatest American philosopher of an earlier generation. From the point of view of contemporary conventional opinion among Anglophone philosophers, this assessment is somewhat eccentric—though not quite idiosyncratic. There is no question that other American philosophers of the time were more influential than Sellars—of those with a large overlap of interests, W. V. O. Quine (1908–2000) being preeminent among them. But one can also gauge the importance of a philosopher by the wealth of ideas, connections, and projects he bequeaths, by their power and fecundity, their capacity for further development, their potential for further illumination. Peirce's scattered, fitful, frustrating writings remain a trove of mostly still-buried treasures. I find in Sellars's more systematic, sustained, if sometimes equally frustrating, writings correspondingly rich veins of philosophical ore.

It was obvious to his contemporaries that Sellars was not only an immensely talented philosopher, but one distinguished from his fellow analysts of the time both by his overtly *systematic* ambitions and by the self-consciously *historical* roots of his thought. Although his range of historical reference was very wide, the most important figure for Sellars always was Kant. The subtitle of his most systematic work, his 1966 John Locke lectures, is "Variations on Kantian Themes." Being avowedly interested in and influenced by Kant was unusual among analytic philosophers during the period of Sellars's *floruit* in the late fifties and early sixties. Bertrand Russell and G. E. Moore had forged the fighting faith of analytic philosophy in opposition to the then-dominant

British Idealism inspired by Hegel (the passion of their youth), which they properly saw as developing themes already implicit in Kant's transcendental idealism. The recoil from Kant in Sellars's philosophical culture circle was not universal. Of those with most influence on Sellars, C. I. Lewis was a self-professed neo-Kantian, who did more than anyone else to keep the teaching of the first Critique alive in American graduate schools of philosophy. And Sellars was in an ideal position to see how deeply influenced by his neo-Kantian background Rudolf Carnap was—perhaps better situated in this regard than Carnap himself.

The efforts in the late sixties of John Rawls in America and Peter Strawson in Britain ensured that Kant would be recovered for later generations not only for the Anglophone canon but as a party to contemporary philosophical conversation. Sellars's development of Kantian ideas in application to issues of current philosophical interest has yet to have its hearing, however. In Chapter 1 of this work, I talk about two major Kantian axes of Sellars's thought: his metalinguistic version of the Kantian idea of categories ("pure concepts of the Understanding") and his scientific naturalism as a version of Kant's distinction between phenomena and noumena. On the first topic, following out clues he finds in Carnap, he gives a metalinguistic reading of Kant's thought that, besides concepts used in empirical description and explanation, there are also concepts whose expressive role it is to make explicit necessary features of the framework that makes empirical description and explanation possible. On the second topic, he brings down to earth Kant's transcendental distinction between empirical appearances and noumenal reality by understanding it in terms of the distinction between what is expressible using the descriptive and explanatory resources of the "manifest image" of the common-sense lifeworld and what is expressible using the descriptive and explanatory resources of ideal natural science (natural science as it is at the Peircean "end of inquiry," construed as a regulative ideal).

One of Kant's big ideas is that what distinguishes judgments and intentional actions from the performances of nondiscursive creatures is that judgments and intentional actions are things we are in a distinctive sense *responsible* for, they are *commitments* of ours, they are exercises of *authority* on the part of their subjects. As such normative statuses, they are things our *rational entitlement* to which is always potentially at issue. That is, they come with a standing obligation to have *reasons* for them. Sellars takes over this idea, saying in one of the orienting passages of *Empiricism and the Philosophy of Mind*:

> [In] characterizing an episode or a state as that of *knowing*, we are not giving an empirical description of that episode or state; we are placing it in the logical space of reasons, of justifying and being able to justify what one says.[1]

Sellars draws from Kant the insight that epistemic, semantic, and intentional vocabulary is all "fraught with ought," as he puts it. Understanding what we are doing when we offer empirical descriptions and explanations requires appreciating the normative character of the space of reasons in which those descriptions and explanations are situated.

Early on he sets the goal of clearing room for a view that goes beyond what he refers to as 'descriptivism' or 'factualism', a view that sees all claims as 'empirical' in a narrow sense.

> [O]nce the tautology 'The world is described by descriptive concepts' is freed from the idea that the business of all non-logical concepts is to describe, the way is clear to an *ungrudging* recognition that many expressions which empiricists have relegated to second-class citizenship in discourse are not *inferior*, just *different*.[2]

His particular target in the essay from which this passage is drawn is alethic modal vocabulary: the language of subjunctive conditionals and of the expression of the laws of nature. The normative vocabulary whose expressive

---

1. In Herbert Feigl and Michael Scriven (eds.), *Minnesota Studies in the Philosophy of Science*, vol. I (Minneapolis: University of Minnesota Press, 1956); reprinted in Sellars's *Science, Perception, and Reality* (London: Routledge and Kegan Paul, 1956; reissued Atascadero, CA: Ridgeview, 1991); reprinted as a monograph, with an Introduction by Richard Rorty and a Study Guide by Robert Brandom (Cambridge, MA: Harvard University Press, 1997), §36. Hereafter *EPM*.

2. "Counterfactuals, Dispositions, and the Causal Modalities," in H. Feigl, M. Scriven, and G. Maxwell (eds.), *Minnesota Studies in the Philosophy of Science*, vol. II (Minneapolis: University of Minnesota Press, 1957), §79. Hereafter CDCM.

role is to make explicit the liability to demands for justification implicit in the application of concepts in claims to empirical knowledge and judgment generally equally fall within the scope of this dictum. Modal and normative vocabulary, together with ontologically categorizing vocabulary such as 'property', 'universal', and 'proposition' are not for Sellars to be understood as in the first instance describing the empirical world. They rather serve the function I described above as categorial in Kant's sense: making explicit features of the framework within which empirical description and explanation are possible.

In his earliest published writings, from 1947–48, Sellars announces himself a convert to what he calls "the new way of words"—going so far as to use that expression in two of his titles.[3] In general he means the methodological approach that Michael Dummett expresses by the slogan "Philosophy of language is first philosophy," and that Richard Rorty called the "linguistic turn." His own formulation is that "philosophy is properly conceived as the *pure theory of empirically meaningful languages.*"[4] This broad methodological approach comprises the dual commitments to understanding discursive (in the Kantian sense of concept-using) creatures first and foremost as language-using creatures, and to approaching philosophical problems through careful attention to the use of the vocabularies in which they are framed. The avatar of the new way of words for Sellars is Carnap. The feature of Carnap's views that made the scales fall from Sellars's eyes is his specification of a particular kind of vocabulary that is neither ground-level empirical descriptive vocabulary nor to be relegated to a sort of second-class status: *metalinguistic* vocabulary. The principal idea Sellars takes over from Carnap is that a properly ungrudging acknowledgment of the nondescriptive expressive role that some respectable forms of discourse might play can take the form of a metalinguistic reading of them. In this book, I pursue further what Sellars makes of this idea, in the first part of Chapter 1 and Chapters 4, 5, and 7.

When asked in conversation what he hoped the eventual effect of his work would be, Sellars replied that he hoped to begin moving analytic philosophy

---

3. "Realism and the New Way of Words" and "Epistemology and the New Way of Words," both reprinted in J. Sicha (ed.), *Pure Pragmatics and Possible Worlds: The Early Essays of Wilfrid Sellars* (Atascadero, CA: Ridgeview, 1980). Hereafter *PPPW*.

4. On the first page of "Epistemology and the New Way of Words," *PPPW*, p. 31.

from its Humean to its Kantian phase. Although he is best known for the strictures he put on empiricist epistemology by criticizing what he called the "Myth of the Given" that lies at its core, some of Sellars's most interesting ideas are constructive suggestions as to how Kantian insights can inform our thought about language. The project of updating Kant in the spirit of the new way of words, of bringing about a post-empiricist Kantian phase of analytic philosophy, is one still well worth engaging in today. Sellars's enterprise seems to me all the more interesting and promising because he combines these two lines of thought with a third: *pragmatism* of a recognizably late-Wittgensteinian sort. By 'pragmatism' in this connection I mean that the project of offering a metalinguistic reading of framework-explicating nondescriptive concepts such as modal, normative, and ontological ones is conducted in terms of *pragmatic* metavocabularies: vocabularies for talking about the *use* of expressions, about discursive social practices. One of the principal aims of this book is to recover a strand of Sellars's thought that is in danger of being overlooked: the essential role that pragmatism plays in working out his metalinguistic form of neo-Kantianism. (It is a central topic of Chapters 1, 3 through 5, and 7.)

One reason this line of thought is easily overlooked is that Sellars never explicitly identified himself with pragmatism. The tradition of American philosophy from which he thought of himself as converting to Carnapian logical analysis in the forties was rather that of his father, Roy Wood Sellars, and the circle of other (now little read) philosophers with whom he debated issues of direct realism, representational realism, and critical realism: figures such as Edwin Bissell Holt, William Pepperell Montague, and Ralph Barton Perry. This group defined itself in no small part by its opposition to Deweyan pragmatism, on the one hand, and to the neo-Hegelian idealists downstream from Josiah Royce, on the other. Nonetheless, like Quine—who also never thought of himself as a pragmatist—Sellars, if I read him right, did assail empiricism from a pragmatist direction. That he nonetheless never thought of himself as a pragmatist is due, I think, to his emerging from the particular cultural background he did. He says:

> I cut my teeth on issues dividing Idealist and Realist and, indeed, the various competing forms of upstart Realism. I saw them at the beginning through my father's eyes, and perhaps for that reason never got

into Pragmatism. He regarded it as shifty, ambiguous, and indecisive.... Pragmatism seemed all method and no result.[5]

I owe to Richard Rorty the idea that in spite of this attitude, Sellars should nonetheless be thought of as pursuing a pragmatist argument. In a line of thought taken up and developed with great panache by Michael Williams, Rorty saw Sellars and Quine as mounting complementary assaults on the epistemological foundationalism central to both traditional and logical empiricism.[6] According to this story, modern foundationalists respond to the traditional epistemological Agrippan trilemma by rejecting the possibilities of an infinite regress of justification and of circular (or "coherentist") justification and embracing a distinguished set of regress-stopping beliefs. Doing so requires two sorts of "epistemically privileged representations" (in Rorty's phrase).[7] The regress on the side of *premises* is to be stopped by appeal to certain knowledge in the form of the *sensory given*. The regress on the side of justifying *inferences* is to be stopped by appeal to certain knowledge in the form of formulations of connections among claims that are *analytic* of their *meanings*. These two sorts of regress-stoppers, one on the side of *content* and the other of *form*, correspond to the two components of logical empiricism.

Sellars argues that only what is conceptually contentful can serve as evidence, can provide reasons for other beliefs. And he argues that even belief-types whose tokens arise noninferentially must be inferentially related to other concepts and belief-types in order to be conceptually contentful. Belief-tokens playing the functional role of reports, of noninferentially acquired discursive entry moves, do not form an autonomous stratum of discourse. They can be understood as conceptually contentful only in virtue of their inferential connections to token beliefs that do *not* play this reporting functional role, but are arrived at as the conclusion of inferences. This

---

5. *Naturalism and Ontology* (Atascadero, CA: Ridgeview, 1979), p. 1. I am grateful to Boris Brandhoff for pointing out this passage.

6. Michael Williams, *Groundless Belief*, 2nd ed. (Princeton, NJ: Princeton University Press, 1999; originally published by Blackwell in 1977). *Locus classicus* for Sellars's argument is *EPM* (1956) and for Quine's, "Two Dogmas of Empiricism," in *From a Logical Point of View* (Cambridge, MA: Harvard University Press, 1953).

7. In his classic *Philosophy and the Mirror of Nature* (Princeton, NJ: Princeton University Press, 1979).

picture rules out the semantic atomism on which the foundational epistemological role of the sensory given was premised. Quine makes a corresponding argument concerning claims supposed to be independent of factual claims because made true by meanings alone. He looks in vain for a difference in the *use* of claims whose truth turns on matters of empirical fact and those whose truth turns solely on the meanings of terms. More deeply, he finds reason to deny the supposed *independence* of meaning claims from factual claims. Not only do the meanings in question depend on very general matters of fact, that meaning-analytic claims can be held onto in spite of changes in empirical commitments is at best a local and temporary function of the role they play in the whole "web of belief."

Both these lines of argument begin by looking at the *use* of expressions in virtue of which they express the conceptual contents they do. In each case, that *pragmatic* investigation yields the conclusion that it is playing a distinctive kind of functional role in a larger conceptual system that confers on states, judgments, or expressions the epistemic privilege on which foundationalists rely. But the epistemological uses to which foundationalists want to put these "privileged representations," on the side of perceptual experience and meaning, require that such representations form an autonomous stratum, in the sense that these representations could have the contents they do independently of their relation to the riskier factual claims to which they are inferentially related. The pragmatic investigation rules out the semantic atomism that is presupposed by the claim of semantic autonomy. This line of thought, leading from pragmatic functionalism through semantic holism to deny epistemological foundationalism, is the common *pragmatist* core of Sellars's and Quine's complementary mid-century assaults on empiricism. (I discuss the role of pragmatism in *EPM* further in Chapter 3.)

In a break with tradition, Sellars considers pragmatics not as a discipline on a level with and alongside syntax and semantics, but as the genus of which they are species. That is, he calls the "pure theory of empirically meaningful languages," with which he identified philosophy in the passage cited above from "Epistemology and the New Way of Words," *pure pragmatics,* and says, continuing that passage, that "pure semantics, as it now exists, is but a fragment of such a theory." His idea is that pragmatics is the study of the *use* of language. Semantics, the study of meaning, is an attempt to codify certain aspects of such use, as is syntax. When Sellars takes over from Carnap the idea that the way to work out an "ungrudging recognition that many expressions which empiricists have relegated to second-class citizenship in discourse are not *inferior,* just *different*" is to understand such potentially philosophically problematic concepts as those expressed by alethic modal vocabulary, normative vocabulary, intentional vocabulary, and ontological-categorial vocabulary (such as 'property' and 'proposition') as *metalinguistic,* the metalanguages he has in mind are *pragmatic* metalanguages. "Pure pragmatics" is the project of developing a *general* pragmatic metavocabulary for specifying the use of *any* language in which empirical description is possible. His argument for semantic holism (and hence against epistemological foundationalism) is an argument conducted in such a pragmatic metavocabulary. This order of explanation is the pragmatist strand in Sellars's thought.

The Sellarsian philosophical project I see as still worth our attention is interesting because it is an attempt to weave together these three strands: the "new way of words," a form of pragmatism specifically adapted to the linguistic turn, and a specifically Kantian successor to empiricist theories of concepts and the discursive generally. It aims to construct a philosophy of language, thought of as first philosophy, in the form of a "pure pragmatics," that is, to transpose Kant's semantic insights into a pragmatist key. Sellars did not succeed in developing a pure pragmatics in this sense. But he made important progress in assembling key metaconceptual elements of an antidescriptivist, post-empiricist Kantian philosophy of language. In Chapter 1, I concentrate on some Kantian themes that unify Sellars's later work, and how that work can be understood as putting in place the lineaments of a pragmatist expressivism that is a worthy successor to the empiricism he inherited. Later chapters go into more detail concerning the ideas and arguments introduced there. My concern throughout is not just to expound or interpret Sellars's ideas, but to work with them, to try to develop and improve them so as better to address the topics with which he was concerned, and with which we are still concerned today.

2. Contingencies of Biography

I acknowledged at the outset of this Introduction that taking a serious philosophic interest in Sellars's writings must still be counted a somewhat eccentric attitude these days. I suppose that not a few of my contemporaries might well think that in my case this focus is a product of my having spent my entire professional career since graduate school at the University of Pittsburgh, where Sellars is revered (in my view, of course, justly). Such an explanation would get things almost exactly backwards. I followed Sellars to Pitt, and since I've been there I have made it my business to make his ideas more generally known—not the least by seeing to it that our doctoral students are at least exposed to those ideas.

When I came to the Yale philosophy department as an undergraduate in 1968, Sellars had been gone for five years, having left for Pitt in 1963. He enjoyed a reputation for depth and brilliance, but left behind no-one who taught his work. Still, he was enough of a 'figure' to motivate me to burrow into *Empiricism and the Philosophy of Mind* on my own. It seemed to me to offer a fresh perspective on both the topics of its title, and to hold the promise to illuminate many further ones. I attended a lecture that Rorty gave at Yale (his graduate *alma mater*) in which he talked a lot about Sellars, and I became convinced that Sellars's work offered a perspective that might make possible the synthesis of my two great interests at the time: technical analytic philosophy of language (I had come to philosophy from mathematics, in which I did a joint major) and classical American pragmatism, particularly Peirce.

When I applied to graduate school, Pittsburgh and Princeton were at the top of my list (though I did apply to Harvard, too—as a backup): Pittsburgh principally because of Sellars and Princeton in no small part because of Rorty. In the end, the strength of the philosophy of language and logic at Princeton convinced me to go there. Saul Kripke, Donald Davidson (whose regular appointment was at Rockefeller, but who often taught seminars at Princeton), and Dana Scott were the big attractions on this front—though ironically Dana left to go to Carnegie Mellon, in Pittsburgh, the year I arrived. Though I was disappointed by this defection, it resulted in my taking every course David Lewis offered, and persuading him to cosupervise my dissertation (with Rorty). (I believe I am the only student on whom they ever collaborated in this capacity.) Rorty did teach Sellars often in his graduate seminars—these were the years during which he worked on a mimeographed "Study Guide" to *EPM*, which (with his permission) I used as the basis for the much more extensive one I later contributed to my edition of that classic work for Harvard University Press. My appreciation of and interest in

Sellars's work grew in step with my greater understanding of it. The bulk of my philosophical energy and attention in these years, though, was devoted to the philosophy of language. On this front the great task seemed to be to absorb and somehow synthesize the disparate influences percolating at Princeton in those years: the Quinean tradition downstream from *Word and Object*, in which Gilbert Harman (also a reader of Sellars) was passionately interested, the new modal semantics pursued in such different ways by Kripke and Lewis, Rorty's pragmatism (in which he took himself to be making common cause with Sellars, Davidson, and some aspects of Quine), and Michael Dummett, whose monumental *Frege's Philosophy of Language*, which appeared in 1974, was the single most important and influential contemporary work of philosophy for me during that time. Sellars was on a back burner, but never far from my mind.

When, in the fall of 1975, Pitt advertised a job, I realized that it was the opportunity of my life. Having regretfully turned away from Pitt and the opportunity to study with Sellars in favor of Princeton and all its opportunities, there was now the possibility of going to Pitt as Sellars's colleague—which would never have been possible had I gone there for my degree. (Though Anil Gupta, who got his degree from Pitt the same year I got my degree from Princeton, has finally found his way back—showing both that it can be done and how hard it is to leave.) To my immense gratification (both then and since), that is how things worked out.

I was soon to discover, however, that being an admirer of Sellars is one thing, and being a colleague of his something else. I had met him only once, when Rorty invited him to talk to one of his seminars at Princeton, and our interaction on that occasion was purely intellectual. I had no contact with him during the hiring process at Pitt—though my later experience of departmental dynamics strongly suggests that unless he had thought well enough of my work, no offer would have been forthcoming. My first face-to-face interaction with Sellars once I took up my duties fit a pattern with which I was to become familiar: cautious démarches on my part and basically friendly responses gruffly delivered on his. I addressed him as "Professor Sellars," and he replied that since we were colleagues he insisted I address him only as 'Wilfrid'. It took me a long time to feel at all comfortable doing so. The next time he spoke to me was a couple of weeks later, when he stopped me in the hall, looked me up and down, and demanded,

"Why do you dress like the guy who pumps my gas?" Wilfrid himself was always nattily dressed, typically in a style he had adopted during his Oxford days in the middle thirties. (I once saw him wearing spats.) I was twenty-six years old and did not (and do not today) dress like that. At a faculty cocktail party he hosted at his handsome house on the hill overlooking the campus I expressed admiration for the multi-thousand-gallon rough stone aquarium that dominated both the living room and the rear patio onto which it extended, injudiciously referring to it as a "fish pond." "It's for the water lilies—the fish are just a necessary evil of the ecology," he growled. I learned (too late) that he was a connoisseur of water lilies (Nymphaeaceae), devoting many hours to cultivating rare types, and especially esteeming their lily pads. In the end, I decided it was helpful to think of him as belonging in a box with one of the great literary heroes of my youth, Nero Wolfe—with his water lilies in place of Wolfe's orchids.

During my second year, a graduate student came to my office with some questions about an article I had extracted from a central chapter of my dissertation. It was a speculative construction inspired by some ideas of Dummett, called "Truth and Assertibility." We had a good talk, and at the end I asked him how he had happened to be reading it. He said that it had been the assigned reading and topic of discussion in Sellars's seminar that week. I knew nothing about this. When next I saw Wilfrid, I asked whether it was true that he had talked about some of my stuff in his seminar. He asked me why I wanted to know. I said he must know how thrilled I would be to hear it and how much it would mean to me. His retort was "It's none of your damn business what I talk about in my seminar."

The best table-talk I was exposed to was before and after Sellars's weekly poker games—which I joined for a while until the action got too intense for my meager skills and interest. When he wanted to be, Sellars was immensely charming and witty. He was a great bon vivant, well read on any number of nonphilosophical topics (not just water lilies) and a lively conversationalist. As an example, he originated the incompatible food triad challenge. He starts off by observing that it is a common occurrence that three *propositions* can be jointly incompatible, even though each pair of them is compatible. His own works are full of these, most famously the inconsistent triad in the opening sections of *EPM*. But even in ordinary life, we find examples such as "A is a green apple," "A is a ripe apple," and "A is a McIntosh apple." His challenge is to find a *perceptual* analog, specifically in the category of taste. By any standard of compatibility, find three foods each pair of which are compatible, but all three of which together are *not* compatible. This problem has achieved a small notoriety, and even a small literature of its own. The best solution I know is Beer, Whiskey, and 7-Up. Beer and Whiskey are a boilermaker, Whiskey and 7-Up is a Seven and Seven, Beer and 7-Up is a Shandy. But the three together are disgusting. In any case, given that the phenomenon of irreducible inconsistent triads is so ubiquitous in the *conceptual* realm, why is it so rare in the *perceptual* realm? Or is that too general a claim, because this is specific to the gustatory modality? Is there no olfactory analog? What would tactile, auditory, or visual versions look like?

On a number of occasions in these early years at Pitt I would make an appointment with his secretary to talk to him about his work. His office was not with the rest of ours; to begin with we were even in a different building, though the philosophy department eventually moved to the Cathedral of Learning where his office was. The reason is that when Wilfrid was being recruited from Yale in 1963, on the third and final campus visit he made, his final meeting was with the Provost, in the Provost's office. Sellars would tell the story this way. The Provost (the architect of the new philosophy department at Pitt, Charles Peake) said, "Professor Sellars, you have been wined and dined during your recruitment. I hope you know how important it is to us that we persuade you to join us. Is there anything that might make a difference to your decision that has *not* been addressed?" Wilfrid responded, "There is one thing, which I almost hesitate to mention, because one is supposed just to focus on the life of the mind. I do like my creature comforts, and a nice office would make a big difference." The Provost said, "I am so glad you brought that up. That is something we can do something about. What would you consider a nice office?" Wilfrid looked around the Provost's office and said, "This is a really nice office." Peake did not miss a beat: "Wilfrid, it's now *your* office." There was nothing Sellars appreciated so much as a grand gesture, and as he told the story, he accepted the position on the spot.

We had our best philosophical talks on these occasions in his office, but I have to say that they were largely unsatisfactory. For a surprisingly long time the form they took was that I would ask him a question about his views, and he would refer me to something he had written. I would say that I had read that, and still had the question. He would refer me to something else, which

I had typically also read. Eventually he would recommend some piece that I had *not* read, and send me off to do so. It became clear that Sellars just was not accustomed to talking about his work with people who were knowledgeable about it. He only rarely taught his own stuff in graduate seminars. His work seems to have been a largely solitary undertaking. We know now, from the correspondence in his Nachlass, that he did keep up a substantive weekly epistolary philosophical conversation with his father.

What Sellars and I talked about mostly was picturing. The idea of a nonnormative tracking relation between the use of discursive sign-designs and elements of the objective world—indeed, the idea of such a representational relation that extends well beyond the discursive realm to include animals and then-conjectured robots—appears already in Sellars's earliest papers and continues throughout his life. I was never able to understand how he understood such matter-of-factual picturing relations to be related to the normatively characterizable discursive practices that (he and I agreed) alone deserved to be thought of in genuinely *semantic* terms. Eventually he confessed that he did not take himself clearly to understand the relation, either. But he always insisted that there must be some such relation, and remained convinced that the dimension he called "picturing" must play an absolutely central role in our world-story of ourselves as knowers-and-agents-in-the-world. We both saw that it is in a story about how sign-designs can lead a double life, on the one hand as items caught up in a web of causal relations supporting subjunctively robust conditionals, and on the other as normatively characterizable as having proper and improper uses ("according to rules" as he thought of them, in good Kantian fashion) that his response must be found to the danger that a broadly Kantian approach to the discursive simply replaces a dualism of mind and matter with one of norm and fact. I was quite critical of his characterization of this amphibiousness, without having positive suggestions as to how one might better conceive it. I would not claim to have an adequate story about it today, but the issue has come to assume an importance for me of the same magnitude as it did for Sellars. The culminating Chapter 6 of *Between Saying and Doing* (the "far-off divine event towards which my whole creation moves"), "Intentionality as a Pragmatically Mediated Semantic Relation," sketches a way of thinking about deontic normative vocabulary and alethic modal vocabulary as articulating two aspects of the phenomenon of intentionality, downstream from what I call the normative and modal Kant-Sellars theses.

And at the center of my reading of, and interest in, Hegel's Absolute Idealism is a corresponding claim about the complementary relation between the deontic normative sense of "material incompatibility" (Hegel's "determinate negation") that applies to commitments of a single subject and the alethic modal sense that applies to properties of a single object. Subjects (exhibiting the structure Kant picked out as the "synthetic unity of apperception") *ought* not undertake incompatible commitments (in judging and acting) and objects *can* not exhibit incompatible properties. It is by treating commitments as incompatible in the first sense that subjects acknowledge properties as incompatible in the second sense. Although of course there would still *be* incompatibilities among objective properties even if there never had been normative discursive subjects, one cannot *understand* what it *means* to call properties incompatible in the alethic modal sense except by reference to the practices and activities of concept-mongering subjects. An important aspect of this view is expounded in Chapter 5 of this book.

What Sellars and I talked about more productively, from my point of view, was semantics, because that was what I most cared about. There were whole stretches of his corpus that we did *not* talk about. One topic that did not come up was modality—which I now see as the key to the issues we *did* discuss. Sellars really wrote only one piece on modality, "Counterfactuals, Dispositions, and the Causal Modalities." It is long and insightful, but in important ways, inconclusive. He never really figured out how to articulate the sense in which modal vocabulary should be thought of as "metalinguistic." I discuss his tribulations in this regard, and how I think they should be resolved, in Chapter 3 below. At the time I was not much interested in modality, in spite of having thought a lot about it as Lewis's student and having co-authored a book extending possible worlds semantics, since my principal aim then was to develop an *alternative* to understanding semantics in terms of modality. And Sellars was very conscious of the unsatisfactory condition of his own thought on this topic. We also did not talk about what is perhaps the most polished and well worked-out portion of his corpus: the treatment of nominalism about universals and other abstract entities. I simply could not understand why the author of *EPM* thought this was a topic of central philosophical significance. It seemed to me at best a minor, if pretty, *application* of a broadly functionalist inferentialist semantics. I finally come to terms with this part of his corpus in Chapter 7.

Another topic that loomed large in his corpus that we did not discuss, because I could see no productive way to do so, was his views about sensa. Particularly during the period when we spoke regularly, Sellars was concerned—I sometimes thought obsessed—with the question of what the scientific successor-notion might be to immediate phenomenal sensory experiences (his "sensa"). He had become convinced that the structural continuity of phenomenal color experience—the famous pink ice-cube thought experiment—could be leveraged into an argument that quantum mechanics could not be the form of the ultimate scientific description of reality. This was one motive for the development of his late ontology of pure processes.[8] I could not and cannot see the philosophical interest of this idea. If it was, indeed, a consequence of the scientific naturalism expressed in his famous *scientia mensura*, the claim that "in the dimension of describing and explaining the world, science is the measure of all things, of what is that it is, and of what is not that it is not,"[9] then this conclusion about the possibility of an armchair refutation of a relatively mature mathematized scientific theory seemed to me a *reductio* of that position. I have come to think of this descriptive privileging of natural science as the unfortunate result of a misplaced, if intelligibly motivated, attempt to naturalize Kant's transcendental distinction between phenomena and noumena in terms of the relations between what he called the "manifest image" and the "scientific image" of knowers and agents in the world. I develop this diagnosis of the origins of his idea and sketch the line of thought that leads me to reject it, in the second half of Chapter 1, and in Chapter 7 further expand on the argument concerning identity and modality, deriving from what I take to be Sellars's own better wisdom, upon which that line of thought principally depends.

When Sellars's scientific naturalism without descriptivism did come up—apart from what seems to me to be in any case the disastrous bridge (a bridge too far) to sensa (even though it anticipates some discussions in contemporary consciousness studies)—it was in connection with picturing. For it seemed to me that that contentious notion ran together issues about nonnormative representation relations with this scientific naturalism, and that

---

8. In his Carus lectures, "Foundations for a Metaphysics of Pure Process," published in *The Monist* 64(1) (1981): 3–90.
9. *EPM* §41.

progress might be made if we could disentangle them. Alas, we never (and, I believe, he never) did. By contrast, one place we *were* together—a point of mutually reassuring agreement—was with his scientific *realism* about theoretical entities. Sellars sensibly opposed instrumentalism about the ontological status of theoretically postulated entities, a position always tempting to empiricists (in his time, bracketed by Quine on "posits" early on and by van Fraassen in Sellars's last decade). The distinction between observable and theoretical things is, Sellars argues in *EPM*, *methodological* rather than *ontological*. It concerns how we know about things, rather than what kind of things they are. (Running these together he called the "Platonic fallacy.") Theoretical things are, by definition, ones we can only entitle ourselves to claims about by *inference*, whereas observable things are *also* accessible noninferentially. But this status is contingent and mutable, subject to historical development. Sellars had usefully applied this lesson to the philosophy of mind (and then to semantics). The "philosophical behaviorism" he favored—in opposition to the "logical behaviorism" (epitomized by Ryle), which he rejected—essentially consists in the analogy:

mental vocabulary : behavioral vocabulary
::
theoretical vocabulary : observational vocabulary.

Mental and intentional vocabulary need not and should not be thought of as *definable* in behavioral terms, but the point of introducing it is to *explain* facts statable in behavioral vocabulary. Two important sorts of mistakes are obviated by this way of thinking about things. In semantics, it permits one to reject the instrumentalism of Dummett's middle period, when he refused to postulate semantic theoretical entities ("meanings") that could not be defined in terms of what one had to be able to *do* to count as grasping or deploying them, specified in a rather restricted behavioral vocabulary. This "manifestability requirement" runs together the sensible idea that the point of postulating semantic entities is to explain behavior (specified, I want to say, with Wittgenstein, in a fairly richly normative vocabulary) with the optional and objectionable instrumentalism that insists on definability in behavioral terms. Second, it opens the way to *philosophical* theorizing that involves postulating unobservables (entities and properties available only inferentially) in both the philosophy of mind and semantics, subject to the methodological pragmatism that insists that the point of such theorizing must be explaining behavior, without the need to identify such philosophical theorizing with *scientific* theorizing. This permits one to accept, as Sellars does, the only claim that occurs verbatim in both the *Tractatus* and the *Philosophical Investigations*, namely, that "philosophy is not one of the natural sciences." Sellars and I were deeply together on the legitimacy of and need for systematic philosophical theorizing in this sense—as among my more immediate teachers, Lewis decidedly was and Rorty decidedly was not.

One main thing I took away from our talks did not concern Sellars's substantive philosophy, though. With only a few exceptions, he really did not add much in conversation to what I could already glean from his writings. The clarifications he offered when pressed were almost always in terms he had worked out in print. My main takeaway concerned not his philosophical views but his attitude toward his work and its reception. It became very clear that underneath Sellars's gruff, grumpy exterior (epitomized in some of the vignettes I recount above about our early interactions) was a vast reservoir of professional bitterness. He *knew* he had done philosophical work of the first importance, and deeply felt that it and he had not been appropriately acknowledged. I could not understand how the satisfaction he should take in having written what he had written would not be enough, all on its own, to compensate for any complaints he might have about his reception thus far, and to engender confidence that eventually his work would be duly appreciated. (I thought then as I more or less do now that anyone who had written *EPM* should die happy.) He longed for people to understand and appreciate his work as he understood and appreciated Kant's, but expressed the worry that it might take centuries in his case, as he thought it had in Kant's. I protested that I was on the case—but somehow he did not find that fact sufficiently reassuring.

It was only many years later, thinking about the shape his career had taken, that I began to understand the likely sources of his radical disaffection, and to sympathize somewhat. Sellars always found philosophical writing exceptionally difficult. He did not publish his first papers until he was thirty-five years old—late enough that his lack of publications was a serious issue in his academic career, and a contrast with his successful and productive philosopher father of which he was acutely aware. And the earliest papers are a mess, their narrative lines almost wholly swamped by detours and digressions. He later said he couldn't describe the flower in the crannied wall without, like Tennyson, seeing the whole world in it.[10] Major pieces written just after he turned forty are much more intelligibly written, including the classics "Inference and Meaning" (1953) and "Some Reflections on Language Games" (1954). There is no question, however, that his professional breakthrough came with what a half-century later is still visible as his masterpiece: the three lectures he gave at the University of London in 1956 that were later published as *Empiricism and the Philosophy of Mind*. The lectures were attended by a substantial selection of the most distinguished contemporary English philosophers (Ryle was his host). His lectures were a smash success, establishing him, in English eyes, as *the* coming American philosopher. Sellars cherished his student days at Oxford as a Rhodes scholar—it was when he decisively turned to philosophy as a career. So the approbation of the English philosophers was particularly satisfying. The London lectures also led immediately to his appointment at Yale, then the second most prestigious philosophy department in the country. Students flocked to him, and his work became the topic of a large number of Ph.D. dissertations. The years from the writing of *EPM* to the publication in 1963 of his first collection of papers, *Science, Perception, and Reality*, were incredibly productive. It is when he did much of his best work: besides *EPM* and the paper on modality it includes his classic "Phenomenalism," the groundbreaking trio of papers on nominalism ("Grammar and Existence: A Preface to Ontology," "Naming and Saying," "Abstract Entities"), "Being and Being Known," and his manifesto "Philosophy and the Scientific Image of Man."

In 1965, nine years after his triumphant London lectures, Sellars was invited back to England, to give the prestigious John Locke lectures at Oxford. Sellars worked hard on this lecture series, recognizing the invitation as the honor it is and wanting to confirm the acknowledged promise of

---

10. Flower in the crannied wall,

> I pluck you out of the crannies,
> I hold you here, root and all, in my hand,
> Little flower—but if I could understand
> What you are, root and all, and all in all,
> I should know what God and man is. (1863)

EPM by producing a masterpiece that would give substance and impetus to the development he desired and intended of Anglophone philosophy from its Humean empiricist youth to its mature Kantian phase. But his Oxford homecoming was a disaster. The first lecture was well attended, as everyone came to "see the elephant." But the material he presented in that lecture was exceptionally difficult. He had decided to emulate Kant's opening of the first Critique with the transcendental aesthetic. I do not myself think Kant did himself or his project any favors by starting this way, but be that as it may, Sellars certainly did not. After numerous readings, I was for many years not able to make much of this first chapter of the book that resulted, *Science and Metaphysics: Variations on Kantian Themes*, until John McDowell finally managed to explain it in his Woodbridge lectures. The thought of trying to follow this material as a lecture in real time is mind-boggling. In any case, the effect of that initial experience was devastating: the audience stayed away in droves. (John McDowell, then an undergraduate, attended only the first lecture, and professes not to have understood a word of it. He later, however, thought deeply about it, devoting his Woodbridge lectures at Columbia to discussing its ideas.) The last three of the six lectures were delivered in the same cavernous auditorium that had accommodated hundreds for the first lecture, but to an audience comprising only a half-dozen who had been hastily rounded up. It was a humiliation, and Sellars never got over it. When I visited him in his hospital room during the last week of his life he spontaneously brought up this experience as a turning-point in his life, something that had permanently darkened his outlook.

His Oxford experience was desperately disappointing to Sellars, but it came to epitomize a larger sea-change in his position in the discipline of which he could not help but feel the effects, while being too close to it to discern the causes. For he gave those lectures at the midpoint of a decade marked out in American philosophy by the publication of Quine's *Word and Object* in 1960 and Kripke's delivering the Princeton lectures published as *Naming and Necessity* in 1970. Sellars was forty-four when *EPM* came out and promised to secure him recognition as a preeminent philosopher of his generation. In the years that followed he continued to produce extraordinary work. But when he looked around a bare nine years later, after the debacle of his Locke lectures, he found himself confronted by a philosophical community that had decisively turned its attentions in other directions. Never again would he get the attention that he had had, and had earned. The Kantian *Kehre* of analytic philosophy was not taking place—indeed, it barely registered as a possibility. Sellars, I think, never knew what hit him. His writing in the seventies is vastly improved stylistically. He made great progress as a communicator in this medium. But nobody much seemed to care.

So the trajectory of Sellars's professional career was quite distinctive, unusual, and in the event disturbing to him. Although he began graduate study at a suitably early age (when he graduated from college and went to Oxford), and had been raised in a philosophical household (his father was department chair at Michigan), he began publishing only pretty late: he was thirty-five. Of course the war intervened, but he always claimed that his wartime service spent devising search-patterns for anti-submarine planes in the Atlantic gave him plenty of time for philosophical reflection. He achieved real recognition, and even celebrity only in 1956, when he was forty-four years old. There followed his greatest years of philosophical creativity and flourishing, during which he had every right to think he would take his rightful place as a preeminent figure in the discipline. But a mere nine years later, by 1965, when he was only fifty-three, it all seemed to come crashing down, and the rest of his life seemed anticlimactic. He was never again to reach the creative philosophical heights of those golden years, nor to achieve the professional recognition they seemed to promise. By the time I knew him, he had soured; his world tasted of ashes.

Sellars's own professional idiosyncrasies contributed significantly to the marginalization of his work that was set in motion by other, larger forces in the discipline. He was rightly known as a charismatic lecturer to undergraduates and a masterful Socratic seminar leader for doctoral students. Philosophers who were interested in his work but daunted by the difficulty of his writing naturally often responded by inviting him to give colloquium presentations, figuring they would come away at least with enough of an idea of what he was doing to be able to make a start on reading him. But Sellars firmly hewed to the view that it is disrespectful of one's colleagues to present finished work in a lecture that is not addressed primarily to students. He believed it implied that the lecturer thought conversation with his audience could contribute nothing to the thought-process the results of which he merely reported. (Is that in fact even true of a finished piece of writing?) So he only ever presented work in progress, the first crude and still confused formulations of ideas that were as yet inchoate. If he was hard to understand in his writings, when he knew what he thought, things were much worse when his complex thoughts were delivered raw, unformed, and untamed. These occasions were by no means always unsuccessful (he secured ongoing audiences at Notre Dame and Arizona, for instance, where his interlocutors were willing to invest sufficient effort across a number of occasions). But all too often they were, unnecessarily, discouraging philosophers who started with some motivation to try to figure him out. The result is that while Sellars always had readers and admirers, he remained a relatively unusual acquired taste within the larger philosophical community. To a first approximation, only people who had actually been taught by Sellars or been taught by people who had been taught by him, and the handful who had for some other reason been strongly motivated independently to put the effort into his work, appreciated his ideas. He never understood why that should be so, and he resented it.

Although Sellars seldom taught his own work, it has nonetheless been a part of the Pitt curriculum for many years. When I joined the department I went into rotation with my colleague Joe Camp in teaching a core seminar in epistemology (eventually one of those required of all doctoral students). He taught *EPM* early in the course, and when it was my turn, I did, too. It fit in perfectly with my Rorty-derived view that Sellars in *EPM* and Quine in "Two Dogmas of Empiricism" had between them dismantled the "privileged representations" postulated by empiricist foundationalists in order to stop regresses of justification. Sellars attacked the idea that one could stop justificatory regresses on the side of premises by finding an autonomous foundation in experiential episodes of the sensory given, and Quine attacked the idea that one could stop justificatory regresses on the side of inferences by appeal to those that were good simply in virtue of the meanings of the terms. Both of these assaults turned on pragmatist-functionalist claims about how expressions must be used or what role they must play in order to count as having contents of the sort empiricist epistemological arguments required. I also taught *EPM* in my undergraduate courses in the philosophy of mind. (It is in this connection that, with his permission and encouragement, I reworked Rorty's valuable study guide that I had used at Princeton into the altogether more substantial—and possibly also ideologically biased—form that appears in the Harvard University Press edition of *Empiricism and the Philosophy of Mind* that I edited.) When John McDowell joined the department in the mid-eighties, he continued this tradition of reading *EPM* in graduate courses. I never mentioned to Wilfrid that we were teaching *EPM* regularly—I had somehow gotten the impression it was none of his business what we taught in our seminars. In later years, though *EPM* was no longer a constant fixture in core courses, it came up often enough in other courses at Pitt that our graduate students remained very likely to have read it carefully. As they have grown up and fanned out across the profession, many of them have also been moved to teach *EPM* to their students. Appreciation of this master-work of Sellars is no longer exclusively a Pittsburgh phenomenon. I would like to think that Sellars would be gratified at the resurgence of interest in his work that we have begun to see in recent years.

3. The Present Volume

Empiricism as Sellars criticizes it in *EPM* is a kind of epistemological and, ultimately, semantic foundationalism. The argument he mounts against it turns on the denial of the *autonomy* of the stratum of experience the empiricist appeals to as the basis in terms of which empirical knowledge and indeed empirical meaningfulness are to be explained. The commitment to the autonomy of the empiricist basis—its independence from that which is to be explained in terms of it—is part of what Sellars means by saying that what he is objecting to is "the whole framework of Givenness." The argument comprises three interwoven strands. One principle element is the Kantian, antidescriptivist appreciation of the normative character of knowledge and meaning:

> [In] characterizing an episode or a state as that of *knowing,* we are not giving an empirical description of that episode or state; we are placing it in the logical space of reasons, of justifying and being able to justify what one says.[11]

The empiricist experiential Given must have a *normative* role: providing reasons or evidence for claims about how things empirically are. The issue he

---

11. *EPM* §36.

presses concerns the context within which something can (even potentially) have that sort of normative significance. Another major strand in the argument is then the denial of the *semantic atomism* implicit in the idea of an autonomous experiential stratum that can play an evidential role relative to objective empirical claims about what properties things have. Sellars's *inferentialist* approach to semantics is crucial to the holist alternative he presents. He understands conceptual content as essentially involving the inferential relations that such a content stands in to other such contents: its role in reasoning. On this view one cannot have *one* concept without having *many*. The conceptual contentfulness of experience, essential not only semantically but to the possibility of experience playing an evidential role by providing reasons for further claims (for Sellars, two sides of one coin), depends on the *inferential* relations such experiences stand in (at least to one another), and is not in principle intelligible just in terms of the role of experiences as *non*inferentially elicited responses. For Sellars experiences can underwrite *descriptions,* rather than merely classificatory *labels* only if and insofar as they are located "in a space of implications."[12] A stratum of experience construed as independent of any inferential relations does not qualify as *conceptually* contentful in the sense required for it to play an *evidential* role. The final strand in the argument is a pragmatic one. Semantic atomism fails because it ignores the *use* or *functional role* of expressions or experiential episodes (perhaps construed as tokenings in a language of thought) in virtue of which they deserve to count as contentful at all. In "Phenomenalism" Sellars also presents an important further argument against empiricism that turns on the implicitly modal character of empirical descriptive concepts (a Kantian point). I discuss this argument in Chapter 3.

I have always thought that these broadly Kantian anti-empiricist arguments of Sellars go deep enough to warrant serious attention to and admiration of his writings. And I have always admired Sellars's systematic theoretical ambitions. But I did not think I had a good grasp of the large-scale architecture of the "synoptic vision" he was constructing. In his methodological manifesto, "Philosophy and the Scientific Image of Man," Sellars characterizes philosophy as the attempt to understand "how things in the broadest possible sense of the term hang together in the broadest possible

---

12. CDCM §108.

sense of the term." For a dismayingly long time, I did not really see how all the pieces of his work hung together, even in the broadest possible sense of the term. I thought I had a good grip on the semantic and epistemological lessons of *EPM*, which I took to be the core of his philosophical contribution. But lots of the rest of the topics he addressed—his nominalism about abstract entities, his treatment of modality, his scientific naturalism, and much else seemed rather far removed from that core. I now think I do see how all these elements "hang together," and that sense is one of the things that I hope to convey in this book.

The key, it now seems to me, is to think about what, apart from the ideas he weaves together in *EPM*, Sellars gets from Kant. (In retrospect, this should perhaps all along have been the obvious strategy.) Chapter 1 is entitled "Categories and Noumena: Two Kantian Axes of Sellars's Thought." It sets out the broad outlines of two master-ideas that I see Sellars as taking from Kant and developing in his own way and for his own time. Together, I think they define the space in which the apparently disparate elements of Sellars's story "hang together." The first is a refinement of Sellars's anti-descriptivism. From the Kantian categories, the "pure concepts of the Understanding," Sellars distills the idea that besides concepts whose principal use is empirical description and explanation, there are concepts whose principal expressive role is rather to make explicit essential features of the framework within which empirical description and explanation are possible. From Carnap he takes the idea that the function of such concepts is broadly metalinguistic. Sellars does a lot of work sharpening his characterization of this distinctive conceptual role. Among the kinds of concepts that Sellars sees as playing such a role are alethic modal concepts, normative concepts, semantic and intentional concepts, and ontological-categorial concepts such as "property," "universal," and "proposition," along with the names of particular universals ("circularity," "redness") and propositions ("The fact that snow is white"). Although Sellars never puts the point quite this way, I think his treatment of all of these kinds of vocabulary—which the narrowly descriptivist empiricist fails to understand as "not inferior to, but merely different from" ordinary empirical descriptive vocabulary—belong together in a box with something like the Peircean label "A New Theory of the Categories." I say why I think that in the first half of Chapter 1. The absolutely central case of alethic modality is discussed in Chapters 3 through 6, where the categorial function is elaborated under the heading "the Kant-Sellars thesis about modality." There I not only try to understand Sellars's view, but also to develop and extend it, and to investigate some important consequences of accepting it. In Chapter 4 I also consider briefly how normative vocabulary and what it expresses fits into the picture. Chapter 7 then uses the idea of a new, broadly metalinguistic theory of the categories as a lens through which to view Sellars's nominalism, worked out in impressive detail in three long essays written between 1959 and 1963.

The second half of the first, orienting chapter offers a diagnosis of where Sellars's philosophical naturalism goes wrong, inviting him down a path that led to such extravagances as his doctrine of sensa. Sellars shaped his scientific naturalism as a detranscendentalized version of Kant's noumena/phenomena distinction. Whereas I think Sellars's new version of the categories is a great idea, eminently worthy of further development and exploitation in our own time, I think understanding the relation between the empirical descriptive resources of natural science, on the one hand, and the empirical descriptive resources of essentially every other form of discourse, on the other, on the model of noumena and phenomena—as representing ultimate reality by contrast to mere appearance—has disastrous consequences. I say how I think this works in Sellars, and why I think it is a bad way for him to develop his naturalism, in the second half of Chapter 1. I do not revisit it in the rest of the book, though the earlier argument turns on points that are further developed there, particularly in Chapter 6.

I think the structure of Sellars's project becomes much clearer when it is thought about as working within the axes defined by what he makes of the two Kantian ideas discussed in my first chapter. There I recommend adding this division to Rorty's distinction between left-wing and right-wing Sellarsians. In the body of this work I address primarily the categorial idea, since I am interested not only in interpreting Sellars, but also and primarily in developing those of his ideas that seem to me to provide the richest resources for thinking about philosophical problems today. Although there is of course much interest in philosophical naturalism, I do not know how to contribute helpfully to this discussion by drawing on what seems to me the deformation of Sellars's original naturalist motivation that resulted from forcing it into the mold of the phenomenon/noumenon distinction.

Chapter 2 offers a simplified exposition of what I take to be the principal arguments of *EPM*, showing how they arise out of a particular picture of what it is to use descriptive vocabulary *observationally*, that is, to make empirical *reports*. Chapter 3 deepens the discussion of the arguments against empiricism in *EPM* by placing them in the context of some of Sellars's other, nearly contemporary articles. It traces further, into those neighboring works, some strands of argumentation that intersect and are woven together in his critique of empiricism in its two principal then-extant forms: traditional and twentieth-century logical empiricism. One of those arguments, from his essay "Phenomenalism," turns on the fact that the use of the ordinary empirical descriptive vocabulary employed to say how things objectively are—the target vocabulary of phenomenalist attempts to reduce it to a purely experiential base vocabulary—implicitly involves alethic *modal* commitments. Modality has been anathema to a line of empiricist thought common to Hume and to Quine, and here Sellars exploits that fact as guiding us to a fatal flaw in phenomenalist forms of empiricism.

Chapter 4 pursues the topic of modality, following Sellars following Kant on the categorial status of modal concepts, filling in the sketch offered in the first half of Chapter 1. Specifically, this chapter looks at what I call the "modal Kant-Sellars thesis." This is the claim that in being able to use ordinary empirical descriptive vocabulary, one already knows how to do everything that one needs to know how to do, in principle, to use alethic modal vocabulary—in particular subjunctive conditionals. This is a thesis concerning the *use* of modal vocabulary; so it is a thesis in pragmatics, rather than semantics. And it concerns the relation between the use of modal vocabulary and the *use* of empirical descriptive vocabulary. It asserts a kind of pragmatic dependence, in the form of claiming the sufficiency of one set of practices or abilities for another. It is a way of making specific the idea that the use of modal vocabulary is "broadly metalinguistic." As I reconstruct it, it is the claim that the use of modal vocabulary can be *elaborated from* the use of descriptive vocabulary, and that it serves to *make explicit* features that are *implicit in* the use of descriptive vocabulary. This is a very special general *expressive role* that modal vocabulary can be taken to play. In fact, as Chapter 4 argues, the *normative* Kant-Sellars thesis claims that deontic normative vocabulary also plays an expressive role of this kind.

Chapter 5 further investigates and develops the particular kind of *pragmatic modal expressivism* that the previous chapter developed from Sellars's views. It addresses the crucial question of what sort of derivative descriptive role alethic modal vocabulary could be taken to play, compatible with understanding its use in the first instance in terms of the pragmatic expressive role it plays relative to vocabulary whose principal use is for description and explanation. That is, it considers what kind of *modal realism* is compatible with a broadly Sellarsian *modal expressivism* of the sort discussed in the previous chapter.

Chapter 6 then looks at some radical consequences for our views about sortals and identity that I argue follow from the broadly Sellarsian understanding of the expressive role distinctive of modal vocabulary epitomized in the modal Kant-Sellars thesis—as elaborated from and explicative of the use of empirical descriptive vocabulary. This chapter fills in the argument sketched in the second half of Chapter 1 against thinking of the objects and properties described in the manifest image as mere appearances of the reality that consists of the objects and properties described in the scientific image. For, it is claimed, when we appreciate the modal commitments implicit in the use of *all* empirical descriptive vocabulary, we see that strongly cross-sortal identity claims—those that link items falling under sortal predicates with different criteria of identity and individuation—are *never* true. Appearances to the contrary are due to the idea that one can restrict the properties governed by the indiscernibility of identity to *nonmodal* properties. But the claim that what is made explicit by alethic modal vocabulary is implicit in the use of even the most apparently nonmodal descriptive vocabulary says that this idea is mistaken. In the sense that would be required, there are no "nonmodal" properties. The claim that strongly cross-sortal identities are never true is a radical one. But if it is right, it rules out the sort of identities that are asserted by a scientific naturalism that endorses Sellars's *scientia mensura* and interprets it as requiring that when manifest-image expressions refer at all, they must refer to items referred to by expressions belonging to the scientific image. This is but one of the consequences for metaphysics of this consequence of the categorial character of modal concepts.

Finally, in Chapter 7, I consider Sellars's metalinguistic expressive nominalism about universals and other abstract entities. Here the focus is not on modality, but on a quite different range of concepts whose use Sellars understands as another important species of the same categorial pragmatic expressive genus as modal and normative vocabulary. Sellars's discussion of what is involved in talk about properties is not much considered in the large contemporary metaphysical literature on properties. That is a shame. He has a lot to offer.

What I think is right about what Sellars does here is the progress he makes in specifying a distinctive expressive role that ontologically categorizing vocabulary plays relative to the use of empirical descriptive vocabulary: the kind of functional classification he thinks it is performing. Sellars himself draws invidious nominalistic ontological conclusions from his characterization of the expressive role of this sort of vocabulary. He takes his account of that expressive role to show that it is wrong to think we are describing anything when we talk about properties, or referring to anything when we use terms like "circularity" or "redness." That is his nominalism. I close by arguing that he fails to show that we should draw these ontological conclusions from his convincing expressivist analysis of the use of this sort of vocabulary. This conclusion opens up space for elaboration of a kind of realism about universals and propositions that would be compatible with Sellars's expressivist account of the use of such vocabulary, by analogy to the reconciliation of modal expressivism and modal realism that proceeded by showing how what is expressed by modal vocabulary admits a *parasitic* descriptive function, which is argued for in Chapter 5. Alas, I am not currently in a position to elaborate an antinominalist realism about abstracta that would occupy the space opened up by my critical argument. (Such further clues as I have are contained in the argument at the end of "The Significance of Complex Numbers for Frege's Philosophy of Mathematics," which is Chapter 9 of *Tales of the Mighty Dead*, together with the discussion of the Julius Caesar problem in Chapter 8 of *TMD*.) The book leaves off within sight of the tantalizing possibility of such a realism compatible with pragmatic expressivism in this area, too, but without seeking to enter that Promised Land.

The attentive reader will notice that some quotations and discussions of the lessons I think should be learned from them are repeated across chapters. This is typically because they are central to my understanding of Sellars's enterprise and contribution. I have left them in place in spite of the repetition for the sake of clarity in the local narratives.

That there can be shown to be a kind of pragmatically metalinguistic expressive role common to Sellars's account of modality and the analysis of abstract-entity-talk that leads him to his special kind of ontological nominalism is a central criterion of adequacy of the account I have given in the first chapter of how disparate parts of Sellars's work are bound together by employing a common strategy of understanding important classes of concepts as playing expressive roles analogous to those of Kant's "pure categories of the Understanding," when that idea is transposed into a pragmatic metalinguistic key. That these various parts of Sellars's corpus are tied together in this way is not something he ever explicitly *says*. It is my description of what he in fact *does*. That the systematic character of Sellars's work can be illuminated by following this categorial Ariadne's thread from one region to another is the hypothesis I am arguing for in this book. In good Hegelian fashion, I am trying to understand Sellars better than he understood himself—and then to figure out where to go on from there. The title of this book, *From Empiricism to Expressivism*, is an attempt to characterize in general terms the trajectory that led him to a Kant-inspired pragmatic expressivism from the criticisms he mounted of empiricism—and has led me to try to push that line of thought further.

I wish that I could have figured out this story in time to try it out on Wilfrid. I feel as though I finally know what I *should* have been saying to him all those years ago. Now, it seems to me, we could *really* have a talk. But one of the happy features of conversations between philosophers is that they need not stop when one—or even both—of the parties dies. This one hasn't yet.

CHAPTER ONE

Categories and Noumena: Two Kantian Axes of Sellars's Thought

Part I: On the Way to a Theory of the Categories

1. Introduction

Several decades ago, Richard Rorty suggested that philosophical admirers of Wilfrid Sellars could be divided into two schools, defined by which of two famous passages from his masterwork *Empiricism and the Philosophy of Mind* are taken to express his most important insight:

> In the dimension of describing and explaining the world, science is the measure of all things, of what is that it is, and of what is not that it is not. (§41)

or

> [In] characterizing an episode or a state as that of *knowing*, we are not giving an empirical description of that episode or state; we are placing it in the logical space of reasons, of justifying and being able to justify what one says. (§36)[1]

---

1. In Herbert Feigl and Michael Scriven (eds.), *Minnesota Studies in the Philosophy of Science*, vol. I (Minneapolis: University of Minnesota Press, 1956); reprinted in Sellars's *Science, Perception, and Reality* (London: Routledge and Kegan Paul, 1956; reissued Atascadero, CA: Ridgeview, 1991); reprinted as a monograph, with an Introduction by Richard Rorty and a Study Guide by Robert Brandom (Cambridge, MA: Harvard University Press, 1997). Hereafter *EPM*.

The first passage, often called the *"scientia mensura,"* expresses a kind of scientific naturalism. Its opening qualification is important: there are other discursive and cognitive activities besides describing and explaining. The second passage says that characterizing something as a knowing is one of them. And indeed, Sellars means that in characterizing something even as a believing or a believable, as conceptually contentful at all, one is doing something other than describing it. One is placing the item in a normative space articulated by relations of what is a reason for what. Meaning, for him, is a normative phenomenon that does not fall within the descriptive realm over which natural science is authoritative.

Rorty called those impressed by the scientific naturalism epitomized in the *scientia mensura* "right-wing Sellarsians" and those impressed by the normative nonnaturalism about semantics expressed in the other passage "left-wing Sellarsians." Acknowledging the antecedents of this usage, he used to express the hope that right-wing and left-wing Sellarsians would be able to discuss their disagreements more amicably and irenically than did the right-wing and left-wing Hegelians, who, as he put it, "eventually sorted out their differences at a six-month-long seminar called 'the Battle of Stalingrad.'" According to this botanization, I am, like my teacher Rorty and my colleague John McDowell, a left-wing Sellarsian, by contrast to such eminent and admirable right-wing Sellarsians as Ruth Millikan, Jay Rosenberg, and Paul Churchland.

While I think Rorty's way of dividing things up is helpful, I want here to explore a different perspective on some of the same issues. I, too, will focus on two big ideas that orient Sellars's thought. I also want to say that one of them is a good idea and the other one on the whole is a bad idea—a structure that is in common between those who would self-identify as either right- or left-wing Sellarsians. And the one I want to reject is near and dear to the heart of the right-wing. But I want, first, to situate the ideas I'll consider in the context of Sellars's neo-Kantianism: they are his ways of working out central ideas of Kant's. Specifically, they are what Sellars makes of two fundamental ideas that are at the center of Kant's transcendental idealism: the metaconcept of *categories,* or *pure concepts of the understanding,* and the distinction between *phenomena* and *noumena.* The latter is a version of the distinction between appearance and reality, not in a light epistemological sense, but in the ontologically weighty sense that is given voice by the *scientia mensura*. I cannot say that these fall under the headings, respectively, of What Is Living and What Is Dead in Sellars's thought, since the sort of scientific naturalism he uses to interpret Kant's phenomena/noumena distinction is undoubtedly very widespread and influential in contemporary Anglophone philosophy. My aim here is threefold: to explain what I take it Sellars makes of these Kantian ideas, why I think the first line of thought is more promising than the second, and the way forward from each that seems to me most worth developing.

When asked what he hoped the effect of his work might be, Sellars said he would be happy if it helped usher analytic philosophy from its Humean into its Kantian phase. (*A propos* of this remark, Rorty also said, not without justice, that in these terms my own work could be seen as an effort to help clear the way from analytic philosophy's incipient Kantian phase to an eventual Hegelian one.)[2] Sellars tells us that his reading of Kant lies at the center of his work. He used that theme to structure his John Locke lectures, to the point of devoting the first lecture to presenting a version of the Transcendental Aesthetic with which Kant opens the *Critique of Pure Reason*. Those lectures, published as *Science and Metaphysics: Variations on Kantian Themes*, are Sellars's only book-length, systematic exposition of his views during his crucial middle period. The development of Kantian themes is not only self-consciously used to give that book its distinctive shape, but also implicitly determines the contours of Sellars's work as a whole. I think the best way to think about Sellars's work is as a continuation of the neo-Kantian tradition. In particular, I think he is the figure we should look to today in seeking an appropriation of Kant's theoretical philosophy that might be as fruitful as the appropriation of Kant's practical philosophy that Rawls initiated. On the theoretical side, Sellars was the greatest neo-Kantian philosopher of his generation.[3]

In fact, the most prominent neo-Kantians of the previous generation, C. I. Lewis and Rudolf Carnap, were among the most immediate influences on

---

2. In his Introduction to my Harvard University Press edition of *Empiricism and the Philosophy of Mind*.

3. His only rival for this accolade, I think, would be Peter Strawson, who certainly did a lot to make us realize that a reappropriation of some of Kant's theoretical philosophy might be a viable contemporary project. But I do not think of Peter Strawson's work as *systematically* neo-Kantian in the way I want to argue that Sellars's is.

Sellars's thought. Kant was the door through which Lewis found philosophy and, later, the common root to which he reverted in his attempt to reconcile what seemed right to him about the apparently antithetical views of his teachers, William James and Josiah Royce. (Had he instead been trying to synthesize Royce with Dewey, instead of James, he would have fetched up at Hegel.) In his 1929 *Mind and the World Order*, Lewis introduced as a central technical conception the notion of the sensory "Given," which Sellars would famously use (characteristically, without mentioning Lewis by name) as the paradigm of what he in *EPM* called the "Myth of the Given." (Indeed, shortly after his 1946 *An Analysis of Knowledge and Valuation*, which Sellars also clearly has in mind in *EPM*, Lewis wrote a piece addressing the question "Is the Givenness of the Given Given?" His answer was No: It is a necessary postulate of high philosophical theory, which dictates that without a sensory Given, empirical knowledge would be impossible.)

We shall see in subsequent chapters that Sellars modeled his own Kantian "metalinguistic" treatments of modality and the ontological status of universals explicitly on ideas of Carnap. Although, like Lewis, Carnap is not explicitly mentioned in *EPM*, his presence is registered for the philosophical cognoscenti Sellars took himself to be addressing there by the use of the Carnapian term "protocol sentence" (as well as Schlick's "Konstatierung") for noninferential observations. Unlike Lewis, Carnap actually stood in the line of inheritance of classical nineteenth-century German neo-Kantianism. His teacher, Bruno Bauch, was (like Heidegger) a student of Heinrich Rickert in Freiburg—who, with the older Wilhelm Windelband, led the Southwest or Baden neo-Kantian school. In spite of these antecedents, Bauch was in many ways closer to the Marburg neo-Kantians, Hermann Cohen and Paul Natorp, in reading Kant as first and foremost a philosopher of the natural sciences, mathematics, and logic. I suppose that if one had asked Carnap in what way his own work could be seen as a continuation of the neo-Kantian tradition of his teacher, he would first have identified with this Marburg neo-Kantian understanding of Kant, and then pointed to the *logical* element of his logical empiricism—itself a development of the pathbreaking work of Frege, Bauch's friend and colleague at Jena when Carnap studied with both there—as giving a precise and modern form to the conceptual element in empirical knowledge, which deserved to be seen as a worthy successor to Kant's own version of the conceptual.

If Lewis and Carnap do not immediately spring to mind as neo-Kantians, that is because each of them gave Kant an empiricist twist, which Sellars was concerned to undo. If you thought that Kant thought that the classical empiricists' Cartesian understanding of the sensory contribution to knowledge was pretty much all right, and just needed to be supplemented by an account of the independent contribution made by a conceptual element, you might well respond to the development of the new twentieth-century logic with a version of Kant that looks like Lewis's *Mind and the World Order* and *An Analysis of Knowledge and Valuation,* and Carnap's *Aufbau* (and for that matter, Nelson Goodman's *Structure of Appearance*). That assumption about Kant's understanding of the role played by sense experience in empirical knowledge is exactly what Sellars challenges in *EPM*.

One of the consequences of his doing that is to make visible the neo-Kantian strand in analytic philosophy that Lewis and Carnap each, in his own way, represented—and which Sellars and, in our own time, John McDowell further developed. Quine was a student of both Lewis and Carnap, and the Kantian element of the common empiricism he found congenial in their thought for him drops out entirely—even though the logic remains. His Lewis and his Carnap are much more congenial to a narrative of the history of analytic philosophy initiated by Bertrand Russell and G. E. Moore, according to which the movement is given its characteristic defining shape as a recoil from Hegel (seen through the lenses of the British Idealism of the waning years of the nineteenth century). They understood enough about the Kantian basis of Hegel's thought to know that a *holus bolus* rejection of Hegel required a diagnosis of the idealist rot as having set in already with Kant. This narrative does pick out one current in the analytic river—indeed, the one that makes necessary the reappropriation of the metaconceptual resources of Kant's theoretical philosophy in the late twentieth and early twenty-first centuries. But it was never the whole story.[4] The neo-Kantian tradition comprising Lewis, Carnap, and Sellars can be thought of as an undercurrent, somewhat occluded from view by the empiricist surface.

---

4. Paul Redding begins the process of recovering the necessary counter-narrative in the Introduction to his *Analytic Philosophy and the Return of Hegelian Thought* (Cambridge: Cambridge University Press, 2010).

2. Categories in Kant

Many Kantian themes run through Sellars's philosophy. I am going to focus on two master-ideas, each of which orients and ties together a number of otherwise apparently disparate aspects of his work. The first is the idea that besides concepts whose characteristic expressive job it is to describe and explain empirical goings-on, there are concepts whose characteristic expressive job it is to make explicit necessary structural features of the discursive framework within which alone description and explanation are possible. Failing to acknowledge and appreciate this crucial difference between the expressive roles different bits of vocabulary play is a perennial source of distinctively philosophical misunderstanding. In particular, Sellars thinks, attempting to understand concepts doing the second, framework-explicating sort of work on the model of those whose proper use is in empirical description and explanation is a fount of metaphysical and semantic confusion.[5] Among the vocabularies that play the second sort of role, Sellars includes *modal* vocabulary (not only the alethic, but also the deontic species), *semantic* vocabulary, *intentional* vocabulary, and *ontological-categorial* vocabulary (such as 'proposition', 'property' or 'universal', and 'object' or 'particular'). It is a mistake, he thinks, to understand the use of any of these sorts of vocabulary as fact-stating in the narrow sense that assimilates it to *describing* how the world is. It is a corresponding mistake to recoil from the metaphysical peculiarity and extravagance of the kinds of facts one must postulate in order to understand statements couched in these vocabularies as fact-stating in the narrow sense (e.g. normative facts, semantic facts, conditional facts, facts about abstract universals) by denying that such statements are legitimate, or even that they can be true. (Though to say that they are true is not, for Sellars, to describe them.) Both mistakes (the dogmatic metaphysical and the skeptical), though opposed to one another, stem from the common root of the *descriptivist fallacy*. That is the failure to see that some perfectly legitimate concepts do not play a narrowly descriptive role, but rather a different, explicative one with

---

5. Distinguishing two broadly different kinds of *use* bits of vocabulary can play does not entail that there are two corresponding kinds of *concepts*—even in the presence of the auxiliary Sellarsian hypothesis that grasp of a concept is mastery of the use of a word. Though I suppress the distinction between these two moves in these introductory formulations, it will become important later in the story.

respect to the practices of description and explanation. Following Carnap, Sellars instead analyzes the use of all these kinds of vocabulary as, each in its own distinctive way, "covertly metalinguistic."

In opposing a Procrustean descriptivism about the expressive roles locutions can play, Sellars makes common cause with the later Wittgenstein. For Wittgenstein, too, devotes a good deal of effort and attention to warning us of the dangers of being in thrall to ("bewitched by") a descriptivist picture. We must not simply assume that the job of all declarative sentences is to state facts ("I am in pain," "It is a fact that...."), that the job of all singular terms is to pick out objects ("*I* think...."), and so on. In addition to tools for attaching, detaching, and in general reshaping material objects (hammer and nails, saws, draw-knives, ...), the carpenter's tools also include plans, a foot-rule, level, pencil, and toolbelt. So, too, with discursive expressive ⁵tools⁵. Wittgenstein's expressive pluralism (language as a motley) certainly involves endorsement of the anti-descriptivism Sellars epitomizes by saying

> [O]nce the tautology 'The world is described by descriptive concepts' is freed from the idea that the business of all non-logical concepts is to describe, the way is clear to an *ungrudging* recognition that many expressions which empiricists have relegated to second-class citizenship in discourse are not *inferior,* just *different.*⁶

But Sellars differs from Wittgenstein in characterizing at least a broad class of nondescriptive vocabularies as playing generically the *same* expressive role. They are broadly metalinguistic locutions expressing necessary features of the framework of discursive practices that make description (and—so—explanation) possible. Of this broad binary distinction of expressive roles, with ordinary empirical descriptive vocabulary on one side and a whole range of apparently disparate vocabularies going into another class as "metalinguistic," there is, I think, no trace in Wittgenstein.⁷

---

6. "Counterfactuals, Dispositions, and the Causal Modalities," in H. Feigl, M. Scriven, and G. Maxwell (eds.), *Minnesota Studies in the Philosophy of Science*, vol. II (Minneapolis: University of Minnesota Press, 1957), §79. Hereafter CDCM.

7. The best candidate might be the discussion of "hinge propositions" in *On Certainty*. But the point there is, I think, different. In any case, Wittgenstein does not *generalize*

The division of expressive roles that I am claiming for Sellars binds together modal, semantic, intentional, and ontological-categorial vocabulary in opposition to empirical descriptive vocabularies and traces back to Kant's idea of "pure concepts of the understanding," or categories, which play quite a different expressive role from that of ordinary empirical descriptive concepts. The expressive role of pure concepts is, roughly, to make explicit what is implicit in the use of ground-level concepts: the conditions under which alone it is possible to apply them, which is to say, use them to make judgments. Though very differently conceived, Kant's distinction is in turn rooted in the epistemological difference Hume notices and elaborates between ordinary empirical descriptive concepts and concepts expressing lawful causal-explanatory connections between them. Hume, of course, drew skeptical conclusions from the observation that claims formulated in terms of the latter sort of concept could not be justified by the same sort of means used to justify claims formulated in terms of empirical descriptive concepts.

Kant, however, looks at Newton's formulation of the best empirical knowledge of his day and sees that the newly introduced concepts of <u>force</u> and <u>mass</u> are not intelligible apart from the laws that relate them. If we give up the claim that F equals m*a then we do not mean <u>force</u> and <u>mass</u>, but are using some at least slightly different concepts. (Galileo's geometrical version of the—late medieval—observable concept of <u>acceleration</u> *is* antecedently intelligible.) This leads Kant to two of his deepest and most characteristic metaconceptual innovations: thinking of statements of laws formulated using alethic modal concepts as making explicit rules for reasoning with ordinary empirical descriptive concepts, and understanding the contents of such concepts as articulated by those rules of reasoning with them.

This line of thought starts by revealing the semantic presuppositions of Hume's epistemological arguments. For Hume assumes that the contents of ordinary empirical descriptive concepts are intelligible antecedently to and independently of taking them to stand to one another in rule-governed inferential relations of the sort made explicit by modal concepts. Rejecting that semantic atomism then emerges as a way of denying the intelligibility of

---

the particular expressive role he is considering to anything like the extent I am claiming Sellars does.

the predicament Hume professes to find himself in: understanding ordinary empirical descriptive concepts perfectly well, but getting no grip thereby on the laws expressed by subjunctively robust rules relating them. Even though Kant took it that Hume's skeptical epistemological argument rested on a semantic mistake, from his point of view Hume's investigation had uncovered a crucial *semantic* difference between the expressive roles of different kinds of concepts. Once his attention had been directed to them, he set himself the task of explaining what was special about these *non*descriptive concepts.

Two features of Kant's account of the expressive role distinctive of the special class of concepts to which Hume had directed his attention are of particular importance for the story I am telling here. They are *categorial* concepts, and they are *pure* concepts. To say that they are 'categorial' in this context means that they make explicit aspects of the *form* of the conceptual as such. For Kant concepts are functions of judgment, that is, they are to be understood in terms of their role in judging. Categorial concepts express structural features of empirical descriptive judgments. What they make explicit is implicit in the capacity to make any judgments at all. This is what I meant when I said above that rather than describing how the world is, the expressive job of these concepts is to make explicit necessary features of the framework of discursive practices within which it is possible to describe how the world is. The paradigm here is the alethic modal concepts that articulate the subjunctively robust consequential relations among descriptive concepts.[8] It is those relations that make possible *explanations* of why one description applies because another does. That force *necessarily* equals the product of mass and acceleration means that one can explain the specific acceleration of a given mass by describing the force that was applied to it. (Of course, Kant also thinks that in articulating the structure of the judgeable as such, these concepts *thereby* articulate the structure of what is empirically *real:* the structure of *nature,* of the *objective world.* But this core thesis of his understanding of empirical realism within transcendental idealism is an optional additional claim, not entailed by the identification of a distinctive class of concepts as categories of the understanding.)

To say that these concepts are 'pure' is to say that they are available to concept-users (judgers = those who can understand, since for Kant the

---

8. Note that these concepts are *not* those Kant discusses under the heading of "Modality" but rather concern the hypothetical form of judgment.

understanding is the faculty of judgment) *a priori*.[9] Since what they express is implicit in any and every use of concepts to make empirical judgments, there is no *particular* such concept one must have or judgment one must make in order to be able to deploy the pure concepts of the understanding. To say that judgers can grasp these pure concepts *a priori* is *not* to say that they are *immediate* in the Cartesian sense of nonrepresentational. Precisely not. The sort of self-consciousness (awareness of structural features of the discursive as such) they make possible is mediated by those pure concepts. What was right about the Cartesian idea of the immediacy of self-consciousness is rather that these mediating concepts are available to every thinker *a priori*. Their grasp does not require grasp or deployment of any *particular* ground-level empirical concepts, but is *implicit* in the grasp or deployment of *any* such concepts. The way I will eventually recommend that we think about this distinctive *a prioricity* is that in being able to deploy ordinary empirical descriptive concepts one already knows how to do everything one needs to know how to do in order to be able to deploy the concepts that play the expressive role characteristic of concepts Kant picks out as "categorial" (as well as some that he does not).

3. Categories in Sellars

Sellars's development of Kant's idea of pure concepts of the understanding is articulated by two master-ideas. First, his successor metaconception comprises concepts that are in some broad sense *metalinguistic*.[10] In pursuing this line he follows Carnap, who, besides ground-level empirical descriptive vocabulary, allowed metalinguistic vocabulary as also legitimate in formal languages regimented to be perspicuous. Such metalinguistic vocabulary allows the formulation of explicit rules governing the use of descriptive locutions. Ontologically classifying terms such as 'object', 'property', and 'proposition' are "quasi-syntactical" metavocabulary corresponding to overtly syntactical expressions in a proper metalanguage such as 'singular

---

9. I take it that Kant always uses *"a priori"* and *"a posteriori"* as adverbs, modifying some verb of cognition, paradigmatically "know."
10. In Chapter 3 I discuss the sense in which "metalinguistic" should be understood in such formulations.

term', 'predicate', and 'declarative sentence'. They are used to formulate "L-rules," which specify the structure of the language in which empirical descriptions are to be expressed.[11] Alethic modal vocabulary is used to formulate "P-rules," which specify rules for reasoning with particular empirically contentful descriptive vocabulary. Carnap's neo-Kantianism does not extend to embracing the metaconcept of categories, which he identifies with the excesses of transcendental idealism. But in the expressions Carnap classifies as overtly or covertly metalinguistic, Sellars sees the raw materials for a more thoroughly Kantian successor conception to the idea of pure categories of the understanding.

The second strand guiding Sellars's reconceptualization of Kantian categories is his *semantic inferentialist* approach to understanding the contents of descriptive concepts. Sellars picks up on Kant's rejection of the semantic atomism characteristic of both the British empiricism of Locke and Hume that Kant was reacting to and of the logical empiricism of Carnap that Sellars was reacting to.[12] The way he works out the anti-atomist lesson he learns from Kant is in terms of the essential contribution made to the contents of ordinary empirical descriptive concepts by the inferential connections among them appealed to in *explanations* of why some descriptions apply to something in terms of other descriptions that apply to it.

> Although describing and explaining (predicting, retrodicting, understanding) are *distinguishable,* they are also, in an important sense, *inseparable.* It is only because the expressions in terms of which we describe objects, even such basic expressions as words for perceptible characteristics of molar objects, locate these objects in a space of implications, that they describe at all, rather than merely label. The descriptive and explanatory resources of language advance hand in hand.[13]

---

11. Chapter 7 discusses Sellars's view about this kind of locution.
12. "Another feature of the empiricist tradition is its 'logical atomism,' according to which every basic piece of empirical knowledge is logically independent of every other. Notice that this independence concerns not only *what* is known, but the *knowing* of it. The second dimension of this 'atomism' is of particular importance for understanding Kant's rejection of empiricism. . . ." Sellars, "Toward a Theory of the Categories," in *Essays in Philosophy and Its History* (Dordrecht: D. Reidel, 1974), §16.
13. CDCM §108.

This is a rich and suggestive passage. It is worth unpacking the claims it contains. It is framed by a distinction between a weaker notion, labeling, and a stronger one, describing. By 'labeling' Sellars means discriminating, in the sense of responding differentially. A linguistic expression is used as a label if its *whole* use is specified by the *circumstances* under which it is applied—the *antecedents* of its application. We might distinguish between three kinds of labels, depending on how we think of these circumstances or antecedents. First, one could look at what stimuli as a matter of fact elicit or in fact have elicited the response that is being understood as the application of a label. Second, one could look *dispositionally* at what stimuli *would* elicit the application of the label. Third, one could look at the circumstances in which the label is *appropriately* applied. What the three senses have in common is that they look only *up*stream, to the situations that have, would, or should prompt the use of the label. The first provides no constraint on future applications of the label—*que sera sera*—as familiar gerrymandering arguments about "going on in the same way" remind us. The second doesn't fund a notion of mistaken application. However one is disposed to apply the label is proper, as arguments summarized under the heading of "disjunctivitis" make clear. Only the third, normatively richer sense in which the semantics of a label consists in its circumstances of *appropriate* application (however the proprieties involved are understood) makes intelligible a notion of *mis*labeling.

Sellars wants to distinguish labeling in *all* of these senses from *describing*. The idea is that since labeling of any of these sorts looks only to the *circumstances* in which the label is, would be, or should be applied, expressions used with the semantics characteristic of labels address at most one of the two fundamental aspects of the use characteristic of descriptions. The rules for the use of labels tell us something about what is (or would be or should be) in effect so described, but say nothing at all about what it is described *as*. That, Sellars thinks, depends on the *consequences* of applying one description rather than another. The semantics of genuine descriptions must look downstream, as well as upstream. It is this additional feature of their use that distinguishes descriptions from labels. Here one might quibble verbally with Sellars's using 'label' and 'description' to describe expressions whose semantics depends on only one or on both of these dimensions of use. But it seems clear that a real semantic distinction is being marked.

Making a further move, Sellars understands those consequences of application of descriptions as essentially involving *inferential* connections to other descriptive concepts. This is what he means by saying that what distinguishes descriptions from labels is their situation in a "space of implications." We can think of these implications as specifying what other descriptions do, would, or should *follow from* the application of the initial, perhaps responsively elicited, description. As he is thinking of things, a description (correctly) applies to a range of things (for descriptive concepts used observationally, including those that are appropriately noninferentially differentially responded to by applying the concept), which are described *by* it. And it describes them *as* something from which a further set of descriptions (correctly) follows. Crucially, these further descriptions can themselves involve applications of descriptive concepts that also have *non*inferential (observational) circumstances of application. Descriptive concepts that have *only* inferential circumstances of application he calls 'theoretical' concepts.

In the opening sentence of the passage Sellars includes *understanding* as one of the phenomena he takes to be intricated with description in the way explaining is. Understanding a descriptive concept requires being able to place it in the "space of implications," partly in virtue of which it has the content that it does. This is in general a kind of knowing *how* rather than a kind of knowing *that:* being able to distinguish in practice the circumstances and consequences of application of the concept, when it is appropriately applied and what follows from so applying it. Grasping a concept in this sense is not an all-or-none thing. The ornithologist knows her way around inferentially in the vicinity of terms such as 'icterid' and 'passerine' much better than I do. A consequence of this way of understanding understanding is that one cannot grasp one concept without grasping many. This is Sellars's way of developing Kant's anti-atomist semantic insight.

Taking a further step (undertaking a commitment not yet obviously entailed by the ones attributed so far), Sellars also thinks that the inferences articulating the consequences of concepts used descriptively must always include *subjunctively robust* inferences. That is, the inferences making up the "space of implications" in virtue of which descriptive concepts have not only potentially atomistic circumstances of application but also non-atomistic relational consequences of application must extend to what other descriptions *would be* applicable if a given set of descriptions *were* applicable. For what Sellars means by 'explanation' is understanding the applicability of some descriptions as *explained by* the applicability of others according to just this kind of inference. This is, of course, just the sort of inferential connection that Hume's empiricist atomistic semantics for descriptive concepts, construing them as labels, could not underwrite. Sellars's conception of descriptions, as distinguished from labels, is his way of following out what he sees as Kant's anti-atomist semantic insight. *Modal* concepts make explicit these *necessary* inferential-consequential connections between descriptive concepts. They thereby perform the expressive role characteristic of Kantian categories: expressing essential features of the framework within which alone genuine description is possible.

All of this is meant to explicate what Sellars means by saying that "the descriptive and explanatory resources of language advance hand in hand." In addition to Kant's idea, Sellars here takes over Carnap's idea of understanding concepts whose paradigm is modal concepts as (in some sense) *metalinguistic*. The principal class of genuinely intelligible, nondefective nondescriptive vocabulary Carnap allows in *The Logical Syntax of Language* is syntactic metavocabulary and what he there calls "quasi-syntactical" vocabulary, which is covertly metalinguistic.[14] For Sellars, the *rules* which modal vocabulary expresses are rules for deploying linguistic locutions. Their "rulishness" is their subjunctive robustness. Following out this line of thought, Sellars takes it that "grasp of a concept is mastery of the use of a word." He then understands the metalinguistic features in question in terms of rules of *inference*, whose paradigms are Carnap's L-rules and P-rules. His generic term for the inferences that articulate the contents of ordinary empirical descriptive concepts is "material inferences." The term is chosen to contrast with inferences that are 'formal' in the sense of depending on *logical* form. In another early essay he lays out the options he considers like this:

... we have been led to distinguish the following six conceptions of the status of material rules of inference:

(1) Material rules are as essential to meaning (and hence to language and thought) as formal rules, contributing to the architectural detail of its structure within the flying buttresses of logical form.

14. R. Carnap, *The Logical Syntax of Language*, (London: Kegan Paul, 1937), §§63–70.

(2) While not essential to meaning, material rules of inference have an original authority not derived from formal rules, and play an indispensable role in our thinking on matters of fact.

(3) Same as (2) save that the acknowledgment of material rules of inference is held to be a dispensable feature of thought, at best a matter of convenience.

(4) Material rules of inference have a purely derivative authority, though they are genuinely rules of inference.

(5) The sentences which raise these puzzles about material rules of inference are merely abridged formulations of logically valid inferences. (Clearly the distinction between an inference and the formulation of an inference would have to be explored).

(6) Trains of thought which are said to be governed by "material rules of inference" are actually not inferences at all, but rather activated associations which mimic inference, concealing their intellectual nudity with stolen "therefores."[15]

His own position is that an expression has conceptual content conferred on it by being caught up in, playing a certain role in, material inferences:

> . . . it is the first (or "rationalistic") alternative to which we are committed. According to it, material transformation rules determine the descriptive meaning of the expressions of a language within the framework provided by its logical transformation rules. . . . In traditional language, the "content" of concepts as well as their logical "form" is determined by the rules of the Understanding.[16]

By "traditional language" here, he means Kantian language. The talk of "transformation rules" is, of course, Carnapian. In fact in this essay Sellars identifies his "material rules of inference" with Carnap's "P-rules."

---

15. Sellars, "Inference and Meaning," in J. Sicha (ed.), *Pure Pragmatics and Possible Worlds: The Early Essays of Wilfrid Sellars* (Atascadero, CA: Ridgeview, 1980), Reprinted in Kevin Scharp and Robert Brandom (eds.), *In the Space of Reasons: Selected Essays of Wilfrid Sellars* (Cambridge, MA: Harvard University Press, 2007), p. 317. Hereafter *PPPW*.

16. Sellars, "Inference and Meaning," *PPPW*, p. 336.

'Determine' is crucially ambiguous between 'constrain' and 'settle'—the difference corresponding to that between what I have elsewhere called 'weak' and 'strong' semantic inferentialism.

As already indicated, the material inferential rules that in one or another of these senses "determine the descriptive meaning of expressions" are for Sellars just the subjunctively robust, hence explanation-supporting ones. As he puts the point in the title of a long essay, he construes "Concepts as Involving Laws, and Inconceivable without Them." This is his response to Quine's implicit challenge in "Two Dogmas of Empiricism" to say what feature of their use distinguishes inferences determining conceptual contents from those that simply register matters of fact. Since empirical inquiry is generally required to determine what laws govern concepts such as copper, temperature, and mass, Sellars accepts the consequence that it plays the role not only of determining facts but also of improving our conceptions—of teaching us more about the concepts that articulate those facts by teaching us more about what really follows from what.

On this way of understanding conceptual content, the modal concepts that express the lawfulness of connections among concepts and so underwrite subjunctively robust implications—concepts such as law, necessity, and what is expressed by the use of the subjunctive mood—have a different status from those of ordinary empirical descriptive concepts. Rather than in the first instance describing how the world is, they make explicit features of the framework that makes such description possible. Because they play this distinctive framework-explicating role, what they express must be implicitly understood by anyone who can deploy *any* ground-level descriptive concepts. As I would like to put the point, in knowing how to (being able to) use any ordinary empirical descriptive vocabulary, each interlocutor already knows how to do everything she needs to know how to do in order to be able to deploy the modal locutions that register the subjunctive robustness of the inferences that determine the content of the descriptive concepts that vocabulary expresses. This is what Kant's idea that the pure concepts of the understanding are knowable *a priori* becomes when transposed into Sellars's framework.

The two lines of thought that orient Sellars's treatment of alethic modality, semantic inferentialism and a metalinguistic understanding of the expressive role characteristic of modal locutions, are epitomized in an early formulation:

I shall be interpreting our judgments to the effect that A causally necessitates B as the expression of a rule governing our use of the terms 'A' and 'B',[17]

where the rule in question is understood as a rule licensing subjunctively robust inferences. I have been filling in the claim that this overall approach to modality deserves to count as a development of Kant's notion of categories, pure concepts of the understanding, as concepts that make explicit features of the discursive framework that makes empirical description possible. Sellars himself, however, does not discuss this aspect of his work under that heading. When he talks about categories he turns instead to his nominalism about abstract entities. The central text here is "Toward a Theory of the Categories" of 1970.[18] The story he tells there begins with Aristotle's notion of categories (though he waves his hands wistfully at a discussion of its origins in Plato's *Sophist* that he feels he cannot shoehorn into the paper) as ontological *summa genera*. There he opposes an unobjectionable hierarchy:

Fido is a dachshund.
Fido is a dog.
Fido is a brute.
Fido is an animal.
Fido is a corporeal substance.
Fido is a substance.

to a potentially problematic one:

X is a red.
X is a color.
X is a perceptual quality.
X is a quality.[19]

---

17. Sellars, "Language, Rules, and Behavior," *PPPW*, footnote 2 to p. 296.
18. In L. Foster and J. W. Swanson (eds.), *Experience and Theory* (Amherst: University of Massachusetts Press, 1970), pp. 55–78; reprinted in *Essays in Philosophy and Its History*. Hereafter TTC.
19. TTC §10–11.

Categories and Noumena

The next decisive move in understanding the latter hierarchy he attributes to Ockham, whom he reads as transposing the discussion into a metalinguistic key. Ockham's strategy, he tells us, is to understand

(A) Man is a species.

as

(B) Man is a sortal mental term.[20]

while construing mental items as "analogous to linguistic expressions in overt speech."

This sketch sets up the transition to what Sellars makes of Kant's understanding of categories:

> What all this amounts to is that to apply Ockham's strategy to the theory of categories is to construe categories as classifications of conceptual items. This becomes, in Kant's hands, the idea that categories are the most generic functional classifications of the elements of judgments.[21]

At the end of this development from Aristotle through Ockham to Kant, he concludes:

> [I]nstead of being *summa genera* of entities which are objects 'in the world,' ... categories are *summa genera* of conceptual items.[22]

The account he goes on to expound in this essay, as well as in his other expositions of his nominalism about terms for qualities or properties, construes such terms metalinguistically, as referring to the inferential roles of the base-level concepts as used in empirical descriptions. I explain how I understand the view and the arguments on this topic in "Sellars's Metalinguistic Expressivist Nominalism" (Chapter 7 of this volume). Without going into

20. TTC §16.
21. TTC §22.
22. TTC §23.

that intricate view further here, the point I want to make is that although Sellars does not say so, the metaconceptual role he here explicitly puts forward as a successor-concept to Kant's notion of <u>category</u> is generically the same as that I have argued he takes alethic modal locutions to play. It is this capacious conception I want to build upon and develop further.

4. Categories Today

The general conception of pure categorial concepts that I have been attributing to Sellars, based on the commonalities visible in his treatment of alethic modal vocabulary and of abstract ontological vocabulary, develops Kant's idea by treating some vocabularies (and the concepts they express) as "covertly metalinguistic." This Sellarsian conception represents his development of Carnap's classification of some expressions as "quasi-syntactic." The underlying insight is that some important kinds of vocabularies that are not strictly or evidently metalinguistic are used not (only) to describe things, but in ways that (also) depend on the use of *other* vocabularies—paradigmatically, empirical descriptive ones.

The lessons I draw from the strengths and weaknesses of Sellars's successor-conception of the "pure concepts of the Understanding" are fourfold. That is, I think he is pointing toward an expressive role characteristic of some concepts and the vocabularies expressing them that has four distinctive features. First, these concepts express what I will call "pragmatically mediated semantic relations" between vocabularies. Second, these concepts play the expressive role of making explicit essential features of the use of some other vocabulary. Third, the proper use of these concepts can be systematically elaborated from the use of that other vocabulary. Fourth, the features of vocabulary(concept)-use they explicate are universal: they are features of any and every autonomous discursive practice. I think there are concepts that play this distinctive fourfold expressive role, and that a good thing to mean today by the term "category" is metaconcepts that do so.

Carnap and Tarski introduced the expression "metalanguage" for languages that let one talk about languages, with the examples of syntactic and semantic metalanguages. In his earliest writings, Sellars also talks about "pragmatic metalanguages," meaning languages for talking about the *use* of languages—rather than the syntactic or semantic properties of expressions.

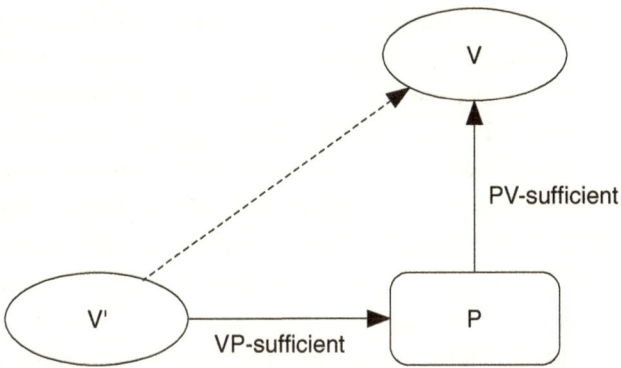

Figure 1.1 Meaning-use diagram representing the pragmatically mediated semantic relation of a pragmatic metavocabulary, V', to another vocabulary, V. P are the practices-or-abilities to deploy the vocabulary V.

These were to be the languages in which we conduct what he called "pure pragmatics." During and after Sellars's most important work in the *anni mirabiles* of 1954–63, however (possibly influenced by Carnap), he shifts to using the expression "semantics" to cover essentially the same ground. I think that this was a step backwards, and that it is one of the obstacles that prevented him from getting clear about the sense in which he wanted to claim that such locutions as alethic modal vocabulary and singular terms purporting to refer to universals ("circularity") and their kinds ("property") are "covertly metalinguistic." One vocabulary serving as a pragmatic metavocabulary for another is the most basic kind of pragmatically mediated semantic relation between vocabularies. It deserves to be called such because the *semantics* of the pragmatic metavocabulary depends on the *use* of the vocabulary for which it is a pragmatic metavocabulary. The relation itself is aptly called a "semantic" relation in the special case where one vocabulary is sufficient to specify practices or abilities whose exercise is sufficient to confer on another vocabulary the meanings that it expresses. We could represent such a semantic relation, mediated by the practices of using the second vocabulary that the first vocabulary specifies, as in Figure 1.1.[23]

23. I introduce, develop, and apply these "meaning-use diagrams" in *Between Saying and Doing: Towards an Analytic Pragmatism* (Oxford: Oxford University Press, 2008).

The pragmatically mediated semantic relation between vocabularies V′ and V, indicated by the dashed arrow, obtains when vocabulary V′ is expressively sufficient to *specify* practices-or-abilities P (that semantic fact about V′ with respect to P is here called "VP-sufficiency") that are sufficient to *deploy* the vocabulary V with the meanings that it expresses when so used. In asserting that this relation between vocabularies obtains, one is claiming that if all the sentences in V′ used to specify the practices-or-abilities P are true of P, then anyone engaging in those practices or exercising those abilities as specified in V′ is using the expressions of V with their proper meanings. This semantic relation between what is expressible in the two vocabularies is mediated by the practices P that the first specifies and which are the use of the second. This particular pragmatically mediated semantic relation holds when the vocabulary V′ allows one to *say* what one must *do* in order to *say* what can be said in the vocabulary V. In that sense V′ makes *explicit* (sayable, claimable) the practices-or-abilities *implicit* in using V. This is the explicative relation I mention as the second component of the complex expressive role that I am offering as a candidate for a contemporary successor-(meta)concept to Kant's (meta)concept of category. There are other pragmatically mediated semantic relations besides being a pragmatic metavocabulary in this sense, and others are involved in the categorial expressive role. The result will still fall under the general rubric that is the first condition: being a pragmatically mediated semantic relation.

One such further pragmatically mediated semantic relation between vocabularies holds when the practices PV-sufficient for deploying one vocabulary, though not themselves PV-sufficient for deploying a second one, can be systematically elaborated into such practices. That is, in being able to deploy the first vocabulary, one already knows how to do everything one needs to know how to do, in principle, to deploy the second. But those abilities must be suitably recruited and recombined. The paradigm here is *algorithmic* elaboration of one set of abilities into another. Thus, in the sense I am after, the capacities to do multiplication and subtraction are algorithmically elaborable into the capacity to do long division. *All* you need to learn how to do is to put together what you already know how to do in the right way—a way that can be specified by an algorithm. The diagram for this sort of pragmatically mediated semantic relation between vocabularies is shown in Figure 1.2.

Categories and Noumena

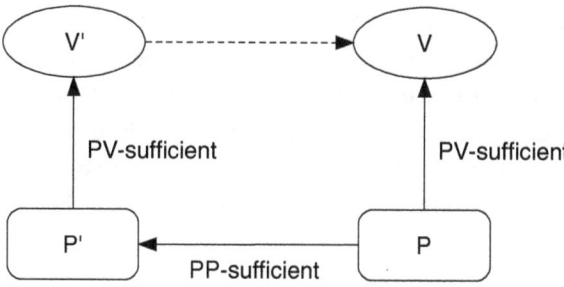

Figure 1.2 Meaning-use diagram representing the relation between two vocabularies, V' and V, that holds if the practices-or-abilities sufficient to deploy vocabulary V can be elaborated into practices sufficient to deploy vocabulary V'.

The dotted arrow indicates the semantic relation between vocabularies V' and V. It is the relation that holds when all the relations indicated by solid arrows hold—that is, when the practices-or-abilities sufficient to deploy vocabulary V can be elaborated into practices sufficient to deploy vocabulary V'. In this case, the semantic relation in question is mediated by two sets of practices-or-abilities: those sufficient to deploy the two vocabularies.

A concrete example of vocabularies standing in this pragmatically mediated semantic relation, I claim, is that of *conditionals* in relation to ordinary empirical descriptive (OED) vocabulary. For using such OED vocabulary, I claim (following Sellars following Kant), requires distinguishing in practice between materially good inferences involving descriptive predicates and ones that are not materially good. One need not be either infallible or omniscient in this regard, but unless one makes *some* such distinction, one cannot count as deploying the OED vocabulary in question. But in being able practically to distinguish (however fallibly and incompletely) between materially good and materially bad inferences, one knows how to do everything one needs to know how to do, in principle, to deploy conditionals. For conditionals can be introduced by recruiting those abilities in connection with the use of sentences formed from the old vocabulary by using the new vocabulary. On the side of circumstances of application (assertibility conditions), one must acknowledge commitment to the conditional p→q just in case one takes the inference from p to q to be a materially good one. And on the side of consequences of application, if one acknowledges commitment to the conditional p→q, then one must take the inference from p to q to be a materially good one. These rules constitute an algorithm for elaborating the ability to distinguish materially good from materially bad inferences using OED vocabulary (or any other vocabulary, for that matter) into the ability appropriately to use conditionals formed from that vocabulary: to distinguish when such conditionals are assertible, and what the consequences of their assertibility is.

My idea for a successor-concept to what Sellars (with hints from Carnap) made of Kant's metaconception of pure concepts of the Understanding is that they must play *both* of these expressive roles, stand in *both* sorts of pragmatically mediated semantic relations to another vocabulary. It must be possible to *elaborate* their use from the use of the index vocabulary, and they must *explicate* the use of that index vocabulary. Speaking more loosely, we can say that such concepts are both *elaborated from* and *explicative of* the use of other concepts—in short that they are el-ex, or just LX with respect to the index vocabulary.

The fourth condition I imposed above is that the concepts in question must be *universally* LX, by which I mean that they must be LX for every autonomous discursive practice (ADP)—every language game one could play though one played no other. That is, the practices from which their use can be elaborated and of which their use is explicative must be essential to talking or thinking at all. This universality would distinguish categorial concepts, in the sense being specified, from metaconcepts that were elaborated from and explicative of only some parasitic fragment of discourse—culinary, nautical, or theological vocabulary, for instance. I take it that any autonomous discursive practice must include the use of ordinary empirical descriptive vocabulary. If so, being LX for OED vocabulary would suffice for being *universally* LX, LX for every ADP.

Putting all these conditions together yields the diagram (shown in Figure 1.3) of the pragmatically mediated semantic relation between vocabularies that obtains when vocabulary V′ plays the expressive role of being universally LX by being elaboratable from and explicative of practices necessary for the deployment of ordinary empirical descriptive vocabulary.

The fact that the rounded rectangle labeled P″, representing the practices from which vocabulary V′ is elaborated and of which it is explicative, appears inside the rounded rectangle representing practices sufficient

Categories and Noumena

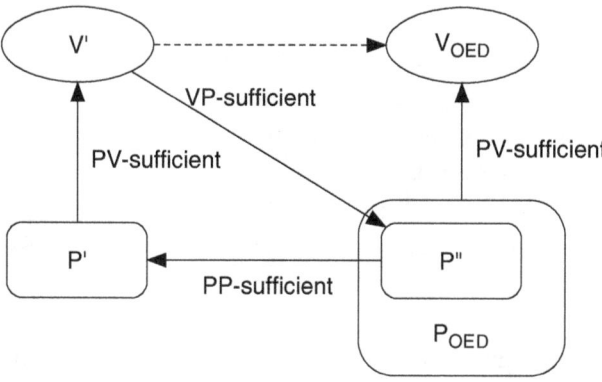

Figure 1.3 Meaning-use diagram representing the pragmatically mediated semantic relation between vocabularies that obtains when vocabulary V' plays the expressive role of being universally LX.

to deploy ordinary empirical descriptive vocabulary indicates that the practices P" are a necessary part of the practices sufficient to deploy OED vocabulary, but need not comprise all such practices. Thus, distinguishing materially good from materially bad inferences involving them is necessary for deploying ordinary empirical descriptive vocabulary (rather than mere labels), but there is a lot more involved in doing so—using such vocabulary observationally, for instance. Different categorial metaconcepts can be LX for different essential features of the use of empirical descriptive vocabulary. Thus alethic modal vocabulary explicates the subjunctive robustness of the inferences explicated by conditionals. "Quasi-syntactic" abstract ontological vocabulary such as 'property' and 'proposition' explicates structural features of descriptive sentences.

Diagramming the expressive role of being LX for practices necessary to deploy OED vocabulary provides an analysis that breaks down the claim that some vocabulary plays a categorial role into its component sub-claims. To show that alethic modal vocabulary, for instance, stands in this pragmatically mediated semantic relation to ordinary empirical descriptive vocabulary one must show that there are some practices-or-abilities (in this case, to reason subjunctively or counterfactually) that are 1) a necessary component of practices-or-abilities that are 2) PV-sufficient to deploy OED vocabulary, 3) from which one can elaborate practices-or-abilities that are 4) PV-sufficient to deploy vocabulary (alethic modal vocabulary) 5) that is VP-sufficient to explicate or specify the original practices-or-abilities. Although there is by design considerable elasticity in the concepts vocabulary, practices-or-abilities, and the various sufficiency and necessity relations between them, the fine structure of the distinctive expressive role in question is clearly specified.

What credentials does that expressive role have to pick out a worthy successor metaconcept to what Sellars made of Kant's categories or pure concepts of the Understanding? At the beginning of my story I introduced the idea behind the Kantian categories as the idea that besides the concepts whose principal use is in giving empirical descriptions and explanations, there are concepts whose principal use is in making explicit features of the framework that makes empirical description and explanation possible. The expressive task characteristic of concepts of this latter class is to articulate what Kant called the "transcendental conditions of experience." The concepts expressed by vocabularies that are LX for empirical descriptive vocabulary perform this defining task of concepts that are categories. As explicative of practices necessary for deploying vocabularies performing the complex expressive task of description and explanation (distinguishable only in the context of their complementary relations within a pragmatic and semantic context that necessarily involves both), this kind of vocabulary makes it possible to *say* what practitioners must be able to *do* in order to describe and explain how things empirically are. They do this by providing a pragmatic metavocabulary for describing and explaining. This is a central feature (the 'X' in 'LX') of the complex pragmatically mediated semantic relation between categorial metaconcepts and ordinary empirical descriptive vocabulary.

One feature of the concepts performing this explicative function that Kant emphasizes is that they are "*pure* concepts of the Understanding." (I take it that the "of" should be understood as expressing both the subjective and objective genitives—as in "Critique of Pure Reason." These concepts both belong to the Understanding and address it, being both discursive and metaconceptual.) To say that they are pure concepts is to say that they are graspable *a priori*.[24] The feature of the LX model that corresponds to the

---

24. Kant does admit also impure *a priori* principles.

a prioricity of Kant's categories is that the use of LX metaconcepts can be elaborated from that of the empirical descriptive vocabularies for which they are LX. As I have put the point, in knowing how to deploy OED vocabulary, one already knows how to do everything one needs to know how to do to deploy vocabulary that is LX for it—such as alethic modal vocabulary, conditionals, and ontological classificatory vocabulary. If we take it, as per Sellars, that grasp of a concept is mastery of the use of a word, then one need not *actually* grasp concepts that are LX for descriptive vocabulary in order to deploy descriptive vocabulary. But in effect, *all* one is missing are the words for them. The circumstances and consequences of application of LX concepts can be formulated by rules that appeal only to abilities one already has in virtue of being able to use OED vocabulary. (Think of the sample rules for conditionals sketched above.) In that sense, the LX concepts are *implicit in* the descriptive concepts. It is not that one must or could grasp these concepts *before* deploying descriptive concepts. It is rather that nothing more is required to grasp them than is required to deploy descriptive concepts, and there are no particular descriptive concepts one must be able to deploy, nor any particular descriptive claims that one must endorse, in order to possess abilities sufficient to deploy the universally LX metaconcepts.

The class of concepts that are arguably universally LX (LX for every autonomous discursive practice because LX for OED vocabulary) overlaps Kant's categories in important ways—most notably in the alethic modal concepts that make explicit subjunctively robust consequential relations among descriptive concepts. But the two do not simply coincide. Besides modal vocabulary, as I argue in *Between Saying and Doing*, logical vocabulary, indexical and demonstrative vocabulary, normative vocabulary, and semantic and intentional vocabulary all should be thought of as LX for OED vocabulary. In spite of this extensional divergence, the fact that vocabulary that is LX for descriptive vocabulary in general principle shares with Kant's categories the two crucial features of being explicative of such vocabulary and being graspable *a priori* makes the idea of universally LX metaconcepts a worthy successor to Kant's breakthrough idea. The fact that Sellars's own development of this idea of Kant's takes such important steps in this direction convinces me that his version of the categories was a progressive step, and a Good Idea.

Part II: Phenomena and Noumena

1. Introduction

I said at the outset that my aim in this chapter is to identify and assess two Kantian ideas that are central to Sellars's thought: what he makes of Kant's metaconcept of <u>categories</u> and what he makes of Kant's distinction between phenomena and noumena. Dividing things up this way provides a different perspective on Sellars from that provided by Rorty's left-wing/right-wing analysis, but like that one it invites one to take sides. I have now sketched how I see a theory of the categories as implicit in Sellars's treatment of modality and of ontologically categorizing vocabulary (even though he only makes the connection in the latter case). Subsequent chapters will further consider both his expressivist account of modality and his nominalist expressivism about properties, qualities, or universals. I have also indicated in general why I think his development of Kantian categories is a good idea, in terms of how I think it can be deepened and developed. I turn now to the second Kantian idea, which I think fares less well in Sellars's hands—and which for that reason I will not discuss further in the rest of this work.

Sellars identifies noumena, things as they are in themselves, the way things really are, with the eventual deliverances of natural science.

> As I see it, in any case, a consistent scientific realist must hold that the world of everyday experience is a phenomenal world in the Kantian sense, existing only as the contents of actual and obtainable conceptual representings, the obtainability of which is explained not, as for Kant, by things in themselves known only to God, but by scientific objects about which, barring catastrophe, we shall know more and more as the years go by.[25]

Science is to tell us what there really is; it is "the measure of all things, of those that are, that they are, and of those that are not, that they are not." Descriptions and explanations couched in other vocabularies present only appearances: phenomena. Where those appearances are appropriately

---

25. *Science and Metaphysics: Variations on Kantian Themes,* The John Locke Lectures for 1965–66 (London: Routledge and Kegan Paul, 1968), p. 173; reprinted by Ridgeview, 1992.

related to the realities described and explained by ultimate science, they are intelligible as appearances *of* those realities. Where they are not so related, they are *mere* appearances: illusions to be seen through or gotten over.

Sellars develops this idea in the context of his contrast between what he calls the "manifest image" and the "scientific image."[26] The scientific image consists exclusively of descriptions and explanations. That is why the *scientia mensura* begins with the crucial qualification "*In the dimension of describing and explaining the world,* science is the measure of all things, of what is that it is, and of what is not that it is not." That the expressive resources called on in description and explanation "advance hand in hand," so that these two come as a package, as we have seen him claiming, is the basis of the categorial status of the alethic modal vocabulary whose home language game is explanation. That alethic modal vocabulary has this categorial status is what in Chapters 4 through 6 I call the "Kant-Sellars thesis about modality." But essential as these activities of describing and explaining are, there is and must be more to discursive practice than just description and explanation. As Sellars says in the crucial anti-descriptivist passage I quoted at the beginning of Part I,

> [O]nce the tautology 'The world is described by descriptive concepts' is freed from the idea that the business of all non-logical concepts is to describe, the way is clear to an *ungrudging* recognition that many expressions which empiricists have relegated to second-class citizenship in discourse are not *inferior,* just *different.*[27]

So far in this chapter I have concentrated on the broadly metalinguistic nondescriptive functions performed by concepts that are categorial in being elaborated from and explicating of ordinary empirical descriptive concepts, which Sellars and I take to be essential to any autonomous discursive practice.[28] But Sellars emphasizes—and this is the doctrine seized upon by those Rorty calls "left-wing Sellarsians"—that besides the modal and ontological

---

26. In "Philosophy and the Scientific Image of Man," reprinted in *In the Space of Reasons.*
27. CDCM §79.
28. That and how metalinguistic categorical functioning of expressions can be compatible with *also* playing a descriptive role is explored for the central case of alethic modal vocabulary in Chapter 5, "Modal Expressivism and Modal Realism: Together Again."

vocabulary I have been discussing, *normative* vocabulary, too, is essential to any autonomous discursive practice.

Vocabulary that is, as Sellars puts it, "fraught with ought" is, in its core prescriptive function, for him the paradigm of a kind of locution whose principal use is *non*descriptive. Normative vocabulary accordingly is not drawn upon in articulating the scientific image of things. It belongs exclusively to the manifest image. In fact I think that normative vocabulary is categorial, in the sense I elaborate at the end of Part I: it can be elaborated from and is explicative of features necessarily exhibited by any autonomous discursive practice. As I shall use the term 'descriptive', it is a necessary condition of something's counting as descriptive vocabulary that there not be any other vocabulary to which it stands as pragmatic or semantic metavocabularies stand to the vocabularies for which they are metavocabularies, or as LX vocabularies stand to the vocabularies of which they are LX. That is, they must not be "metalinguistic" in the broad sense to which Sellars gives that term.[29] Because language used prescriptively is also an essential element of any autonomous discursive practice, the merely descriptive and explanatory language that makes the scientific image explicit does not comprise an autonomous discursive practice. It is and must necessarily remain parasitic, embedded in the wider context of the manifest image, on which it depends pragmatically and semantically. I take it that Sellars is right about this—an insight he shares with the Heidegger of *Sein und Zeit*.

But the language of the manifest image—the language of the ordinary lifeworld, both before and after the advent of modern science—deployed in any autonomous discursive practice, *also* deploys vocabulary to describe and explain its world. The question addressed by the *scientia mensura* concerns the relations between the descriptions and explanations whose home is in the manifest image and those whose home is in the scientific image.

---

29. More generally, no vocabulary whose use is properly characterized by a complex meaning-use diagram of the sort used to botanize "broadly metalinguistic" expressive roles in *Between Saying and Doing* will count as 'descriptive' in the sense I discuss in this part of the chapter. For our rough-and-ready purposes, we can treat any vocabulary that does not play such a role and occurs essentially in declarative sentences as descriptive. If it is suitably inferentially related to noninferential observation reports, then it counts as *empirical* descriptive vocabulary. (I'm not going to try here to fill in the notion of suitability being appealed to.)

The general tenor of Sellars's view is that the latter trump the former. But the *scientia mensura* passage goes farther than this vague and general claim. In assigning ultimate authority over *existence* claims to the technical language of eventual natural science (it is authoritative regarding "what is that it is, and ... what is not that it is not") this passage assigns the scientific image the role of arbiter of what is *real*, and consigns the descriptions of the manifest image to the role of expressing merely how things *appear*. Where for Kant, the deliverances of natural (Newtonian) science, no less than the descriptions of the manifest image, describe an empirical nature that belongs to the realm of phenomena, Sellars's detranscendentalized, naturalized version of the distinction has science limning the realm of the noumena. Kant's contrast between the phenomenal and the noumenal is reconstrued by Sellars to concern the relations between the descriptive resources of the manifest image and the descriptive resources of the scientific image. It is this Sellarsian development of this Kantian contrast with which I want to take issue. (So the stance I will be taking is anti-right-wing, but not because it appeals to left-wing premises—though I endorse these, too.)

This view is sometimes loosely referred to (even by Sellars himself) as Sellars's "scientific realism." That is a potentially misleading characterization. For one thing to mean by talk of his scientific *realism* is the view he opposes to *instrumentalism* about theoretical entities (which in turn must be strictly distinguished from the *nominalism* he endorses concerning *abstract* entities). Instrumentalism is the semantic and ontological view that only descriptive terms with observational reporting uses refer to anything. Purely theoretical terms—those without noninferential reporting uses—are understood as being merely calculational devices for making inferences that connect observables. As against such instrumentalism, Sellars understands the difference between terms with observational uses and purely theoretical terms to be *methodological*, rather than *ontological*. That is, the difference concerns *how* we know about something, rather than the *kind of thing* we know about. (Running these issues together is "the Platonic fallacy.") Purely theoretical objects are ones that are only epistemically accessible to us by means of inference, while observable objects are also epistemically accessible to us via noninferential reports—that is, judgments elicited by the exercise of reliable differential dispositions to respond to stimuli that are (for the most part) nonlinguistic.[30] Understood thus methodologically, the status of an object as theoretical or observable can change over time. When Pluto was first postulated, it was as a theoretical entity about which we could know only by making inferences from perturbations in the orbit of Neptune. With improvements in telescopy, looking at the calculated position of the hypothetical planetoid yielded the first observations of Pluto. It became, for the first time, observable. But *it* did not change ontological status; only its relation to us changed. Astronomers had been referring to the same planetoid, and knew things about it such as its orbit and mass, before it became observable—and would have done even if it had *never* become observable. A comparable story could be told about Mendelian genes.

I think Sellars is simply and evidently correct in endorsing scientific realism about theoretical entities, as opposed to any sort of instrumentalism. He applies this view in the philosophy of mind to yield important conclusions. For he understands behaviorism as instrumentalism about mental or psychological entities. Among the initially theoretical, postulated entities that later become observable on Sellars's account are thoughts and sense impressions, according to the Myth of Jones at the end of *Empiricism and the Philosophy of Mind*. It is of the essence of his "philosophical behaviorism," as opposed to Ryle's "logical behaviorism" (which requires strict definability of mental-theoretical vocabulary in terms of behavioral-observable vocabulary), to be realistic in this sense about theoretical entities postulated to explain observable behavior. Sellars distinguishes himself from Wittgenstein in just this way. (Dummett succumbs to a correspondingly objectionable instrumentalism in semantics when he insists on the "manifestability in linguistic behavior" of all features of meanings postulated to explain such behavior. One can understand the criteria of adequacy of semantic theories that postulate meanings as involving the success of the explanations of proper linguistic behavior they enable without insisting, instrumentalistically, that they can be *nothing but* proprieties of linguistic behavior, as Dummett has done. In this he follows Wittgenstein, who seems

---

30. I discuss Sellars's views about observation and observability further in Chapter 2, "The Centrality of Sellars's Two-Ply Account of Observation to the Arguments of *Empiricism and the Philosophy of Mind*."

to have thought that accepting the right of semantic theories to postulate unobservables would violate the claim—the only one to appear verbatim in both the *Tractatus* and the *Investigations*—that "Philosophy is not one of the natural sciences.")

But it is important to realize that scientific realism in this anti-instrumentalist sense in no way implies the reductive scientific naturalism expressed by the *scientia mensura*. Indeed, it is hard even to formulate auxiliary hypotheses which, conjoined with realism about theoretical entities, would entail the unique ontological authority of the descriptive vocabularies of the natural sciences. (If one claimed that *only* theoretical terms refer to what really exists, the converse of instrumentalism, one might be able to derive the stronger conclusion. But that would have the perverse consequence that it is *in principle* impossible to observe anything real. Such an extravagant anti-empiricist claim is in any case far from anything Sellars endorses.) Insisting that purely theoretical vocabulary (vocabulary whose circumstances of application are solely inferential) is in principle no less apt for having genuinely referential uses and being used to make true claims than terms that have observational uses (that is, that also have noninferential circumstances of application) does not involve any commitment to the differential ontological authority of some descriptive vocabulary (whether observational or theoretical) over other descriptive vocabulary. Anti-instrumentalist scientific realism is an *egalitarian* ontological thesis (opposed to the inegalitarianism of instrumentalism), while the whole point of the *scientia mensura* is ontological *in*egalitarianism. It is true that Sellars identifies the systematic methodology of postulating unobservables as a key feature differentiating the scientific from the manifest image. But even if this view were taken to the extreme of identifying every episode of such postulation, from pre-Socratic elements-theorists down to the present day (including the genius Jones), as the eruption of science within everyday life—the scientific image emerged, after all, *within* the manifest image—insisting on the at-least-equal ontological status of theoretical entities relative to observable ones does not underwrite the ontological privileging of scientific descriptive terms (including those with observational uses) over everyday ones. (The epistemological and methodological advantages of the scientific method of postulating unobservables is another matter.)

2. The Issue

The question Sellars's neo-Kantian reappropriation of the phenomena/noumena distinction addresses is how to understand the relations between the descriptive vocabulary native to the manifest image and the descriptive vocabulary native to the scientific image. The *scientia mensura* claims that the latter exercises final normative ontological authority over what does and does not really exist. I take it that this means that descriptive terms from the manifest image refer to things specifiable in descriptive terms from the scientific image, if they refer at all. The two images amount to two different realms of senses, picking out (if anything) the same referents—namely those picked out by the descriptive terms of the scientific image. This is what I shall mean by the "sense/reference scientific naturalist rendering of the phenomena/noumena distinction." I do not see what else it could mean to accord to natural science the status of being the measure of what is and what is not, i.e. of what exists and what does not. So if some nonscientific descriptive term refers to anything real (rather than presenting a mere appearance), it is only because it corefers with some scientific descriptive term (possibly a complex one). Coreference of terms is identity of objects. So to exist, the claim is, requires being identical to some object specifiable in the language of eventual natural science.

I don't think that is right, and I don't think a suitably enlightened naturalism requires such a commitment. I am not here going to try to demonstrate that Sellars is wrong on this point. I want instead to sketch the reasons that lead me to that conclusion, and to indicate briefly how we might think otherwise about things. The topic is a huge one, and I think it is something like as important for the philosophical enterprise as Sellars took it to be. So it is hardly the sort of issue it so much as makes sense to think of settling. Before outlining my rationale for thinking that Sellars is wrongheaded in pursuing the line of thought epitomized in the *scientia mensura*, though, I want to pause briefly to acknowledge that in the context of the present project there is a certain perversity involved in adopting the stance I am adopting. For of the two Kantian currents of thought in Sellars's thought I am concerned to identify and assess in this chapter, it is precisely his version of ontological scientific naturalism that has the most resonance on the contemporary philosophic scene. The idea of identifying a suitable successor-concept to

Kant's pure concepts of the Understanding and justifying its importance for understanding issues of recognized philosophical significance today is not one structuring much current research. Yet it is this idea, perhaps only implicit in Sellars's writings, that I want to recommend. The idea that expressly guides much of what he did—the idea of the ultimate ontological authority of natural science—which *does* motivate a lot of philosophers writing today, on the contrary, I want to disparage. This constellation of attitudes amounts to a peculiar strategy for one who wants, as I do, to argue that Sellars's work provides rich resources that can and ought to be mined by philosophers going forward. Nonetheless, it is precisely the less familiar and congenial ideas that seem to me the most valuable here.

Coreference claims and identity claims are different ways of making explicit intersubstitution licenses. The indiscernibility of identicals is one-half of Leibniz's Law articulating the content of identity claims (the other being the identity of indiscernibles). To say the objects referred to by expressions flanking an identity sign are indiscernible is to say that what is true of the one is true of the other: they have the same properties and stand in the same relations. And that is to say that a sentence of the form 'a=b' licenses inferences from sentences of the form 'Pa' to those of the form 'Pb', and *vice versa*. But there is a question of the scope or extent of this intersubstitution license. For 'a=b' does not license *every* inference from a sentence that can be written " . . . a____ " to " . . . b____ " and *vice versa*. For even though

1) Bob Dylan is (=) Bob Zimmerman,

from

2) No-one has ever doubted that everyone who believes that Bob Dylan wrote *Blowing in the Wind* believes that Bob Dylan wrote *Blowing in the Wind*,

it does not follow that

3) No-one has ever doubted that everyone who believes that Bob Dylan wrote *Blowing in the Wind* believes that Bob Zimmerman wrote *Blowing in the Wind*.

In the formal mode (in Carnap's terminology) we can say either that

4) "No-one has ever doubted that everyone who believes that Bob Dylan wrote *Blowing in the Wind* believes that . . . wrote *Blowing in the Wind*,"

is not a predicate that expresses a property, or that identity claims do not entail indiscernibility with respect to all properties. Quine regiments this distinction by saying that (4) is a context that is *referentially opaque:* coreference of terms does not license intersubstitution *salva veritate.* By contrast

5) " . . . is less than 6 feet tall,"

is a *referentially transparent* context, that is, one with respect to which identity claims *do* license intersubstitution.[31] Granted that there is a distinction between referentially opaque and referentially transparent contexts—which is to say between properties with respect to which identicals are indiscernible—how is the distinction to be drawn? In particular, where do sentential contexts containing alethic modal vocabulary belong?

3. A Diagnosis

Once upon a time, there was a doctrine I'll call "extensionalism" and Quine was its prophet. It has two parts: a view about a class of predicates (and the properties they express), called 'extensional', and a corresponding view about identity. The view about identity is that identicals are indiscernible only with respect to extensional predicates/properties. So for instance, modal predicates are not extensional in the privileged sense, and so are referentially opaque. The defining feature of extensional predicates/properties is that

---

31. 'Context' here means what in Chapter 7 of *Making It Explicit* (and Chapter 4 of *Articulating Reasons*) I call "sentence-frames" and Dummett calls "complex predicates." Frege thought of them as "concepts," which he understood in terms of thoughts (expressible by declarative, that is, assertible, sentences) with holes in them. They were "unsaturated" (ungesättigt). We can think of them, less puzzlingly, as expressed by equivalence classes of sentences, each of which can be turned into any other by substituting one singular term for another in what then shows up as an argument-place.

what they apply to in a given possible world, for instance, the actual world, depends only on what is true at that world. (Of course, this would not be Quine's favored way of specifying this feature.) They are in this sense modally *insulated,* in that their conditions of applicability (what they describe) are insulated from facts about what *would* happen if. . . . Extensionalism was inspired by model-theoretic semantics for some formal languages. In this sort of semantics, what a predicate applies to in a model depends only on that model, not on what is happening in other models. The extension of a predicate, what it applies to, can be identified just with a subset of the domain of that model. Possible worlds semantics, introduced on the basis of an extensional understanding of the basic predicates, then can introduce intensions, as functions from possible worlds (thought of as constrained models) to the extensions of predicates that are extensional in each world. On that basis one can for the first time come to understand predicates that are not modally insulated, but are, as I will say *modally involved* in the sense that what they apply to in a world *does* depend on what is happening in other possible worlds. But, the thought is, expressions that corefer in a world need not be indiscernible with respect to *these* properties. The intersubstitution inferences licensed by simple identity claims (those that are not themselves modally qualified by some such operator as 'necessarily') extend only to extensional contexts, that is, contexts that are modally insulated.

Quine himself was notoriously skeptical about the ultimate intelligibility of nonextensional locutions. But extensionalism as I am using the term does not require this additional attitude. It is defined rather by taking its semantic starting-point from a conception of extensional sentential contexts and the properties they express that treats them as nonmodal, in the sense of being modally insulated, and understanding identity exclusively in terms of such modally insulated properties.[32] One might be an extensionalist in this sense and acknowledge intensional properties, such as modal ones, that are modally involved, so long as they are understood in terms of functions taking worlds as arguments, whose ranges are extensional contexts and properties, which *are* modally purely local. Quine's anti-modal semantic hyperextensionalism requires substantial further commitments beyond this view. There

---

32. It should not cause confusion to use the term "modally insulated" indifferently to refer to a property of sentential contexts and of the properties they express.

is room for more moderate expressions of the prejudice that modal vocabulary is in some way second-class with respect to nonmodal vocabulary, that do not extend to this hyperextensionalism. For instance, extensionalist semantics can manifest itself in the intuition, still shared by many, that the modal facts at a world must supervene on the nonmodal facts at that world, that is, that at each world the facts statable using modally insulated locutions must determine the facts statable using modally involved ones. (According to the extensionalist way of thinking about modality, which analogizes possible worlds to set-theoretic models, all the modal facts across *all* the worlds taken together in any case supervene on all the nonmodal facts across all the worlds. The metalanguage of possible worlds semantics is itself conceived as having an extensional semantics.)

4. An Argument

The contrast between modally insulated (extensional) predicates and modally involved ones—a contrast that need not, contra Quine, be understood as invidious—is essential to this extensionalist semantic picture. And it is accordingly essential to understanding the indiscernibility of identicals, hence identity and coreference, in terms of intersubstitution licenses that extend only to extensional contexts, that is, contexts expressing modally insulated properties. The idea of modally insulated predicates and the properties they express conflicts directly with a central lesson Sellars draws from Kant, however. That lesson is that modal vocabulary makes explicit features implicit in the use of *all* ordinary empirical descriptive vocabulary. That is just the kind of vocabulary that seems most apt for an extensionalist semantic analysis, and for which it is most important to the extensionalist program that such an analysis can be offered.

6) The chunk of iron has a mass of 1 kilogram.
7) The shadow is perfectly circular.
8) That lion is sleeping lightly.
9) The second patch of paint is red.

These are all sentences the extensionalist would take as paradigms of extensional attributions of modally insulated properties. But Sellars, following

Kant, disagrees. Endorsing what I have called "the modal Kant-Sellars thesis," epitomized in the title of one of Sellars's essays, "Concepts as Involving Laws, and Inconceivable without Them," he insists that every empirical descriptive concept has modal consequences.[33] That is, its correct application has necessary conditions that would be expressed explicitly using subjunctive conditionals, and hence depends on what is true in other possible worlds besides the one in which it is being applied.

(6) cannot be true unless

6′) A force of 1 Newton would accelerate the chunk of iron at 1 meter/second/second.

is also true. (7) has as a consequence that

7′) If a straight line were to intersect the shadow, it would intersect the boundary of the shadow at exactly one point or exactly two points, but not three points.

(8) has as necessary conditions that

8′) Some moderate stimulus (e.g. a sufficiently loud noise, bright light, or hard jostling) would wake the lion.

(9) entails

9′) The patch would look red under standard conditions, and would look brown to a standard observer under green light.

All descriptive predicates have subjunctively robust consequences because, as Sellars says, being located in a space of such explanation-supporting

---

33. It is a measure of the pervasiveness of this insight in Sellars's thought that this was the first philosophy essay that Sellars wrote that was eventually published—even though others were published before it was.

implications is just what distinguishes *descriptions* from mere labels.[34] Describing something in the actual situation *always* involves substantial commitments as to how it *would* behave, or what else *would* be true of it, in other *possible* situations.

If this is right, then there are no predicates/properties that are extensional in the sense of being modally insulated. *All* empirical descriptive properties are modally involved. And if for that reason extensionalism about predicates/properties should be rejected, then extensionalism about identity must go with it. So accepting the modal Kant-Sellars thesis has substantial consequences, in particular for how we ought to think about identity.[35] Before extracting some of those consequences, it is accordingly worth looking more closely at the thesis itself. I have emphasized so far that even the best candidates for modally insulated predicates/properties have subjunctive consequences: consequences for what *would* be true of what they apply to *if* some other circumstances *were* different. Those consequences are necessary conditions of the applicability of the predicates/properties in question: under circumstances in which they do not hold, the predicate does not apply, the property is not instantiated. We can get some insight into why this must be so by looking at what is involved in a descriptive property being *determinate*.

Properties come in families: shape-properties, color-properties, mass-properties, atomic-number-properties, biological-species-properties, and so on. Though properties from different families are different, they are often compatible. *Spherical, red, made entirely of steel, having a mass of 1 kilogram* are all different properties, but one object can have all or any combination of them. By contrast, two properties from the same such family are not only different, they are *exclusively* different. One object cannot be both spherical and cubical, entirely steel and entirely wood. It cannot have

---

34. As quoted in Part I above, Sellars says:

   Although describing and explaining (predicting, retrodicting, understanding) are *distinguishable,* they are also, in an important sense, *inseparable.* It is only because the expressions in terms of which we describe objects, even such basic expressions as words for perceptible characteristics of molar objects, locate these objects in a space of implications, that they describe at all, rather than merely label. The descriptive and explanatory resources of language advance hand in hand. (CDCM §108).

35. This line of thought is the topic of Chapter 6, "Sortals, Identity, and Modality: The Metaphysical Significance of the Modal Kant-Sellars Thesis."

a mass of 1 kilogram and a mass of 5 kilograms, be monochromatically red and monochromatically green. These are incompatible properties, not just different ones. A property is the property it is in part because of its location in this space of compatible families of incompatible properties. Part of what we mean when we say that a property is determinate, is some specific or particular property, is that its possession rules out the possession of a definite set of other properties, which define its family, and is compatible with properties from a definite set of other families.[36] This is true even with determinable properties that are not fully determinate: for instance, *orange*, as opposed to *Pantone 17-1463 (Tangerine Tango)*. Indeed, the difference between more determinable and more determinate properties consists in part in the range of other determinables that they exclude or are incompatible with. The incompatibilities among properties are essential to the individuation of objects, since objects (particulars) are units of account for incompatibilities of properties (universals). If a=b, then it cannot be that Pa and Qb, for incompatible properties P and Q. But if a≠b, it is possible that Pa and Qb. To be an object (a single object) is to exclude incompatible properties. This structure is what underwrites the Aristotelian argument that properties and objects are distinguished by the fact that properties can have converses (contradictories) but objects cannot. The converse of a property P would be a property P' possessed or exhibited by all and only objects that do not possess or exhibit P. In this sense, *nonred* is the converse of *red*. Symmetrically, the converse of an object *a* would be an object *a'* that had all and only the properties that *a* does not have. But there is no such object, because that set of properties includes incompatible (contrary) ones. If *a* has a mass of 1 kilogram, *a'* would have to have a mass of 5 kilograms, and a mass of 10 kilograms, and so on. And if *a* has the property of not being identical to *b* and not being identical to *c*, which are not identical to each other, then *a'* would have to have the property of being identical to both *b* and *c*.

This aristotelian metaphysical structure of properties and objects is articulated by the distinction between *mere* difference (exhibited by *red* and

---

36. Of course things are more complicated than this: some specific members of different families can be incompatible; incompatibility is not merely a binary relation; there are relational properties as well as monadic ones. But the point I am making arises already in the simplest cases, and comparable phenomena occur in the more complex ones.

spherical) and *exclusive* difference (exhibited by *red* and *green*, and by *spherical* and *cubical*).[37] This is the structure not only of the ordinary empirical descriptive properties of common sense and Sellars's manifest image, but also of the empirical observable and theoretical descriptive properties of the advanced natural sciences, including physics, chemistry, and biology. The alternative to this aristotelian metaphysical framework of objects and properties is a tractarian one that makes do with mere difference. Such a scheme admits no constraints on the coinstantiation of properties by (in the *Tractatus* itself, elementary) objects. The asymmetry of objects and properties essential to the aristotelian framework is abolished: objects, no less than properties, do have converses. For all I know, a coherent metaphysics could be erected on such a bizarre tractarian ontological base. But it would not be the structure of the metaphysics of descriptive properties inherent in either the manifest or the scientific image.

And the broadly aristotelian metaphysical understanding of objects and properties does not admit of modally insulated properties. The exclusions essential to the determinate identity of properties—and equally to the determinate identity of objects—are subjunctively robust exclusions. Possession of any and every descriptive property in this world or situation has consequences and presuppositions concerning what is possible in other worlds and situations.[38] All such properties are modally involved. The aristotelian metaphysical framework of objects and properties entails the modal Kant-Sellars thesis and contradicts extensionalism about any empirical descriptive properties. In denying the existence of modally insulated properties, it also denies the extensionalism about identity that consists in restricting the indiscernibility entailed by identity of objects to properties that are modally insulated. All empirical descriptive properties are modal properties, in the sense that they have both subjunctive circumstances and subjunctive consequences of possession or exhibition—that is, ones that depend on what *would* be true if various facts *were* different.

---

37. In Hegel's insightful discussion of this structure in the Perception chapter of the *Phenomenology,* these are "gleichgültige Verschiedenheit" and "ausschließende Verschiedenheit": indifferent and exclusive difference.

38. Among the properties being excluded by the qualifier "descriptive" here are properties such as being such that 2+2=4.

The view I am asserting here bears many similarities to what is sometimes known as "dispositionalism" in the contemporary metaphysics of properties. (One *locus classicus* for such views is Huw Mellor's "In Defence of Dispositions.")[39] This umbrella-term covers a host of different, more specific views. I think that rather than expressing the central tenet around which these views cluster by saying that all properties are dispositional properties (which risks confusions of the sort associated with what Whitehead identified as the "fallacy of lost contrast"), it is better to say that even predicates expressing the most paradigmatically categorical of properties ('wooden', 'circular') have as consequences the kind of subjunctive conditionals that were often appealed to as the defining feature of dispositional properties. All descriptive predicates express what Sellars in *EPM* calls "mongrel categorical-hypothetical" properties. In general, many, perhaps most, of the currently most controverted issues concerning dispositional properties concern the relation between them and subjunctive conditionals. Worries about the relations between conventional dispositional properties ('visible', 'toxic', 'fragile') and so-called 'canonical' dispositional properties, which are regimented so as to require the truth of only a single subjunctive conditional ("In circumstances C, would respond with manifestation M") are of this sort. So, too, are issues about finkish and reverse-finkish dispositions—in which the stimulus circumstances of some disposition D are the same as the stimulus circumstances triggering a higher-order disposition of some system to gain or lose disposition D—as well as cases of mimicking, in which the corresponding subjunctive conditionals are true even though the disposition is lacking, and cases of antidotes, where the disposition is present though the subjunctive conditional fails (as when something fragile is carefully packed).[40] These are all important and difficult issues, but they arise in the context of attempts to *analyze* or *define* dispositions in terms of subjunctive conditionals. The claim I am making, that the applicability of any and every

---

39. *The Philosophical Review*, 83 (1974), pp. 157–181. More recently, dispositionalist views are expounded and defended in A. Chakravartty, *A Metaphysics for Scientific Realism: Knowing the Unobservable* (Cambridge: Cambridge University Press, 2007) and A. Bird, *Nature's Metaphysics: Laws and Properties* (Oxford: Oxford University Press, 2007).

40. D. Lewis, "Finkish Dispositions," *The Philosophical Quarterly* 47 (1997): 143–158. For a more recent survey, see M. Fara, "Dispositions and Habituals," *Noûs* 39 (2005): 43–82.

empirical descriptive predicate has subjunctive conditional consequences, that is, necessary conditions, does not require addressing these issues.

Two remarks about how I am thinking of subjunctive conditionals and dispositional properties are in order here, however, so as to forestall other concerns that have arisen in connection with contemporary metaphysical investigations into these topics. First, the subjunctive conditionals associated with dispositional properties codify inferences that, like almost all material inferences, are *nonmonotonic*. That is, they are not robust under arbitrary addition of auxiliary premises. So as I would want us to think about such conditionals, the claim

10) If this organism were to ingest a toxic substance, it would be harmed,

is not incompatible with the truth of

11) If this organism were to ingest a toxic substance, and it had been given an antidote to that substance, it would not be harmed.

The ubiquity of nonmonotonicity is evident in the ordinary informal reasoning of the garden, kitchen, and workshop, in the more institutionalized reasoning of the law court and the medical examining-room, and in the special sciences. I have urged elsewhere that the expressive role of *ceteris paribus* clauses not be thought of as somehow *removing* or *repairing* nonmonotonicity—turning nonmonotonic inferences into ones that are robust under arbitrary addition of collateral hypotheses. (The proper name for a Latin phrase whose rehearsal can do something magical like that is 'spell'.) Rather, the effect of including a *ceteris paribus* clause in a conditional is explicitly to *acknowledge* the nonmonotonicity of the inference it codifies: to mark that although one is endorsing the inference from *these premises* to the conclusion, one is *not* thereby claiming that the conclusion still follows from every larger premise-set that includes these premises as a proper subset. We philosophers and logicians do not have very good conceptual tools for dealing with the nonmonotonicity of inferences and of the conditionals that codify those inferences. Improving those tools is a central philosophical challenge, particularly, but not exclusively, for semantic inferentialists. The current primitive state of our thought about the phenomenon of nonmonotonicity is, however, no reason for ignoring it. The literature that addresses the relations between dispositional properties and subjunctive conditionals would be very different if those conditionals were thought of as nonmonotonic, as I think we ought.

The claim that all empirical descriptive properties are modally involved is one thing to mean by saying that all such properties involve a dispositional element or possess a dispositional aspect. This can seem paradoxical. How are the circumstances of manifestation and what counts as manifestation of a disposition to be specified if only vocabulary that is dispositional in the sense of having subjunctive conditionals as necessary conditions and consequences of application is available? To dispel this sense of paradox, it should suffice to emphasize that all the properties traditionally thought of as categorical are included in the scope of the denial of modally insulated properties. So they are still available in specifying the circumstances of manifestation of dispositions, and what counts as manifesting them. In particular, properties that are dispositional in the sense of being modally involved include standard observables. Indeed, *observable* is of course itself a dispositional property. And surely *observable* and *visible* (in the sense of things that can be observed or seen under some circumstances) are the paradigms of observable properties. What would it mean to say that one could not in general see whether something is visible by looking at it? But even if by 'visible' we mean "would (or could) be seen if viewed under standard conditions" one can still often see that something is visible—although this observation is, like others, fallible. Moving only slightly further afield, there is nothing wrong in principle with claims such as

12) I can see that the cup is fragile,
13) I can see that you are angry,
14) This fruit tastes toxic.

One might in any particular case be wrong. But as with 'red' and 'purple finch', the application of dispositional terms can be the exercise of a reliable differential responsive reporting disposition. That is enough for observability, as I argue on Sellars's behalf in Chapter 2 ("The Centrality of Sellars's Two-Ply Account of Observation to the Arguments of *Empiricism and the Philosophy of Mind*"). Dispositions are in principle open to being observable in the same way and by the same sort of process by which the difference between potsherds being Toltec and their being Aztec, which might start out as a purely theoretical difference, epistemically accessible to an inquirer only via complex processes of inference from more easily observable features, can also come to be an observable difference, for a sufficiently trained and experienced archaeologist or anthropologist.

5. Consequences for Strongly Cross-Sortal Identities

The modal Kant-Sellars thesis says that all empirical descriptive properties are modally involved. If, accordingly, there are no modally insulated properties, then the properties with respect to which identicals must be taken to be indiscernible cannot be restricted to modally insulated ones, on pain of emptying of significance the intersubstitution licenses that articulate the expressive role characteristic of identity claims as such. But allowing modally involved properties into the class of properties with respect to which identicals must be indiscernible has radical consequences. Only under very special circumstances will identities relating items falling under different sortals be true. The statue is not identical to the lump of clay, even if the lump has never been in any other shape than the statue, and never will be. For the lump *would* survive if the statue were squashed, and the statue would not. They are not indiscernible with respect to this modal property. Material constitution is not identity. This is, of course, a conclusion many others have come to. But it is not the end of the significance of the modal Kant-Sellars thesis for identity.

The contents of sortal predicates differ from those of nonsortal predicates in determining not only circumstances and consequences of appropriate *application*, but also criteria of *identity* and *individuation*. They determine when two candidate objects a and b, which are both Ks, are the *same* K. True identities can also relate singular terms that fall under different sortals.

15) Kitten a (at t) is (=) cat b (at time t'),

can be a true identity. That is because the sortals 'kitten' and 'cat' differ only in their criteria of application, not in their criteria of identity. When (15) holds, a is the same cat as b. Kittens are cats (young ones), and if a and b

are kittens, they are the same kitten if and only if they are the same cat. (It is sometimes said that 'kitten' is a phase-sortal of 'cat'.) I'll say that identity claims relating terms falling under different sortals that share criteria of identity are only *weakly* cross-sortal.

16) Passenger *a* is (=) person *b*,

by contrast, is a *strongly* cross-sortal identity claim. For although passengers are something like time-slices of persons, they are counted differently (unlike kittens and cats). U.S. airlines flew 730 million domestic passengers in 2011, while the population of the U.S. (the number of persons) was only 311 million. When I flew round-trip between Pittsburgh and Boston, I remained one person, but was counted as two passengers. If my airline counted me as (playing the role of) passenger #17863 of the week on the way out and passenger #19242 on the way back, these are different passengers. Some have wanted to say that this shows that different passengers can be the same person, that all of

17) Passenger *a* = Bob B.,
18) Passenger *b* = Bob B.,
19) Passenger *a* ≠ passenger *b*,

can be true.

I think it follows from our argument thus far that this cannot be right. For "passenger *a*" and "the person Bob B." are terms specifying objects that differ in their modal properties, reflecting the different criteria of identity associated with their governing sortals. If Bob B. had never been on an airplane, he would not have been passenger *a*, but would still have been Bob B. Strongly cross-sortal identities relating terms falling under descriptive sortals with different criteria of identity and individuation differ in the (nonmonotonic) subjunctive conditionals that are necessary conditions of the applicability of those sortals, and so of those terms. So they are not indiscernible with respect to (modally involved) properties that identity claims assert they must share—on pain of rendering incoherent the intersubstitution license that is the distinguishing expressive role in virtue of which something counts as an *identity* claim. So strongly cross-sortal identity claims are *never* true. (I argue for this claim at greater length in Chapter 6: "Sortals, Identity, and Modality: The Metaphysical Significance of the Modal Kant-Sellars Thesis.") It is important to notice that this claim, strong though it is, does not entail that identity claims such as

20) Barack Obama is the 44th President of the United States,

cannot be *contingently* true, under its *de dicto* reading, even though both

21) Barack Obama might never have won any election,

and

22) The 44th President of the United States must have won an election,

read *de dicto*, can both be true contingently. But this difference in modal properties is not to the point, since (20) is not a strong cross-sortal identity claim of any kind. Both the terms involved fall under the sortal 'person'. "President of the United States" is a kind of phase-sortal. Grover Cleveland was both the 25th and the 27th President, but

23) The 25th President of the United States = The 27th President of the United States,

is true, as we can see when we ask, "How many different Presidents has the United States had?" The question means "How many different people have been President?" The case is not analogous to that of passengers.

Of course, all this is controversial (though with the aid of some plausible auxiliary hypotheses about how sortals work, it follows from the widely accepted Kripkean doctrine that all true identity claims are necessarily true), and raises a host of subsidiary questions. But I am deriving the conclusion that no identity claims involving terms that fall under descriptive sortals exhibiting different criteria of identity and individuation (that is, no strongly cross-sortal identity claims) are true from the claim that all descriptive properties are modally involved (so that we cannot require that identicals be indiscernible only with respect to modally insulated properties), via the claim that differences in criteria of identity and individuation entail differences in modal profile—that is, differences in the possession of properties whose applicability or possession entails nonmonotonic subjunctive conditionals. I think this is a strong argument. But it does not rule out in principle the possibility of partitioning modally involved predicates into two classes X and Y, insisting that only those from class X are referentially transparent (indiscernible with respect to identity, within the scope of the intersubstitution license made by identity claims), and then claiming further that some strongly cross-sortal identities come out true because the predicates/properties that modally distinguish the sortals includes only those from class Y. All I can do is point out how demanding the criteria of adequacy are for such an attempted partition, downstream of the modal Kant-Sellars thesis. Some candidates for the distinguished class X of identity-relevant predicates/properties can be immediately dismissed: nonrelational properties won't do. The notion of <u>intrinsic</u> properties is a candidate, but it was designed to be restricted to modally insulated properties—and I don't share the metaphysical faith that we can make sense of the notion of <u>natural</u> properties that Lewis retreated to in order to define intrinsicness.[41] But considering such alternatives would take us too far afield.

If all this is right, then the relation between the objects referred to in the manifest image and those referred to in the scientific image cannot be identity. For the identities in question would all be strongly cross-sortal. The sortals of the manifest image come with criteria of identity and individuation that essentially involve nonmonotonic subjunctive conditionals couched in other descriptive terms belonging to the manifest image. Think about the criteria of identity and individuation for such descriptive sortals articulating denizens of the manifest image as 'credenza', 'violin', 'yawl', 'rocker panel', 'shrub', 'mortgage lien', 'stock market crash', 'ciborium', 'frock', 'crepe', 'tragedy'. One cannot specify whether one has one or more of things of these kinds without appealing to their criteria of application, which are in turn couched in a plethora of further manifest image descriptive vocabulary

---

41. It might seem that the modal realism of Chapter 5, "Modal Expressivism and Modal Realism: Together Again," and the conceptual realism I have endorsed elsewhere, must involve commitment to such a distinguished class of properties that are 'natural'. I do not think that it does. In any case, I take it that even if the idea of properties that are "written in Nature's own language" were sustainable, such properties would not be modally insulated. If they were, we could not appeal to them to *describe* how things are.

drawn from the relevant domains: home decorative, musical, nautical, automotive, legal, and so on. One cannot say under what (possibly counterfactual) conditions something would or would not still be a K, and the same K, without using other terms of these kinds. For identities relating items of these kinds to items of kinds specified in the vocabulary of an eventual natural science not to be strongly cross-sortal, the subjunctive conditionals specified in the two kinds of vocabulary will have to match. That is not going to happen. The manifest-image kinds mentioned above are basically identified and individuated *functionally,* by their relations to things of other such functional kinds in complex systems articulated by social norms.[42]

One consequence that emerges particularly clearly from these considerations can be summarized in a slogan that is only slightly hyperbolic: *Nothing* is identical to the mereological sum of things of other kinds (e.g. fundamental particles). This is obvious, because mereological sums are indifferent to the spatial rearrangement of their parts—and that is not true, for instance, of things of *any* of the kinds listed above. Nor are they identical to specifiable spatiotemporal constellations of their parts or particles. For not even a wildly disjunctive specification in the language of physics will underwrite the right subjunctive conditionals to agree in criteria of application and identity with those determined by the manifest-image kinds. Even if one could say, holding a great deal constant, what arrangements of particles *would* count as a stock market crash or a mortgage lien, *what* one would have to hold constant to do so would itself have to be specified at least in part using other manifest-image sortals and descriptive predicates.

6. A Weaker Version of the Naturalistic Construal of the Phenomena/Noumena Distinction

The modal Kant-Sellars thesis, epitomized in Sellars's titular claim that empirical descriptive concepts involve laws and are inconceivable without them, is an essential element of the successor notion of Kantian categories that I discussed in Part I as one of Sellars's best ideas. I have been arguing

---

42. The issue here is not at all one of *vagueness,* but of mismatch of criteria of identity and individuation. The issues Wilson discusses in *Wandering Significance* are of much greater relevance than is classic *sorites* vagueness.

here that it is incompatible with the way he wants to develop another Kantian theme: the distinction between phenomena and noumena. This idea is his way of working out the ontological privileging "in the dimension of describing and explaining" of scientific descriptive vocabulary over the descriptive vocabulary of the manifest image announced in the *scientia mensura*. The particular version of his idea that I have been considering might be called the "identity version of a sense/reference construal of the scientific naturalist rendering of the phenomena/noumena distinction." It is the idea that the descriptive vocabulary of the manifest image refers, if it refers at all, to items more adequately specified in the descriptive vocabulary of an eventual or ideal science.[43] Such a view is committed to there being true identity claims relating the descriptive terms in the vocabulary of the manifest image that refer at all and descriptive terms drawn from the vocabulary of the scientific image. These will in general be what I have called "strongly cross-sortal" identity claims: claims relating terms whose governing sortals are governed by quite different criteria of identity and individuation. (If there were any doubt about that, we can see that this is what he has in mind from some of the examples he considers: 'person' having as its scientific-image successor neurophysiologically specifiable "core persons," his envisaging of an eventual scientific ontology of pure processes, and so forth.) I have been arguing that the modal Kant-Sellars thesis implies that strongly cross-sortal identities are never true. The different criteria of identity and individuation associated with the sortals involved underwrite divergent subjunctive conditional

---

43. I have bracketed concerns about Sellars's commitments to a Peircean end-of-inquiry science, conceived of as the limit asymptotically approached by properly conducted empirical theorizing. In fact I think it is very difficult to make sense of this notion, for the same reasons I have offered in objecting to Crispin Wright's similar appeal to 'superassertibility' as assertibility by current justificatory standards and evidence that is robust under arbitrary improvements in or additions to our information. Firmness under revisions by adding information is an epistemically valuable property (a characterization of something we ought to aim at) only if 'information' is restricted to *true* claims. If not, if it just means something like then-warranted, it will include lots of *false* claims. And there is no reason to esteem epistemically claims commitment to which would be robust under the addition of arbitrary false claims, even if warrantedly believed. Such accounts of what inquiry aims at seem bound to be either circular (because implicitly invoking notions of truth—perhaps in the guise of information—or improvement) or normatively unsatisfactory, because not specifying properties of our views we have reason to aspire to achieving.

properties. That is just what it means for the identities in question to be *strongly* cross-sortal. The weaker half of Leibniz's Law, the indiscernibility of identicals, tells us that identicals must not have different properties. The modal Kant-Sellars thesis tells us that we cannot read this principle so as systematically to exclude these subjunctive conditional properties.

I conclude that the identity version of the sense/reference construal of the scientific naturalist rendering of the phenomena/noumena distinction is untenable, and should be recognized to be so by Sellars's own lights. The very argument that I take to show this, though, shows just how demanding the task of working out the underlying motivation in terms of *identity* of what is described in the manifest-image vocabulary and the scientific-image vocabulary really is. It is too demanding. Is a weaker, more plausible construal available? Sellars's idea that meaning claims should be understood as functional classifications—the point of his introducing his favorite technical device, dot-quotes, epitomized in the title of his 1973 "Meaning as Functional Classification"[44]—shows that a way forward is available to him. For it suggests that we should understand the 'sense' part of the sense/reference version of the phenomena/noumena distinction functionally. Then the 'reference' end would naturally be understood in terms of what *realizes* the function or plays the role specified by the sense component. (There is a way of reading that claim according to which it is what Sellars calls "sign designs" that do that. But that is not the sense that is helpful here.) The idea would be to understand Sellars's scientific naturalism—of which the *scientia mensura* would then be thought of as a somewhat incautious formulation—as privileging scientific vocabulary with respect to specifications of what, if anything, really plays the roles specified in the descriptive vocabulary of the manifest image. The claim would be that it is in this sense, much looser than that of identity, that manifest-image descriptions should be taken to be *about* things better specified in scientific-image descriptions.

One particularly clear way to work out this thought is the one suggested by David Lewis (and adopted by the Canberra planners). Think of the whole set of empirical descriptions specified in manifest-image vocabulary that would be endorsed by the application of current justificatory practices as a theory. Ramsify that theory by replacing each bit of descriptive vocabulary in it by a

---

44. Reprinted in *In the Space of Reasons*.

variable bound by a quantifier ranging over predicates or sortals. That yields a specification of the functional roles played by that descriptive vocabulary in the manifest-image theory. Then look for the "best realizers" of those roles that are specifiable in the descriptive vocabulary of the scientific image. These will be the terms that make the resulting theory most (approximately) true. Those best realizers, described in the favored vocabulary, are then what we take the manifest-image talk to have really been about. The very strong and implausible claim that a person is (=) her functioning nervous system is replaced by the much weaker and (so) more plausible claim that the best realizer, specified in the language of neurophysiology, of the functional role played by the concept person, is the functioning nervous system of a human being.

This now-popular way of understanding a whole range of metaphysical claims is available to Sellars in his own terms. Given the difficulties attendant upon the identity version of his suggested scientific naturalist construal of the phenomena/noumena distinction, diagnosed above, this strategy of looking for the best realizers specifiable in the favored vocabulary for functional roles resulting from Ramsifying away the questionable vocabulary of the manifest image seems like a more charitable way of working out Sellars's idea. Satisfying as such an irenic outcome would be, I think this way of working out the naturalistic impulse or insight is less attractive than it might first appear. For it is in substantial tension with *another* compelling argument that Sellars made.

7. Another Sellarsian Argument

In Chapter 3 below ("Pragmatism, Inferentialism, and Modality in Sellars's Arguments against Empiricism") I discuss an argument Sellars offers in his essay "Phenomenalism." He is considering the prospects for the phenomenalist project of substituting claims about subjunctively robust relations among "sense contents" or phenomenal properties of the sort taken to be expressed by claims about how things look for claims couched in the vocabulary of enduring physical objects. A paradigm is C. I. Lewis's idea (in *An Analysis of Knowledge and Valuation*)[45] that one might replace physical object talk with "non-terminating judgments" that are infinite sequences

---

45. C. I. Lewis, *An Analysis of Knowledge and Valuation* (La Salle, IL: Open Court, 1950).

of "terminating judgments" consisting of conditionals whose consequents employ only phenomenal vocabulary. The familiar (and once popular) idea is that part of what it means to say

24) There is a currently unobserved tomato on the table in the next room,

is

25) If I *were* to walk into the next room and look at the table, I *would* be visually presented with a red-orange round bulgy surface.

Sellars points out that such approaches are caught in a dilemma. Their reductive aim requires commitment to the idea that

> there are inductively confirmable generalizations about sense contents which are 'in principle' capable of being formulated without the use of the language of physical things.... [46]

But "this idea is a mistake," he says, because

> the very selection of the complex patterns of actual sense contents in our past experiences which are to serve as the antecedents of the generalizations in question presuppose our common sense knowledge of ourselves as perceivers, of the specific physical environment in which we do our perceiving and of the general principles which correlate the occurrence of sensations with bodily and environmental conditions. We select those patterns which go with our being in a certain perceptual relation to a particular object of a certain quality, where we know that being in this relation to an object of that quality normally eventuates in our having the sense content referred to in the consequent.

That is, in order to formulate subjunctive conditionals about the sense contents I would be presented with under various circumstances, the

---

46. "Phenomenalism," in *In the Space of Reasons*, p. 331.

circumstances have to be specified—as I did in the tomato example above—in the very language of enduring physical objects that one is aiming to analyze. It just is not true that if I were only to *seem* to walk into the next room and to *seem* to look at the table, I *would* be visually confronted by a red-orange round bulgy surface. *That* antecedent can be satisfied by just *imagining* going and looking, and I can imagine almost *any* result. Subjunctive conditionals formulated entirely in phenomenal vocabulary are not even true *ceteris paribus*. On the other hand, if in order to make the subjunctive conditionals true appeal is made to enduring-physical-object talk, then the reductive analytic purpose of the phenomenalist is not served.

Of course in *EPM* Sellars offers other reasons to doubt the autonomy of phenomenal 'looks' talk to objective 'is' talk. But this argument is independent of his critique there of the conceptions of sensory givenness on which phenomenalists such as C. I. Lewis, the Carnap of the *Aufbau*, and Goodman in *The Structure of Appearance* rely. The claim I want to make is that a version of this "Phenomenalism" argument applies to the project of Ramsifying away manifest-image descriptive vocabulary and seeking best realizers specified in scientific-image descriptive vocabulary. Both the phenomenalist reductive project and this functionalist rendering of scientific naturalism seek to explain the use of some target vocabulary (object-directed, ordinary empirical description) in terms of the use of a privileged base vocabulary (phenomenal experience talk, scientific description). The phenomenalist looks directly to underwrite subjunctive conditionals whose consequents are expressed in the privileged vocabulary, while the functionalist naturalist looks to reproduce as far as possible the subjunctive conditionals that articulate the criteria of identity and individuation of sortals in the target vocabulary by means of conditionals couched in the privileged vocabulary. The Sellarsian argument we are considering presents both with a dilemma: either the process being considered eliminates *all* the target vocabulary from its end product, or it does not. The argument claims that neither option is satisfactory. In the case of phenomenalism, full eliminability of the target vocabulary can be bought only at the cost of the evident falsity of the subjunctive conditionals into which object talk is translated, and less than full eliminability vitiates the analysis by conceding that subjective phenomenal talk is not, after all, autonomous relative to objective talk.

In the case at hand, the question is whether the envisaged Ramsification of a world-theory formulated in manifest-image descriptive vocabulary is to be thought of as Ramsifying away *all* the ordinary empirical descriptive and explanatory vocabulary, or only *some* of it. As with the phenomenalism example, if some manifest-image descriptive vocabulary must remain unRamsified, the commitment to the *general* authority of scientific over everyday vocabulary "in the dimension of describing and explaining" claimed by the *scientia mensura* will not have been vindicated. Just as description and explanation, whether in scientific or manifest-image terms, are not (and are acknowledged by Sellars not to be) autonomous, but depend on being embedded in the lifeworld of the manifest image, so *scientific* description and explanation would have been conceded not to be autonomous even within the realm of description and explanation.

So the functionalist way of reading Sellars's scientific naturalist rendering of Kant's phenomena/noumena distinction seems to be committed to Ramsifying away *all* the manifest-image descriptive and explanatory vocabulary before seeking best realizers specifiable in scientific-image vocabulary. In the case of phenomenalism, Sellars's claim is that the subjunctive conditionals that result aren't in general true, so the account fails. What sort of subjunctive conditionals result if one abstracts away from all the ordinary descriptive vocabulary? One of the lessons we have learned from worrying this issue in the literature is that they will be massively multiply realized. The purely formal structure that results from *full* Ramsification of a theory, no matter how complex, typically has purely numerical realizers (models), for instance. And even if the realizers are specified in a physical object vocabulary, wildly gerrymandered realizers can still be constructed, in addition to the "intended" models.

One common response to this observation is to require that the *causal* relations among items in the target vocabulary not be Ramsified. What is wanted is the best realizers in the favored vocabulary of the causal roles played by items initially specified in the manifest-image vocabulary. Talk of "causation" here is, I take it, a somewhat dark way of indicating that the Ramsified theory must still underwrite the (defeasible) subjunctive conditionals appealed to in explanations. That is, indeed, a reasonable constraint. But it leads right back to the other horn of the dilemma: among the subjunctive conditionals that must be underwritten are those articulating the criteria of identity and individuation (as well as the criteria and consequences of application) of the manifest-image sortals appealed to in the explanations that are part and parcel of content of the descriptive vocabulary of the manifest image. These inevitably have manifest-image sortal vocabulary at least in their antecedents. In this individuating role, that vocabulary is not eliminable in such conditionals in favor of strongly cross-sortal vocabulary. (One *can* specify equivalents of sortals such as "cat" by means of phase-sortals such as "kitten," "young cat," "middle-aged cat," "old cat," or suitably regimented versions of them. But that is precisely because these are *not strongly* cross-sortal relative to "cat." Trying the same trick with sortals that don't just apply to, but individuate time-slices of persons, for instance functional ones such as "passenger" gives the wrong results.)

Here is a diagnosis: Sellars puts forward his scientific naturalist version of Kant's phenomena-noumena distinction in terms of the overriding authority of the scientific over manifest-image vocabulary of description-and-explanation against the background of a hierarchical picture of explanation that seemed much more plausible at the time than it does now. We can think of that picture as having two parts. First is a unity-of-science view, championed by Neurath and Carnap among others, that sees the sciences as forming a reductive explanatory hierarchy, with fundamental physics at the bottom, chemistry built on it, biology on it, the special natural sciences above them, and psychology and the social sciences hovering somehow above them, at least insofar as they deserve to count as "real" sciences. The ideal is to be able to do all the explanatory work of the upper levels by appeal only to vocabulary and laws of the lower levels. Second is the idea, often conjoined with the first and championed most famously perhaps by Quine, that common sense (the "manifest image"), too, belongs in this hierarchy, at least insofar as it gets anything right. Sellars's *scientia mensura* expresses a version of this second idea. But it cannot be *more* plausible than the first idea, of which it is an analogous extension.

Yet today, hardly any philosopher of science would subscribe to the explanatory hierarchy central to the unity-of-science idea (the *methodological* unity of science is a different issue). It now seems clear that science works at many explanatory levels, and that generalizations available at one level cannot be replaced by those formulable in the vocabulary of other levels. The seminal argument is Jerry Fodor's classic 1974 piece "Special Sciences: The Disunity of Science as a Working Hypothesis."[47] Of a piece with his line of thought

---

47. *Synthese* 28: 97–115.

is Putnam's 1975 argument that one cannot demonstrate, in the theory and vocabulary of quantum mechanics, that one cannot put a rigid, solid square peg with 1" sides in a round hole of 1" diameter.[48] Rigidity and solidity, the concepts needed to apply geometry to this case, are not concepts reconstructable at the level of QM. The generalizations they permit are orthogonal to those of QM—which, however, could perhaps (in principle) be appealed to in explaining the rigidity under a range of circumstances of some specific material. Dennett's writings about "Real Patterns" offer a fundamental conceptual diagnosis of why explanatory incommensurability across levels should be considered to be the norm. In *Wandering Significance* Mark Wilson analyzes cases in which attempts at explanatory reductions of engineering concepts such as rigidity to more fundamental physical concepts are obliged to go in circles—precisely because the antecedents of the subjunctive conditionals required to apply the more fundamental physical concepts must be specified in part in the engineering language.[49] As far as I am aware, the principal source of dissent from the near consensus on the explanatory heterogeneity and incommensurability of the various sciences (sometimes called the "Many Levels" view) comes from variants of Kim's suggestion that the higher-level descriptive properties expressed by the vocabularies of the special sciences could be understood to be equivalent to infinite disjunctions of all nomically possible extensions of the predicates, specified in the language of fundamental physics.[50] In the present context it suffices to point out that Kim assumes that the content of descriptive predicates and sortals is exhausted by what it applies to, a view Sellars explicitly rejects in favor of one that sees the *explanatory* role of descriptive predicates as at least equally essential to their contents.

---

48. H. Putnam, "Philosophy and Our Mental Life" (Chapter 14), *Mind, Language and Reality: Philosophical Papers*, vol. II (Cambridge: Cambridge University Press, 1975). I have slightly altered the example.

49. Mark Wilson, *Wandering Significance* (Oxford: Oxford University Press, 2008). No-one who has thought about the wealth of examples Wilson presents will be tempted by the simple-minded picture of explanatory reductionism of the special sciences that I am joining the common contemporary philosophical wisdom in rejecting. For expository reasons I have regretfully indulged here in what Wilson properly excoriates as the "Theory T fallacy."

50. For instance in J. Kim, "Multiple Realizability and the Metaphysics of Reduction," *Philosophy and Phenomenological Research* 52 (1992): 1–26. Reprinted in Kim's *Supervenience and Mind* (Cambridge: Cambridge University Press, 1993), pp. 309–336.

I conclude that even within the natural sciences, a version of the dilemma Sellars presents in "Phenomenalism" prevails. If one Ramsifies away all higher-level descriptive-explanatory vocabulary, the resulting roles are unmanageably multiply realized. No "best realizer" emerges. To preserve explanatory power, subjunctive conditionals must be underwritten whose specification requires antecedents specified in the descriptive vocabulary of the special sciences. But then that vocabulary is not being supplanted for explanatory purposes by the lower-level vocabulary. If for this reason we should reject the idea that the descriptive vocabulary of the special sciences can be dispensed with in favor of that of fundamental physics without loss of explanatory power, all the more reason to think that is true of the descriptive vocabulary of the manifest image, in favor of natural scientific vocabulary generally. For in that case we have descriptions and corresponding explanations addressed to (to repeat some examples offered above) artifacts such as credenzas, violins, yawls, rocker panels, ciboria, and frocks. Further, we have social phenomena such as stock market crashes, mortgage liens, elections, paparazzi, and internet memes. The same considerations that make visible the explanatory irreducibility of the special sciences dictate the extension of that claim to explanations involving these manifest-image sortals.

The result is that the functionalist way of reading Sellars's scientific naturalist rendering of Kant's phenomena/noumena distinction fares no better than the sense/reference identity way of reading it. It just is not the case that everything we talk about in the manifest image that exists at all ("of those that are, that they are, and of those that are not, that they are not") is something specifiable in the language of an eventual natural science. The manifest image is not best thought of as an appearance, of which the world as described by science is the reality. By contrast to what Sellars makes of Kant's idea of categories, his way of developing Kant's distinction between the phenomenal world and the noumenal world is not a good idea.

8. Expressive Pragmatic Naturalism

Is there really *nothing* to be made of Sellars's naturalism, even by his own lights? Is it *just* a bad idea? This would be an ironic conclusion to draw. For the Kantian idea of his that I have praised, the idea of "pure concepts of the Understanding" as not themselves descriptive, but as having the distinctive expressive role of making explicit necessary features of the framework of description (which includes explanation), is not one that looms large in contemporary philosophy. Whereas we live in a philosophical age so pervaded by naturalism that it becomes an almost invisible sustaining medium—like the air we breathe, which we see only indirectly, when it is polluted or when moving in gusts of wind. We could endorse a substantially weakened version of Sellars's slogan: claiming not that science is the "measure of all things," but just that in the dimension of description and explanation, when science *collides with* common sense, when common sense descriptions and explanations are *contradicted by* science, that the superior authority of science should be acknowledged. No doubt. But this is an anodyne concession. For the considerations I have advanced on Sellars's behalf against the stronger commitment expressed in the *scientia mensura*, rooted in the significance for identity and individuation of the Kant-Sellars thesis about the categorial status of modality with respect to descriptive vocabulary, and in the significance of the incommensurability of explanatory levels for the prospects of functionalist reductions-by-realization, teach us that such collisions and contradictions will be the exception, not the rule. After all, many theologians are quite comfortable making the corresponding concession regarding religious discourse vis-à-vis scientific.

Supervenience is another weak form of naturalism. Although he did not address more recent versions of the doctrine, Sellars endorses some version of what he calls "emergentism" with the remark

> Emergence is one form taken by a negative answer to the question: "Could a world which includes minds be described with the same primitive predicates (and laws) as a mindless universe?"[51]

The trouble is that at least the supervenience component of such a view, which he here insists on, is far too weak a form of scientific naturalism to satisfy naturalists such as Sellars—as has become abundantly clear from subsequent investigations.[52]

---

51. "Realism and the New Way of Words," in *PPPW*. Henceforth RNWW.
52. A classic defense of this view is Terry Horgan's "From Supervenience to Superdupervenience: Meeting the Demands of a Material World," *Mind* 102(408) (1993): 555–586.

There is, though, a potentially much more robust kind of naturalism available to Sellars, and it is the kind to which he started out committed. In his early writings Sellars used the phrase "pure pragmatics" to describe the study of the *use* of language, in virtue of which its symbols are meaningful, rather than just what he calls "sign designs" (Wittgenstein's "signpost considered just as a piece of wood").

> *The Pragmatic Metalanguage.* . . . [M]etalanguages of this type alone are meta-*languages* in the complete sense of the term, for they alone deal with languages *as languages,* that is as *meaningful* symbols. Syntactics and semantics as epistemological rather than empirical disciplines are abstractions from pure pragmatics, and are misunderstood in a way that leads directly to psychologism when their fragmentary character is overlooked. It is with some hesitation that I speak of these meta-languages as pragmatic, for they have nothing to do with language as expressive or persuasive, or with such other concepts of empirical psychology as have come to be characterized as the subject-matter of a science of pragmatics. Pure pragmatics or which is the same thing, epistemology, is a formal rather than a factual matter. In addition to the concepts of pure syntactics and semantics, pure pragmatics is concerned with other concepts which are *normative* as opposed to the factual concepts of psychology, as 'true' is normative as opposed to 'believed' or 'valid' is normative as opposed to 'inferred'.[53]

This rich passage has a number of striking features. First, he considers both syntax and semantics to be *aspects* of "pure pragmatics," rather than studies to be laid alongside pragmatics at the same level. That other way of thinking of them—the dominant view when he wrote these words in 1948, as it is now—which overlooks their "fragmentary character" with respect to pragmatics, he claims leads to psychologism. The whole passage is framed by a distinction between 'pure', 'formal', 'epistemological', 'normative' disciplines and 'empirical', 'factual' (elsewhere: 'descriptive') ones. He makes clear that he thinks of the difference in terms of the *metalinguistic* character

53. RNWW, p. 69.

of the former, in the distinctively *categorial* sense of 'metalinguistic' explored in the first part of this chapter. It is not that syntax and semantics belong exclusively to the factual-descriptive disciplines; even "pure semantics" is to be understood as fragmentary with respect to "pure pragmatics." Sellars explicitly marks that he uses "pragmatics" broadly, to pick out systematic theories of the *use* of language, rather than more narrowly as addressing issues having to do with convenience of communication (as in Grice), effects of context on interpretation, and so on.

The sort of naturalism I see as implicit in Sellars's early writings is a broadly naturalistic approach to pure pragmatics—and so to pure semantics and other formal, epistemological, normative metalinguistic disciplines addressing aspects of the *use* of language in virtue of which it deploys *meaningful* symbols. What he is groping for, I think, is a *pragmatic* naturalism that is not a kind of *descriptivism*.[54] Descriptivist naturalisms in this area he would see as ignoring the normative character of the metalinguistic expressive roles characteristic of the expressions of pure pragmatics (including pure semantics and syntax), and so collapsing the pure into the empirical, the formal into the factual. That is what Sellars, following Frege, calls "psychologism." The key to a nondescriptivist naturalism is, first, focusing, to begin with, more broadly on *pragmatics* rather than more narrowly on *semantics* and, second, to appreciate the categorial metalinguistic expressive roles of the nondescriptive vocabulary—including the normative vocabulary—deployed in articulating the pragmatic theory of the use of ordinary empirical descriptive vocabulary. For while that vocabulary is not itself descriptive vocabulary, its use is implicit in the use of ordinary empirical descriptive vocabulary. (The 'L' in 'LX' indicates that its use is *elaborated from* the use of OED vocabulary.) Its expressive role is to make explicit features implicit in the use of ordinary empirical descriptive vocabulary. (The 'X' in 'LX' indicates that its use is *explicative of* the use of OED vocabulary.) In this sense, nothing over and above the use of the language of the descriptivist naturalist is invoked by the nondescriptivist naturalist.

In a number of works over the last decade, Huw Price has argued that there are two substantially different strategies a naturalist can adopt in

---

54. "It would be foolish for me to pretend that I have done more than grope in the right direction." RNWW, p. 77.

offering a naturalistic understanding of some region of discourse.[55] What he calls "object naturalism" concerns the objects and properties the vocabulary in question allows us to talk and think about, how it represents the objective world as being. Object naturalism seeks to solve what Frank Jackson calls the "location problem": to locate the truth-makers of claims in the target discourse in the world as specified in a favored naturalistic vocabulary—perhaps that of fundamental physics, or of the special sciences.[56] The *scientia mensura* is a paradigmatic statement of the fighting faith of object naturalism. What Price calls "subject naturalism," by contrast, is a *pragmatic* naturalism, rather than a representational *semantic* naturalism. The subject naturalist makes no assumptions about whether the target vocabulary admits of a properly representational semantics. (Price himself does not think representational semantics are appropriate for *any* discourses—but one need not follow him in his radical anti-representationalism to pursue subject naturalism.) What the subject naturalist wants is a naturalistic account of the discursive practices of *using* the target vocabulary *as* meaningful in the way it is meaningful. Rather than a naturalistic *semantic* metavocabulary, the subject naturalist seeks a naturalistic *pragmatic* metavocabulary.[57]

---

55. Starting off in "Naturalism without Representationalism," in David Macarthur and Mario de Caro (eds.), *Naturalism in Question* (Cambridge, MA: Harvard University Press, 2004), pp. 71–88, and more fully in his books *Naturalism without Mirrors* (Oxford: Oxford University Press, 2011) and *Expressivism, Pragmatism, and Representationalism* (Cambridge: Cambridge University Press, 2013).

56. Frank Jackson, *From Metaphysics to Ethics: A Defence of Conceptual Analysis* (Oxford: Oxford University Press, 2000).

57. As will be evident from what follows, Huw undertakes two commitments I am not willing to undertake, one explicitly and one implicitly:

   a) The explicit one is to anti-representationalism as opposed to nonrepresentationalism. I think *some* expressions *should* be given a representationalist semantics. But not *all* should.

   b) The implicit commitment of his is to using a wholly naturalistic metalanguage to specify linguistic *use*, in a distinctive sense of 'naturalistic' that identifies it as a subset of *descriptive* vocabulary. I think normative vocabulary, too, is available. And I think normative vocabulary is categorial: it, like modal vocabulary, necessarily comes in play along with descriptive vocabulary, not that one must have it whenever one has descriptive vocabulary, but that one must have the phenomena that it makes explicit wherever one has descriptive vocabulary. My slogan here is: naturalism need not entail descriptivism—the view that only descriptive

An object naturalist might be puzzled about arithmetic vocabulary. What, she wants to know, are the numbers referred to by numerals? They don't show up in the physicist's inventory of the furniture of the world—though the use of arithmetic and other mathematical vocabulary is certainly essential to the practice of physics. Can we locate them by identifying them with occult constellations of familiar physical objects?[58] If they are not physical objects but "abstract objects," how are they to be understood to be related to the objects studied by the physicist? The subject naturalist is untouched by these worries. The subject naturalist's question is how to understand the practices of counting and doing arithmetic in virtue of which (natural) number talk means what it does. If we can explain, in naturalistically acceptable terms, how it is possible to teach and learn to count and calculate using numerals, ontological difficulties of the sort that exercise the object naturalist should be taken at most to throw doubt on the aptness of this sort of discourse to the kind of representationalist semantic treatment that can then be seen to be the source of those difficulties. So long as we can understand the discursive practices of using the target vocabulary naturalistically—can offer a naturalistic pragmatic theory of that discourse—there need be no fear that anything is going on that is puzzling from a naturalistic point of view.

Subject naturalism is Wittgensteinian rather than Carnapian naturalism. In his later work, Wittgenstein dispels distinctively metaphysical puzzlement about the nature of certain kinds of *things* (pains, numbers) by refocusing attention on the corresponding kinds of *talk* (pain-talk, number-talk). If the practices of evincing and ascribing pains can be made sense of in common-sense terms, without having to invoke any mysterious abilities, if we can understand how such practices arise, and are taught and learned, then worries on the part of the naturalist about the peculiarity of the things we take ourselves to be talking *about* (such as the Cartesian privacy of pains) seem out of place. In this case, Rorty's eliminative materialism completes the job Wittgenstein begins. Identifying, as the title of one of his famous early essays puts it, "Incorrigibility as the Mark of the Mental," in the distinctively

---

vocabulary is licit, that other expressive roles are second-class (though the categorial ones are, in a certain sense, parasitic on the descriptive).

58. As Hartry Field does in *Science without Numbers* (Princeton, NJ: Princeton University Press, 1980).

Cartesian sense (unknown to the Greeks and medievals) he first offers an analysis of the incorrigibility and privacy of mental events as reflecting a distinctive kind of *authority* accorded to certain sincere first-person avowals. He then offers what amounts to a social-engineering account of the social practices by which authority of this distinctive kind can be instituted and accorded by a community to certain performances. The final step is then to describe how such discursive practices, having arisen out of a situation in which this distinctive kind of authority did not exist, could themselves evolve so as to outgrow it—if, for instance, the community comes to allow the overriding in some circumstances of sincere first-person avowals of being in pain on the basis of cerebroscopical evidence. A picture according to which the practices of pain avowal and attribution are seen as reflecting the antecedent metaphysical nature of what is being avowed and attributed is replaced by one in which the practices themselves are explained, without appeal to metaphysically puzzling entities they are taken to report.

Subject naturalism is so called because it is naturalistic about the subjects who engage in discursive practices, rather than the objects they talk and think about. It is a *pragmatic* naturalism—naturalism about the *use* of language—rather than a *semantic* naturalism concerned with the purported referents of linguistic expressions. Wittgenstein is fond of reminding us that not all grammatically singular terms perform the job of picking out objects, and not all declarative sentences are in the fact-stating line of work. When in doubt, his counsel is not to be wedded to a particular semantic picture, but to look at the actual use of the expression. If it can be unproblematically characterized—in particular, if we can see how otherwise unremarkable abilities and practices can be recruited and deployed so as to add up to the discursive practice-or-ability in question—then the demands of naturalism should count as having been satisfied.

Asking what constraints should be imposed on a pragmatic metavocabulary shows that we should distinguish two species of subject naturalism. Descriptivist subject naturalism restricts the pragmatic metavocabulary it employs to empirical descriptive vocabulary, whether that of common sense, the special sciences, or fundamental physics. This is the same range of options available to object naturalists. But pragmatic naturalism need not be descriptivist. It can be not what the young Sellars called "empirical pragmatics," but what in the passage I cited above he called "pure pragmatics." The difference lies in the pragmatic metavocabulary used. Once we have appreciated the distinctive expressive role characteristic of categorial concepts—pure concepts that make explicit what is implicit in the use of empirical descriptive vocabulary—another option emerges. A pragmatic metavocabulary can include vocabulary that is elaborated from and explicative of the use of any empirical descriptive vocabulary (and hence of any autonomous discursive practice—since, I take it, any ADP must include the use of empirical descriptive vocabulary). This includes not only alethic modal vocabulary, but also, as I argue in Chapter 4, normative vocabulary. In this regard, I am with the left-wing Sellarsians—but on grounds that, as the passage cited above shows, Sellars emphasized throughout his career. The principal expressive role of universally LX vocabulary is nondescriptive. (I argue in Chapter 5 that this is compatible with such vocabulary *also* playing a descriptive role—albeit one that can only be understood against the background of its basic categorial expressive role.)

Nonetheless, nondescriptive expressive pragmatic naturalism counts as a *naturalism* insofar as the *use* and *content* of the nondescriptive pragmatic metavocabulary it employs is intelligible entirely in terms of the use of whatever kind of descriptive vocabulary is favored (privileged) by a particular variety of naturalism (e.g. the vocabulary of the special sciences, fundamental physics, or even ordinary empirical descriptive vocabulary). The use of descriptive vocabulary can not only be *described,* it can be *made explicit.* The botanization of pragmatically mediated expressive roles presented in *Between Saying and Doing* and exploited in Chapter 4 shows that *expression* is a much wider category than *description*—a claim Sellars is much concerned to emphasize when he is wearing his anti-descriptivist hat. Universally LX vocabularies are a special kind of pragmatic metavocabulary. The masteridea of *nondescriptivist pragmatic subject naturalism* is that one ought to be able to employ in one's pragmatic metavocabulary not only any vocabulary playing this distinctive categorial expressive role with respect to empirical descriptive vocabulary, but indeed any vocabulary whose use can itself be specified by such an LX pragmatic metavocabulary. For this kind of pragmatic naturalism, it can be specifications of use, of discursive practices, in pragmatic metavocabularies "all the way down"—or rather, all the way up the hierarchy of pragmatic metavocabularies, metametavocabularies, and so on. Besides *describing* discursive practice, we can *explicate* it. And the practices of doing that, too, can be explicated. If the base language underlying all this explication (as opposed to that employed in doing so) is that of empirical description, the enterprise deserves to be thought of as naturalistic in an extended sense.[59] This is what I would make of Sellars's "pure pragmatics": an expressive pragmatic (subject) naturalism that avoids scientism by rejecting its genus, descriptivism.

My conclusion is that Sellars's best wisdom on the topic of naturalism is contained in his early ideas about pure pragmatics. What is aspired to is not the object naturalism expressed in the *scientia mensura* passage. It is a subject naturalism, specifically a *pragmatic* naturalism. Further, it is a *pure* pragmatic naturalism, rather than an empirical, factual, or descriptive naturalism (all, for the early Sellars, ways of picking out the same pragmatic metavocabulary). In keeping with the best way of working out his ideas about Kantian categories, I recommend we think about this nondescriptivist pragmatic naturalism as an *expressive* pragmatic naturalism. The pragmatic metavocabulary centers around vocabulary that is both elaborated from and explicative of essential features of the use of empirical descriptive vocabulary. At this point the motivation for according a unique global ontological or metaphysical privilege to *scientific* descriptive vocabulary as opposed to the ordinary empirical descriptive vocabulary of the manifest image lapses—tied, as it is, to the object naturalist framework. With it, commitment to the in-principle replaceability of that ordinary empirical descriptive vocabulary by the descriptive vocabulary of eventual natural science is also seen to be mistaken. As I quoted in Part I, Sellars formulated his anti-descriptivist creed like this:

> [O]nce the tautology 'The world is described by descriptive concepts' is freed from the idea that the business of all non-logical concepts is to describe, the way is clear to an *ungrudging* recognition that many expressions which empiricists have relegated to second-class citizenship in discourse are not *inferior,* just *different.*[60]

---

59. In another early essay, "Epistemology and the New Way of Words," Sellars says "philosophy is properly conceived as the *pure theory of empirical languages,*" observing that pure semantics is only a proper part of it; *PPPW,* p. 31.

60. CDCM §79.

I want to claim that we have now seen that the way is clear to an *ungrudging* recognition that many manifest-image descriptive expressions which scientific naturalists have relegated to second-class citizenship in discourse are not *inferior*, just *different*. We need no longer look forward, as Sellars unfortunately thought we were obliged to do, to a future in which descriptive concepts such as person have been superseded by successor-concepts expressed in the language of neurophysiology.

Conclusion

The general view I have been elaborating and defending in this chapter is that Sellars's thought can be understood as articulated by two developments he saw himself as offering of central themes of Kant. The first is what Sellars made of Kant's notion of "pure categories of the Understanding." The second is what he made of Kant's distinction—a constitutive element of his transcendental idealism—between phenomena and noumena. Under the first heading, Sellars appreciated that besides concepts whose primary function is the empirical description and explanation of objective features of the world, there are concepts whose expressive role is to make explicit aspects of the discursive framework within which empirical description and explanation are possible. Under the second heading, Sellars claimed that "in the dimension of describing and explaining," ordinary empirical descriptive vocabulary expresses how things merely appear (phenomena), while "science is the measure of all things, of what is that it is, and of what is not that it is not," i.e. what there really is (noumena). Put crudely, my claim has been that the first is a Good Idea, and the second is a Bad Idea. Somewhat less crudely, it is that Sellars's own better wisdom regarding the first master-idea should have motivated a different way of working out his naturalist insight. On the critical side, what I have called the "modal Kant-Sellars thesis" and his argument against phenomenalist reductionism should have shown him that both the identity version of the sense/reference reading of the *scientia mensura* and the functional best-realizers version of it were not workable. On the positive side, his understanding of "pure pragmatics" and his metalinguistic way of working out the Kantian idea of categories open up space for and point to a nondescriptivist expressive, pragmatic, subject naturalism that accords well with his early conceptions and avoids the difficulties of principle that afflict the scientific object naturalism to which he ended up committed.

At the beginning of this chapter I mentioned Sellars's description of his philosophical aspiration to move analytic philosophy from its Humean to its Kantian phase. Probably the most important dimension of that desirable transformation is the normative insight Rorty appealed to in picking out left-wing Sellarsianism: that in characterizing an episode in intentional terms we are not describing it, but placing it in a normative space of justifying and reasoning. Sellars's thought is animated throughout by an appreciation of Kant's fundamental insight that what distinguishes judgments and intentional actions from the responses of nondiscursive creatures is that they are things subjects are in a distinctive way *responsible* for. What they are responsible for *doing* is having reasons for them. About this crucial normative, rational dimension demarcating specifically discursive activities, Sellars was never a scientific naturalist. In the first half of this chapter, I was concerned to point to another, perhaps less appreciated strand in Sellars's neo-Kantianism: his metalinguistic pragmatic expressivism, as it is on display in the way he develops Kant's notion of "pure categories of the Understanding." (In Chapter 7 I argue that it is the key to his nominalism about universals and "abstract objects" more generally.) In the second half of this chapter I diagnosed Sellars's rendering of Kant's transcendental distinction between phenomena and noumena as involving, in effect, backsliding into a basically Humean metaphysics of kinds (of a sort not unpopular in contemporary analytic metaphysics). Following out the consequences of the modal Kant-Sellars thesis pointed the way toward a more Kantian metaphysics of kinds. I ended by recommending a shift in attention from the metaphysical issues of object naturalism to a more Wittgensteinian pragmatic expressivism as a nondescriptivist subject naturalism, inspired by Sellars's early "pure pragmatics" and informed by how it is possible to develop his ideas about Kantian categories in terms of pragmatic metavocabularies.

I am very aware that arguments I have offered—particularly in criticizing various versions of the sense/reference scientific object naturalist understanding of the phenomena/noumena distinction—are defeasible. I have not tried to armor them against the objections or defend them against the alternatives that abound in the massive literature on the relevant topics. I do not pretend that I have offered knock-down arguments. I take it that argument in philosophy, as in ordinary life and in such more institutionalized fora as the law court and the medical examining room, is in general nonmonotonic, that is defeasible: probative rather than dispositive. That it is is of course no reason not to offer arguments, nor a reason to denigrate or despise them. For it is by exploring the inferential network by following argumentative paths that we come to understand. My hope is that the perspective provided by tracing the trajectory through issues of identity and individuation associated with sortals that begins with the modal Kant-Sellars thesis affords some such insight. But as Sellars says at the end of one of his first published papers: "It would be foolish for me to pretend that I have done more than grope in the right direction."[61]

61. RNWW, p. 77.

CHAPTER TWO

The Centrality of Sellars's Two-Ply Account of Observation to the Arguments of *Empiricism and the Philosophy of Mind*

Empiricism and the Philosophy of Mind (*EPM*) is one of the great works of twentieth-century philosophy. It is rich, deep, and revolutionary in its consequences. It cannot, however, be ranked among the most *perspicuous* of philosophical writings. Although it is fairly easy to discern its general tenor and tendency, the convoluted and digressive order of exposition pursued in the essay has obscured for many readers the exact outlines of such a fundamental concept as givenness—with the result that few could at the end of their reading accurately trace its boundaries and say what all its species have in common, being obliged instead to content themselves with being able to recognize some of its exemplary instances. Again, I think that partly for this reason, readers of *EPM* seldom realize just how radical is its critique of empiricism—just how much of traditional empiricist ways of thinking must be rejected if Sellars's arguments are accepted. And if the full extent of the work's conclusions is hard to appreciate, all the more difficult is it to follow its argumentative path through all its turnings. In what follows my aim is to lay out one basic idea of Sellars's, which I see as underlying three of the most important arguments he deploys along the way to his conclusions. My concern here will not be in how those arguments contribute to his overall enterprise, but rather in how they are rooted in a common thought. Sellars does not make this basic idea as explicit as one would like, and does not stop along the way to observe how each of the three individual arguments depends on it. But if I am right, we will understand the essay better by being able to identify and individuate this thread in the tapestry.

The master-idea I want to start with is Sellars's understanding of observational capacities: the ability to make noninferential reports of, or to form perceptual judgments concerning, perceptible facts. My claim is that he treats them as the product of two distinguishable sorts of abilities: the capacity reliably to discriminate behaviorally between different sorts of stimuli and the capacity to take up a position in the game of giving and asking for reasons. The three central strategic moves in the essay I will seek to understand in terms of that two-factor approach to observation are, first, the way he dissolves a particular Cartesian temptation by offering a novel account of the expressive function of 'looks' talk; second, his rationalist account of the acquisition of empirical concepts; and third, his account of how theoretical concepts can come to have observational uses.

1. Sellars's Two-Ply Account of Observation

If we strip empiricism down to its core, we might identify it with the insight that knowledge of the empirical world depends essentially on the capacity of knowing organisms to respond differentially to distinct environing stimuli. I'll call this claim *'basic'*, or 'stripped down' empiricism; it could equally well be called the *trivial* thesis of empiricism.[1] Surely no rationalist or idealist has ever denied *this* claim. While differential responsiveness is obviously a necessary condition for empirical knowledge, it is clearly nothing like a sufficient condition. A chunk of iron responds differentially to stimuli, for instance, by rusting in some environments and not in others. To that extent, it can be construed as *classifying* its environments, taking or treating them as being of one of two kinds. In the same way, as Hegel says, an animal takes something as food by "falling to without further ado and eating it up."[2] But this sort of classificatory taking something *as* something should not yet be classed as a *cognitive* matter, on pain of losing sight of the fundamental ways in which genuine observationally acquired knowledge differs from what is exhibited by merely irritable devices such as thermostats and land mines.

---

1. I would call it "minimal empiricism," except that John McDowell, in the Introduction to the paperback edition of *Mind and World* (Cambridge, MA: Harvard University Press, 1996) has adopted that term for a *much* more committal thesis.

2. *Phenomenology*, paragraph 109, in the numeration of A. V. Miller's translation (Oxford: Oxford University Press, 1979).

A parrot could be trained to respond to the visible presence of red things by uttering the noise "That's red." We might suppose that it is disposed to produce this performance under just the same circumstances in which a genuine observer and reporter of red things is disposed to produce a physically similar performance. There is an important respect in which the parrot and the observer are alike. We could call what they share a *reliable differential responsive disposition* (which I'll sometimes shorten to 'RDRD'). RDRDs are the first element in Sellars's two-ply account of observational knowledge. At least in the basic case, they are characterizable in a naturalistic, physicalistic vocabulary.³ The concept of an RDRD is meant to capture the capacity we genuine knowers share with artifacts and merely sentient creatures such as parrots that the basic thesis of empiricism insists is a necessary condition of empirical knowledge.

The second element of Sellars's two-ply account of observational knowledge is meant to distinguish possessors of genuine observational belief and knowledge from merely reliable differential responders. What is the crucial difference between the red-discriminating parrot and the genuine observer of red things? It is the difference between *sentience* and *sapience*. For Sellars's purposes in *EPM*, the difference between merely differentially responding artifacts and genuinely sentient organisms does not make an essential cognitive or epistemological difference. *All* we need pay attention to in them is their exercising of reliable differential responsive dispositions. But he is very concerned with what distinguishes both of these sorts of things from genuine observers. His thought is that the difference that makes a difference is that candidates for observational knowledge don't just have reliable dispositions to respond differentially to stimuli by *making noises,* but have reliable dispositions to respond differentially to those stimuli by *applying concepts.* The genuine observer responds to visible red things by coming to believe, claiming, or reporting *that* there is something red. Sapient awareness differs from awareness in the sense of mere differential responsiveness (the sort exhibited by any organism or device that can for instance be said in the full sense to be capable of avoiding obstacles) in that the sapient being

---

3. They would not be so characterizable in cases where the response is specified in, say, normative or semantic vocabulary—for instance, as *correctly* using the word 'red', or as applying the *concept* red.

responsively classifies the stimuli as falling under concepts, as being of some conceptually articulated kind.

It is obvious that everything turns on how one goes on to understand concept application or the conceptual articulation of responses. For Sellars, it is a linguistic affair: grasping a concept is mastering the use of a word. Then we must ask what makes something a use of a word, in the sense relevant to the application of concepts. Sellars's answer is that for the response reliably differentially elicited by the visible presence of a perceptible state of affairs to count as the application of a concept, for it to be properly characterized as a reporting or coming to believe *that* such-and-such is the case, is for it to be the making of a certain kind of move or the taking up of a certain kind of position in a game of giving and asking for reasons. It must be committing oneself to a content that can both serve as and stand in need of *reasons,* that is, that can play the role both of premise and of conclusion in *inferences.* The observer's response is conceptually contentful just insofar as it occupies a node in a web of inferential relations.

What the parrot lacks is a *conceptual understanding* of its response. That is why it is just making noise. Its response means nothing to the parrot—though it may mean something to us, who *can* make inferences from it, in the way we do from changes in the states of measuring instruments. The parrot does not treat red as entailing colored, as entailed by scarlet, as incompatible with green, and so on. And because it does not, uttering the noise 'red' is not, for the parrot, the adopting of a stance that can serve as a reason committing or entitling it to adopt other stances, and potentially in need of reasons that might be supplied by still further such stances. By contrast, the observer's utterance of 'That's red', is making a move, adopting a position, in a game of giving and asking for reasons. And the observer's grasp of the conceptual content expressed by her utterance consists in her practical mastery of its significance in that game: her knowing (in the sense of being able practically to discriminate, a kind of knowing *how*) what follows from her claim and what it follows from, what would be evidence for it and what is incompatible with it.

Although Sellars does not carefully distinguish them, two different strands can be discerned within this second element of his account. First is the idea that for performances (whether noninferentially elicited responses or not) to count as *claims,* and so as expressions of *beliefs* or *judgments,* as candidates for *knowledge*, they must be in what he calls "the dimension of endorsement."[4] This is to say that they must have a certain sort of pragmatic significance or force: they must express the endorsement of some content by the candidate knower. They must be the adoption of a certain kind of normative stance: the undertaking of a *commitment*. Second, that the commitment is a *cognitive* commitment, the endorsement of a *conceptual content*, is to be understood in terms of its *inferential* articulation, its place in the "space of reasons," its being a move in the "game of giving and asking for reasons."[5] This is to say at least that in making a claim one commits oneself to its suitability as a premise from which conclusions can be drawn, a commitment whose entitlement is always at least potentially liable to demands for vindication by the exhibition of other claims that can serve as reasons for it.

This two-factor account of perceptual judgments (claims to observational knowledge) is a version of a broadly Kantian strategy: insisting on the collaboration of capacities characterizable in terms of receptivity and spontaneity. It is a pragmatic version, since it is couched in terms of know *how*: practical abilities to respond differentially to nonlinguistic stimuli, and to distinguish in practice what inferentially follows from or serves as a reason for what. The residual empiricism of the approach consists in its insistence on the need for the exercise of some of our conceptual capacities to be the exercise of RDRDs. Its residual rationalism consists in its insistence that the responses in question have cognitive significance, count as applications of concepts, only in virtue of their role in reasoning. What otherwise would appear as language-entry moves, without language-language moves, are blind. What otherwise would appear as language-language moves, without language-entry moves, are empty. (I say "what otherwise would appear" as moves because such blind or empty moves do not for Sellars qualify as moves in a *language* game at all.)[6]

---

4. Sellars's discussion begins at *EPM* §16. All references are to section numbers of Sellars's *Empiricism and the Philosophy of Mind*, reprinted with an Introduction by Richard Rorty and a Study Guide by Robert Brandom (Cambridge, MA: Harvard University Press, 1997).
5. See for instance *EPM* §36.
6. The idiom of "language-language" moves and "language-entry" moves is drawn from Sellars's "Some Reflections on Language Games," in *Science, Perception, and Reality* (London: Routledge and Kegan Paul, 1963). Reprinted in *In the Space of Reasons*.

It follows from this two-pronged approach that we must be careful in characterizing perceptual judgments or reports of observations as 'noninferential'. They are noninferential in the sense that the particular acts or tokenings are noninferentially *elicited*. They are not the products of a process of inference, arising rather by the exercise of reliable capacities to noninferentially respond differentially to various sorts of perceptible states of affairs by applying concepts. But *no* beliefs, judgments, reports, or claims—in general, no applications of concepts—are noninferential in the sense that their content can be understood apart from their role in reasoning as potential premises and conclusions of inferences. Any response that does not at least potentially have an inferential significance—which cannot, for instance, serve as a premise in reasoning to further conclusions—is cognitively idle, a wheel on which nothing else turns.

This rationalist claim has radical consequences. It means that there can be no language consisting only of noninferential reports, no system of concepts whose *only* use is in making perceptual judgments. Noninferential reports do not form an autonomous stratum of language: a game one could play though one played no other. For that they are *reports* or *claims*, expressions of *beliefs* or *judgments*, that they are applications of *concepts* at all, consists in their availability to serve as premises and conclusions of inferences. And this is so no matter what the subject matter of the reports might be—even if what is reported, that of which one is noninferentially aware, is one's own current mental states. Awareness that reaches beyond mere differential responsiveness—that is, awareness in the sense that bears on *cognition*—is an essentially inferentially articulated affair.

So observational concepts, ones that have (at least some) noninferential circumstances of appropriate application, can be thought of as *inference laden*. It does not follow, by the way, that they are for Sellars for that reason also *theory laden*. For, as will appear below, Sellars understands theoretical concepts as those that have only inferential circumstances of appropriate application—so that noncompound claims in which they occur essentially are ones that one can only become entitled to as the result of an inference. His rationalist rendering of the notion of conceptual contentfulness in terms of role in reasoning only commits Sellars to the claim that for any concept to have noninferential uses, it must have inferential ones as well. He is prepared to countenance the possibility of an autonomous language game in which every concept has noninferential as well as inferential uses. Such a language game would be devoid of theoretical terms.

2. 'Looks' Talk and Sellars's Diagnosis of the Cartesian Hypostatization of Appearances

One of the central arguments of *EPM* applies this two-legged understanding of the use of observational concepts to the traditional understanding of claims about how things *look* as reports of *appearances*. The question he addresses can be variously put. In one form it is the question of whether looks-red comes before is-red conceptually (and so in the order of explanation). Put in a form more congenial and comprehensible to a pragmatist—that is, in a form that concerns our abilities to *do* something—this becomes the question of whether the latter can be defined in terms of the former in such a way that one could learn how to use the defining concept (looking-ϕ) first, and only afterwards, by means of the definition, learn how to use the defined concept (is-ϕ). Since Sellars understands grasp of a concept in terms of mastery of the use of a word, this then becomes a question about the relation between practices of using "looks-ϕ" talk and the practices of using "is-ϕ" talk. This is a relatively clear way of asking about an issue that goes to the heart of the Cartesian project of defining the ontological realm of the mental in terms of the epistemic privileged access in the sense of incorrigibility of mental occurrences.

Descartes was struck by the fact that the appearance/reality distinction seems not to apply to appearances. While I may be mistaken about whether something *is* red (or whether the tower, in the distance, *is* square), I cannot in the same way be mistaken about whether it *looks* red to me now.[7] While I may legitimately be challenged by a doubter: "Perhaps the item is not *really* red; perhaps it only *seems* red," there is no room for the further doubt, "Perhaps the item does not even *seem* red; perhaps it only *seems* to seem

---

7. I might be mistaken about whether *red* is what it looks, that is, whether the property expressed by the word 'red' is the one it looks to have. But that, the thought goes, is another matter. I cannot be mistaken that it looks that way, like *that*, where this latter phrase is understood as having a noncomparative use. It *looks-red*, a distinctive phenomenal property, which we may inconveniently only happen to be able to pick out by its association with a word for a real-world property.

red." If it seems to seem red, then it really does seem red. The *looks, seems,* or *appears* operators collapse if we try to iterate them. A contrast between appearance and reality is marked by the distinction between looks-ϕ and ϕ for ordinary (reality-indicating) predicates 'ϕ'. But no corresponding contrast is marked by the distinction between looks-to-look-ϕ and looks-ϕ. Appearances are reified by Descartes as things that really are just however they appear. He inferred that we do not know them mediately, by means of representings that introduce the possibility of *mis*-representing (a distinction between how they really are and how they merely appear, i.e. are represented as being). Rather, we know them *immediately*—simply by having them. Thus appearings—thought of as a realm of entities *reported* on by noninferentially elicited claims about how things *look* (for the visual case), or more generally *seem,* or *appear*—show up as having the ideal qualifications for epistemologically secure foundations of knowledge: we cannot make mistakes about them. Just *having* an appearance ("being appeared-to ϕ-ly," in one of the variations Sellars discusses) counts as *knowing* something: not that something is ϕ, to be sure, but at least that something *looks-, seems-,* or *appears*-ϕ. The possibility accordingly arises of reconstructing our knowledge by starting out only with knowledge of this sort—knowledge of how things look, seem, or appear—and building up in some way to our knowledge (if any) of how things really are (outside the realm of appearance).

This project requires that concepts of the form looks-ϕ be intelligible in principle in advance of grasping the corresponding concepts ϕ (or is-ϕ). Sellars argues that Descartes got things backwards. 'Looks' talk does not form an autonomous stratum of the language—it is not a language game one could play though one played no other. One must already be able to use 'is-ϕ' talk in order to master 'looks-ϕ' talk, which turns out to be parasitic on it. In this precise practical sense, is-ϕ is *conceptually* (Sellars often says 'logically') *prior* to looks-ϕ.

His argument takes the form of an account of how 'looks' talk can arise piggy-backed on 'is' talk. In *EPM* Sellars does not try to support the strong modal claim that the various practices *must* be related in this way. He thinks that his alternative account of the relation between these idioms is so persuasive that we will no longer be tempted by the Cartesian picture. It is an interesting question, which I will not pursue here, whether his story can be turned into an even more compelling argument for the stronger claim he wants to make. What he offers us is the parable of John in the tie shop.

At the first stage, John has mastered the noninferential use of terms such as 'green' and 'blue'. So he can, typically, reliably respond to green things by applying the concept <u>green</u>, to blue things by applying the concept <u>blue</u>, and so on. To say that his responsive dispositions are reliable is to say that he usually turns out to be right—so the inference from his being disposed to call something 'green' or 'blue' to its being green or blue is a generally good (though not infallible) one.

At the next stage, electric lights are installed in the shop, and John discovers that they make him prey to certain sorts of systematic errors. Often, when under the electric lights inside his shop he observes something to be green, it turns out in fact—when he and others examine it outside in daylight—to be blue. Here it is obviously important that John have access to some ways of entitling himself to the claim that something is blue, besides the term he is initially disposed to apply to it. This can include his dispositions to respond to it outside the shop, together with his beliefs about the circumstances in which ties do and do not change color, the assessments of others, and the fact that the proper use of color terms was originally keyed to daylight assessments. At this point, John becomes cautious. When viewing under the nonstandard conditions of electric lighting, he does not indulge his otherwise reliable disposition to respond to some visible ties by calling them green. Instead he says something like "I'm disposed to call this green, and if I didn't know that under these circumstances I'm not a reliable discriminator of green things, I would give in to that temptation and call it green."

At the final stage, John learns under these circumstance to substitute the expression "It *looks* green" for this long expression of temptation withstood. Using the expression "looks-ϕ" is doing two things: first, it is evincing the same usually reliable differential responsive disposition that in other circumstances results in the claim that something *is*. But second, it is *withholding* the endorsement of the claim that something is green. In other words, it is doing something that agrees with an ordinary noninferential report of green things on the first component of Sellars's two-ply account of observation reports—sharing an RDRD—but disagrees with it on the second component, withholding endorsement instead of undertaking the commitment.

The idea is that where collateral beliefs indicate that systematic error is likely, the subject learns not to make the report 'x is ϕ', to which his previously inculcated responsive dispositions incline him, but to make a new kind of claim: 'x *looks* (or seems) ϕ'. The Cartesian temptation is to take this as a new kind of report. This report then is naturally thought of as reporting a minimal, noninferentially ascertainable, foundationally basic item, an appearing, about which each subject is incorrigible. Sellars's claim is that it is a mistake to treat these as reports at all—since they *evince* a disposition to call something ϕ, but do not do so. They do not even *report* the presence of the disposition—that is, they are not ways of *saying* that one has that disposition.

This analysis of what one is doing in using 'looks' explains the incorrigibility of 'looks' talk. One can be wrong about whether something *is* green because the claim one endorses, the commitment one undertakes, may turn out to be incorrect. For instance, its inferential consequences may be incompatible with other facts one is or comes to be in a position to know independently. But in saying that something *looks* green, one is not endorsing a claim, but *withholding* endorsement from one. Such a reporter is merely evincing a disposition to do something that for other reasons (e.g. suspicion that the circumstances of observation lead to systematic error) he is unwilling to do—namely, endorse a claim. Such a reporter cannot be wrong, because he has held back from making a commitment. This is why the *looks, seems,* and *appears* operators do not iterate. Their function is to express the withholding of endorsement from the sentence that appears within the scope of the operator. There is no sensible contrast between 'looks-to-look ϕ' and 'looks-ϕ', of the sort there is between 'looks-ϕ' and 'is-ϕ', because the first 'looks' has already withheld endorsement from the only content in the vicinity to which one might be committed (to something's being ϕ). There is no further withholding work for the second 'looks' to do. There is nothing left to take back. Since asserting 'x looks ϕ' is not undertaking a propositionally contentful commitment—but only expressing an overrideable disposition to do so—there is no issue as to whether or not that commitment (which one?) is correct.

Sellars accordingly explains the incorrigibility of appearance claims, which had so impressed Descartes. He does so in terms of the practices of using words, which are what grasp of the relevant appearance concepts must amount to, according to his methodological linguistic pragmatism. But once we have seen the source and nature of this incorrigibility—in down-to-earth, practical, resolutely nonmetaphysical terms—we see also why it is precisely unsuited to use as an epistemological foundation for the rest of our (risky, corrigible) empirical knowledge. For, first, the incorrigibility of claims about how things merely *look* simply reflects their emptiness: the fact that they are not really claims at all. And second, the same story shows us that 'looks' talk is not an autonomous language game—one that could be played though one played no other. It is entirely parasitic on the practice of making risky empirical reports of how things actually are. Thus Descartes seized on a genuine phenomenon—the incorrigibility of claims about appearances, reflecting the non-iterability of operators like *looks, seems,* and *appears*—but misunderstood its nature, and so mistakenly thought it available to play an epistemologically foundational role for which it is in no way suited.

3. Two Confirmations of the Analysis of 'Looks' Talk in Terms of the Two-Ply Account of Observation

Sellars finds that the analysis of 'looks' talk in terms of the two-pronged account of perceptual judgments is confirmed by its capacity to explain features of appearance-talk that are mysterious on the contrasting Cartesian approach.

i) The apple over there is red.
ii) The apple over there looks red.
iii) It looks as though there were a red apple over there.

Utterances of these sentences can express the same responsive disposition to report the presence of a red apple, but they endorse (take responsibility for the inferential consequences of) different parts of that claim. (i) endorses both the existence of the apple and its quality of redness. (ii) endorses only the existence of the apple. The 'looks' locution explicitly cancels the qualitative commitment or endorsement. (iii) explicitly cancels both the existential and the qualitative endorsements. Thus, if someone claims that there is in fact no apple over there, he is asserting something incompatible with

(i) and (ii), but not with (iii). If he denies that there is anything red over there, he asserts something incompatible with (i), but not with (ii) or (iii). Sellars's account of the practice of using 'looks', in terms of the withholding of endorsement when one suspects systematic error in one's responsive dispositions, can account for the difference in scope of endorsement that (i)–(iii) exhibit. But how could that difference be accounted for by an approach that understands 'looks' talk as reporting a distinctive kind of particular, about which we are incorrigible?

Sellars finds a further confirmation of his account of 'looks' talk—and so of the two-factor account of observational capacities that animates it—in its capacity to explain the possibility of reporting a merely *generic* (more accurately, merely determinable) look. Thus it is possible for an apple to look red, without its looking any specific shade of red (crimson, scarlet, etc.). It is possible for a plane figure to look many-sided without there being some particular number of sides (say 119) which it looks to have. But if 'looks' statements are to be understood as reports of the presence before the eye of the mind of a particular which *is,* how can this possibility be understood? Particulars are completely determinate. A horse has a particular number of hairs, though as Sellars points out, it can *look* to have merely 'a lot' of them. It is a particular shade of brown (or several shades), even though it may look only darkly colored. So how are such generic, merely determinable, looks possible? Sellars's account is in terms of scope of endorsement. One says that the plane figure looks 'many-sided' instead of '119-sided' just in case one is willing only to endorse (be held responsible for justifying) the more general claim. This is a matter of how far one is willing to trust one's responsive dispositions, a matter of the epistemic credence one feels they deserve or are able to sustain. Particulars, even if they are sense contents, cannot be colored without being some determinate color and shade. How then can the sense datum theorist—who wants to say that when something *looks* ϕ to S, something in S *is* ϕ—account for the fact that something can look colored without looking to be any particular color, or look red without looking to be any particular shade of red? So Sellars's account of 'looks' talk in terms of endorsement can account for two aspects of that kind of discourse that no theory that invokes a given can explain: the scope distinctions between qualitative and existential lookings, and the possibility of merely generic or determinable lookings.

4. A Rationalist Account of the Acquisition of Empirical Concepts

It is characteristic of empiricism as Sellars understands (and rejects) it, that it countenances a notion of awareness or experience meeting two conditions. First, it goes beyond mere differential responsiveness in having some sort of cognitive *content*—that is, content of the sort that under favorable circumstances amounts to knowledge. This is the idea of a notion of awareness or experience *of* a red triangle in one's visual field that can at the same time be (or be one's evidence for) knowledge *that* there is a red triangle in one's visual field. Second, this sort of awareness is *preconceptual:* the capacity to be aware in this sense or have experiences of this sort is prior to and independent of the possession of or capacity to apply concepts. The idea of a kind of awareness with these two features is what Sellars calls the "Myth of the Given."

Whatever difficulties there may be with such a conception—most notably the incoherences Sellars rehearses in the opening sections of *EPM*—it does provide the basis for a story about concept acquisition. Concepts are understood as acquired by a process of *abstraction,* whose raw materials are provided by exercises of the primitive capacity for immediate, preconceptual awareness.[8] One may—and Sellars does—raise questions about whether it is possible to elaborate this story in a coherent fashion. But one ought also to ask the corresponding question to the empiricists' rationalist opponents. Rationalists like Sellars claim that *all* awareness is a conceptual affair. Being aware of something, in any sense that goes beyond mere responsiveness in its potential cognitive significance—paradigmatically in its capacity to serve as *evidence*—is bringing it under a concept. Sense experience cannot be the basis for the acquisition of concepts, since it presupposes the capac-

---

8. It is tempting to think that on this line concepts are related to the contents of preconceptual experiences as universals to particulars. But as Sellars points out, the empiricists in fact took as primitive the capacity to be aware already of *repeatables,* such as redness and squareness. This might suggest that the relation is better understood as one of genus to species. But scarlet is not strictly a *species* of the genus red, since there need be no way to specify the relevant differentiae without mentioning the species. (Compare the relation between the phenomenal property of redness and that of being colored.) So the relation between immediately experienceable contents and the concepts under which they are classified is better understood as that of *determinate* repeatable to *determinables* under which it falls.

ity to apply concepts. So how *do* knowers acquire concepts? At this point in the dialectic, classical rationalists such as Leibniz threw up their hands and invoked innate ideas—denying that at least the most basic and general concepts *were* acquired at all. Sellars owes either a defense of innatism, or an alternative account of concept acquisition.

Sellars rejects innatism. Grasp of a concept is mastery of the use of a word, so concepts are acquired in the process of learning a language. But if we don't acquire the concept green by noticing green things, since we must already have the concept in order to notice green things as such (by applying the concept to them), how is it possible for us to learn the use of the word 'green', and hence acquire the concept? We each start by learning the corresponding RDRDs: being trained to respond to visibly green things by uttering what is still for the novice just the *noise* 'green'. This much, the parrot can share. Besides these language-entry moves, the language learner must also master the inferential moves in the vicinity of 'green': that the move to 'colored' is OK, and the move to 'red' is not, and so on. Training in these basic language-language moves consists in acquiring more RDRDs, only now the stimuli, as well as the responses, are utterances.

If a two year old wobbles into the living room and utters the sentence "The house is on fire," we will not generally take him to have claimed or expressed the belief that the house is on fire. He does not know what he is saying—in the sense that he does not yet know what he would be committing himself to by that claim, or what would be evidence for it or against it. If a five year old child utters the same sentence, though, we may well take the utterance to have the significance of a claim, the expression of a belief. We take it to be the adoption of a stance in the dimension of endorsement, to be the undertaking of a commitment, by *holding* the child responsible for her claim: asking for her evidence, asking her what she thinks we should do about it, and so on. For it is now presumed that she can tell what she is committing herself to, and what would entitle her to that commitment, and so knows what she is saying, what claim she is endorsing, what belief she is expressing. When the child masters enough of the inferential moves in the vicinity of a responsively elicited utterance of "That is red," she is taken to have endorsed a claim, and so to have applied a concept.

On the inferential account of distinctively conceptual articulation, grasping a concept requires mastering the inferential connections between the appropriate use of some words and the appropriate use of others. So on this account there is no such thing as grasping just one concept: grasping *any* concept requires grasping *many* concepts. Light dawns slowly over the whole.

How good must one be at discriminating the appropriate antecedents and consequents of using a word in order to count as grasping the concept it expresses? Sellars does not explicitly address this question in *EPM*, but I think his view is that whether or not one's utterance has the significance of endorsing a claim, and so of applying a concept, is a question of how it is treated by the other members of the linguistic community. The normative status of committing oneself—taking up a position in the dimension of endorsement—is a social status. One must be good enough at anticipating and fulfilling one's responsibilities in order to be *held* responsible, and so for one's remarks to be accorded authority, in the sense of being treated as providing suitable premises for inferences by others. How much is enough is not a metaphysical matter of recognizing the crossing of some antecedently specifiable boundary, but a social matter of deciding when to recognize a performance as authoritative and hold the performer responsible. It is a question that belongs in a box with the question when writing one's name at the bottom of a piece of paper counts as committing oneself to pay the bank a certain sum of money every month for thirty years. Some seventeen year olds may actually understand what they would be committing themselves to better than some twenty-two year olds. But the community is not therefore making a metaphysical mistake in treating the latter but not the former as able genuinely to commit themselves.

Sellars account of concept acquisition starts with reliable differential responsive dispositions to respond to environing stimuli by uttering sentences. What is then required is that one's utterance come to have the significance of making a move in the game of giving and asking for reasons. That requires two elements: the practical inferential know-how required to find one's way about in the inferential network connecting different sentences, and the social acknowledgment of that know-how as sufficient for one's performances to have the significance in the linguistic community of commitments to or endorsements of the inferentially articulated claims expressed by those sentences. This story is structured and motivated by Sellars's two-pronged account of observation reports, as noninferentially elicited endorsements of inferentially articulated claims.

5. Giving Theoretical Concepts an Observational Use

As a final example of the work Sellars calls on his two-pronged analysis of observational capacities to do in *Empiricism and the Philosophy of Mind* we might consider his account of how theoretical concepts can acquire an observational use. His reason for addressing the issue is that he wants to make intelligible the idea that some sorts of paradigmatic mental occurrences—thoughts and sense impressions—might first become available to us purely theoretically, and only later come to be observable by us. For showing that such a development in our capacities *is* intelligible provides a means of confounding the Cartesian idea of immediate (that is, noninferential) observability as *essential* to the very idea of mental occurrences. But my concern here is with the general point, rather than this particular application of it.

The first point to realize is that, as I mentioned above, according to Sellars's view, the distinction between theoretical objects and observable objects is *methodological,* rather than *ontological.* That is, theoretical and observable objects are not different kinds of thing. They differ only in how we come to know about them. Theoretical objects are ones of which we can only have *inferential* knowledge, while observable objects can also be known noninferentially. Theoretical concepts are ones we can only be entitled to apply as the conclusions of inferences, while concepts of observables also have noninferential uses. But the line between things to which we have only inferential cognitive access and things to which we also have noninferential cognitive access can shift with time, for instance as new instruments are developed. Thus when first postulated to explain perturbations in the orbit of Neptune, Pluto was a purely theoretical object; the only claims we could make about it were the conclusions of inferences. But the development of more powerful telescopes eventually made it accessible to observation, and so a subject of noninferential reports. Pluto did not then undergo an ontological change. All that changed was its relation to us.[9]

It might be objected to this view that when the issue of the ontological status of theoretical entities is raised, they are not considered merely as

---

9. Notice that this realism about theoretical entities does not entail scientific realism in the sense that privileges science over other sorts of cognitive activity, although Sellars usually discusses the two sorts of claims together.

objects in principle like any others save that they happen at the moment to be beyond our powers of observation. They are thought of as *unobservable* in a much stronger sense: permanently and in principle inaccessible to observation. But Sellars denies that anything is unobservable in this sense. To be observable is just to be noninferentially reportable. Noninferential reportability requires only that there are circumstances in which reporters can apply the concepts in question (the dimension of inferentially articulated endorsement) by exercising reliable differential dispositions to respond to the objects in question (the causal dimension), and know that they are doing so. In this sense, physicists with the right training can *noninferentially* report the presence of mu mesons in cloud chambers. In this sense of 'observation', nothing real is in principle beyond the reach of observation. (Indeed, in Sellars's sense, one who mastered reliable differential responsive dispositions noninferentially to apply *normative* vocabulary would be directly observing normative facts. It is in this sense that we might be said to be able to *hear*, not just the noises someone else makes, but their *words* and, indeed, *what they are saying*—their *meanings*.) It is an empirical question what circumstances we can come reliably to respond to differentially. The development of each new sort of measuring instrument potentially expands the realm of the here-and-now observable.

Once one sees that observation is not based on some primitive sort of preconceptual awareness, the fact that some observation reports are riskier than others and that when challenged we sometimes retreat to safer ones from which the originals can be inferred, will not tempt one to think that the original reports were in fact the products of inference from those basic or minimal observations. The physicist, if challenged to back up his report of a mu meson, may indeed justify his claim by citing the distinctively hooked vapor trail in the cloud chamber. This is something else observable, from which the presence of the mu meson can, in the right circumstances, be inferred. But to say that is not to say that the original report was the product of an inference after all. It was the exercise of a reliable differential responsive disposition keyed to a whole chain of reliably covarying events, which includes mu mesons, hooked vapor trails, and retinal images. What makes it a report of mu mesons, and not of hooked vapor trails or retinal images, is the inferential role of the concept the physicist noninferentially applies. (It is a consequence of something's being a mu meson, for instance, that it is *much* smaller than a finger, which does *not* follow from something's being a hooked vapor trail.) If *mu meson* is the concept the physicist applies noninferentially, then if he is sufficiently reliable, when correct, that is what he *sees*. His retreat, when a question is raised, to a report of a hooked vapor trail, whose presence provides good inferential reason for the original, noninferentially elicited claim, is a retreat to a report that is safer in the sense that he is a *more* reliable reporter of hooked vapor trails than of mu mesons, and that it takes less training to be able reliably to report vapor trails of a certain shape, so that is a skill shared more widely. But the fact that an inferential justification can be offered, and that the demand for one may be in order, no more undermines the status of the original report as noninferentially elicited (as genuinely an observation) than does the corresponding fact that I may under various circumstances be obliged to back up my report of something as red by invoking my reliability as a reporter of red things in these circumstances—from which, together with my disposition to call it red, the claim originally endorsed noninferentially may be inferred.

Thus one can start with grasp of a concept that consists entirely in mastery of its use as a premise and conclusion in inferences—that is, as a purely theoretical concept—and by the addition of suitable RDRDs come to be able to use them observationally, perhaps in observations whose standard conditions include not only such items as good light (as in the tie shop case) but also the presence of various sorts of instruments. This argument once again appeals to and depends upon Sellars's understanding of observational capacities as the product of reliable noninferential responsive dispositions and mastery of inferential norms.

6. Conclusion: On the Relation between the Two Components

Sellars's primary explanatory target in *Empiricism and the Philosophy of Mind* is our knowledge of the current contents of our own minds. He wants to rethink our understanding of the way in which we experience or are aware of what we are thinking and how things perceptually seem to us. The point I have been trying to make in this essay is that the master-idea that guides his argument is a particular way of thinking, not about our knowledge of the contents of our own minds, but about our observational knowledge of ordinary empirical states of affairs. It is because he understands perceptual awareness of a red apple in front of one as he does that Sellars rejects a host of traditional ways of thinking about awareness of having a sense impression of a red apple or the thought that there is a red apple in front of one.

I have claimed Sellars understands the sort of perceptual awareness of external objects that is expressed in observation reports as the product of exercising two different sorts of capacities: the capacity reliably to respond differentially to stimuli (which we share both with merely sentient creatures such as parrots and with merely irritable devices such as thermostats and land mines) and the capacity to take up positions and make moves in a game of giving and asking for reasons. I have rehearsed the way I see some of the major arguments and conceptual moves in the essay as rooted in this two-ply conception: the account of the use of 'looks' talk that underlies the incorrigibility of sincere contemporaneous first-person reports of how things perceptually seem to one, including the treatment of scoped and generic 'looks' claims, Sellars's approach to the issue of concept acquisition, which caused so much trouble for traditional rationalists, and his rendering of the distinction between theoretical and observational concepts.

I would like to close with some observations and questions about the relations between the two kinds of ability whose cooperation Sellars sees as required for observation. The two sorts of capacities define dimensions of perceptual awareness that are in a certain sense orthogonal. We saw in the discussion of concept acquisition the broad outlines of a story about how one might move from possession of mere RDRDs to the capacity to apply observational concepts. And we saw in the discussion of theoretical and observational concepts how one might move from the purely inferential capacity to apply a concept, by the addition of suitable RDRDs, to mastery of a fully observational concept. That is, we saw in the case of particular observational concepts how one could have either of the two components without the other, and then move to having both.

But this shows only *local* independence of the two components: that one can have the RDRD of an observational concept without having the concept, and one can have a concept without having the RDRD needed to be able to apply it observationally. The corresponding global independence claim is not true. Purely theoretical concepts do not form an *autonomous* language game, a game one could play though one played no other. For one must be able to respond conceptually to the utterances of others in order to be talking at all. So one could not play the game of giving and asking for reasons at all unless one could apply at least *some* concepts noninferentially, in the making of observation reports. But this does not mean that there could not be an *insulated* region of purely theoretical concepts, say those of pure mathematics—'insulated' in the sense that they had no inferential connection to anything inferentially connected to a concept that had an observational use. I don't say that any actual mathematics is like this, though it may be. Pure mathematics, I think, is in principle *applicable* to ordinary empirical objects, both those accessible through observation and those (now) accessible only inferentially. Applying an abstract mathematical structure to concrete objects is using the former to guide our inferences concerning the latter. But this relation ought not to be assimilated to that between theoretical objects and observable objects. It is not clearly incompatible with a kind of inferential insulation of the game of giving and asking for reasons concerning the mathematical structures. I think there are many interesting issues in the vicinity that are as yet not fully explored.[10]

It might seem that there could be no interesting question concerning the potential independence of RDRDs, corresponding to this question about the potential independence of the game of giving and asking for reasons. For it seems obvious that there can be reliable differential responsive dispositions without conceptual capacities. That is what mere sentients and artifacts have. But I think in fact there is a subtle question here, and I want to end by posing it. To begin with, what is obvious is at most that the RDRDs corresponding to *some* observational concepts can be exhibited by creatures who lack the corresponding concepts. And we might doubt even this. The story of John in the tie shop reminds us that our dispositions actually to call things red can be quite complex, and interact with our background beliefs—for instance about what are standard conditions for observing red things, and what conditions we are in—in complex ways. Though this claim goes beyond what Sellars says, I think that learning about systematic sources of error can lead us to alter not just how we express our dispositions (substituting 'looks-ϕ' for 'is-ϕ'), but eventually even those dispositions themselves. I think, though I

---

10. See, for instance, McDowell's discussion in "Brandom on Inference and Representation," *Philosophy and Phenomenological Research* 57(1) (1997): 157ff, and my reply at pp. 189ff.

cannot say that I am sure (a condition that itself ought to give some sorts of Cartesians pause), that familiarity with the Müller-Lyer illusion has brought me to a state in which one of the lines no longer even *looks* to me to be longer than the other. The more theoretically laden our concept of standard conditions for some sort of observation are (think of the mu meson case, where those conditions involve the presence of a cloud chamber), the less likely it is that a creature who could deploy no concepts whatsoever could master the RDRDs of a sophisticated observer.

Besides creatures who lack concepts entirely (because they are not players in any game of giving and asking for reasons), we could ask about which RDRDs are in principle masterable by concept users who for some reason lack the specific concepts that for the genuine observer are keyed to the RDRDs in question. It might be, for all I know, that by suitable reinforcement I could be trained to sort potsherds into two piles, which I label with the nonsense terms 'ping' and 'pong', in such a way that I always and only put Toltec potsherds in the 'ping' pile and Aztec ones in the 'pong' pile. What would make my noises *nonsense* is that they do not engage inferentially with my use of any other expressions. And we might suppose that I do not have the concepts Toltec and Aztec. If told to substitute the labels 'Toltec' and 'Aztec' for 'ping' and 'pong', I would then be a kind of idiot savant with respect to the noninferential applicability of those concepts (which I would still not grasp). Perhaps there are no conceptual limits to such idiot savantry. But I find it hard to conceive of cases in which someone who lacks all the relevant concepts nonetheless can acquire the RDRDs necessary to serve as a measuring device (not, by hypothesis, a genuine reporter) of observable instances of the applicability of thick moral concepts such as courage, sensitivity, cruelty, justice, and so on. Of course, unless one endorses something like Sellars's account of what is required for something to be observable, it will seem that such properties are not suitable candidates for being observable by *anybody*, never mind by idiot savants. But for those of us who do accept his approach, this sort of question is one that must, I think, be taken seriously. That is the thought I want to leave you with at the end of this chapter.

CHAPTER THREE

Pragmatism, Inferentialism, and Modality in Sellars's Arguments against Empiricism

1. Introduction

In this chapter I want to place the arguments of *Empiricism and the Philosophy of Mind* into the context of some of Sellars's other, nearly contemporary articles, by tracing further, into those neighboring works, some strands of argumentation that intersect and are woven together in his critique of empiricism in its two principal then-extant forms: traditional and twentieth-century logical empiricism. Sellars always accepted that observation reports resulting noninferentially from the exercise of perceptual language-entry capacities play both the privileged epistemological role of being the ultimate court of appeal for the justification of empirical knowledge claims and therefore (given his inferentialist semantics) an essential semantic role in determining the contents of the empirical concepts applied in such judgments. But in accord with his stated aspiration to "move analytic philosophy from its Humean into its Kantian phase," he was severely and in principle critical of empiricist ambitions and programs in epistemology and (especially) semantics that go beyond this minimal, carefully circumscribed characterization of the cognitive significance of sense experience. Indeed, I think the lasting philosophical interest of Sellars's thought lies primarily in the battery of original considerations and arguments he brings to bear against all weightier forms of empiricism. Some, but not all, of these are deployed in the opening critical portions of *Empiricism and the Philosophy of Mind*, where the ground is cleared and prepared for the constructive theorizing of the last half. But what is on offer there is only part of Sellars's overall critique of empiricism. We accordingly court misunderstanding of what is there if we do not appreciate the shape of the larger enterprise to which it contributes.

In an autobiographical sketch, Sellars dates his break with traditional empiricism to his Oxford days in the thirties. It was, he says, prompted by concern with understanding the sort of conceptual content that ought to be associated with "logical, causal, and deontological modalities." Already at that point he says that he had the idea that

> what was needed was a functional theory of concepts which would make their role in reasoning, rather than supposed origin in experience, their primary feature.[1]

This telling passage introduces two of the master-ideas that shape Sellars's critique of empiricism. The first is that a key criterion of adequacy with respect to which its semantics will be found wanting concerns its treatment of *modal* concepts. The second is that the remedy for this inadequacy lies in an alternative broadly functional approach to the semantics of these concepts that focuses on their *inferential roles*—as it were, looking *downstream* to their subsequent *use*, as well as *upstream* to the circumstances that elicit their application.

This second, inferential-functionalist, semantic idea looms large in *Empiricism and the Philosophy of Mind*. In fact, it provides the raw materials that are assembled and articulated into Sellars's positive account of the semantics of the concepts applied in reporting thoughts and sense impressions. Concern with the significance of *modality* in the critique of empiricism, however, is almost wholly absent from that work (even though it is evident in articles Sellars wrote even earlier). I do not think that is because it was not, even then, an essential element of the larger picture of empiricism's failings that Sellars was seeking to convey, but rather because it was the result of a hard-won but ultimately successful divide-and-conquer expository strategy. That is, I conjecture that what made it possible for Sellars finally to write *Empiricism and the Philosophy of Mind* was figuring out a way to articulate the considerations he advances there *without* having also at the same time to explore the issues raised by empiricism's difficulties with modal concepts. Whether or not that conjecture about the intellectual-biographical

---

1. "Autobiographical Reflections (February, 1973)," in H. N. Castañeda (ed.), *Action, Knowledge, and Reality*, (Indianapolis, IN: Bobbs-Merrill, 1975), p. 285.

significance of finding a narrative path that makes possible the separation of these aspects of his project is correct, I want to claim that it is important to understand what goes on in *Empiricism and the Philosophy of Mind* in the light of the fuller picture of the expressive impoverishment of empiricism that becomes visible when we consider what Sellars says when he *does* turn his attention to the semantics of modality.[2]

There is a third strand to the rope with which Sellars first binds and then strangles the excessive ambitions of empiricism. That is his methodological strategy of considering *semantic* relations among the meanings expressed by different sort of vocabulary that result from *pragmatic* dependencies relating the practices one must engage in or the abilities one must exercise in order to count as using those bits of vocabulary to express those meanings. This is the *pragmatist* element in Sellars's multi-front assault on empiricism. It makes a significant contribution to the early, critical portion of *EPM*, though Sellars does not overtly mark it, as he does the contribution of his inferential functionalism to the later, more constructive portion. The concern with what one must *do* in order to *say* (so, to think) various kinds of things remains implicit in what Sellars *does*, rather than explicit in what he *says about* what he *does*. As we will see, both the pragmatist and the inferentialist ideas are integral to his critique of empiricist approaches to modality and to his constructive suggestions for a more adequate treatment of modal vocabulary.

2. The Inferentialist and Pragmatist Critique of Empiricism in *EPM*

I think of the classical project of analytic philosophy in the twentieth century as being the exploration of how the meanings expressed by some target vocabularies can be exhibited as in some sense a logical elaboration of the meanings already expressed by some base vocabularies. The conception of the desired semantic relation between vocabularies (the sense of 'analysis') varied significantly within this broadly defined semantic project, including definition, paraphrase, translation, reduction in various senses,

---

2. *Empiricism and the Philosophy of Mind*, reprinted with an introduction by Richard Rorty and a study guide by Robert Brandom (Cambridge, MA: Harvard University Press, 1997). Hereafter *EPM*.

supervenience, and truth-making, to name just a few prominent candidates. I take it to be integral to the analytic philosophical project during this period that however that semantic relation is conceived, *logical* vocabulary is taken to play a special role in elaborating the base vocabulary into the target vocabulary. The distinctively twentieth-century form of *empiricism* can be understood as one of the *core programs* of this analytic project—not in the sense that every participant in the project endorsed some version of empiricism (Neurath, for instance, rejects empiricism where he sees it clashing with another core semantic program that was dearer to his heart, namely naturalism), but in the sense that even those who rejected it for some target vocabulary or other took the possibility of an empiricist analysis to be an important issue, to set a legitimate philosophical agenda.

Construed in these terms, twentieth-century empiricism can be thought of as having proposed three broad kinds of empiricist base vocabularies. The most restrictive kind comprises *phenomenalist* vocabularies: those that specify how things subjectively *appear* as opposed to how they objectively are, or the not-yet-conceptualized perceptual *experiences* subjects have, or the so-far-uninterpreted sensory *given* (the data of sensation: sense data). A somewhat less restrictive genus of empiricist base vocabularies limits them to those that express *secondary qualities,* thought of as what is *directly perceived* in some less demanding sense. And a still more relaxed version of empiricism restricts its base vocabulary to the *observational* vocabulary deployed in noninferentially elicited perceptual reports of observable states of affairs. Typical target vocabularies for the first, phenomenalist, class of empiricist base vocabularies include those expressing empirical claims about how things really or *objectively* are—that is, those expressing the applicability of any objective empirical concepts. Typical target vocabularies for secondary-quality empiricism include any that specify *primary qualities* or the applicability of concepts that are not response-dependent. And typical target vocabularies for observational vocabulary empiricism include *theoretical* vocabulary. All species of empiricism are concerned with the possibility of underwriting a semantics for the modal vocabulary used to express laws of nature, probabilistic vocabulary, normative vocabulary, and other sophisticated vocabularies of independent philosophical interest. The standard empiricist alternatives are either to show how a given target vocabulary can be semantically elaborated from the favored empiricist base vocabulary, on the one hand, or to show how to live with a local skepticism about its ultimate semantic intelligibility, on the other.

At the center of Sellars's critique of empiricism in *EPM* is an argument against the weakest, least committive, observational version of empiricism (a critique that then carries over, *mutatis mutandis*, to the more demanding versions). That argument depends on both his inferential-functionalist semantics and on his pragmatism. Its fundamental strategy is to show that the proposed empiricist base vocabulary is not *pragmatically* autonomous, and hence not *semantically* autonomous. Observational vocabulary is not a vocabulary one could use though one used no other. Noninferential reports of the results of observation do not form an autonomous stratum of language. In particular, when we look at what one must *do* to count as making a noninferential report, we see that that is not a practice one could engage in except in the context of *inferential* practices of using those observations as *premises* from which to draw inferential *conclusions,* as *reasons* for making judgments and undertaking commitments that are *not* themselves observations. The contribution to this argument of Sellars's inferential functionalism about semantics lies in underwriting the claim that for *any* judgment, claim, or belief to be contentful in the way required for it to be *cognitively, conceptually,* or *epistemically* significant, for it to be a potential bit of *knowledge* or *evidence,* to be a *sapient* state or status, it must be able to play a distinctive *role in reasoning*: it must be able to serve as a *reason for* further judgments, claims, or beliefs, hence as a *premise* from which they can be *inferred.* That role in reasoning, in particular, what those judgments, claims, or beliefs can serve as reasons or evidence *for,* is an essential, and not just an accidental component of their having the semantic content that they do. And that means that one cannot count as understanding, grasping, or applying concepts *non*inferentially in observation unless one can also deploy them at least as premises in *inferences* to conclusions that do *not,* for that very reason, count as *non*inferential applications of concepts. Nor, for the same reason, can any discursive practice consist entirely of noninferentially acquiring *premises,* without any corresponding practice of drawing *conclusions.* So noninferential, observational uses of concepts do not constitute an autonomous discursive practice: a language game one could play though one played no other. And this conclusion about the pragmatic dependence of observational uses of vocabulary on inferential ones holds no matter what the subject-matter of those observations is: whether it is observable features of the external environment, how things merely appear to a subject, or the current contents of one's own mind.

Here the pragmatist concern with what one must *do* in order to be able to *say* (or think) something combines with semantic inferentialist-functionalism about conceptual content to argue that the proposed empiricist base vocabulary is not pragmatically autonomous—since one must be able to make claims inferentially in order to count as making any noninferentially. If that is so, then potentially risky inferential moves cannot be seen as an in-principle optional superstructure erected on a semantically autonomous base of things directly known through observation.

Although this is his most general and most powerful argument, Sellars does not limit himself to it in arguing against the substantially more committive forms of empiricism that insist on phenomenalist base vocabularies. In addition, he develops a constructive account of the relations between (at least one principle species of) phenomenalist vocabulary and objective vocabulary that depends on pragmatic dependences between what one must *do* in order to deploy each kind, to argue once again that the proposed empiricist base vocabulary does not form a semantically autonomous stratum of the language. This is his account of the relation between 'looks' talk and 'is' talk.

It develops out of his positive account of what one must *do* in order to use vocabulary observationally. To apply the concept green noninferentially one must be able to do at least two sorts of things. First, one must be able reliably to respond differentially to the visible presence of green things. This is what blind and color-blind language users lack, but non-language-using pigeons and parrots possess. Second, one must be able to exercise that capacity by reliably responding differentially to the visible presence of green things by applying the *concept* green. So one must possess, grasp, or understand that concept. "Grasp of a concept is mastery of the use of a word," Sellars says, and his inferential functionalism dictates that this must include the *inferential* use of the word: knowing at least something about what follows from and is evidence for or against something's being green. This the blind or color-blind language user has, and the pigeon and parrot do not. Only the performances of the former can have the pragmatic significance of taking up a stand in the space of reasons, of committing themselves to something that has a *conceptual*, that is, inferentially articulated, content.

The point of Sellars's parable of John in the tie shop is to persuade us that the home language game of the 'looks' or 'seems' vocabulary that expresses how things merely appear to us, without undertaking any commitment to how they actually are, is one that is pragmatically parasitic on the practice of making in-principle risky reports of how things objectively are. For what one must *do* in order to count as saying how things merely *look*, Sellars claims, is to *evince* the reliable differential disposition to respond to something by claiming that it is green, while *withholding* the endorsement of that claim (because of one's collateral beliefs about the situation and one's reliability in it). If that is what one is doing in making a 'looks' claim, then one cannot be wrong about it in the same way one can about an 'is' claim, because one has withheld the principal commitment rather than undertaking it. And it follows that phenomenalist 'looks' talk, which expresses how things merely appear, without further commitment to how things actually are, is not an autonomous discursive practice—not a language game one could play though one played no other—but is in fact pragmatically parasitic on objective 'is' talk.

My point in rehearsing this familiar argument is to emphasize the role played both by Sellars's pragmatist emphasis on what one must be able to *do* in order to count as *saying* various kinds of things—*using* vocabulary so as to express certain kinds of meanings—and by his inferentialist-functionalist insistence that the role some vocabulary plays in *reasoning* makes an essential contribution to its semantic content. Although Sellars does not go on to make this argument, the way these two lines of thought conspire to undermine the semantic autonomy of candidate empiricist base vocabularies provides a template for a parallel objection to secondary-quality empiricism. For at least a necessary condition on anything's being a secondary-quality concept is that it have an observational role that supports the introduction of corresponding 'looks' talk, so that mastery of that 'looks' talk can be taken to be essential to mastery of the concept—as 'looks-green' arguably is for mastery of the concept green, but 'looks-square' is *not* for mastery of the concept square. What would be needed to fill in the argument against secondary-quality empiricism via the non-autonomy of its proposed base vocabulary, would be an argument that nothing could count as mastering a vocabulary consisting entirely of expressions of this sort, apart from all inferential connections to primary-quality concepts that did not have this structure.

3. Pragmatism and Phenomenalism

Thus far I have confined myself to offering a general characterization of anti-empiricist arguments that appear in *Empiricism and the Philosophy of Mind*. None of them involve empiricism's treatment of modality. Now I want to put those arguments in a somewhat different frame, by conjoining them with one that is presented elsewhere, and which *does* turn on the significance of modal concepts. The previous arguments concerned the suitability of some vocabulary to serve as the *base* vocabulary of an empiricist analysis—since plausible motivations for caring about such an analysis typically require that it be semantically autonomous. This one turns on the criteria of adequacy of the analysis itself. My remarks in this section concern Sellars's arguments in his essay "Phenomenalism," which can be regarded as a kind of companion piece to *EPM*. (Later I will discuss another contemporary essay that I think should be thought of as yoked together with these two in a troika.) The first, modal, point is one that Sellars registers there, but does not linger on—his principal concern being rather with a second point, concerning another aspect of the vocabulary in which phenomenalist analyses would have to be couched. But given my purposes here, I want to make a bit more of the modal point than he does.

The basic idea of a phenomenalist-empiricist semantic analysis of ordinary objective vocabulary is that the expressive work done by talk of mind-independent objects and their properties and relations can be done by talk of *patterns* in, *regularities* of, or *generalizations* concerning sense experiences characterized in a phenomenalist vocabulary. Saying that the curved red surface I am experiencing is an experience *of* an apple that has parts I am *not* experiencing—a similarly bulgy, red back and a white interior, for instance—is properly understood as saying something about what I *would* experience if I turned it around or cut it open. That it continued to exist in the kitchen when I left the room is a matter of what I *would* have experienced *had* I returned. The first, obvious, observation is that an account of objective reality in terms of the *powers* of circumstances to *produce*, or my *dispositions* to *have*, sensations, experiences, beings-appeared-to and so on essentially involves *modal* concepts. The patterns, regularities, or generalizations in subjective appearances that are supposed to constitute objective realities are modally robust, counterfactual-supporting patterns, regularities, or generalizations. Talk of what I actually *do* experience will not by itself underwrite claims about unexperienced spatial or temporal parts of empirical objects. Twentieth-century logical empiricism promised to advance beyond traditional empiricism because it could call on the full expressive resources of *logical* vocabulary to use as the 'glue' sticking sensory experiences together so as to construct simulacra of external objects. But *extensional* logical vocabulary is not nearly expressively powerful enough for the phenomenalist version of the empiricist project. So the phenomenalist conditional "terminating judgments," into an infinite set of which C. I. Lewis proposes (in his *Analysis of Knowledge and Valuation*) to translate the "non-terminating judgments" of ordinary objective empirical discourse, have to use his modal notion of *strict* or necessary implication.[3] And similar points could be made about other phenomenalist reductionists such as Ayer. The consequence of this observation to which I want to draw attention is that one cannot use such a strategy in one's phenomenalist empiricist analysis, translation, or reduction of objective talk *and* at the same time be a Humean skeptic about what *modal* vocabulary expresses. So essential features of the only remotely plausible *constructive* strategy of phenomenalist empiricism are simply incompatible with the most prominent *skeptical* consequences about modal concepts characteristically drawn both by traditional and twentieth-century logicist empiricism.

This is a powerful argument. Sellars's principal concern in his essay "Phenomenalism," however, is with a subsequent point. The conditionals codifying the patterns, regularities, or generalizations concerning sense experience that correspond to judgments about how things objectively are must not only be subjunctive, counterfactually robust conditionals, but in order to have any hope of being materially adequate (getting the truth-conditions even approximately correct) their *antecedents* must themselves be expressed in *objective* vocabulary, *not* in *phenomenalist* vocabulary. What is true (enough) is that if I were *actually* to turn the apple around, cut it open, or return to its vicinity in the kitchen I *would* have certain sense experiences. It is *not* in general true that if I merely *seem* to do those things I am guaranteed to have the corresponding experiences. For, phrased in such phenomenalist terms, the antecedent is satisfied in cases of imagination,

---

3. La Salle, IL: Open Court, 1946.

visual illusion, dreaming, hallucination and so on that are precisely those *not* bound by the supposedly object-constituting rules and regularities. As Sellars summarizes the point:

> To claim that the relationship between the framework of sense contents and that of physical objects can be construed on the [phenomenalist] model is to commit oneself to the idea that there are inductively confirmable generalizations about sense contents which are 'in principle' capable of being formulated without the use of the language of physical things.... [T]his idea is a mistake.[4]

It is a mistake because

> the very selection of the complex patterns of actual sense contents in our past experiences which are to serve as the antecedents of the generalizations in question presuppose our common sense knowledge of ourselves as perceivers, of the specific physical environment in which we do our perceiving and of the general principles which correlate the occurrence of sensations with bodily and environmental conditions. We select those patterns which go with our being in a certain perceptual relation to a particular object of a certain quality, where we know that being in this relation to an object of that quality normally eventuates in our having the sense content referred to in the consequent.

This argument then makes evident

> the logical dependence of the framework of private sense contents on the public, inter-subjective, logical space of persons and physical things.[5]

So the phenomenalist vocabulary is not autonomous. It is not a language game one can play though one plays no other. In particular, the uses of it that might plausibly fulfill many of the same pragmatic functions as ordinary

---

4. "Phenomenalism," in Kevin Scharp and Robert Brandom (eds.), *In the Space of Reasons* (Cambridge, MA: Harvard University Press, 2007), p. 331.
5. "Phenomenalism," p. 328.

objective empirical talk themselves presuppose the ability to deploy such objective vocabulary.

As Sellars points out, the lessons learned from pressing on the phenomenalist version of empiricism apply more generally. In particular, they apply to the more liberal version of empiricism whose base vocabulary is observational, including observations of enduring empirical objects, and whose target vocabulary is theoretical vocabulary. To begin with, if talk of theoretical entities is to be translated into or replaced by talk of patterns in, regularities of, or generalizations about observable entities, they must be *lawlike, counterfactual*-supporting regularities and generalizations. They must permit inferences to what one *would* observe if one *were* to find oneself in specified circumstances, or to prepare the apparatus in a certain way. For, once again, the patterns, regularities, or generalizations about observations the assertion of which an instrumentalist empiricist might with some initial plausibility take to have the same pragmatic effect as (to be doing the same thing one is doing in) deploying theoretical vocabulary must reach beyond the parochial, merely autobiographically significant contingencies of what subjects happen actually to observe. The theory is that electrical currents cause magnetic fields regardless of the presence of suitable measuring devices. And that can only be made out in terms of what is observ*able*, that is *could* be observed, not just what *is* observed. And that is to say that the instrumentalist-observational form of empiricism is also incompatible with Humean-Quinean skepticism about the intelligibility of what is expressed by alethic modal vocabulary.

And an analog of the second argument against phenomenalist forms of empiricism also applies to instrumentalist forms. For, once again, the *antecedents* of the counterfactual conditionals specifying what *could* or *would* have been observed *if* certain conditions *had* obtained or certain operations *were* performed cannot themselves be formulated in purely observational terms. The meter-needle *would* have been observably displaced if I had connected the terminals of a volt-ohmeter to the wire, but that something *is* a VOM is *not* itself a fact restatable in purely observational terms. Even leaving apart the fact that it is a *functional* characterization not equivalent to any specification in purely *physical* terms, a description of the construction of some particular kind of VOM is still going to help itself to notions such as being made of copper, or being an electrical insulator (another bit of vocabulary that is both functional and theoretical). To satisfy the semantic ambitions of the instrumentalist it is not enough to associate each theoretical claim with a set of jointly pragmatically equivalent counterfactual-supporting conditionals whose *consequents* are couched wholly in observational vocabulary. All the theoretical terms appearing in the *antecedents* of those conditionals must be similarly replaced. No instrumentalist reduction of any actual theoretical claim has ever been suggested that even attempts to satisfy this condition.

Though Sellars does not, and I will not, pursue the matter, one expects that corresponding arguments will go through, *mutatis mutandis,* also for the kind of empiricism that seeks to understand the use of primary-quality vocabulary wholly in terms of the use of secondary-quality vocabulary. What we mean by talk of primary qualities will have to be cashed out in terms of its *powers* to produce, or our *dispositions* to perceive, secondary qualities—that is, in terms of modally robust, counterfactual-supporting generalizations. And it will be a challenge to specify the antecedents of a materially adequate set of such conditionals wholly in the official secondary-quality vocabulary.

4. Sellars's Pragmatism and Modality

The arguments I have considered so far set limits to the semantic ambitions of phenomenalist and instrumentalist forms of analytic empiricism, first by focusing on the *pragmatic* preconditions of the required semantic autonomy of the proposed empiricist base vocabularies, and second by looking in more detail at the specific sorts of *inferential* patterns in the base vocabulary in terms of which it is proposed to reconstruct the circumstances and consequences of application of items in the various target vocabularies. Here it was observed that the material adequacy of such reconstructions seems to require the ineliminable involvement of terms from the target vocabulary, not only on the right side, but also on the left side of any such reconstruction—in the *definiens* as well as in the *definiendum.* Modality plays a role in these arguments only because the material adequacy of the reconstruction also turns out to require appeal to counterfactually robust inferences in the base vocabulary. Insofar as that is so, the *constructive* semantic projects of the phenomenalist, instrumentalist, and secondary-quality forms of empiricism are at odds with the local semantic skepticism about what is expressed by alethic modal vocabulary that has always been a characteristic cardinal *critical* consequence of empiricist approaches to semantics, as epitomized for its traditional phase by Hume and for its logicist phase by Quine.

In another massive, pathbreaking essay of this period, "Counterfactuals, Dispositions, and the Causal Modalities"[6] (completed in February of 1957), Sellars argues directly against this empiricist treatment of modality, completing what then becomes visible as a two-pronged attack on the principal contentions and projects of empiricism, only the opening salvos of which were fired in *Empiricism and the Philosophy of Mind*.[7] His principal target here is the "tendency to assimilate all discourse to describing," which he takes to be primarily "responsible for the prevalence in the empiricist tradition of 'nothing-but-ism' in its various forms (emotivism, philosophical behaviorism, phenomenalism)."[8] The form Sellars addresses in this essay is the Humean one that one can find in statements of laws of nature, expressed in alethic modal vocabulary that lets us say what is and is not necessary and possible, "nothing but" expressions of matter-of-factual regularities or constant conjunctions (though he claims explicitly that considerations corresponding to those he raises for causal modalities are intended to apply to logical and deontological modalities as well).[9] His arguments are directed

---

6. In H. Feigl, M. Scriven, and G. Maxwell (eds.), *Minnesota Studies in the Philosophy of Science*, vol. II (Minneapolis: University of Minnesota Press, 1957), pp. 225–308. Hereafter CDCM.

7. As in *EPM* (and even, though to a lesser extent, in "Phenomenalism"), in this essay Sellars describes himself not as denying empiricism, but rather as correcting it, protecting its core insights from the damage done by their overextension. But he also makes it clear that the result of such rectification is a Kantian view that gives equal weight to rationalist insights, when they are suitably reconstructed. So for instance he says:

> It is my purpose to argue that the core truth of Hume's philosophy of causation is not only compatible with, but absurd without, *ungrudging* recognition of those features of causal discourse as a mode of rational discourse on which the 'metaphysical rationalists' laid such stress, but also mis-assimilated to describing." (CDCM §82)

And the final sentence of the essay invokes the "profound truth" of Kant's conception of reason, "which empiricism has tended to distort."

8. CDCM §103.
9. CDCM §103.

against the view that holds modal vocabulary semantically unintelligible, on grounds of inability to specify what it is saying about what the world is like, how it is describing things as being, insofar as by using it we are asserting something that goes beyond endorsing the existence of nonmodally characterizable universal descriptive generalizations.

Hume found that even his best understanding of actual observable empirical *facts* did not yield an understanding of *rules* relating or otherwise governing them. Those facts did not settle which of the things that *actually* happened *had* to happen (given others), that is, were (at least conditionally) *necessary*, and which of the things that did *not* happen nonetheless were *possible* (not ruled out by laws concerning what did happen). The issue here concerns the justifiability and intelligibility of a certain kind of *inference*: modally robust, counterfactual-supporting inferences, of the kind made explicit by the use of modal vocabulary. Hume (and, following him, Quine) took it that epistemologically and semantically fastidious philosophers face a stark choice: either show how to explain modal vocabulary—the circumstances of application that justify the distinctive counterfactual-supporting inferential consequences of application—in nonmodal terms, or show how to live without it, to do what we need to do in science without making such arcane and occult supradescriptive commitments.

This demand was always the greatest source of tension between empiricism and naturalism, especially the scientific naturalism that Sellars epitomized in the slogan "Science is the measure of all things, of those that are, that they are, and of those that are not, that they are not." For modern mathematized natural science shorn of concern with laws, counterfactuals, and dispositions—in short of what is expressed by alethic modal vocabulary—is less than an impotent Samson; it is an inert, unrecognizable, fragmentary remnant of a once-vital enterprise. Sellars's general recommendation for resolving this painful tension (felt particularly acutely by, and one of the principal issues dividing, the members of the Vienna circle) is to relax the exclusivism and rigorism he traces to empiricism's semantic descriptivism (in a passage we have found reason to quote more than once already):

> [O]nce the tautology 'The world is described by descriptive concepts' is freed from the idea that the business of all non-logical concepts is to describe, the way is clear to an *ungrudging* recognition that many

expressions which empiricists have relegated to second-class citizenship in discourse are not *inferior,* just *different.*[10]

Sensitized as we now are by Sellars's diagnoses of *semantic autonomy* claims as essential to various empiricist constructive and reconstructive projects, both in *EPM* and in the "Phenomenalism" essay, and familiar as we now are with his criticisms of them based on the inferentially articulated *doings* required to use or deploy various candidate base vocabularies, it should come as no surprise that his objections to critical empiricist suspicions of and hostility toward modality follow the same pattern. For the Humean-Quinean empiricist semantic challenge to the legitimacy of modal vocabulary is predicated on the idea of an independently and antecedently intelligible stratum of empirical discourse that is purely descriptive and involves no modal commitments, as a semantically autonomous background and model with which the credentials of modal discourse can then be invidiously compared.

In this case, as in the others, the argument turns both on the *pragmatism* that looks to what one is doing in deploying the candidate base vocabulary—here "purely descriptive" vocabulary—and on the nature of the *inferential* articulation of that vocabulary necessary for such uses to play the expressive role characteristic of that vocabulary. The argument in this case is subtler and more complex than the others, however. First, I take it that Sellars does *not* deny the intelligibility-in-principle of purely descriptive discourse that contains no explicitly modal vocabulary. Sellars is, frustratingly but characteristically, not explicit about his attitude toward the pragmatic autonomy in principle of such purely descriptive discourse. He says:

> The idea that the world can, in principle, be so described that the description contains no modal expression is of a piece with the idea that the world can, in principle, be so described that the description contains no prescriptive expression. For what is being called to mind is the ideal of statement of 'everything that is the case' which, however, serves *through and through only* the purpose of stating what is the case. And it is a logical truth that such a description, however many modal

---

10. CDCM §79.

expressions might properly be used in *arriving at* it or in *justifying* it, or in showing the *relevance* of one of its components to another, could contain no modal expression.[11]

Sellars's view about this ideal is complex: there is a sense in which it is intelligible, and a sense in which it is not. Such a discourse would be unreflective and unselfconscious in a way ours is not. For reasons that will emerge, it would belong to what at the end of the essay he calls the stage of human language "when linguistic changes had *causes*, but not *reasons*, [before] man acquired the ability to reason about reasons."[12]

The second reason the argument must be subtler here is that there are special difficulties involved in, and corresponding delicacies required for, working out the general pragmatist-inferentialist strategy so as to apply it to this case, by specifying the relation between the expressive role distinctive of modal vocabulary, on the one hand, and what one is *doing* (in particular, the inferential commitments one is undertaking) in using ordinary, nonmodal, descriptive vocabulary itself, on the other.

The pragmatic dependency relation that lies at the base of Sellars's argument is the fact that

> although describing and explaining (predicting, retrodicting, understanding) are *distinguishable*, they are also, in an important sense, *inseparable*. It is only because the expressions in terms of which we describe objects, even such basic expressions as words for perceptible characteristics of molar objects, locate these objects in a space of implications, that they describe at all, rather than merely label. The descriptive and explanatory resources of language advance hand in hand.[13]

Descriptive uses of vocabulary presuppose an inferentially articulated "space of implications," within which some descriptions show up as reasons for or explanations of others. Understanding those descriptions requires placing them in such a space. This pragmatist claim about what else one must be

---

11. CDCM §80.
12. CDCM §108.
13. CDCM §108.

able to *do*—namely, *infer, explain,* treat one claim as a *reason* for another—in order for what one is doing to count as *describing* connects to the use of *modal* vocabulary via the following principle:

> To make first hand use of these [modal] expressions is to be about the business of explaining a state of affairs, or justifying an assertion.[14]

That is, what one is *doing* in *using* modal expressions is explaining, justifying, or endorsing an inference. So what one is doing in saying that As are *necessarily* Bs is endorsing the inference from anything's being an A to its being a B.

The first sort of difficulty I alluded to above stems from the fact that there are other ways of endorsing such a pattern of inference besides *saying that* all As are necessarily Bs. One's endorsement may be *implicit* in other things one *does,* the reasoning one engages in and approves of, rather than *explicit* in what one *says*. So from the fact (assuming, as I shall, that it is a fact) that the activity of describing is part of an indissoluble pragmatic package that includes endorsing inferences and the fact that what one is doing in making a modal claim is endorsing an inference, it does not at all follow that there can be no use of descriptive vocabulary apart from the use of modal vocabulary. The second difficulty stems from the fact that although Sellars may be right that what one is *doing* in making a modal claim is endorsing a pattern of inference, it is clear that one is not thereby *saying that* an inference is good. When I say, "Pure copper necessarily conducts electricity," and thereby unrestrictedly endorse inferences from anything's being pure copper to its conducting electricity, I have nevertheless *said* nothing about any inferences, explanations, justifications, or implications—indeed, I have said something that could be true even if there had never been any inferences or inferrers to endorse them, hence no describers or discursive practitioners at all.[15] These two observations set the principal criteria of adequacy both for Sellars's positive working-out of the pragmatist-inferentialist treat-

---

14. CDCM §80.
15. Sellars connects this obvious fact with an observation:

> Idealism is notorious for the fallacy of concluding that because there must be minds in the world in order for *us* to have reason to make statements about the world, therefore there is no sense to the idea of a world which does not include minds. (CDCM §101)

ment of modal vocabulary, and for his argument that the purely descriptive base vocabulary invoked by the empiricist critic of the semantic credentials of modal vocabulary lacks the sort of discursive autonomy the empiricist criticism presupposes and requires.

Sellars's central rhetorical strategy in this essay is to address the issue of what is expressed by modal claims about necessary connections by offering

> a sympathetic reconstruction of the controversy in the form of a debate between a Mr. C (for Constant Conjunction) and a Mr. E (for Entailment) who develop and qualify their views in such a way as to bring them to the growing edge of the problem.[16]

Officially, he is even-handed in his treatment of the vices and virtues of the empiricist, who denies that the use of modal vocabulary can express any legitimate semantic content beyond that expressed by a descriptive, extensional universal generalization, and the rationalist, who understands that content in terms of entailments expressing rules of reasoning. In fact, however, as becomes clear when he launches into his own account, he is mainly concerned to develop a version of the rationalist account. As the second half of the essay develops, Sellars marks his abandonment of the disinterested pose by an uncharacteristically explicit expository shift:

> It is now high time that I dropped the persona of Mr. E, and set about replying to the challenge with which Mr. C ended his first critique of the entailment theory.[17]

---

16. CDCM, Introduction.

17. CDCM §85. In fact, Sellars's 'defense' of Mr. C (see the passage from §82 quoted in Note 7 above) consists of showing what concessions he needs to make to Mr. E. This proceeds first by Mr. C's qualification that "'A causes B' *says* that (x)[Ax→Bx] and *implies* that the latter is asserted on inductive grounds" (CDCM §62), followed by the necessity of conceiving "of induction as establishing principles *in accordance with which* we reason, rather than as major premises *from which* we reason" (CDCM §83). As will appear, the former concession, introducing the notion of what is contextually implied by contrast to what is explicitly said, is then dialectically made available to be pressed into service by Mr. E. This bit of dialectic is a pretty rhetorical flourish on Sellars's part, but I doubt that in the end it reflects any deep feature of the confrontation between the empiricist and rationalist approaches to modality.

Doing that requires careful investigation of the differences between and relations among four different sorts of item:

- Practical endorsement of the propriety of an inference from things being A to their being B;
- The explicit statement that one may infer the applicability of 'B' from the applicability of 'A';
- The statement that A physically entails B;
- The statement that As are necessarily Bs.

The first is the sort of thing Sellars takes to be pragmatically presupposed by the activity of describing, that is, deploying descriptive vocabulary. The second fails to capture such practical endorsements, because of the possibility of asserting such statements regarding the *expressions* 'A' and 'B' without understanding what they express.[18]

The third sort of statement expresses Mr. E's initial stab at an analysis of the fourth. It is the answer to the question: what sort of entailment is it that modal statements are supposed to express?

> Mr. E has a ready answer.... [I]t might... be called 'natural' or 'physical' entailment, for while any entailment is a logical relation, we can distinguish within the broad class of entailments between those which are, and those which are not, a function of the specific empirical contents between which they obtain. The latter are investigated by general or formal logic (and pure mathematics). Empirical science, on the other hand, to the extent that it is a search for *laws*, is the search for entailments of the former kind. (Putative) success in this search finds its expression in statements of the form 'It is (inductively) probable that A physically entails B.'[19]

---

18. As Sellars says:

> But one can know that Turks, for example, ought to withdraw '...' when they commit themselves to '—' without knowing the language, whereas the statement that '*p* entails *q*' contextually implies that the speaker not only knows the language to which '*p*' and '*q*' belong, but, in particular, knows how to use '*p*' and '*q*' themselves. (CDCM §81)

19. CDCM §56.

The virtue of statements like "A physically entails B" is that they do plausibly codify the practical endorsement of an inference that is implicit in what one does in the form of something one can explicitly *say*, without bringing in irrelevant commitments concerning particular expressions, the activity of inferring, or discursive practitioners. The remaining difficulty is that they seem plainly not to have the same content, not to say the same thing, as explicitly modal statements of objective necessity.

Sellars's response to this problem is to acknowledge that modal statements do not *say that* some entailment holds, but to distinguish between what is *said* by using a bit of vocabulary and what is *'contextually implied'* by doing so. Sellars says very little about this latter notion, even though it bears the full weight of his proposed emendation of the rationalist account. It is recognizably the same distinction he had appealed to earlier, in "Inference and Meaning," as the distinction between what one *says* by making a statement and what one thereby *conveys*. There his example is that in asserting "The sky is clear today," I *say* that the sky is clear today, but *convey* that I *believe* that it is clear.[20] That otherwise uninterpreted example suggests to me that what Sellars has in mind is the distinction between *semantic* and *pragmatic* inferences. That is the distinction between inferences underwritten by the *contents* of what is *said* or asserted, on the one hand, and inferences underwritten by what one is *doing* in saying them, on the other. The inference from "The sky is clear" to "It is not raining" is of the first sort; the inference from my asserting "The sky is clear" to "Brandom believes the sky is clear" is of the second sort. Inferences of these two kinds may generally be distinguished by the Frege-Geach embedding test: look to see whether those who make the inference in question also endorse the corresponding conditional. "If the sky is clear, then it is not raining" is generally true, while "If the sky is clear, then Brandom believes it is clear" is not generally true. (Compare the inference from my *saying*, "That is an ugly tie you are wearing" to "Bob is annoyed with me.")

---

20. Sellars, "Inference and Meaning," in J. Sicha (ed.), *Pure Pragmatics and Possible Worlds: The Early Essays of Wilfrid Sellars* (Atascadero, CA: Ridgeview, 1980), p. 280. Hereafter *PPPW*.

5. Kantian Pragmatism about Modality

If that is in fact the distinction Sellars is after, then it seems to me that the view he is expounding and defending can be put less paradoxically if we do not take a detour through entailment statements, but concern ourselves directly with the relation between the endorsement of patterns of inference and modal statements. The underlying rationalist insight is a pragmatist-inferentialist one: what one is *doing* in making a modal claim is endorsing a pattern of inference. Modal vocabulary makes possible new kinds of *sayings* that have the *pragmatic effect* of endorsing inferences. To say that is not yet to say what they *say*, it is only to say what one is *doing by* saying them. But it does settle the *pragmatic significance* of such modal claims, in the sense of their appropriate circumstances and consequences of application.[21]

---

21. It is the attempt to specify this peculiar and distinctive sort of pragmatically mediated relation between vocabularies that leads Sellars to say things like

> It is sometimes thought that modal statements do not describe states of affairs in the world, because they are *really* metalinguistic. This won't do at all if it is meant that instead of describing states of affairs in the world, they describe linguistic habits. It is more plausible if it is meant that statements involving modal terms have the force of *prescriptive* statements about the use of certain expressions in the object language. Yet there is more than one way to '*have the force of*' a statement, and failure to distinguish between them may snowball into a serious confusion as wider implications are drawn. (CDCM §81)

and

> Shall we say that modal expressions are metalinguistic? Neither a simple 'yes' nor a simple 'no' will do. As a matter of fact, once the above considerations are given their proper weight, it is possible to acknowledge that the idea that they are metalinguistic in character oversimplifies a fundamental insight. For our present purposes, it is sufficient to say that the claim that modal expressions are 'in the metalanguage' is not too misleading if the peculiar force of the expressions which occur alongside them (represented by the 'p' and the 'q' of our example) is recognized, in particular, that they have 'straightforward' translation into other languages, and if it is also recognized that they belong not only 'in the metalanguage', but in discourse about thoughts and concepts as well. (CDCM §82)

and

> We must here, as elsewhere, draw a distinction between what we are committed to concerning the world by virtue of the fact that we have reason to make a certain assertion, and the force, in a narrower sense, of the assertion itself. (CDCM §101)

If one practically endorses the pattern of inference that treats classifying or describing anything at all as an A as sufficient grounds ("all on its own," as Sellars says, in order to capture the way the pattern of inferences in question is counterfactually robust) for concluding that it is a B, then one is committed to the claim that all As are necessarily Bs. And commitment to that claim is commitment to practically ratify that pattern of inference. Assuming, as Sellars has claimed, that using ordinary, nonmodal, descriptive vocabulary requires practically endorsing such patterns of inference ("situating descriptions in a space of implications"), anyone who has the practical ability to deploy "purely descriptive" vocabulary already knows how to do everything he needs to know how to do to deploy modal vocabulary as well. He need not actually do so, since practically undertaking those inferential commitments does not require that one have available a language with vocabulary permitting one to *do* that by *saying* something. But *all* a practitioner lacks in such a circumstance is the *words* to hook up to discriminative and responsive abilities he already possesses. In this precise sense, the ability to deploy modal vocabulary is *practically implicit* in the ability to deploy nonmodal descriptive vocabulary.

Sellars has claimed that the activity of describing is unintelligible except as part of a pragmatic package that includes also not just the making of inferences, but the making of *counterfactually robust* inferences: the sort of inferences involved in *explanation*, and licensed by explicitly modal statements of *laws*. He sums up the claim admirably in the title of another one of his earliest papers: "Concepts as Involving Laws, and Inconceivable without Them."[22] Grasp of a concept is mastery of the use of a word, Sellars says. And for descriptive concepts, that use includes not only sorting inferences (however fallibly and incompletely) into materially good and materially bad ones, but also, among the ones one takes to be materially good, to distinguish (however fallibly and incompletely) between counterfactual circumstances under which they do, and counterfactual circumstances under which they do not, *remain* good. Part of taking an inference to be materially good is having a view about which possible additional collateral premises or auxiliary hypotheses would, and which would not, infirm it. Chestnut trees produce

22. *PPPW*, pp. 87–124.

chestnuts—unless they are immature, or blighted. Dry, well-made matches strike—unless there is no oxygen. The hungry lioness would still chase the antelope if it were Tuesday or the beetle on the distant tree crawled slightly further up the branch, but not if the lioness's heart were to stop beating. The point is not that there is any particular set of such discriminations that one must be able to make in order to count as deploying the concepts involved. It is that if one can make *no* such practical assessments of the counterfactual robustness of material inferences involving those concepts, one could not count as having mastered them.

Against the background of this pragmatist-inferentialist claim about what is involved in the ordinary descriptive use of concepts, Sellars's claim, as I am reading him, is that explicitly modal "lawlike" statements are statements that one is committed or entitled to whenever one is committed or entitled to endorse such patterns of counterfactually robust inference, and commitment or entitlement to which in their turn commit or entitle one to the corresponding patterns of inference. Saying that about them settles what one needs to *do* to *use* such modal statements. It does *not* say how one is thereby *describing* the world as being when one does. It does not, in particular, *describe* a pattern of inference as good (though that saying does, in its own distinctive way, *express endorsement* of such a pattern). It does not do those things for the simple reason that the use of modal expressions is *not* in the first instance *descriptive*.[23] It codifies explicitly, in the form of a statement, a feature of the use of descriptive expressions that is indissolubly bound up with, but not identical to, their descriptive use. Nonetheless, in knowing how to use vocabulary descriptively, one knows how to do everything one needs to know how to do in order to use modal vocabulary. And that is enough to show that one cannot actually be in the Humean predicament presupposed by the empiricist challenge to the intelligibility of modal vocabulary. For one cannot know how to use vocabulary in matter-of-factual descriptions ("The cat is on the mat") and not have any grip on how to use modal, counterfactual, and dispositional vocabulary ("It is necessary for live cats to breathe"; "The cat could still be on the mat if the mat were a

---

23. Sellars says:

> [Mr. E.] conceives of induction as establishing principles *in accordance with which* we reason, rather than as major premises *from which* we reason. (CDCM §83)

slightly different shade of blue, but not if it turned into soup"; "The cat would leave the mat if she saw a mouse"). Although *explicitly* modal *vocabulary* is an in-principle optional superstructure on practices of deploying descriptive vocabulary, what it expresses cannot be mysterious in principle to those who can engage in those base-level practices.

In taking this line, Sellars quite properly sees himself as reviving a central idea of Kant's. The ability to use empirical descriptive terms such as 'mass', 'rigid', and 'green' already presupposes grasp of the kind of properties and relations made explicit by modal vocabulary. It is this insight that leads Kant to the idea of 'pure' concepts or 'categories', including the alethic modal concepts of necessity and possibility that articulate causal laws, which must be available *a priori* because and in the sense that the ability to deploy them is presupposed by the ability to deploy ordinary empirical descriptive concepts. The categories, including modality, are concepts that make explicit what is implicit in the empirical descriptive use of any concepts at all. Though the details of *which* laws, the statements of which express counterfactually robust patterns of inference, actually obtain is an empirical one, *that* empirical descriptions are related by *rules* in the form of laws, which do support counterfactually robust inferences, is *not* itself an empirical matter, but a truth about the framework of empirical description. I want to call the underlying insight "the Kant-Sellars thesis about modality." It is the claim that in being able to use nonmodal, empirical descriptive vocabulary, one already knows how to do everything one needs to know how to do in order to deploy modal vocabulary, which accordingly can be understood as making explicit structural features that are always already implicit in what one *does* in describing.

6. Conclusion

Articulating and justifying his version of the Kant-Sellars thesis about modality is Sellars's constructive response to the empiricist tradition's "nothing-but-ism" about modality: its demand that what is expressed by modal claims either be shown to be expressible in nonmodal terms, or be dispensed with entirely by semantically fastidious philosophers and scientists. This complements and completes his demonstration, in the "Phenomenalism" essay, that this critical consequence of an overambitious empiricism is in any case incompatible with any constructive empiricist effort to reconstruct or replace the use of target vocabularies such as objective-descriptive vocabulary, primary-quality vocabulary, and theoretical vocabulary in terms of the favored empiricist base vocabularies, if that effort is subject to even the most minimal criteria of material adequacy. Together, these arguments show what Sellars eventually made of his early intuition that the soft underbelly of empiricism, in both its traditional and its twentieth-century logistical form, is its semantic treatment of modality.

My overall aim in this chapter has been to place the arguments against empiricism presented in the first half of *Empiricism and the Philosophy of Mind* in the larger context opened up by laying them alongside the further battery of arguments aimed at the same target that derive from consideration of that tradition's views about modality. And I have been concerned to show that the methodological strategies that guide all of these discussions are Sellars's *pragmatist* insistence on looking at what one must be able to *do* in order to deploy empirical descriptive vocabulary, and his *rationalist* commitment to the necessary *inferential* articulation of the concepts expressed by the use of such vocabulary. I think that even fifty years on, there is still a lot of juice to be squeezed out of these ideas.

But I want to close with another, perhaps more frivolous suggestion. Every sufficiently engaged reading becomes a rewriting, and I have been offering here, *inter alia*, the outline of a different narrative strategy that Sellars could have adopted in the late 1950s. Under some such title as *The Limits of Empiricism*, he could have re-presented the material that in fact appeared first as roughly the first half of *Empiricism and the Philosophy of Mind*, and the second halves of each of "Phenomenalism" and "Counterfactuals, Dispositions, and Causal Modalities," organized around and introduced in terms of the themes I have traced here. It is interesting to speculate about how his reception might have been different—and about where we would find ourselves today—had this been the shape of Sellars's first book.

CHAPTER FOUR

Modality and Normativity: From Hume and Quine to Kant and Sellars

1. The Modal Revolution

The status and respectability of alethic *modality* was always a point of contention and divergence between naturalism and empiricism.[1] It poses no problems in principle for *naturalism*, since modal vocabulary is an integral part of all the candidate naturalistic base vocabularies. Fundamental physics is above all a language of *laws;* the special sciences distinguish between true and false *counterfactual* claims; and ordinary empirical talk is richly *dispositional*. By contrast, modality has been a stumbling-block for the *empiricist* tradition ever since Hume forcefully formulated his epistemological and ultimately semantic objections to the concepts of law and necessary connection.

Those traditional reservations about the intelligibility of modal notions were underscored, reinforced, and confirmed for twentieth-century versions of empiricism, which had been distinguished, strengthened, and made more precise by the addition of the semantic logicist model of the conceptual articulation of empirical content. Extensional, first-order quantificational languages could express *regularities* and *generalizations* with hitherto undreamed of power and precision. But for philosophers from Russell through Carnap to Quine, that just made it all the more urgent to explain, or explain away, the *lawlikeness* or counterfactual-supporting *necessity* distinctive of at least *some* of those generalizations,

---

1. This tension was a principal source of conflict within the Vienna Circle, dividing Neurath and Schlick, for instance, with Carnap trying to mediate.

which demonstrably extended beyond what can be captured by the expressive resources of that logical vocabulary.[2]

This confluence of traditional empiricist with logicist difficulties concerning the content expressed by modal vocabulary had the result that for roughly the first two-thirds of the twentieth century, Anglophone philosophy regarded alethic modal vocabulary with extreme suspicion, if not outright hostility. It ranked, with normative vocabulary, as among the most mysterious and philosophically puzzling forms of discourse, the source of central standing and outstanding philosophical problems, as a prime candidate for the analytic project of semantic clarification in favored terms or, failing that, principled elimination from perspicuous discourse, as Quine famously recommended.

But philosophical attitudes toward modality underwent a remarkable, in many ways unprecedentedly radical transformation during the twentieth century. For starting in the second half of the century and accelerating through the last third, modal vocabulary became the analytic semanticist's best friend, and an essential part of the contemporary philosopher's metaconceptual tool-kit. I think it is worthwhile reminding ourselves just how surprised and astonished philosophers who lived and moved and had their being in the earlier milieu would have been to discover that by the end of their century, when questions were raised about the semantics of some vocabulary—for instance, normative, intentional, or even semantic vocabulary itself—not only the dominant strategy, but the very first recourse would be to appeal to *modal* notions such as dispositions, counterfactual dependencies, and nomological relations to explain the questionable conceptual contents. Just how—they would want to know—did what seemed most urgently in need of philosophical explanation and defense suddenly become transformed so as to be unproblematically available to explain other puzzling phenomena? Surely such a major transformation of *explanandum* into *explanans* could not be the result merely of a change of fashion, the onset of amnesia, or the accumulation of fatigue? But if not, what secret did we find

---

2. We now know, thanks to Danielle Macbeth's *Frege's Logic* (Cambridge, MA: Harvard University Press, 2005), that Frege's own Begriffsschrift notation did not share the expressive impoverishment with respect to modality exhibited by the extensional first-order logic that Russell and, following him, everyone else drew from it.

out, what new understanding did we achieve, to *justify* this change of philosophical attitude and practice?

Two answers to this question lie ready to hand. First, there was a formal-semantic revolution in modal logic. And second, the Anglophone tradition more or less gave up empiricism in favor of naturalism. I think both those explanations are right, as far as they go, both as a matter of historical fact and in the order of justification. But it is important to understand exactly *which* questions those developments *did* offer responsive answers to, and to which they did *not*.

As to the first point, I think there is a widespread tendency to think that, to paraphrase Alexander Pope,

Modality and Nature's laws lay hid in night,
God said: "Let Kripke be!" and all was light.

But that cannot be right. Kripke's provision of a complete extensional semantic metavocabulary for intensional modal logical vocabulary—and its powerful development, by others such as Montague, Scott, Kaplan, Lewis, and Stalnaker, into a general intensional semantics for nonlogical vocabulary—*is* an adequate response to worries stemming from the *extensional* character of the *logical vocabulary* in which semantics had been conducted. That is, it addresses the difficulties on the *semantic logicist* side of the classical project of analysis that stem from the expressive impoverishment of first-order logical vocabulary. But these formal developments do *not* provide an adequate response to residual *empiricist* worries about the intelligibility of modal concepts. For the extensionality of the semantic metalanguage for modality is bought at the price of making free use of modal primitives: most centrally, the notion of a <u>possible</u> world (as well as that of <u>accessibility</u> relations among such *possibilia*). As Quine emphasized, the modal vocabulary whose use is essential to this semantic approach evidently falls within the circle of terms and concepts to which empiricist suspicions and questions apply. That is, even putting *ontological* issues aside, whether possible worlds are thought of as abstract objects, as concrete particulars spatiotemporally unconnected to our universe, or as *sui generis* possibilia, both the *epistemological* question of how we are to understand the possibility of our *knowing* anything about such items (and their accessibility relations), and the question how, if the possibility of such *cognitive* contact is mysterious, the idea of our having the *semantic* contact necessary so much as to *talk* or *think* about them can be made intelligible, are wholly untouched by this formal apparatus and remain every bit as pressing as before.

2. The Modal Kant-Sellars Thesis

How urgent those questions are depends on whether we have grounds to accept criticisms of the empiricist program that undermine the basis for its relegation of modal vocabulary to a suspect, second-class status. I think that the best justification for our new comfort with modal idioms is indeed to be found in the principled rejection of some of the crucial presuppositions of the empiricist critique of the credentials of modal concepts. We can now see that the operative core of both Quine's and Sellars's arguments against empiricism consists in objections to its underlying *semantic atomism*.[3] Arguing that meaning must at least determine inferential role and noticing that what follows from or is evidence for or against a claim depends on what other claims are available as auxiliary hypotheses or collateral premises, Quine concludes that the smallest unit of meaning is not a sentence, even in the case of observation sentences, but what he calls a 'theory': the whole constellation of all sentences held true, articulated by their inferential relations both to one another and to sentences not held true. Sellars argues that even observational beliefs acquired noninferentially through perception can be understood as *conceptually* contentful—and hence potentially cognitively significant—only in virtue of their inferential relations to other possible beliefs. He concludes that noninferential reports, no matter what their subject matter, cannot constitute an autonomous discursive practice: a language game one could play though one played no other.

It is clear, I take it, how these anti-atomist arguments bear against empiricist foundationalism: the layer-cake picture of a semantically autonomous base of perceptual experience or reports thereof, on which is erected a semantically optional superstructure, in effect, of theories inferentially based on those observations. And insofar as empiricist worries about the status of laws, necessary connections, dispositions, and counterfactual possibilities

---

3. In their classic papers of the 1950s, "Two Dogmas of Empiricism" and *Empiricism and the Philosophy of Mind*.

are predicated on the difficulty of justifying the inferences that would add them to the supposedly semantically autonomous base of nonmodal reports of actual experiences, Quine's and Sellars's assault on the layer-cake picture, if successful, undercuts those worries by removing the motivation for their ultimately unmeetable constraints on an account of what modal vocabulary expresses. Thought of this way, though, criticism of the semantic presuppositions of the empiricist project does not bear any more directly on its treatment of *modal* vocabulary than on its treatment of any other potentially puzzling candidate for empiricist explication: *theoretical* (that is, nonobservational, exclusively inferentially applicable) vocabulary, *normative* vocabulary, *probabilistic* vocabulary, and so on.

But there is another, much more intimate and immediate *positive* connection between arguments against semantic atomism and our understanding of what is expressed by the use of modal vocabulary. And it is here that I think we can find the best justification for our current relaxed attitude toward and even enthusiastic embrace of modal idioms as suitable tools for serious analytic semantic work. The underlying idea is what I will call the "Kant-Sellars thesis about modality." Hume found that even his best understanding of actual observable empirical *facts* did not yield an understanding of *rules* relating or otherwise governing them. Those facts did not settle which of the things that *actually* happened *had* to happen (given others), that is, were (at least conditionally) *necessary*, and which of the things that did *not* happen nonetheless were *possible* (not ruled out by laws concerning what did happen). Though initially couched as an *epistemological* question about how one could *know* what rules or laws were in play, Hume's worries run deeper, raising the *semantic* question of what it could so much as *mean* to say that the facts are governed or related by rules or laws. Hume (and, following him, Quine) took it that epistemologically and semantically fastidious philosophers faced a stark choice: either show how to explain modality in nonmodal terms or learn to live without it. But that challenge is predicated on the idea of an independently and antecedently intelligible stratum of empirical discourse that is purely descriptive and involves no modal commitments, as a semantically autonomous background and model with which the credentials of modal discourse can then be invidiously compared. One of Kant's most basic ideas, revived by Sellars, is that this idea is mistaken. The ability to use ordinary empirical descriptive terms such as 'green', 'rigid', and 'mass' already presupposes grasp of the kind of properties and relations made explicit by modal vocabulary. Sellars summed up the claim admirably in the title of one of his early papers: "Concepts as Involving Laws, and Inconceivable without Them."[4]

Kant was struck by the fact that the essence of the Newtonian concept of mass is of something that by law *force* is both necessary and sufficient to *accelerate*. And he saw that all empirical concepts are like their refined descendants in the mathematized natural sciences in this respect: their application implicitly involves counterfactual-supporting dispositional commitments to what *would* happen *if*. . . . Kant's claim, put in more contemporary terms, is that an integral part of what one is committed to in applying any determinate concept in empirical circumstances is drawing a distinction between counterfactual differences in circumstances that *would* and those that *would not* affect the truth of the judgment one is making. One has not grasped the concept cat unless one knows that it would still be possible for the cat to be on the mat if the lighting had been slightly different, but not if all life on Earth had been extinguished by an asteroid-strike.[5]

---

4. In J. Sicha (ed.), *Pure Pragmatics and Possible Worlds: The Early Essays of Wilfrid Sellars* (Atascadero, CA: Ridgeview, 1980), pp. 87–124. Hereafter *PPPW*. This slogan is a good place to start in thinking about Kant's point, but in fact Sellars's own view is subtly but importantly different from Kant's. For Sellars, the laws determining the truth of counterfactuals involving the application of a concept are part of the content of the concept. For Kant, modal concepts make explicit not something implicit in the *content* of determinate concepts, but something implicit in their *empirical use,* in *applying* them to make empirical *judgments*. That is why the pure concepts of the understanding—what he calls 'categories', such as possibility and necessity—both are to be understood in terms of the forms of judgment (the table of categories derives from the table of judgments) and express synthetic, rather than analytic necessities. From Kant's point of view, a better slogan than Sellars's would be "The *Use* of Concepts in Empirical *Judgments* as Involving Laws and Inconceivable without Them."

5. It is this observation, unwittingly underscored by Hume (for Kant, the Moses who brought us to within sight of the Promised Land he himself was destined not to enter), that motivates Kant to wheel in his heavy transcendental machinery. For he sought to explain the modal commitments implicit in the application of ordinary empirical concepts by placing the modal concepts of law and necessity in the newly postulated realm of *pure* concepts or categories, which must be graspable *a priori* precisely in the sense that their applicability is presupposed by the applicability of *any* empirical concepts. The concept of vocabularies that are "universally LX," introduced below, is a successor notion along at least one important dimension.

In an autobiographical sketch, Sellars dates his break with traditional empiricism to his Oxford days in the thirties. It was, he says, prompted by concern with the sort of content that ought to be associated with logical, causal, and deontological modalities. Already at that point he had the idea that

> what was needed was a functional theory of concepts which would make their role in reasoning, rather than supposed origin in experience, their primary feature.[6]

Somewhat more specifically, he sees modal locutions as tools used in the enterprise of

> ... making explicit the rules we have adopted for thought and action....
> I shall be interpreting our judgments to the effect that A causally necessitates B as the expression of a rule governing our use of the terms 'A' and 'B'.[7]

In fact, following Ryle,[8] he takes modal expressions to function as *inference licenses*, expressing our commitment to the goodness of counterfactually robust inferences from necessitating to necessitated conditions. If and insofar as it could be established that their involvement in such counterfactually robust inferences is essential to the *contents* of ordinary empirical concepts, then what is made explicit by modal vocabulary is implicit in the use of any such concepts. That is the claim I am calling the "Kant-Sellars thesis." On this view, modal vocabulary does not just add to the use of ordinary empirical observational vocabulary a range of expressive power that is *extraneous*—as though one were adding, say, *culinary* to *nautical* vocabulary. Rather, the expressive job distinctive of modal vocabulary is to articulate just the kind of essential semantic connections among empirical concepts

---

6. In H. N. Castañeda (ed.), *Action, Knowledge, and Reality* (Indianapolis, IN: Bobbs-Merrill, 1975), p. 285.
7. Sellars, "Language, Rules, and Behavior," in *PPPW*, fn. 2 to p. 136.
8. Gilbert Ryle, "'If', 'So', and 'Because'," in Max Black (ed.), *Philosophical Analysis* (Englewood Cliffs, NJ: Prentice Hall, 1950), pp. 302–318.

that Sellars (and Quine) point to, and whose existence semantic atomism is principally concerned to deny.

As I would like to formulate it, the Kant-Sellars thesis begins with the claim that in using ordinary empirical vocabulary, one already knows how to do everything one needs to know how to do in order to introduce and deploy modal vocabulary. If that is right, then one cannot be in the position the atomist (for instance, empiricist) critic of modality professes to find himself in: having fully understood and mastered the use of *non*modal vocabulary, but having thereby afforded himself no grip on the use of *modal* vocabulary, and no access to what it expresses. The Humean-Quinean predicament is accordingly diagnosed as resulting from a failure properly to understand the relation between modal vocabulary and what one must *do* in order to *deploy* nonmodal, empirical, descriptive vocabulary.

The thought that the expressive role characteristic of alethic modal vocabulary is to make explicit semantic or conceptual connections and commitments that are already implicit in the use of ordinary (apparently) nonmodal empirical vocabulary faces at the outset at least two sorts of potentially weighty objection. First, didn't Kripke's semantic investigations of modally rigid designators reveal the sort of necessity they articulate as being *metaphysical,* specifically by contrast to the sort of *conceptual* necessity that Quine, for instance, had worried about and rejected? And second, to talk about what is necessary and possible is not to *say* anything about rules for using linguistic expressions, or about what anyone is committed to, since the objective modal claims in question could have been true even if there had never been language users, linguistic expressions, rules, or commitments.

As to the first objection, the philosophical phase of the modal revolution (developing the earlier logical and semantic phases of that revolution) that Kripke precipitated in "Naming and Necessity" did indeed use the semantic phenomenon of the modal rigidity of some nondescriptive vocabulary to articulate a kind of necessity that is knowable only *a posteriori.* The conclusion that such necessity should not be understood as *conceptual* necessity follows only if one either identifies conceptual content with *descriptive* content (by contrast to the causally-historically acquired content of proper names and demonstratives) or takes it (as Quine, following the tradition, had) that conceptual connections must be knowable *a priori* by those who have mastered those concepts. But both of these are optional commitments, which can and should be rejected by anyone trying to follow out the Kant-Sellars line of thought about modality. McDowell has argued, to my mind, convincingly, that the content expressed by demonstrative vocabulary should be understood as thoroughly conceptual (and that Frege already took it to be so).[9] And in *Making It Explicit*, I articulate a broadly inferential notion of the conceptual that incorporates the indirectly inferential roles of substitution and anaphora—including the anaphoric phenomenon that is modal rigidity.[10]

On the other point, Sellars's forthright response to Quine's pragmatic challenge in "Two Dogmas of Empiricism"—to say what it is about the *use* of expressions that distinguishes inferences underwritten by necessary conceptual relations from those underwritten by contingent matter-of-factual ones—is to identify the concept-articulating inferences as those that are counterfactually robust.[11] He cheerfully embraces the consequence that to discover what is contained in the concept copper one needs empirically to investigate the laws of nature. (This is a kind of semantic 'externalism' that does not need to take on the dangerous and difficult task of making sense of a notion of the 'internal' with which to contrast.) The issue about conceptual necessities here is not an empirical one: who is right about the conceptual? The Kant-Sellars thesis about modality requires deploying a concept of the conceptual that differs in important ways from the traditional one. As long as such a notion can be intelligibly developed and consistently applied, those differences need only be kept firmly in mind, not counted as fatal flaws.

The response to the second objection (that saying what is necessary or possible is not saying anything about how anyone talks) must be to be clearer about the sort of pragmatically mediated semantic relation the Kant-Sellars thesis takes modal vocabulary to stand in to ordinary, nonmodal descriptive vocabulary. The large claim in the vicinity—one that will occupy me not only in this chapter but beyond—is, as Sellars puts it, that "the language of modality is . . . a 'transposed' language of norms."[12] I do not think that

---

9. John McDowell, "De Re Senses," *Meaning, Knowledge, and Reality* (Cambridge, MA: Harvard University Press, 2001).
10. Robert Brandom, *Making It Explicit* (Cambridge, MA: Harvard University Press, 1994), Chapters 6, 7 (especially Sections III and IV), and 8 (Section V).
11. "Is There a Synthetic *A Priori?*," *Philosophical Studies* 20 (1953): 121–138.
12. Sellars, "Inference and Meaning," in *PPPW*, p. 280.

Sellars himself ever manages to say clearly just what sort of 'transposition' he has in mind. He appeals to a distinction between what is *said* by the use of some vocabulary, and what is *conveyed* by its use. While admitting that talk of what is necessary does not *say* anything about what language users ought or ought not to do, he nonetheless insists that it "conveys the same information" as "rules to the effect that we may do thus and so, and ought not do this and that, in the way of manipulating expressions in a language."[13] His (only somewhat helpful) example is that when I say, "The sky is clear," I have both said something about the weather and conveyed something about my beliefs. The point, I take it, is to distinguish what follows *semantically* from the content of what I have *said* from what follows *pragmatically* from my *saying* of it. (Embedding the claims as the antecedents of conditionals will distinguish these two sorts of consequences. "If the sky is clear, then it will not rain" expresses a good inference, whereas "If the sky is clear, then Brandom believes that the sky is clear" does not. For only the semantic content, and not the pragmatic force of the utterance, survives such embedding.)

3. Meaning-Use Analysis of the Modal Kant-Sellars Thesis

We can put ourselves in a position to be clearer about what Sellars is after with his dark notion of what an utterance 'conveys'. The view is that what I am *doing* when I say that it is causally necessary that if this piece of copper is heated to 1084° C, it will melt, is endorsing a certain kind of inference. I am not *saying that* that inference is good; the facts about copper would be as they are even if there were no inferrers or inferrings. When Sellars says, "the language of modality is ... a 'transposed' language of norms," he is saying in the terms I want to use that normative vocabulary codifying rules of inference is a *pragmatic metavocabulary* for modal vocabulary. His 'transposition' is just this pragmatically mediated semantic relation between deontic normative and alethic modal vocabulary.

To get clearer about the notion of a pragmatic metavocabulary, about Sellars's transposition thesis relating modal and normative vocabularies, and about the Kant-Sellars thesis, it will be useful to employ the metaconceptual

---

13. *PPPW*, p. 280.

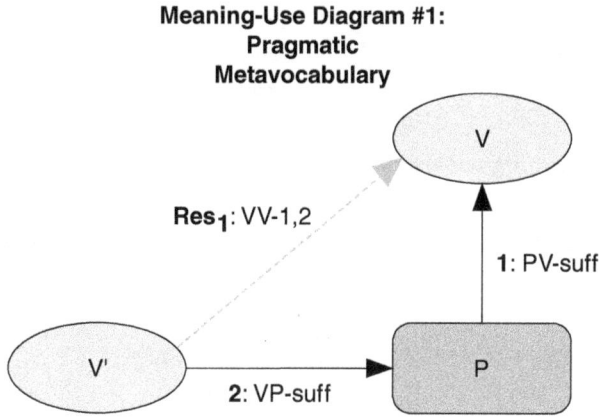

Figure 4.1 Meaning-use diagram of V' as a pragmatic metavocabulary of V.

apparatus for identifying and individuating expressive roles that vocabularies can play relative to one another that I introduced and developed in *Between Saying and Doing*, and sketched here in the first half of Chapter 1. Its basic building blocks are relations between discursive practices and the vocabularies. Practice-vocabulary sufficiency—"PV-sufficiency" for short—obtains when engaging in a specified set of practices or exercising a specified set of abilities is sufficient for someone to count as *deploying* a specified vocabulary. Vocabulary-practice sufficiency—"VP-sufficiency" for short—is the relation that holds between a vocabulary and a set of practices-or-abilities when that vocabulary is sufficient to *specify* those practices-or-abilities. VP-sufficient vocabularies that *specify* PV-sufficient practices let one *say* what it is one must *do* to count as engaging in those practices or exercising those abilities, and so to deploy a vocabulary to *say* something.

PV-sufficiency and VP-sufficiency are two basic *meaning-use* relations (MURs). In terms of those basic relations, we can define a more complex relation: the relation that holds between vocabulary V' and vocabulary V when V' is VP-sufficient to specify practices-or-abilities P that are PV-sufficient to deploy vocabulary V. This VV-relation is the *composition* of the two basic MURs. When it obtains I will say that V' is a *pragmatic metavocabulary* for V. It allows one to *say* what one must *do* in order to count as *saying* the things expressed by vocabulary V. We can present this relation graphically (Figure 4.1) in a *meaning-use diagram* (MUD).

The conventions of this diagram are as follows:

- Vocabularies are shown as ovals, practices-or-abilities as (rounded) rectangles.
- Basic meaning-use relations are indicated by solid arrows, numbered and labeled as to kind of relation.
- Resultant meaning-use relations are indicated by dotted arrows, numbered and labeled as to kind and the basic MURs from which they result.

The idea is that a resultant MUR is the relation that obtains when all of the basic MURs listed on its label obtain.

The meaning-use diagram of the pragmatically mediated semantic relation of being a pragmatic metavocabulary illustrates a distinctive kind of *analysis* of that relation. It exhibits that relation as the resultant, by composition, of the two basic meaning-use relations of PV-sufficiency and VP-sufficiency. A complex MUR is analyzed as the product of operations applied to basic MURs. This is *meaning-use analysis.*

Consider one of the pragmatist criticisms that Sellars addresses to the empiricist core program of the classical analytic project, discussed in Chapters 1 and 2. It turns on the assertion of the *pragmatic dependence* of one set of vocabulary-deploying practices-or-abilities on another. Because he thinks part of what one is *doing* in saying how things merely appear is withholding a commitment to their actually being that way, and because one cannot be understood as *withholding* a commitment that one cannot *undertake,* Sellars concludes that one cannot have the ability to say or think how things *seem* or *appear* unless one also has the ability to make claims about how things *actually are.* In effect, this Sellarsian pragmatist critique of the phenomenalist form of empiricism consists in the claim that the practices that are PV-sufficient for 'is-ϕ' talk are PP-necessary for the practices that are PV-sufficient for 'looks-ϕ' talk.[14] That pragmatic dependence of practices-or-abilities then induces a resultant pragmatically mediated semantic relation between the vocabularies. The meaning-use diagram for this claim is shown

---

14. I discuss this argument in greater detail in the final chapter of *Tales of the Mighty Dead* (Cambridge, MA: Harvard University Press, 2004).

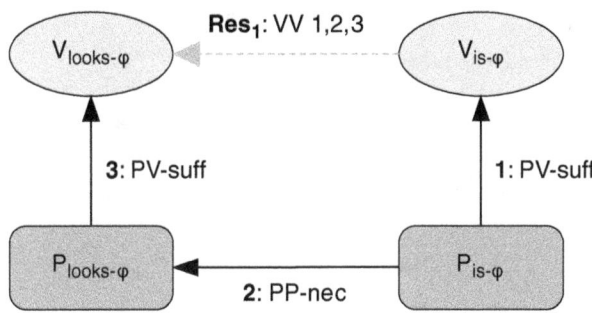

Figure 4.2 Meaning-use diagram: pragmatically mediated semantic presupposition.

in Figure 4.2. The resultant MUR here is a kind of complex, pragmatically mediated VV-necessity, or semantic presupposition.

In fact, although Sellars's argument for the crucial PP-necessity relation of pragmatic dependence of one set of vocabulary-deploying practices-or-abilities on another is different, his argument against the observational version of empiricism—the claim that purely noninferential, observational uses do not form an autonomous discursive practice, but presuppose inferential uses—has exactly the same form (Figure 4.3).

In terms of this apparatus, we can express the reading I am suggesting for Sellars's transposition claim regarding modal and normative vocabulary in a meaning-use diagram (Figure 4.4).

This claim is merely part of the background of what I have been calling the "Kant-Sellars thesis" about modality, however. That thesis comprises two claims:

a) In using ordinary empirical vocabulary, one already knows how to do everything one needs to know how to do in order to introduce and deploy *modal* vocabulary. The capacity to use modal vocabulary can be *elaborated from* capacities one must already have in order to be able to deploy any autonomous vocabulary.

and

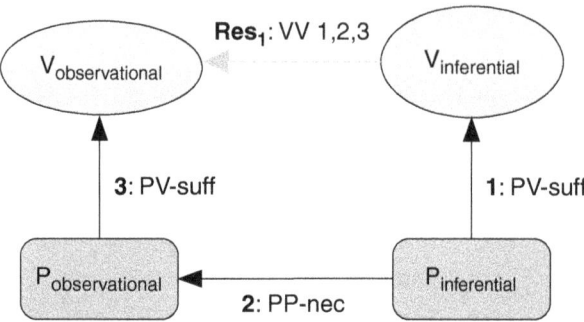

Figure 4.3 Meaning-use diagram representing Sellars's claim that purely observational uses of vocabulary do not form an autonomous discursive practice.

b) The expressive role characteristic of alethic modal vocabulary is to *make explicit* semantic, conceptual connections and commitments that are already *implicit* in the use of ordinary empirical vocabulary.

The first says that some practices that are PV-necessary for the use of any empirical vocabulary are PP-sufficient for practices that are PV-sufficient

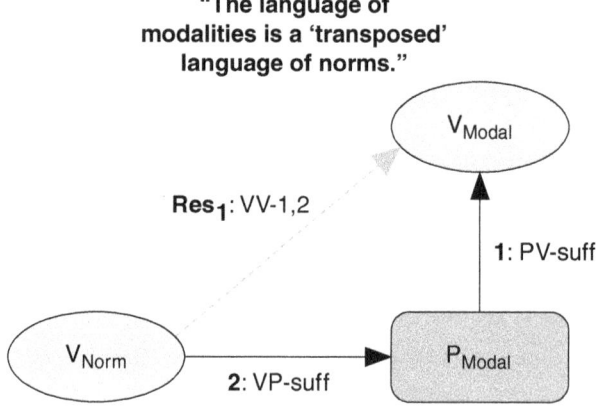

Figure 4.4 Meaning-use diagram: "The language of modalities is a transposed language of norms."

Modality and Normativity

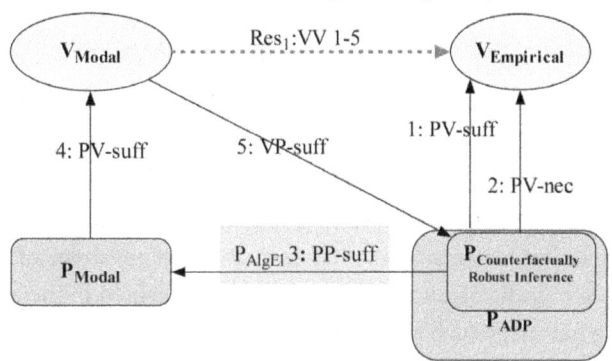

Figure 4.5 The Kant-Sellars Thesis: modal vocabulary is elaborated-explicating (LX).

to deploy modal vocabulary. The second says that that modal vocabulary then makes explicit those aspects of practices-or-abilities that are implicit in the use of any empirical vocabulary. These are ways of saying that modal vocabulary stands to ordinary empirical vocabulary in the complex, pragmatically mediated semantic relation that in *Between Saying and Doing* I call "elaborating-explicating": the meaning-use relation called 'LX' for short. The corresponding MUD is shown in Figure 4.5.

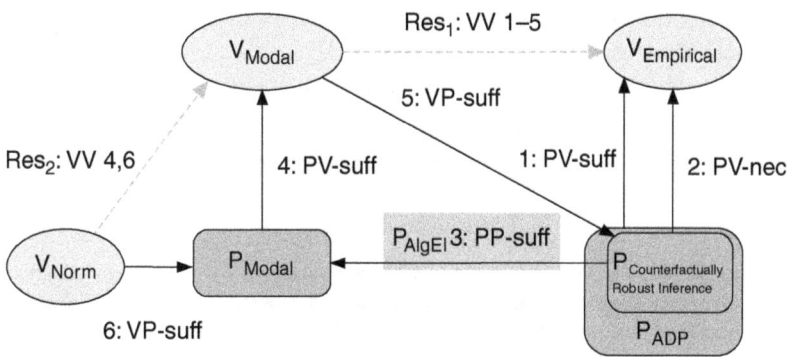

Figure 4.6 Modal, normative, and empirical vocabulary.

Combining these claims yields a MUD asserting relations among modal, normative, and empirical vocabularies (see Figure 4.6).

4. Counterfactual Robustness and the Updating Argument

So far, I have only expounded, explicated, and mentioned some of the consequences of the Kant-Sellars thesis about modal vocabulary, but not sought to *argue* for it. What reason is there to think that it is *true*? The analysis of the Kant-Sellars thesis as asserting a complex pragmatically mediated semantic relation between vocabularies that is the resultant of a definite constellation of basic meaning-use relations, as presented in the MUD, tells us exactly what shape such an argument must have. For it tells us just which *basic* meaning-use relations must be established in order to show that the *resultant* one obtains. The key element in this case will be finding some set of practices that can be argued to be at once contained in or exhibited by every autonomous discursive practice, and PP-sufficient for practices PV-sufficient for deploying explicitly modal vocabulary, which is VP-sufficient to specify the original PV-necessary practices-or-abilities. As the labels on the MUDs indicate, for the argument I will mount, those practices are *counterfactually robust inferential* practices-or-abilities—more specifically, the practical capacity to associate with materially good inferences *ranges of counterfactual robustness*. If it can be established that deploying any ordinary empirical vocabulary presupposes these practices-or-abilities, and that they in turn suffice to introduce explicit modally qualified conditionals that permit the expression of those practical discriminations, then the universal elaborated-explicating (LX) character of modal vocabulary relative to ordinary empirical vocabulary will have been demonstrated.[15]

I have already claimed that any autonomous discursive practice (ADP) must include practices-or-abilities of distinguishing some inferences as materially good from others that are not. For some bit of vocabulary to

---

15. In the idiom of *Between Saying and Doing*, a vocabulary V_1 is *elaborated* from and *explicative* of another vocabulary V_2 just in case a) in deploying V_2 one already knows how to do everything one needs to know how to do, in principle, to deploy V_1 (capacities sufficient to deploy V_1 can be algorithmically elaborated from the capacities necessary to deploy V_2) and b) V_1 makes it possible to *say* what one is *doing* in using V_2.

function as a propositionally contentful declarative sentence is for it to be available to serve as the premise and conclusion of such material inferences. Further, it is the expressive job generically characteristic of *conditional* vocabulary to *codify* endorsements of material inferences: to make them explicit in the form of declarative sentences that can themselves serve as the premises and conclusions of inferences. The philosopher most responsible for getting us to think about conditionals in this way is Gilbert Ryle. In his classic essay "'If', 'So', and 'Because'," in which he introduces the idea of hypothetical statements as inference tickets or licenses, he also points out an intimate connection between them and *modal* claims. He says:

> We have another familiar way of wording hypothetical statements. Although the standard textbooks discuss "modal propositions" in a different chapter from that in which they discuss hypotheticals, the differences between modal and hypothetical statements are in fact purely stylistic. There is only one colloquial way of correctly negating the superstitious hypothetical statement "If a person walks under a ladder, he comes to grief before the day is out," namely, by saying "No, a person may (might, or could) walk under a ladder and not come to grief." And the only colloquial way of putting a question to which an "if-then" statement is the required affirmative answer is to ask, for example, "Can an Oxford Vice-Chancellor not be (or need he be) a Head of College?" . . . [W]e always can reword an "if-then" statement as a statement of the pattern "It cannot be Monday today and not be Tuesday tomorrow." . . . [16]

I think he is right that "It is possible that (p and not-q)" is incompatible with "if p then q" when the latter is used to codify an ordinary material inference such as the inference from a banana's being yellow to its being ripe. Endorsing a material inference does involve a commitment of the sort made explicit by the use of modal vocabulary, about what is and is not possible, and what is at least conditionally necessary.

For this reason, the fact that we cannot intelligibly describe someone as deploying a concept unless he makes some distinction between materially

16. Ryle, "'If', 'So', and 'Because'," p. 313.

good and bad inferences involving it has the consequence that we also cannot understand the practitioner as deploying the concept unless he treats the material inferences he takes to be good as having a certain *range of counterfactual robustness,* that is, as remaining good under various merely hypothetical circumstances. One grasps the claim "the lioness is hungry" only insofar as one takes it to have various consequences (which *would* be true if it *were* true) and rule out some others (which *would not* be true if it *were* true). And it is not intelligible that one should endorse as materially good an inference involving it, such as the inference from "the lioness is hungry" to "nearby prey animals visible to and accessible by the lioness are in danger of being eaten," but be disposed to make no distinction at all between collateral premises that would, and those that would not, if true infirm the inference. One must make *some* distinction such as that the inference would still go through if the lioness were standing two inches to the east of her actual position, the day happened to be a Tuesday, or a small tree ten miles away cast its shadow over a beetle, but not if she were shot with a tranquilizing dart, the temperature instantly plummeted 300 degrees, or a plane crashed, crushing her. The claim is not that one could not fail to assess some or even all of *these particular* counterfactuals correctly and still count as grasping the claim that is their premise, but that one could not so qualify if one made *no* such distinctions.

It may initially be tempting to think that the inferences that are counterfactually robust are all and only those underwritten by *laws.* Thus inferences underwritten by the law that all samples of copper melt at 1083.4° C are counterfactually robust: if this coin (which in fact is silver) *were* made of copper, it *would* melt at 1083.4° C. Whereas inferences underwritten by the accidental regularity that all the coins in my pocket are copper are not counterfactually robust: if I *were* to put this coin (which in fact is silver) in my pocket, it would *not* be copper. There are indeed real and significant differences between these cases, but I think it is important not to think of them in terms of the difference between inferences that *are* counterfactually robust and inferences that are *not.* The difference is rather one of the character of the particular *ranges* of counterfactual robustness. For the accidental generalization that all the coins in my pocket are copper *does* underwrite counterfactuals such as "If I *were* to choose a coin at random from my pocket, it *would* be copper." In fact *every* claim, whether contingent or not, supports *some* counterfactual inferences, and if one grasped *none* of them one would not qualify as understanding those claims.

I think these considerations suffice to establish that autonomous discursive practices *essentially*, and not just *accidentally*, involve the association of ranges of counterfactual robustness with at least some material inferences. If, as Ryle claims, and as is in any case plausible, *modal* vocabulary specifying what is at least conditionally possible and necessary can then be introduced to make explicit those commitments to the at least limited counterfactual goodness of material inferences, then we have what is needed for the modal Kant-Sellars thesis. But I think that if we dig deeper, we can learn more. So rather than leaving things at this point, I want to consider a more detailed line of argument for this, the most potentially controversial element of the complex meaning-use relation that thesis asserts.

For the first premise, I take it to be clear that every autonomous discursive practice must have some vocabulary that can be used *observationally*, in reliably differentially elicited noninferential reports. This is the core of what I have been referring to as "ordinary empirical vocabulary." Second, I have already argued that those who engage in any discursive practices must distinguish in practice between materially good and materially bad inferences—where calling them 'material' just means that the presence of some nonlogical vocabulary is essential to the classification. Recall that this is not to claim that they must have a view about the goodness or badness of every possible candidate material inference; there can be some about which they have no view. And it is not to claim that they always are correct about the goodness of the inferences toward which they do have attitudes. But to count as deploying any vocabulary at all, one must treat some inferences involving it as good and others as bad. Otherwise, one's utterances are wholly devoid of conceptual content; whatever pragmatic significance they may have, it cannot be thought of as *discursive* significance. Even tokenings that are noninferentially elicited by environing stimuli—that is, the applications of observational vocabulary mentioned in the first premise—must have inferential *consequences*, if they are not to be cognitively idle.

The third claim is that material inference is in general *nonmonotonic*. That is, the inference from p to q may be materially good, even though the inference from $p\&r$ to q is not. Monotonicity of inference is of course a familiar feature of inferences within a formal *logical* system, and in mathematical reasoning; and that feature is arguably inherited by fundamental physics. But in the special sciences inferences are almost always *defeasible,* by collateral circumstances that thereby count as 'special'. Each stage in a physician's differential diagnosis is like this: the inference from test result, physical finding, or symptom is surrounded by a nimbus of usually unspoken 'unless'es. And no-one supposes that such probative reasoning can always be turned into dispositive reasoning by making an explicit, exhaustive list of the potential defeasors. Certainly, reasoning in everyday life does not generally admit such completions. If I strike this dry, well-made match, it will light—unless it is done inside a strong magnetic field. But it still will light if, in addition, it is struck inside a Faraday cage—unless there is not enough oxygen. And so on. There need be no definite totality of possible defeasors, specifiable in advance. Even where we have some idea how to enumerate them, unless those provisos are generally left implicit, actually stating the premises so as to draw inferences from them monotonically is impossibly cumbersome in practice.

At this point, one is liable to think of *ceteris paribus* clauses. The careful way to formulate the ordinary inference just mentioned is that if I strike this dry, well-made match, *ceteris paribus,* or other things being equal, it will light. I think that is indeed exactly what we ought to say, and the point I want to make can be made by saying that what such *ceteris paribus* clauses mark is an unavoidable feature of ordinary material inferences. But it is critical to understand what such clauses *do* and do *not* do. They are *not* devices for the wholesale stipulation of the denial of all of the potential defeasors that, even if exhaustively knowable and statable, if denied retail would make the inference unsurveyable. That is, they are not devices that *make* nonmonotonic inferences monotonic. The proper term for a Latin phrase whose utterance could do *that* is '*magic spell*'. If it is thought of as a wholesale proviso covering all possible defeasors, the effect of adding '*ceteris paribus*' to the statement of the inference that if I strike this dry, well-made match, then it will light, would be to say, "unless for some reason it doesn't" or "except in those circumstances when it doesn't." That is not producing an inference that is *monotonic;* it is producing one that is *trivial.* The real expressive function of *ceteris paribus* clauses is not *magically* to *remove* the nonmonotonicity of material inferences, nor to replace them with other monotonic ones, but rather *explicitly* to *acknowledge* their nonmonotonicity: to mark the inference being endorsed as one that has unspecified, but potentially important defeasors.[17]

The fourth premise is that at any given time, many, if not most, of a subject's beliefs could only be justified by exhibiting them as the conclusions of material inferences. We might call a believer "epistemically responsible" insofar as she acknowledges a commitment to being able to justify many, if not most, of her beliefs, under suitable circumstances. My fifth premise is that in order to count as a discursive practitioner, one must be at least minimally epistemically responsible. Present purposes will not require that we attempt to quantify what the minimal level of such responsibility is.

We can draw a preliminary conclusion. The five considerations advanced so far together entail that epistemically responsible believers face a potentially intractable *updating problem*. Every change of belief, no matter how small, is *potentially* relevant to the justification of every prior belief. Acquiring a new belief means acquiring what, for any material inference the believer endorses and relies upon for justification, might possibly turn out to be a defeasor. And giving up any belief means giving up not only a premise that might previously have been relied upon in justification, but also a potential counter-defeasor (for instance, a magnetic field's not being a defeasor to the match's lighting if there is a Faraday cage inside the field).

Now it is not practically feasible explicitly to review all of one's beliefs every time one's beliefs change, in order to check which are and which are not still justifiable. If that were what epistemic responsibility demanded, then it would be a pointless, impossible ideal. Language users who *do* not (because they *can*not) do *that*, must *practically* distinguish, among all the inferences that rationalize their current beliefs, which of them are update *candidates*, in the light of the current change of belief (let us say, for simplicity, a newly added belief). That is practically to associate with the new belief

---

17. For empirical claims involving theoretical vocabulary, this is obvious. For theoretical vocabulary is, by definition, vocabulary that can *only* correctly be applied as the conclusion of an inference. But the justification even of beliefs acquired *non*inferentially, through observation, typically will involve appealing to the reliability of the observer's differential responsive dispositions to endorse such claims under a range of circumstances. The inference from my being a reliable reporter of red things in good light to my responsively elicited claim that something is red being true can be a good material inference. But it is nonmonotonic, defeasible by a whole range of collateral circumstances.

a set of material inferences of which it is a potential defeasor. The potential defeasors in this way associated with each material inference endorsed in turn define (by complementation) the range of counterfactual robustness practically associated with that inference.[18]

I conclude that in view of the nonmonotonicity of material inference, the practical task of updating the rest of one's beliefs when some of them change is tractable in principle only if those who deploy a vocabulary practically discriminate ranges of counterfactual robustness for many of the material inferences they endorse. If that is right, then establishing the modal Kant-Sellars thesis requires further showing how to introduce modal vocabulary on the basis of such counterfactual conditionals, and how to use modal vocabulary to make those counterfactual conditionals explicit. Ryle's remarks suggest a strategy for both: treat "If p were true, q would be true" as equivalent to "It is not possible that p and *not-q*." In *Between Saying and Doing* (Chapter Five) I show how to follow out this strategy in detail, by treating the claim that q follows from p as equivalent to the claim that everything materially incompatible with q is materially incompatible with p—so that to say that "Coda is a dog" entails "Coda is a mammal" is to say that everything incompatible with his being a mammal is incompatible with his being a dog.

5. The Normative Kant-Sellars Thesis

Before turning to that project of connecting material inferential relations with an implicitly modal notion of material incompatibility, however, I want to consider an analog of the Kant-Sellars thesis about *modal* vocabulary that applies instead to *normative* vocabulary.

Kant read Hume's theoretical and practical philosophies as raising variants of a single question. On the side of theoretical reasoning, Hume asks what our warrant is for moving from descriptions of what *in fact* happens to characterizations of what *must* happen and what could not happen. How,

---

18. Somewhat more carefully put: assuming some length restriction ensuring finiteness of the set of logically non-compound sentences involved, the ability to associate with each sentence a set of inferences of which it is a potential defeasor can be algorithmically elaborated into (and hence is PP-sufficient for) the ability to associate with each inference a set of potential defeasors, and hence again, the set of non-defeasors.

he wants to know, can we rationally justify the move from descriptions of matter-of-factual regularities to formulations of necessary laws? On the side of practical reasoning, Hume asks what our warrant is for moving from descriptions of how things are to prescriptions of how they ought to be. How, he wants to know, can we rationally justify the move from 'is' to 'ought'? In Kant's terminology, these are both species of 'necessity': *practical* (including moral) and *natural* necessity, respectively. For him, 'necessary' (notwendig) just means "according to a *rule*." Hume's predicament is that he finds that even his best understanding of *facts* doesn't yield an understanding of *rules* governing and relating those facts, underwriting assessments of which of the things that actually happen (something we can experience) *must* happen (are *naturally* necessary), or *ought* to happen (are *normatively* or *practically* necessary).

As we have seen, on the modal side, Kant's response is that Hume's predicament is not a real one. One cannot in fact fully understand the descriptive, empirical employment of ordinary determinate concepts such as cat without at least implicitly understanding also what is made explicit by the modal concepts that articulate laws. Kant mounts a corresponding line of thought on the side of *normative* or *practical* necessity. Normative concepts make explicit commitments that are implicit in any use of concepts, whether theoretically in judgment or practically in acting intentionally—that is, in endorsing practical maxims. *Judgment* and *agency* are implicitly normative phenomena because they consist in the application of concepts, and applying concepts is undertaking commitments and responsibilities whose *content* is articulated by those concepts. (For Kant, specifically *moral* normative vocabulary makes explicit commitments that are already implicit in the practical use of concepts to endorse maxims, ends, and plans.)

I am not going to go into how Sellars builds on this thought, because I will develop it in a somewhat different way. Suffice it to say that in the light of Kant's parallel responses to Hume's parallel concerns with the credentials of modal and normative vocabulary—concerns couched in epistemological terms, but at base semantic in character—we can formulate a *normative* Kant-Sellars thesis by analogy to the *modal* one. It is the claim that in order to apply or deploy ordinary empirical descriptive vocabulary, including observational vocabulary—and hence, in order to deploy any autonomous vocabulary whatsoever—one must already be able to do everything needed

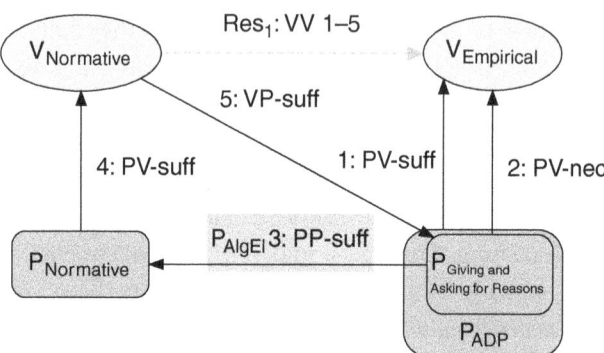

Figure 4.7 Normative Kant-Sellars Thesis: normative vocabulary is elaborated-explicating (LX).

to introduce normative vocabulary. Articulated in terms of meaning-use analysis, it is the claim that there are practices PV-necessary for engaging in any autonomous discursive practice that are PP-sufficient for practices PV-sufficient to deploy normative vocabulary. If, again by analogy to the modal case, we add the claim that normative vocabulary is VP-sufficient to *specify* those aspects of the practices that are PV-necessary for any ADP, we have the full-blown claim that normative vocabulary is elaborated-explicating, or LX, for all autonomous vocabularies. The MUD for the resultant complex meaning-use relation among vocabularies is shown in Figure 4.7.

How might one argue for the normative Kant-Sellars thesis? I have been working all along with the idea that any autonomous set of practices can be intelligible as deploying a vocabulary—that is, as being *discursive* or *linguistic* practices—only insofar as those practices attribute to some performances the pragmatic significance of *assertions,* and that it is a necessary feature of that pragmatic significance that assertions can serve both as premises and conclusions of *inferences.* The notions of asserting and of inferring are on this account essentially and indissolubly linked. This is to say that every autonomous *discursive* practice must include core practices of *giving and asking for reasons.* It is playing a suitable role in such a constellation of practices that makes the sign-designs whose production can have in that context the pragmatic significance of being an assertion—something that can both serve as and stand in need of a reason—qualify as *declarative sentences*. And standing in those inferential (justificatory, evidential) relations is a necessary condition of those sentences being intelligible as expressing *propositional contents*.[19]

It is these core practices of giving and asking for reasons that I propose as being both PV-necessary for every autonomous discursive practice (as I have just been claiming) and PP-sufficient for, in the sense of algorithmically elaboratable into, practices PV-sufficient for the introduction of normative vocabulary, which can then serve explicitly to specify key features of those practices. In particular, I will argue that no set of practices is recognizable as a game of giving and asking for *reasons* for *assertions* unless it involves implicitly (practically) acknowledging at least two sorts of normative status, *commitments* and *entitlements*, and some general structures relating them.

Suppose we have a set of counters or markers such that producing or playing one has the social significance of making an assertional move in the game. We can call such counters 'sentences'. Then for any player at any time there must be a way of partitioning sentences into two classes, by distinguishing somehow those that he is disposed or otherwise prepared to assert (perhaps when suitably prompted). These counters, which are distinguished by bearing the player's mark, being on his list, or being kept in his box, constitute his score. By playing a new counter, making an assertion, one alters one's own score, and perhaps that of others.

Here is my first claim: for such a game or set of toy practices to be recognizable as involving *assertions*, it must be the case that playing one counter, or otherwise adding it to one's score, can *commit* one to playing others, or adding them to one's score. If one asserts, "The swatch is red," one *ought* to add to one's score also "The swatch is colored." Making the one move *obliges* one to be prepared to make the other as well. This is not to say that all players actually *do* have the dispositions they *ought* to have. One might not act as one is committed or obliged to act; one can break or fail to follow this sort of rule of the game, at least in particular cases, without thereby being expelled

---

19. For my purposes here I do *not* need to claim that inferential articulation, broadly construed, is *sufficient* to constitute propositional content. I need only the weaker claim that it is a *necessary* feature: that nothing that could *not* play the role of premise and conclusion of an inference could be intelligible as propositionally contentful.

from the company of players of the asserting game. Still, I claim, assertional games must have rules of this sort: rules of *consequential commitment.*

Why? Because to be recognizable as *assertional,* a move must not be *idle,* it must make a *difference,* it must have *consequences* for what else it is appropriate to do, according to the rules of the game. Assertions express judgments or beliefs. Putting a sentence on one's list of judgments, putting it in one's belief box, must have consequences for how *else* one ought, rationally, to act, judge, and believe. We may be able to construct cases where it is intelligible to attribute beliefs that are consequentially inert and isolated from their fellows: "I just believe that cows look goofy, that's all. Nothing follows from that, and I am not obliged to act in any particular way on that belief." But *all* of our beliefs could not intelligibly be understood to be like this. If putting sentences onto my list or into my box *never* has consequences for what else belongs there, then we ought not to understand the list as consisting of my *judgments,* or the box as containing my *beliefs.*

Understanding a claim, the significance of an assertional move, requires understanding at least *some* of its consequences, knowing what *else* (what other moves) one would be committing oneself to by making that claim. A parrot, we can imagine, can produce an utterance perceptually indistinguishable from an assertion of "That's red." Our nonetheless not taking it to have asserted that sentence, not to have made a move in that game, *is* our taking it that, unaware as it is of the inferential involvements of the claim that it would be expressing, of what it would be committing itself to were it to make the claim, it has not thereby succeeded in committing itself to anything. Making that assertion is committing oneself to such consequences as that the swatch is colored, that it is not green, and so on.

For this reason we can understand making a claim as taking up a particular sort of normative stance toward an inferentially articulated content. It is *endorsing* it, taking *responsibility* for it, *committing* oneself to it. The difference between treating something as a claiming and treating it just as a brute sounding off, between treating it as making a move in the assertional game and treating it as an idle performance, is just whether one treats it as the undertaking of a commitment that is suitably articulated by its consequential relations to other commitments. These are *rational* relations, whereby undertaking one commitment *rationally* obliges one to undertake others, related to it as its inferential consequences. These relations at least partly articulate the *content* of the commitment or responsibility one undertakes by asserting a sentence. Apart from such relations, there is no such content, hence no assertion.

The next claim I want to make is that practices incorporating a game of giving and asking for reasons must involve acknowledgment of a *second* kind of normative status. I have said that making a move in the assertional game should be understood as acknowledging a certain sort of *commitment*, articulated by consequential inferential relations linking the asserted sentence to other sentences. But players of the game of giving and asking for reasons must also distinguish among the commitments an interlocutor undertakes, a distinguished subclass to which she is *entitled*. *Linguistic rationalism* understands *assertions*, the fundamental sort of speech act, as essentially things that can both serve as and stand in need of *reasons*. Giving reasons for a claim is producing other assertions that *license* or *entitle* one to it, that *justify* it. Asking for reasons for a claim is asking for its *warrant*, for what *entitles* one to that commitment. Such a practice presupposes a distinction between assertional commitments to which one *is* entitled and those to which one is *not* entitled. Reason-giving practices make sense only if there can be an issue as to whether or not practitioners are entitled to their commitments.

Indeed, I take it that liability to demands for *justification*, that is, demonstration of *entitlement*, is a major dimension of the *responsibility* one undertakes, the *commitment* one makes, in asserting something. In making an assertion one implicitly acknowledges the propriety, at least under some circumstances, of demands for reasons, for justification of the claim one has endorsed, the commitment one has undertaken. Besides the *committive* dimension of assertional practice, there is the *critical* dimension: the aspect of the practice in which the propriety of those commitments is assessed. Apart from this critical dimension, the notion of *reasons* gets no grip.

So the overall claim is that the sense of endorsement that determines the force of assertional speech acts involves, at a minimum, a kind of *commitment* the speaker's *entitlement* to which is always potentially at issue. The assertible contents expressed by declarative sentences whose utterance can have this sort of force must accordingly be inferentially articulated along both normative dimensions. *Downstream*, they must have inferential *consequences*, commitment to which is entailed by commitment to the original content. *Upstream,* they must have inferential *antecedents,* relations to contents that can serve as premises from which entitlement to the original content can be inherited.

6. Conclusion

If that is right, then discursive practitioners as such must be able in practice to take or treat each other and themselves as exhibiting *normative* statuses: as being *committed* and *entitled* to contents expressed by the declarative sentences whose freestanding utterance has the pragmatic significance of acknowledging a commitment and claiming an entitlement. Since by hypothesis these practitioners can already make assertions, the introduction of normative vocabulary permitting one explicitly to *say that* someone is committed or entitled to a claim requires only that new vocabulary, "S is committed to p" and "S is entitled to p," be deployed with the *circumstances* of application that one can assert these sentences formed using the new normative vocabulary whenever one would in practice respond to S as having the commitment or entitlement labeled with the sentence p, and with the *consequences* of application that whenever one asserts one of these new normative sentences, one must also take or treat S in practice as having the corresponding commitment or entitlement. Introducing vocabulary playing this role requires only the algorithmic elaborative abilities I have called *"response substitution"* (along with the arbitrary formation and permutation of states), together with the sort of basic deontic scorekeeping abilities I have argued one must possess in order to engage in practices of giving and asking for reasons at all. Further, when used with these circumstances and consequences of application, it is clear that when one of these new normative sentences is asserted, the pragmatic significance of that speech act will be to *say that* someone is committed or entitled to a claim, making propositionally *explicit* a practical attitude—taking or treating someone in practice *as* committed or entitled to a claim—that before the advent of the new vocabulary remained *implicit* in what one *did.*

My overall claim is that both the modal and the normative Kant-Sellars theses are true. In order to be able to talk at all, to make claims and inferences, one must already know how to do everything necessary in principle (in the precise sense of 'in principle' given by the notion of algorithmic elaboration) to deploy alethic modal and deontic normative vocabulary. If so, one cannot be stuck in the position Hume took himself to be in: understanding ordinary empirical descriptive vocabulary, but with that providing no grip on the use of modal and normative vocabulary. The *semantic* relations between what is expressed by the use of empirical descriptive vocabulary, on the one hand, and what is expressed by the use of modal and what (something different) is expressed by normative vocabulary, on the other, are essentially *pragmatically mediated* ones. To understand the relation between how things merely *are* and how they *must* be or (a different matter) *ought* to be, one must look at what one is *doing* in *saying* how things are, and what is required to *say* what one is thereby doing. Transposing Kant's response to Hume into this pragmatist key requires the metaconceptual resources of meaning-use analysis, which is what enables us to be clear about the pragmatically mediated semantic relations on which that response depends.

Coming to understand both modal and normative vocabulary as standing in the complex resultant pragmatically mediated semantic relation of being LX to—elaborated from and explicating of practices integral to every autonomous discursive practice will turn out also to be the key to understanding a deep and illuminating feature of the relation of these two vocabularies, not just to vocabulary use in general, but also to each other. It supplies the raw materials for filling out and developing Sellars's suggestive claim that modal vocabulary is a 'transposed' language of norms.

CHAPTER FIVE

Modal Expressivism and Modal Realism: Together Again

A Modal Expressivism

1. Kant saw that in addition to concepts whose principal use is to make it possible for us to describe how things are, there are concepts that make explicit features of the metaconceptual *framework* that makes such description possible. An important class of the framework-explicating concepts (arguably the one that motivated this entire line of thought) comprises *alethic modal* concepts, such as necessity and possibility. These express lawful relations between ground-level descriptive concepts and mark the special status of Newton's laws, their lawfulness, by contrast to the status of merely contingent matters of fact, the role played by statements of initial and boundary conditions for particular applications of those laws. But it is not only in understanding the use of technical scientific concepts that the modal concepts find application. The use of ordinary empirical descriptive concepts such as gold, and cat, and house, no less than the Newtonian concepts of mass, force, and acceleration, is essentially, and not just accidentally, articulated by the modality these modal concepts express.

It is because he believes all this that Kant calls modal concepts (among others) 'pure' concepts: categories. Pure concepts are a species of *a priori* concepts.[1] The sense in which we can think of them as available *a priori* that

---

1. That is, concepts available *a priori*. I take it that Kant's standard usage of "*a priori*" is adverbial, though this is not obvious since the Latin phrase is not grammatically marked as it would be in German. *Exactly* what Kant means by the term 'pure' [rein], as it applies generically to reason, knowledge, understanding, principles, concepts, and intuition is a complex and challenging question. There seems to be some terminological drift across the species,

I want to focus on comprises three claims. First, what they express are structural features of the framework within which alone it is possible to apply *any* concepts, make *any* judgments, including ordinary empirical descriptive ones. Second, in being able to apply any ground-level empirical concepts, one already knows how to do everything one needs to know how to do in order to apply the categorial concepts. Finally, there are no *particular* empirical descriptive concepts one must be able to apply in order to have implicit mastery of what is expressed by categorial concepts such as the modal ones (though perhaps one must have some descriptive concepts or other).

The alethic modality that has this categorial status is something like physical necessitation. It is the modality involved in the "pure principle" that "every alteration must have a cause." But the use of these modal concepts to formulate particular laws of nature results neither in *a priori* principles nor in analytic judgments. Lawlike claims assert modal relations between noncategorial descriptive concepts. They are synthetic, and must be discovered and justified empirically. The crux of Kant's challenge in the first Critique that culminates in the B Deduction, is to show how it is intelligible that categorial concepts, paradigmatically the modal ones, can both articulate structural relations intrinsic and essential to the use of descriptive *concepts* and express *causal* laws of nature that combine the features of being on the one hand universal and necessary and, on the other hand, empirical.

2. A further development of what I want to claim will be retrospectively recognizable as the same line of thought can be found in Frege.[2] His use of Latin letters and his logical sign of generality (used in conjunction with the notation for hypotheticals) express relations between concepts. It has always been an embarrassment for the anachronistic extensional quantificational reading of this notation (due originally to Russell) that Frege says of it, when he first introduces it in the *Begriffsschrift*, that it is the right way

---

and some wavering on how to classify particular examples. (The status of the crucial *a priori* principle that every alteration must have a cause, for instance, is apparently variously characterized at [B3] and [B5].) Being available *a priori* is necessary, but not sufficient [B3].

2. The characterization of Frege's Begriffsschrift that follows is one that I had my eyes opened to by Danielle Macbeth's pathbreaking book *Frege's Logic* (Cambridge, MA: Harvard University Press, 2005).

to express *causal* relations of necessitation.³ For it is a commonplace of the later logistical tradition that merely quantificational relations between concepts cannot distinguish between contingent regularities and lawlike, necessary ones. For that, explicit modal operators must be applied to the quantified conditionals.

But Frege deploys his notation so that the relations between concepts expressed by generalized conditionals *already* have modal force. Relations between concepts of the sort logic lets us express have consequences for relations between their extensions, of the sort our quantificational notation expresses, but his generality locutions (the use of Latin letters and the concavity with German ones) codify relations we think of as intensional. Fregean logical concepts are indeed second- and higher-order concepts, but more than that, the universality they express is rulish. They are in the first instance principles in accordance with which to reason, and only derivatively premises from which to reason.⁴ In addition to permitting the formulation of purely logical relations among logical concepts, Frege's logical vocabulary permits us to assert necessary connections among empirical concepts that themselves can only be discovered empirically: physically or causally necessary connections. In the Preface to the *Begriffsschrift*, Frege says:

> It seems to me to be easier still to extend the domain of this concept-script [Begriffsschrift] to include geometry. We would only have to add a few signs for the intuitive relations that occur there. . . . The transition to the pure theory of motion and then to mechanics and physics could follow at this point. The latter two fields, in which besides rational necessity [Denknotwendigkeit] natural necessity [Naturnotwendigkeit]

---

3. *"This is the way in which causal connections are expressed."* [Italics in the original.] *Begriffsschrift* §12; p. 27 in Jean van Heijenoort (ed.), *From Frege to Gödel: A Source Book in Mathematical Logic, 1879–1931* (Cambridge, MA: Harvard University Press, 1967). Foreshadowed at §5.

4. Following Mill, this is Sellars's way of putting the point, in "Counterfactuals, Dispositions, and the Causal Modalities," in H. Feigl, M. Scriven, and G. Maxwell (eds.), *Minnesota Studies in the Philosophy of Science*, vol. II (Minneapolis: University of Minnesota Press, 1957), pp. 225–308. Hereafter CDCM.

asserts itself, are the first for which we can predict a further development of the notation as knowledge progresses.[5]

The additional signs that such an extension requires do *not* include modal operators. The necessity (whether natural or rational) of the connections between empirical concepts is already contained as part of what is expressed by the *logical* vocabulary, even when it is used to make claims that are not logically, but only empirically true.

The capacity to express modal connections of necessitation between concepts is essential to Frege's overall purpose in constructing his Begriffsschrift. Its aim is to make explicit the contents of concepts. Frege understands that content as articulated by the *inferential* relations between concepts, and so crafted his notation to make those inferential connections explicit. Introducing his project in the third section of the *Begriffsschrift,* he says:

> The contents of two judgments may differ in two ways: either the consequences derivable from the first, when it is combined with certain other judgments, always follow also from the second, when it is combined with the same judgments, or this is not the case. The two propositions "The Greeks defeated the Persians at Plataea," and "The Persians were defeated by the Greeks at Plataea," differ in the first way. . . . I call that part of the content that is the *same* in both the *conceptual content* [begrifflicher Inhalt]. . . . [I]t alone is of significance for my conceptscript [Begriffsschrift].

The principal technical innovation that makes it possible for the Begriffsschrift to express the inferential relations that articulate conceptual content, Frege takes it, is his notation for generality, when used in connection with his conditional (used to express hypothetical judgeable contents). An essential element of that expressive power is the capacity of this notation to express rulish, *modally robust,* inferential relations of necessitation, including, importantly, the natural necessity characteristic of inferences underwritten by *causal* connections. Though he doesn't himself think of it

---

5. van Heijenoort, *From Frege to Gödel,* p. 7. I have emended the translation slightly, where I have noted the original German terms.

this way, Frege is continuing and developing Kant's line of thought concerning the role that modality (including centrally the kind of necessity involved in causation) plays in distinguishing the expressive role of certain concepts that relate ground-level empirical descriptive concepts to one another from the expressive role of those descriptive concepts themselves.

3. Nearer to our own time, this line of thought has been further developed and clarified by Wilfrid Sellars. He lucidly compressed his endorsement of the fundamental Kantian idea that modal concepts make explicit something implicit in the use of ordinary empirical descriptive concepts into the title of one of his earliest essays: "Concepts as Involving Laws, and Inconceivable without Them." But he also offers the outline of a more articulated argument for the claim. We can reconstruct it as follows:

1. "It is only because the expressions in terms of which we describe objects . . . locate these objects in a space of implications, that they describe at all, rather than merely label."[6]
2. It is an essential feature of the inferential relations in which, according to claim (1), descriptive concepts must stand, that they can be appealed to in *explanations* and *justifications* of further descriptions.
3. So: "although describing and explaining (predicting, retrodicting, understanding) are *distinguishable,* they are also, in an important sense, *inseparable.* . . . The descriptive and explanatory resources of language advance hand in hand. . . ."[7]
4. The expressive role distinctive of modal vocabulary is to make explicit these explanatory and justificatory relations.

This line of thought is a way of filling in ideas that Sellars had had since his student days. In an autobiographical sketch, he tells us that he was to begin with concerned to understand the sort of content expressed by concepts of the "logical, causal, and deontological modalities." (Here only what he calls the "causal" modalities are at issue—a point to which I shall return.) His big idea, he tells us, was that what was needed was a functional theory

---

6. CDCM §108.
7. CDCM §108.

of concepts which would make their role in reasoning, rather than supposed origin in experience, their primary feature.[8]

The idea he got from Kant was that the "role in reasoning" distinctive of a key class of alethic modal concepts is to articulate the "role in reasoning" of ordinary empirical descriptive concepts.

The two key moves in an argument of this form are, first, an account of the descriptive use of empirical concepts that exhibits as essential their articulation by inferences that can support explanations and justifications and, second, an account of the central function of at least some alethic modal vocabulary as expressing explanatory and justificatory inferential relations among descriptive concepts. The conclusion of the argument is what I call the "Kant-Sellars thesis about modality": in knowing how to use ordinary empirical descriptive vocabulary, one already knows how to do everything one needs to know how to do in order to be able (in principle) to use alethic modal vocabulary.[9] According to this thesis, one cannot be in the semantic predicament that empiricists such as Hume and Quine envisaged: understanding ordinary empirical descriptive vocabulary perfectly well, but having thereby no grip at all on what is expressed by modal vocabulary.

How does Sellars understand the distinction between "merely labeling," on the one hand, and describing, in the sense he then wants to argue "advances hand in hand" with explaining and justifying, on the other hand? Labeling is attaching signs to, or associating them with, items in the nonlinguistic world. The paradigm of this semantic relation is that between an arbitrary name and its bearer, or a sign and what it signifies—what Sellars elsewhere calls "the 'Fido'-Fido model." Now it is one of the founding insights of analytic philosophy of language that the results of a Procrustean assimilation of *all* semantic relations to this nominalistic model are disastrous. That is a lesson taught originally by Frege, and again by both the Wittgenstein of the *Tractatus* and the Wittgenstein of the *Investigations*, each in his own way. (The mistake lives on in semiotics and in the structuralist heirs of de Saussure. Derrida was sufficiently in the grip of this traditional picture that

---

8. In H. N. Castañeda (ed.), *Action, Knowledge, and Reality* (Indianapolis, IN: Bobbs-Merrill, 1975), p. 285.

9. I discuss this claim at greater length in Chapter 4 of *Between Saying and Doing: Towards an Analytic Pragmatism* (Oxford: Oxford University Press, 2008).

the only alternative to it he could conceive was that signs should be understood to stand exclusively for . . . other signs.) What one will not understand on this model, in the first instance, is what is special about *sentences,* and what they express: claimables, judgeable contents, Fregean thoughts as thinkables. In particular, using the 'Fido'-Fido model to think about the relation between declarative sentences and *true* Fregean thinkables, facts, is fraught with difficulties. Indeed, even the more promising strategy that avoids the nominalistic mistake of modeling the semantics of sentences on that of names while crafting a technical notion of *representation* to be generic across its disparate name-bearer and (true) sentence-fact species requires more subtlety, craft, and guile than is generally appreciated.

Of course, one need not make the nominalistic mistake of assimilating *all* semantic relations to labeling in order to claim that the model applies to *some* uses of linguistic expressions, that is, to claim that there are, after all, labels—even if sentences are not to be counted among them. Sellars is claiming that describing should also not be assimilated to applying a "mere label." Here the relevant grammatical category is not terms or sentences, but predicates. Predicate labels in Sellars's sense can have more content than proper names like 'Fido'. The use of predicates to make observation reports requires the user to exercise a reliable differential responsive disposition. It is tempting to think that reliably responding in a distinctive way to some things and not others is a way of *classifying* them as being of some kind, or as having something in common. What more besides dividing things into groups could be required to count as *describing* them as being of different kinds? The difference between classifying in the sense of labeling and describing emerges when we ask what the things grouped together by their elicitation of a common response are supposed to be described *as*. If the dog reliably barks at some things, and not others (cats, dogs, and squirrels, but not horses; men but not women; motorcycles but not cars; helicopters but not airplanes; church bells but not the neighbor's stereo; and so on) it is *grouping* things, sorting them into two classes. But there need be nothing it is *describing* them *as*. When the metal strip expands in some environments and contracts in others, it is not yet *describing* them as warm or cold.

Sellars's idea is that what one is describing something *as* is a matter of what *follows* from the classification—what *consequences* falling in one group or another has. It is insofar as being grouped one way rather than another can serve as a *premise* in an *inference* that the grouping is intelligible as a *description* and not merely a label. Even in the primitive, noninferential case of the three vervet cries appropriately elicited (as the young ones are trained by their elders) by snakes, eagles, and leopards, it is insofar as they are appropriately responded to (as the young ones are trained by their elders) by jumping, covering, and climbing, respectively, that they begin to be intelligible as describing threats-from-below, threats-from-above, and so on. Reliably differentially elicited responses are intelligible as observation reports, as empirical descriptions, just insofar as they are available to *justify* further claims. It is essential, and not just accidental, to descriptive predicates that they can be used to make claims, which would be expressed by declarative sentences. And it is essential, and not accidental to those claimings that they can serve as *reasons* for further claims. (Of course, this Sellarsian inferentialist way of developing Frege's claims about how we must think of the contents of predicates and sentences as related to one another once we see the inadequacy of nominalistic construals is controversial. I have elaborated and defended it elsewhere, and am merely expounding it here.)

In the same spirit, Michael Dummett argues that the content of a descriptive concept cannot be identified with its circumstances of appropriate application alone. In order to avoid the defects and inadequacies of one sided theories of meaning, one must consider *both* those circumstances of application *and* the appropriate consequences of such application—which is to say also its role as a premise in inferences (both theoretical and practical). It is possible to construct descriptive concepts that share circumstances or consequences of application, but differ in the other component. In such cases, they differ also in their content or meaning. Thinking of the application of substantive nonlogical descriptive concepts as involving a commitment to the propriety of the material inference from their circumstances to their consequences of application is a way of insisting that descriptive concepts count as locating the objects they are applied to "in a space of implications."

Sellars sees modal locutions as tools used in the enterprise of

> . . . making explicit the rules we have adopted for thought and action. . . . I shall be interpreting our judgments to the effect that A

causally necessitates B as the expression of a rule governing our use of the terms 'A' and 'B'.[10]

The rules they express are rules of *inference*. Modal expressions are inference licenses or inference "tickets," in Ryle's terminology.[11] These are what Sellars calls "material," that is, nonlogical inferences. In fact, what these modal locutions make explicit, according to Sellars, are just the implications, situation in a space of which is what distinguishes descriptive concepts from mere labels. Inferences such as "Pittsburgh is to the West of Princeton, so Princeton is to the East of Pittsburgh" articulate the content of the descriptive concepts West and East.

Further, it is the inferential commitments acknowledging such material implicational relations that are appealed to in explanation and justification.

> To make first hand use of these [modal] expressions is to be about the business of explaining a state of affairs, or justifying an assertion.[12]

That is, what one is *doing* in *using* modal expressions ("As are necessarily Bs") is endorsing an inference (from anything's being A to its being B) that can be appealed to in justifying one description on the basis of another, or explaining the applicability of one description by the appealing to the applicability of another: "The raspberries are red *because* they are ripe." This is why the expressive resources of description, on the one hand, and justification and explanation, on the other hand, "advance hand in hand," as Sellars says.

Because he understands the expressive function characteristic of the modal vocabulary he is addressing to be that of making explicit the inferential relations appealed to in justifications and explanations, Sellars takes it that the central use of that vocabulary is in qualifying conditionals,

---

10. Sellars, "Language, Rules, and Behavior," in J. Sicha (ed.), *Pure Pragmatics and Possible Worlds: The Early Essays of Wilfrid Sellars* (Atascadero, CA: Ridgeview, 1980), fn 2 to p. 136. Hereafter *PPPW*.

11. Gilbert Ryle, "'If', 'So', and 'Because'," in Max Black (ed.), *Philosophical Analysis* (Englewood Cliffs, NJ: Prentice Hall, 1950), pp. 302–318. Sellars does not discuss whether "A causally necessitates B" should be understood as expressing a committive, or merely a permissive inference.

12. CDCM §80.

paradigmatically quantified conditionals, rather than their use as operators applying to nonconditional descriptive sentences. What the modal vocabulary expresses is the element of *generality* that Ryle had insisted was present in all endorsements of inferences:

> ... some kind of openness, variableness, or satisfiability characterizes all hypothetical statements alike, whether they are recognized "variable hypotheticals" like "For all x, if x is a man, x is mortal" or are highly determinate hypotheticals like "If today is Monday, tomorrow is Tuesday."[13]

That element of generality would naturally be made explicit in this last example by applying a necessity operator to the conditional. Another way of putting this same point is that the inferential relations among descriptive concepts in virtue of which they can be used to *describe*, and not just *label*, which are appealed to in *justifications* and *explanations* of the applicability of one description on the basis of the applicability of another, and which are made explicit by the use of modally qualified conditionals, are *subjunctive-* and *counterfactual*-supporting inferences. They make explicit the laws that Sellars says concepts involve and are inconceivable without.

This constellation of claims to which Sellars aspires to entitle himself articulates what he makes of the tradition of thinking about modality that Kant initiates and Frege develops in an inferentialist key. It is a story that construes (at least one kind of) modal vocabulary as distinguished by the role it plays in expressing explicitly essential aspects that it makes visible as implicit already in the use of ordinary empirical descriptive vocabulary. Having a ("first hand") use in explicating the framework within which vocabulary use can have the significance of describing—a framework we come to see as necessarily a unified package comprising not only description, but justification and explanation, a framework articulated by subjunctively robust inferential relations among descriptive concepts—sets modal vocabulary off from the descriptive vocabulary, precisely in virtue of the distinctive expressive role it plays with respect to the use of such descriptive vocabulary. This, then, is Sellars's modal expressivism.

---

13. Ryle, "'If', 'So', and 'Because'," p. 311.

4. It is, it should be acknowledged, largely programmatic. Turning the program into a full-blooded account of the use of modal vocabulary would require satisfactory responses to a number of challenges. I remarked above that Sellars's approach focuses on modally qualified conditionals. So, at a minimum, we would need to understand how it might be developed or extended to deal with other uses of modal operators.[14]

A second issue concerns the kind of modality Sellars is telling us about. His topic patently is not *logical* necessity and possibility. Nor is it the sort of *metaphysical* necessity and possibility Kripke introduces us to in "Naming and Necessity." In the principal essay in which he develops his expressivism, Sellars specifies what he is interested in as "causal" modalities.[15] There and elsewhere he talks about them as "physical" modalities. It is clear that he means to be discussing the sort of alethic necessity and possibility that characterizes laws of nature—not only laws of fundamental physics, but also laws promulgated in the special sciences. He seems to think that this is generically the same modality as that involved in ordinary informal explanations of empirical phenomena: of why the car wouldn't start, why the beans burned, why the squirrel couldn't get to the bird-feeder, and so on. It is clearly some such notion of necessity and possibility that Kant was addressing. It is the kind of necessity that is the target of Hume's skeptical epistemological doubts about the possibility of establishing on inductive grounds, and of his consequent semantic doubts about, its ultimate intelligibility. Frege's few, gnomic remarks about the modal force of his generality locutions (the concavity and the use of Latin letters) suggest he was thinking about something like this same notion of necessity.

Sellars also clearly thinks that it is a kind of *conceptual* necessity. The modality he is analyzing characterizes the subjunctively robust inferential connections among empirical concepts in virtue of which (at least in part) they have the descriptive contents that they do. The laws, exhibiting that modality, which such concepts involve (without which, we are told, they are

---

14. Semantic inferentialists think that the use of *any* concept involves commitment to the propriety of all the inferences from the circumstances of appropriate application to the appropriate consequences of application of that concept. Cf. Chapter 1 of Robert Brandom, *Articulating Reasons* (Cambridge, MA: Harvard University Press, 1997). So in that context, a strategy for addressing this challenge might not be far to seek.

15. CDCM.

inconceivable) articulate the contents of those concepts, or at least the framework within which they are intelligible as having those contents. This aspect of Sellars's thought is what he makes of Kant's treatment of alethic modality as a *category,* a *pure* concept. For those, Sellars thinks, are the concepts that make explicit something implicit in the use of any empirical descriptive concepts. This is the *semantic* sense in which they are always available *a priori:* apart from the applicability of any *particular* noncategorial, empirical concepts.

But it is not easy to see how to reconcile these two characterizations of the modality in question: as causal, physical necessity and possibility, and as some sort of conceptual necessity and possibility. In particular, these two conceptions of a kind of alethic modality seem to pull in different directions epistemologically. For laws of nature, or statements about what causally or physically necessitates what (or makes what else causally or physically possible or impossible) must in general be established empirically. But questions of what is conceptually necessary or possible, of what other concepts must or can be applied if some concept *were* to be applied, just in virtue of the contents of the concepts involved, seems to be something one can discover *a priori.* One does not need to know how the world is, only what one means— not what descriptive concepts actually apply to a situation, but only what the contents of those concepts are. We are faced with an inconsistent triad of a form that is familiar to readers of *Empiricism and the Philosophy of Mind:*[16]

1. Physical or causal necessity and possibility are a kind of conceptual necessity and possibility.
2. Physical or causal necessities and possibilities must be established empirically.
3. Conceptual necessities and possibilities can be established *a priori.*

Sellars is fully aware of this difficulty and has a straightforward, if radical, response. He rejects the third element of the triad. A semantic externalist

---

16. Edited by Robert Brandom, with an Introduction by Richard Rorty (Cambridge, MA: Harvard University Press, 1997) §6. Notice that insofar as there is any go to Sellars's reading of Kant on this point, a corresponding issue arises for Kant's view. How is it, exactly, that we can know *a priori that* nature is lawful, but can only know empirically what the laws are?

avant la lettre, he takes it that we cannot discover the contents of our concepts or the meanings of our words just by introspecting. He follows Kant in understanding concepts as rules (norms) we bind ourselves by, without knowing everything about what we are committing ourselves to by applying those concepts. Finding out what applications of descriptive concepts are correct and finding out what inferences connecting those descriptive concepts are correct are two sides of one coin, two aspects of one process of empirical inquiry. Though Quine would not put the point this way, Sellars is at one with him in denying the Carnapian two-phase story (appropriate for formal languages, but not for natural languages) according to which first, by one sort of procedure one has privileged, nonempirical access to, one fixes meanings (concepts, the language) and then subsequently, by another sort of procedure, which is empirical, determines the facts (what to believe, one's theory) as expressed in those meanings (concepts, language). To find out what the contents of the concepts we apply in describing the world really are, we have to find out what the laws of nature are. And that is an empirical matter.

Another challenge to working out Sellars's version of modal expressivism concerns the extent to which, and the sense in which, it should be understood as taking the expressive role characteristic of modal vocabulary to be a *metalinguistic* one. On the one hand, when Sellars says he wants to understand a paradigmatic kind of modal judgment as "the expression of a rule governing our use of the terms 'A' and 'B'," this sounds straightforwardly metalinguistic in a classical sense. (This formulation is from an early paper, and is *not* appealed to in the later 1959 paper that contains his official account.) On the other hand, it cannot be right to say that modal claims should be understood as covertly made in a metalanguage whose mastery requires mastery of terms that *refer to* terms (here, descriptive ones) in an object language—which is the classical Tarski-Carnap sense. For someone (perhaps a monolingual German) could claim, believe, or judge that A causally necessitates B without ever having heard of the English *expressions* that 'A' and 'B' stand for in the example. Further, the claim could be true even if there had never been such expressions, because there had never been any language users. (There would still have been laws of nature, even if there had never been language.) So is the view he is after a metalinguistic expressivism, or not? In light of the considerations just mentioned, Sellars's characteristically nuanced-but-unhelpful assessment is this:

Shall we say that modal expressions are metalinguistic? Neither a simple 'yes' nor a simple 'no' will do.[17]

He wants to say that while modal statements are not metalinguistic in a narrow sense, there is a wider sense in which they are.

It is sometimes thought that modal statements do not describe states of affairs in the world, because they are *really* metalinguistic. This won't do at all if it is meant that instead of describing states of affairs in the world, they describe linguistic habits. It is more plausible if it is meant that statements involving modal terms have the force of *prescriptive* statements about the use of certain expressions in the object language. Yet there is more than one way to '*have the force of*' a statement, and failure to distinguish between them may snowball into a serious confusion as wider implications are drawn.[18]

What distinction does he have in mind?

We must here, as elsewhere, draw a distinction between what we are committed to concerning the world by virtue of the fact that we have reason to make a certain assertion, and the force, in a narrower sense, of the assertion itself.[19]

Sellars acknowledges that modal statements do not *say that* some entailment holds, but distinguishes between what is *said* by using a bit of vocabulary and what is '*contextually implied*' by doing so. Sellars says very little about this latter notion, even though it bears the full weight of his proposed emendation of the rationalist account. This is really all he says about the matter in the only essay he devotes to the exposition of his views about the "causal modalities."

Elsewhere he had put what I think is recognizably the same point in terms of a distinction between what one *says* by making a statement and what

---

17. CDCM §82.
18. CDCM §81.
19. CDCM §101.

(else) one *conveys* by doing so.[20] There his example is that in asserting, "The weather is fine today," I *say* that the weather is fine today, but *convey* that I *believe* that it is fine. This is suggestive, but won't help us out in detail in the modal case. For, first, he doesn't give us any idea what, if anything, *is said* by making a modal claim. Second, assertions are in general expressions of belief, regardless of what their content is. But the case we care about depends on the application of specifically modal concepts in what is said *doing* something specific that one is *not* doing in making assertions generally.

I think Sellars never really figures out how to work out the line of thought he suggests here. After 1959 he never repudiates the views he sketched in "Counterfactuals, Dispositions, and the Causal Modalities," and seems to continue to endorse them. But he never revisits the topic substantially—never says how he thinks one might go on to fill in the expressivist idea he had gestured at there. Doing that is, in effect, left as an exercise to the reader. I conjecture that one reason for this failure is that he labored under the restriction of a further systematic constraint consequent upon other views near and dear to his heart. For he *also* thought that discourse about properties, universals, and even facts was metalinguistic in a broad, nonclassical sense. The problem for him, I think, is that he thought he not only needed to find a specific sense in which modal vocabulary could be understood to be 'metalinguistic', but also a sense of that term that was *generic* between that case and the case of ontological-categorial vocabulary such as 'property' and 'universal'. He *did* work hard, and make significant progress, on delineating the sense in which he thought of that latter sort of vocabulary as metalinguistic, avoiding the pitfalls (mentioned above) involved in understanding it as metalinguistic in the orthodox sense that requires reference to the expressions of an object language. His response turns on the discursive functional roles that dot-quoted expressions refer to, the notion of distributive singular terms, and of the formation of a kind of such terms by instantiating-categorizing quotation to refer to those roles.[21] This is a very sophisticated response

---

20. "Inference and Meaning," *PPPW*, p. 280. This is also an earlier piece (1953), and he does not in CDCM advert to this way of making the distinction.

21. His views are developed in three seminal essays: "Naming and Saying," "Grammar and Existence: A Preface to Ontology," and "Abstract Entities." They are reprinted as Chapters 5, 6, and 7 of K. Scharp and R. Brandom (eds.), *In the Space of Reasons: Selected Essays of Wilfrid Sellars* (Cambridge, MA: Harvard University Press, 2007).

to the corresponding difficulties that arise for calling ontological-categorial expressions 'metalinguistic'. But *that* solution does not *immediately* apply to modal expressions. (Whether some variant of it would work is another question.) And he could not figure out how to specify either the genus that comprises both, or the modal species.

5. Sellars is working with Kant's idea that the expressive role distinctive of alethic modal vocabulary is to make explicit something that is implicit already in the use of ordinary empirical descriptive vocabulary. He picks up Frege's hint that what matters is the specifically *inferential* articulation essential to the conceptual contentfulness of descriptive vocabulary. He develops those thoughts by adding the idea that that expressive role is in some broad but noncanonical sense metalinguistic—a matter of the role such vocabulary plays in endorsing rules of inference governing descriptive vocabulary. And equally importantly, he focuses our attention on the *pragmatic* dimension of that expressive role. That is, he counsels us to look to what we are *doing* when we endorse a modal claim. (Compare: expressivism about normative vocabulary—paradigmatically deontic vocabulary.)

I want to make a couple of suggestions for how one might move forward with what Sellars made of Kant's thought about how the expressive role characteristic of alethic modal vocabulary is related to that of ordinary empirical descriptive vocabulary. One lesson I think we can learn from Sellars's difficulties is that the notion of being 'metalinguistic' or ("about language") is too crude an expressive tool, too undifferentiated a concept, to be helpful in this context. There are, as Sellars intimates, *many* ways in which the use of one vocabulary can depend on that of another, besides any terms of the one vocabulary *referring* to those of the other. Putting together Sellars's *metalinguistic* idea with his *pragmatic* idea, we could consider the possibility that the place to begin thinking about the expressive role of modal vocabulary is with what in *Between Saying and Doing* I call a "pragmatic metavocabulary." This concept takes its place alongside that of a <u>syntactic metavocabulary</u>, which enables one to talk about linguistic expressions themselves (both what Sellars calls "sign designs" and grammatical categories), and a <u>semantic metavocabulary</u>, which enables one to talk about what linguistic expressions refer to or what descriptive concepts let one say. A *pragmatic* metavocabulary enables one to talk about what one is *doing* in *using* linguistic expressions, the speech acts one is performing, the pragmatic force one is investing them with or exercising, the commitments one is undertaking by making claims, the norms that govern linguistic performances, and so on. (This list is something of a motley, meant to correspond to the capaciousness of 'do' and 'use', a reminder that the concept picked out is still generic.) Sellars's model is that modal vocabulary says something that would be said more explicitly in a *semantic* metavocabulary. But by the time his commentary has taken back everything that it turns out needs to be taken back, not much is left of that model. What seems right about the commentary, however, is Sellars's observations about what one is *doing* in making "first hand use" of modal vocabulary: endorsing inferences. Insofar as there is anything to that idea, the more natural strategy would seem to be to take one's model from *pragmatic* metavocabularies. After all, Sellars ends up saying nothing at all about what one *says* in making first-hand use of modal vocabulary. Properly understood, I think, his is not a *semantic* expressivism about alethic modal vocabulary, but a kind of *pragmatic* expressivism about it.

As a first try at expressing the thought that would result from transposition from a semantic into a pragmatic key, we might try this: In making first-hand use of (the relevant kind of) alethic modal vocabulary one is *doing* something distinctive that could be specified explicitly in the right kind of pragmatic metavocabulary, namely endorsing a class of inferences. The pragmatic metavocabulary enables one to *say* what modal vocabulary enables one to *do*. Such a claim does not in itself involve any commitment concerning the relations between the *content* of talk about endorsing inferences and talk about necessity and possibility, never mind commitment to their equivalence. Notice, further, that counterfactuals that suppose the absence of concept users are irrelevant to the assessment of *this* claim. For in that case there would be neither endorsers of inferences nor users of modal vocabulary.

The claim that is on the table so far is evidently too weak to be interesting, though. It does not carve out an expressive role that is *distinctive* of modal vocabulary. For in making an ordinary descriptive claim one is *also* doing something that could be specified in a pragmatic metavocabulary, namely applying descriptive concepts, making a claim, undertaking a doxastic or assertional commitment. And those, the Frege-Sellars inferentialist line goes, essentially involve commitments to the proprieties of inferences. My second suggestion for developing Sellars's modal expressivism is that what is special about (a certain kind of) modal vocabulary is that it stands in a special relation to descriptive vocabulary—a relation that invited its characterization as 'metalinguistic' (with respect to that descriptive vocabulary) in the first place. This relation is that anyone who knows how to use ordinary empirical descriptive vocabulary (e.g. 'red', 'square', 'moving', 'alive', 'electron') already knows how to do everything she needs to know how to do to deploy modal vocabulary. A variant formulation (closely related, but not equivalent) would be that the norms governing the use of ordinary empirical descriptive vocabulary determine the norms governing the use of modal vocabulary. In this sense, modal vocabulary makes explicit (in the form of a new kind of claimable content) something that is implicit already in the *use* of descriptive vocabulary. This claim about the expressive role characteristic of modal vocabulary is vocabulary-specific. For not all vocabularies stand in this relation to some other kind of vocabulary. In particular, there is in general nothing that ordinary empirical descriptive (OED) vocabulary stands to in this expressive relation.

An instructive parallel is with a particular bit of logical vocabulary: the conditional. If Sellars is right that an essential element distinguishing *describing* from mere *labeling* keyed to differential responsiveness is the inferential involvements of the locutions applied (their "situation in a space of implications") then anyone who knows how to use descriptive vocabulary already knows how to do everything he needs to know how to do to use conditionals whose antecedents are formed from those descriptive claimables. For to be able to use the descriptive vocabulary, one must make some distinction (however partial and fallible) between materially good and materially bad inferences involving that vocabulary. And that is sufficient to introduce conditionals as having the circumstances of appropriate application that if one is committed to the propriety of the inference from p to q, then one is committed to the conditional claim "if p then q," and the consequences of application that if one is committed to the conditional claim "if p then q," then one is committed to the material propriety of the inference from p to q. The capacity to use the underlying descriptive vocabulary can be straightforwardly (indeed, algorithmically) transformed into the capacity to use conditionals involving that vocabulary.

What aspect of inference is it that modal vocabulary is supposed to express? My third suggestion for developing the Kant-Sellars approach to modality is an answer to this question. The key fact to appreciate, I think, is that outside of logic and mathematics (and possibly fundamental physics, though I doubt it),[22] in ordinary language and the special sciences, material inference is massively *nonmonotonic*. That is, the fact that the inference from *p* to *q* is a materially good one in some situation does not mean that the inference from *p* and *r* to *q* must also be a good one, in the same situation. If I strike this dry, well-made match, it will light—but not if in addition all the oxygen is removed from the room, or a sufficiently strong magnetic field is applied, or. . . . If I let loose of the leash, the dog will chase the cat—but not if either one is struck by lightning, a bear suddenly blocks the way, or. . . . This phenomenon is ubiquitous and unavoidable, even in less informal contexts: differential medical diagnosis, the application of common or case law, or philosophical argumentation. One cannot secure material inferences from all possible defeasors by explicitly building their denial into the premises, for the class of defeasors is in general open-ended and not antecedently surveyable. Nor can one achieve the same effect wholesale by the use of *ceteris paribus* clauses. As I have argued elsewhere, the expressive role of such clauses is explicitly to acknowledge the nonmonotonicity, hence defeasibility of the qualified inference, not magically to remove it.[23] (As I said in the previous chapter, the technical term for a Latin phrase whose application can do *that* is 'spell'.)

The defeasibility or nonmonotonicity of the material inferences essential to the conceptual contentfulness of descriptive vocabulary means that the use of such vocabulary requires not only making a distinction (however fallibly) between those inferences one endorses and those one does not, but also (as part of that capacity, and also fallibly) between the collateral premises or auxiliary hypotheses whose additions one takes it would, and those that would not, infirm the inference, in the sense that the conclusion would no longer follow. That is, in order to use OED vocabulary, one must associate *some* range of subjunctive and counterfactual robustness with the material inferences that (at least partially) articulate the contents of the descriptive concepts. So, for

---

22. For reasons Mark Wilson elaborates in his original and important book *Wandering Significance* (Oxford: Oxford University Press, 2006).

23. In Chapter 2 of *Articulating Reasons: An Introduction to Inferentialism* (Cambridge, MA: Harvard University Press, 2000).

instance, I might endorse the inference that would be made explicit in a conditional by "If I release my grip on the book, then it will fall to the floor." But for the attribution of such an inferential commitment to me to be sustainable, I must make some distinction between collateral circumstances that would defeat the inference (a table is moved under it, someone else catches it, it dissolves in a puff of smoke, it is snatched up by a passing hawk ...) and those that would not (it is Tuesday, it is slightly cooler today than it was yesterday, my car has been moved slightly further away ...). Of course I might be wrong about whether any of these particular auxiliary hypotheses actually would or would not defeat the inference to the conclusion. But if I make no distinction of this sort at all I should be convicted of not understanding the concepts (book, falling) that I am attempting to apply.

The principal vocabulary we use to make these distinctions explicit is *subjunctive* and *counterfactual* conditionals: "If the lioness *were* to be struck by a spear ... ," "If the book *had been* attached to a large helium-filled balloon. ... " Subjunctives let us express, explore, and communicate the ranges of counterfactual robustness of the inferences we endorse, our commitments concerning what would and would not defeat or infirm those inferences. The subjunctive mood is a principal alethic modal construction. Talk of what is and isn't possible or necessary if ... also lets us mark out regions of monotonicity within the field of material inferences relating applications of descriptive concepts. "If the patient has a positive muscle-contracture test, it does not necessarily follow that he has malignant hyperthermia. It is possible that he has Duchesne's dystrophy. If he has [genetic variant], then it is necessary that he has malignant hyperthermia." "If the wood had been pressure-treated, it would not have split over the winter, but it is possible that its color would have faded."

On this account, subjunctive robustness is the generality or "openness" Ryle found in the inferences made explicit by conditionals, and which is made explicit by modal vocabulary, including the subjunctive mood. It involves a kind of quantification over auxiliary hypotheses that would not, according to the modal claim, infirm the inference or its conclusion.[24] (Frege's account

---

24. Many everyday uses of modal vocabulary to qualify claims suppress the premises from which the claim implicitly is taken to follow, and so court the danger of countenancing the modal fallacy that would infer from p and $\Box(p \to q)$ to $\Box q$. Thereon hangs a tale.

of the significance of his Latin letters indicates that he agrees with Ryle.) The kind of generalization implicit in the use of subjunctive or modal vocabulary is what is invoked in *explanation,* which exhibits some conclusion as the result from an inference that is good as an instance of a *kind,* or in virtue of a *pattern* of good inferences. This is what was intuitively right about the deductive-nomological understanding of explanation. What was wrong about it is that subjunctive robustness need not be underwritten by *laws:* modally qualified conditionals whose quantifiers are wide open. That is, there need not be inferences guaranteed to be *globally* monotonic no matter what collateral premises are thrown in, standing behind every *local* region of monotonicity—every set of collateral premises with respect to which the inference *is* subjunctively robust. Thus singular explanations, for instance, singular causal explanations, need not fall under covering laws to be good explanations. But they do need to involve *some* range of subjunctive (including counterfactual) robustness in order to count as *explanations,* rather than just descriptions of some event. It is because the use of descriptive vocabulary requires commitment to inferences with some range of subjunctive robustness that, as I earlier quoted Sellars as saying:

> Although describing and explaining (predicting, retrodicting, understanding) are *distinguishable,* they are also, in an important sense, *inseparable.* . . . The descriptive and explanatory resources of language advance hand in hand. . . ."[25]

The expressive job characteristic of modal vocabulary is to make explicit this implicit dimension of the use of ordinary empirical descriptive vocabulary.

A Modal Realism

6. This sketch of a program for extending the Kant-Sellars tradition of modal expressivism raises a myriad of questions, some of detail, others more substantial. Rather than beginning to fill in that sketch by addressing some of those questions, I want to confront the ideas that motivate it with

---

25. CDCM §108.

a different set of intuitions: those that motivate a robust modal realism. By "modal realism" I mean the conjunction of the claims that

> MR1) Some modally qualified claims are *true*.
> MR2) Those that are state *facts*.
> MR3) Some of those facts are *objective*, in the sense that they are independent of the activities of concept users: they would be facts even if there never were or never had been concept users.[26]

There are strong reasons to endorse all three of these claims. As to the first, physics tells us things such as "Two bodies acted upon only by gravitational forces necessarily attract one another in direct proportion to the product of their masses and in inverse proportion to the square of the distance between their centers of mass." I take it this claim, for instance, is true. Even if it is not, I take it that *some* claims of this form, purporting to state laws of nature, do, in fact, state laws of nature. Denying this brings one into direct contradiction with the empirical sciences themselves. Supporting such a position would require a strong argument indeed. For the empirical sciences are in the business of making subjunctive- and counterfactual-supporting claims. That is, they offer not only *descriptions*, but *explanations*. Indeed, the descriptions they offer are essentially, and not just accidentally, available to figure in explanations of other descriptions.

The second claim is, I think, true in virtue of the definition of 'fact'. A fact, Frege says, is a thought that is true.[27] He means 'thought' in the sense of something thinkable, not in the sense of a thinking, of course. For there can be unthought facts. On this usage, it is alright to say that facts make thoughts or claims true only in the sense that facts make acts of thinking and claiming true. For the facts just *are* the true thinkables and claimables. Wittgenstein is appealing to this way of using 'fact' when he says: "When we say, and mean, that such-and-such is the case, we—and our meaning—do

---

26. Of course, this is itself a modal claim, expressed counterfactually in the subjunctive mood. That fact is not problematic in the current context. One upshot of the previous discussion is that *any* description of how things objectively are implicitly involves modal commitments.

27. In Gottlob Frege, "The Thought: A Logical Inquiry," *Mind* 65 (1956): 289–311.

not stop anywhere short of the fact; but we mean: this—is—so."[28] On this usage, if there are true modal claims—in the sense of true modal claimables, or modal claimings that are true in that they are claimings of true claimables—then there are modal facts. Modal facts are just facts statable using modal vocabulary, as physical facts are facts statable using physical vocabulary, nautical facts are facts statable using nautical vocabulary, and so on.

The third claim is perhaps the most controversial of these three platitudes. But I think the same principle I implicitly invoked in talking about the first claim underwrites it. Physics tells us that the current laws of nature were already laws of nature before there were human concept users. And although it does not specifically address the issue, it is clearly committed to the claim that the laws would have been the same even if there never had been concept users. Indeed, many of the laws of nature (including all the Newtonian ones) exhibit a temporal symmetry: they hold indifferently at all times. So they are independent of the advent, at some particular time, of concept users. And one of the mainstays of physics over the last century—substantially contributing to its distinctive conceptual shape—is the result of the Noether theorem that tells us (entails) that this fundamental temporal symmetry is mathematically equivalent to the physical principle of conservation of energy.[29] Denying MR3 is denying the temporal symmetry of laws of nature. And the theorem tells us that that means denying the conservation of energy. While there are reasons from the bleeding edge of physics to worry about the universal truth of the principle of conservation of energy, those considerations are irrelevant in the current context: they do not stem from the presence or absence of concept users in our world. I conclude that one cannot deny MR3 without taking issue with substantial, indeed fundamental, empirical issues in physics.[30]

---

28. Ludwig Wittgenstein, *Philosophical Investigations* (Oxford: Basil Blackwell, 1953), §95.

29. Cf. for instance Nina Byers, "E. Noether's Discovery of the Deep Connection between Symmetries and Conservation Laws," in Mina Teicher (ed.), *Israel Mathematical Conference Proceedings: The Heritage of Emmy Noether* (Tel-Aviv: Bar-Ilan University, 1998).

30. I offer a different argument for this same conclusion (not specifically for the modal case, but for a more generic one that comprises it) in Section V of Chapter 5 of *Perspectives on Pragmatism* (Cambridge, MA: Harvard University Press, 2011).

I am claiming that one ought to endorse MR1 and MR3 unless one takes issue with the principle that philosophers thinking metalinguistically about semantics and concept-use ought not, in general, to be in the business of denying claims made by physicists, when the latter are speaking *ex cathedra* on matters that fall within their professional purview. There are some philosophers (Huw Price is one) who are both competent and willing to do so—indeed, in his case, specifically on the matter of the physicists' uncritical use of modal vocabulary. But I am not one of them.

I take it that

There were no true claimings before there were vocabularies, because there were no claimings at all. But it does not follow that there were no true claimables. In fact, we can show that we ought not to say that. Here is an argument that turns on the grammatical transformations that "It is true that . . ." takes.

Physics tells us that there were photons before there were humans. I read a lot about them in Stephen Weinberg's account of the early history of the universe, *The First Three Minutes* (New York: Basic Books, 1988), for instance. So if before time V there were no humans, so no vocabularies, we do not want to deny that

1. There were (at time pre-V) photons.

We can move the tense operator out front, and paraphrase this as

2. It was the case (at time pre-V) that [there are photons].

By the basic redundancy property of 'true', we can preface this with "It is true that . . .":

3. It is true that [It was the case (at time pre-V) that [there are photons]].

Now we can move the tense operator out to modify the verb in "It is true that . . .":

4. Was [It is true (at time pre-V) that [there are photons]].

This is the key move. It is justified by the observation that *all* sentential operators can be treated this way, as a result of deep features of the redundancy of 'true'. Thus one can transform "It is true that Not[*p*]" into Not[It is true that *p*], "It is true that Possibly[*p*]" into "Possibly[It is true that *p*]," and "It is true that Will-be[*p*]" into "Will-be[It is true that *p*]." But now, given how the tense operators work, it is straightforward to derive

5. It was true (at time pre-V) that [there are photons].

And again invoking the features that make 'true' redundant, we get

6. It was the case (at time pre-V) that [It is true that [there are photons]].

These uniformities involving the interaction of 'true' with other sentential operators tell us we are committed by our use of those expressions to either deny that there were photons before there were people—which is to deny well-entrenched deliverances of physics—or to admit that there were truths about photons before there were people to formulate them.

1) If some crucible were heated to a temperature high enough to melt copper, then it would be hot enough to melt aluminum.

is a chemical necessity: a chemical law of nature. It is a modal fact. It is modally, subjunctively, counterfactually independent of the existence of concept users. If that is right, then descriptions of how things objectively are stand in modally robust material (nonlogical) consequential relations to one another. Another such is

2) If the sample were (had been) pure copper, then it would be (would have been) denser than water.

Besides relations of material consequence, descriptive facts we can state can also stand in relations of material incompatibility.

3) A sample's being pure copper is incompatible with its being an electrical insulator. (It is not possible that a sample be both pure copper and an electrical insulator.)

Ways the world can be empirically described as being stand to one another in objective, modally robust relations of material consequence and incompatibility.

7. The modalities this sort of realism addresses are those invoked by the natural sciences and their analogs in less systematic ordinary language. What the kind of modal vocabulary in question expresses is not *logical* possibility and necessity, for the truth of claims such as (1), (2), and (3) depends essentially on their use of the *non*logical empirical descriptive concepts copper, aluminum, temperature, water, density, and so on. Nor is it metaphysical necessity, which abstracts from actual laws of nature and other subjunctive- and counterfactual-supporting dependencies that turn on particular properties things can be described as having.

The modal revolution in late twentieth-century Anglophone philosophy had three principal phases. First was Kripke's revolution in the semantics of modal logical vocabulary. Second was the generalization, by Lewis, Stalnaker, Montague, and Kaplan, among others, of his algebraic possible-worlds apparatus to an intensional semantics for nonlogical expressions. Third was the introduction of the conceptual apparatus that led to the recognition of the possibility of necessities knowable only *a posteriori*, and contingencies knowable *a priori*, in Kripke's "Naming and Necessity." It was this third phase that gave rise to contemporary analytic metaphysics. The kind of modality to which both the modal expressivism of the previous section and the modal realism of this one are addressed is relevant at most to the second phase: the one in which modal notions such as possibility are used to explicate the contents of nonlogical concepts.

There is another line of argument to the conclusion that commitment to modal realism is implicit in commitment to a corresponding realism about claims expressed using ordinary empirical descriptive vocabulary. It will make clearer the relation between one kind of alethic modality and conceptual content. We can begin with a platitude: there is some way the world objectively is. How it objectively is must be discovered by empirical inquiry, and sets a semantic and epistemic standard for assessment of the correctness of our descriptive claimings as potential expressions of knowledge. The question is how to understand the relation of modal facts (if any) to how the world objectively is as describable (at least sometimes) in nonmodal empirical descriptive vocabulary. One might ask a supervenience question here, but the line of thought I am concerned with goes a different way. It asks what modal commitments are implicit already in the idea of an empirically describable world. It focuses on the *determinateness* of the way things objectively are.

To talk about how things objectively are as determinate is to invoke a contrast with how they are not. This idea is summed up in the Spinozist (and scholastic) principle *omnis determinatio est negatio*. This thought is incorporated in the twentieth-century concept of information (due to Shannon),[31] which understands it in terms of the partition each bit establishes between how things are (according to the information) and how they are not. But there are different ways we might follow out this idea, depending on how we think about the sort of negation involved. What I'll call the "Hegelian" model of determinateness insists that it must be understood as what he calls

---

31. Claude E. Shannon and Warren Weaver, *The Mathematical Theory of Communication* (Urbana: University of Illinois Press, 1949).

"exclusive" [ausschließend] difference, and not mere or "indifferent" [gleichgültig] difference.³² Square and circular are exclusively different properties, since possession by a plane figure of the one excludes, rules out, or is materially incompatible with possession of the other. Square and green are merely or indifferently different, in that though they are distinct properties, possession of the one does not preclude possession of the other. An essential part of the determinate content of a property—what makes it the property it is, and not some other one—is the relations of material (nonlogical) incompatibility it stands in to other determinate properties (for instance, shapes to other shapes, and colors to other colors). In fact, Hegel's view is that determinateness is a matter of standing in relations of material incompatibility (his "determinate negation") and material consequence (his "mediation") to other determinates. We might think of these as related by the principle that one property, say metallic, is a consequence of another, copper, in case everything incompatible with being metallic (say, being a mammal) is incompatible with being copper. A property possession of which rules out possession of *no* other properties, and has as a consequence possession of no others, is as such *in*determinate.

One observation we can make about this distinction between exclusive difference and mere difference is that one can define mere difference solely in terms of exclusive difference, but not *vice versa*. For one can say that two properties are *merely* different just in case they are not incompatible with each other, but are materially incompatible with different properties. Square and green are different because they are incompatible with different properties: square is incompatible with circular, and green is not.³³

---

32. The rubric 'Hegelian' here is tendentious, and liable to be alarming. More seriously, it is liable to be unhelpful. For now, treat it as a mere label. I will say what I mean by it—give it some content—as we go along.

33. This definition sounds circular, because of its invocation of the notion of sameness of the properties incompatible with a property. But we can avoid this. Suppose we have labeled properties (say, by real numbers). If an oracle then tells us for each label the set of all labels of incompatible properties, we can sort the labels into equivalence classes, accordingly as the set of incompatible labels they are associated with is the same. These will all be labels of the same property. Two labels that are not in the same incompatibility-equivalence class are then labels of different properties. Some pairs of properties that are different in this sense will then also be exclusively different, if one is a member of the incompatibility set of (a label of) the other.

One reason to endorse this Hegelian conception of determinateness is that it is required to underwrite what might be taken to be an essential aspect of the structural difference between the fundamental ontological categories of *object* and *property*. Aristotle had already pointed out a fundamental asymmetry between these categories. It makes sense to think of each property as coming with a *converse*, in the sense of a property that is exhibited by all and only the objects that do *not* exhibit the index property. Has a mass greater than 5 grams is a property that has a converse in this sense. But it does *not* make sense to think of *objects* as coming with converses, in the analogous sense of an object that exhibits all and only the properties that are *not* exhibited by the index object. This is precisely because some of those properties will be incompatible with one another. Thus my left leg has the properties of not being identical to Bach's second Brandenberg concerto and not being identical to Gottlob Frege. Its converse, if it had one, would have to have the properties of being identical to both.

Now one might deny that this categorial asymmetry is essential to the concepts of object and property. A *Tractarian* conception of (elementary) objects and properties makes do with mere difference. Elementary properties and relations do not stand in relations of material incompatibility or consequence. They are independent, in that the fact that an object exhibits one property or stands in one relation has no consequences for any others it might exhibit or stand in.[34] (*All* the relations of incompatibility and consequence holding between states of affairs in the *Tractatus* hold between non-elementary states of affairs, and are due solely to the *logical* complexity of those states of affairs. There are no material, that is, nonlogical, relations of consequence and incompatibility in that picture.) In this context it is coherent to associate with each elementary object a converse, which exhibits all and only the properties (stands in all and only the relations) that the index object does not. I am not concerned here to argue that the Tractarian conception of object is incoherent or otherwise inadequate just because it has no room for the Aristotelian categorial asymmetry. For my purposes it is sufficient to point out that the Hegelian notion of determinateness, which requires acknowledging the dis-

---

34. There are both textual and conceptual difficulties concerning the status of monadic elementary properties in the *Tractatus*. But the points I am concerned to make go through just as well if we restrict ourselves to relations, so I will ignore both these kinds of difficulty.

tinction between mere difference and exclusive difference, *does* underwrite (is necessary and sufficient for) the Aristotelian point about the difference between objects and properties (or relations).

A Tractarian conception of determinateness is one according to which it is sufficient for properties to be determinate that they are *merely* different from one another, and sufficient for objects to be determinate that they exhibit some merely different properties. Tractarian properties do not stand to one another in relations of determinable properties (e.g. polygonal, colored) and more determinate properties falling under them (circular, green). For the more determinate properties would stand in relations of material consequence to their determinables, and in relations of material incompatibility to other determinates falling under the same determinable. So nothing like the structure—characteristic of shapes and colors, and of biological taxonomies—of properties as falling into determinable families of exclusively different determinates which are merely different from determinates falling under other determinables is available in a Tractarian world.

The Hegelian conception of determinateness as a matter of standing in relations of exclusive difference (material incompatibility, and—so—material consequence) to other determinates, then, has at least these three consequences in its favor:

- The mere difference that articulates the Tractarian world can be defined in terms of exclusive difference, but there is no backwards route;
- Objects and properties that are determinate in this sense exhibit the Aristotelian categorial asymmetry;
- Properties will exhibit the standard structure of compatible determinable families of incompatible determinate properties.

It should be clear that to take the objective world to be determinate in the Hegelian sense—so, to consist of objects and their properties and relations in the Aristotelian sense, and for those properties and relations to exhibit the structure of determinable families of determinates—is to be committed to modal realism. For Hegelian determinateness requires that there be facts about what properties and states of affairs are materially incompatible with which others, and about what material consequential relations they stand in to which others. The determinateness of the fact that this coin is copper consists in part in its being incompatible with the coin being silver and its having as a consequence that it conducts electricity—that is, with its being *necessary* that it is not silver, *possible* that it is green, and *necessary* that it conducts electricity.[35] Metallurgists discover these modal facts as part of the same kind of empirical inquiry through which they discover that this coin is in fact copper. A world without modal facts would be an indeterminate world: a world without objects in the Aristotelian sense, and without properties in the sense that admits a determinate-determinable structure.

The kind of modality in question is that expressed in ordinary conversational language, and in a more systematic and controlled way in the special sciences, both empirical and exact. It is the modality involved in claims such as "No monochromatic patch can be both red and green," "It is impossible for a square plane figure to be circular," "Pure copper at sea-level pressure necessarily melts at 1083.4° C," and "A mammal placed in an evacuated belljar would die of oxygen deprivation." These are not either *logical* modalities, except in an extremely extended sense—though one not without precedent in Anglophone philosophy of the forties and fifties), nor are they oomphier metaphysical modalities in a Kripkean sense.

In laying out Sellars's views I registered that he thinks of what he called the "causal modalities" as characterizing the inferential relations that articulate the contents of empirical descriptive concepts. If we go back to what Hegel made of Kant's views of modality and conceptual content, we find a notion of conceptual content that can help us better understand how this kind of modality can be understood as a *conceptual* modality. On this conception, to be *conceptually* contentful just is to stand in modally robust relations of material consequence and incompatibility (what Hegel calls relations of "mediation" and "determinate negation"). This is a resolutely nonpsychological sense of 'conceptual'. For it makes no reference to concept-*use*—to the *application* of concepts by anyone at all. So if there are laws of nature according to which some properties are incompatible with others (*can*not be exemplified by the same object at the same time) or have others as their consequences (if one is

---

35. Of course there are various provisos that would have to be added to make these claims strictly true, since copper can be alloyed with silver, and so on. I ignore these complications, as beside the point I am after.

exhibited by an object, the other *must* be) then the world as it is objectively, independently of the activity of any knowing and acting subjects, is conceptually articulated. Empirical inquiry is at once the job of determining what judgments are true and what concepts are correct—that is, what really follows from what and what really precludes what. Linguistic terms can *express* concepts, by being used so as to undertake commitments as to what follows from what and what precludes what. But the concepts they express are in no sense *products* of that concept-applying activity.

As we saw, Sellars insists that it is standing in such relations that makes empirical descriptive vocabulary genuinely *descriptive,* that is, expressive of descriptive *concepts,* rather than merely functioning as reliably differentially responsively elicited *labels.* And we have seen that the sort of modal realism I have been sketching has as one of its consequences that empirical descriptive properties and states of affairs stand to one another in relations of material consequence and incompatibility. So Hegel offers us definitions of what it is to be *determinate* and to be *conceptually articulated,* according to which to take the objective world to be determinate is to take it to be *modally* articulated and to be *conceptually* articulated. That is, it commits one both to modal realism and to conceptual realism: the view that the objective world is modally, and *so* conceptually structured, quite apart from its relations to us.

Together

8. The core of the modal realism I have just sketched consists of some claims that express philosophical common sense: there are laws of nature, events sometimes causally necessitate others, there is a determinate way the world objectively is, and its being that way rules out (excludes the possibility) of its being some other ways. These are commitments to which any philosopher ought to want to be entitled. They should be contested only under theoretical duress by exceptionally weighty and compelling arguments. I have elaborated those core claims in the context of others that are *not* commonsensical, most notably that modal realism in this sense entails *conceptual* realism about the objective world. The link between the two classes of claim is forged by the Hegelian nonpsychological definition of the conceptual, as what is articulated by relations of material (that is, in general nonlogical) consequence or necessitation and incompatibility. I think this is a good thing to mean by "conceptual," not the least because of the space it opens up to understand how the sort of causal modalities investigated by the sciences can be thought of as articulating the contents of concepts. That is a deservedly controversial claim. Whatever stance one takes on it, the sense in which I am using the term "conceptual" is, I trust, at least reasonably clear.

But what is the relation between this kind of modal *realism* and the modal *expressivism* I talked about in the first part of this essay? There the expressive role characteristic of modal vocabulary was identified as making explicit the material inferential and incompatibility relations in virtue of which ordinary empirical descriptive (OED) vocabulary expresses the content that it does. This expressive role was distinguished from that of the ground-level empirical descriptive vocabulary, whose principal job it is to say how things objectively are. There is no further vocabulary to which OED vocabulary stands in the same semantically explicative relation as alethic modal vocabulary stands to it.[36] The core of this version of modal expressivism lies precisely in the distinction it insists on between the expressive role distinctive of modal vocabulary and that of vocabulary whose job is describing the world, at least in the narrow, paradigmatic sense in which OED vocabulary describes the world. Modal realism says that modal vocabulary *does* describe the world, does say how things are. So are these two lines of thought simply incompatible? Are we obliged to choose between them?

I think that the modal expressivism of Part I and the modal realism of Part II are not only compatible, but that that account of the *expressive* role distinctive of modal vocabulary is just what is needed to understand the central claims of modal *realism*. The expressivism complements, rather than conflicting with, the realism about the use of modal concepts. How is such a reconciliation to be understood? The first step is to see that modal expressivism (ME) makes claims about what one is *doing* in using modal concepts, while modal realism (MR) makes claims about what one is *saying* by using modal concepts. ME says that what one is doing when one makes a modal claim is endorsing an inference relating descriptive concepts as subjunctively (including counterfactually) robust, or treating two descriptive concepts as incompatible. MR says that when one does that, one is saying (claiming) *that*

---

36. This is the expressive role of being *elaborated from* and *explicative of* the use of OED vocabulary. It is what in *Between Saying and Doing* I call "being LX" for that vocabulary.

possession or exhibition of one empirical property is a consequence of, or is incompatible with, possession or exhibition of another. The claim that ME and MR are *compatible* is the claim that one can *both* be *doing* what ME says one is doing in applying modal vocabulary *and* be *saying* what MR says one is saying by doing that. The claim that they are *complementary* is the claim that an important way to understand what one is *saying* by making modal claims is precisely to think about what one is *doing* by making them.

According to this way of understanding the relations between ME and MR, the claims of modal expressivism are made in a *pragmatic* metavocabulary for modal vocabulary: that is, a vocabulary suitable for specifying the practices, abilities, and performances that make up the *use* of modal vocabulary. And the claims of modal realism are made in a *semantic* metavocabulary for modal vocabulary: that is, a vocabulary suitable for specifying the *meanings* or conceptual *contents* expressed by modal vocabulary. What we have here is an instance of the general question of how to understand the relations between these two complementary aspects of concept application in claims: the use of the concepts and their meaning or content, what one is doing by applying them and what one is saying by applying them. I don't think we have a good general theory of how these dimensions of discourse are related to one another. (I've made a first try at an analytic framework in which such a theory might be embedded, in *Between Saying and Doing*.) Looking more closely at the special case of modal vocabulary—a vocabulary-kind of particular philosophical interest and importance—provides a potentially valuable case study and test bench for approaching the more general question of how to understand the relations between what is said in pragmatic metavocabularies and what is said in semantic metavocabularies addressing the same base vocabulary. Of special interest in this case is the relation between the use and meaning of modal vocabulary in relation to that of ordinary empirical descriptive vocabulary.

Modal expressivism says that what one is doing in making modal claims is not the same thing one is doing in making claims using ordinary empirical descriptive vocabulary. For in the former case, but not the latter, one is (perhaps *inter alia*) committing oneself to subjunctively robust inferential-and-incompatibility relations among descriptive concepts one is not in general thereby applying. Modal realism says that in making modal claims one is saying how things objectively are, describing the objective world.

Reconciling these claims requires specifying a sense of "describing" or "empirical fact-stating" that is broader than that applicable to the primary use of OED vocabulary, but still sufficiently akin to it that the broader sense applicable to modal claims and the narrower sense applicable show up as species of a recognizably descriptive genus.

One broader sense that is available is that provided by *declarativism* about description, which makes it equivalent to "fact-stating" in a very capacious sense. This is the view that identifies facts with whatever is stated by declarative sentences that can be used both free-standingly, to make assertions, and in embedded contexts, paradigmatically as the antecedent of conditionals and in the context of a propositional attitude ascribing locutions. I think this is a perfectly good way to use "fact" and "fact-stating." But in this context, it buys modal realism too cheaply, and hence buys too cheap a version of modal realism. For in this sense "One ought not to be cruel," "Raspberries are preferable to strawberries," and "The value of Picasso's *Guernica* does not lie in its beauty" are all straightforwardly fact-stating (if they were true, they would state facts), and hence descriptive in the declarativist's *very* broad sense. So this usage loses the contrast between description and evaluation (which perhaps is no bad thing, but should be a position reached for more specific reasons than the broad charter of declarativism offers) and between objective description and subjective expression of preference or other attitude. A modal realism worthy of the name should be held to a more demanding standard for what counts as empirical fact-stating or description. I conclude that a proper reconciliation of ME and MR requires crafting a sense of "empirical description" or "empirical fact-stating" that is wider than the narrow senses applicable only to OED vocabulary such as "cat," "red," and "mass of five grams," but not as broad as the declarativist's.[37]

9. Before indicating how that might be done, I want to consider one way in which the modal expressivist line of thought can be seen to be essential to understanding the modal realist line of thought. Modal realism claims that there are objective modal *facts*. One important species of modal facts is *laws*

---

37. Here I've run back and forth indiscriminately between description (or fact-stating) and empirical description as the concept being considered. I think it is the combination that matters for modal realism. These issues will be taken up separately in Sections 9 and 10.

of nature. Modal realism makes essential use of the concepts of fact and law, but does not by itself *explain* those concepts. Modal expressivism does. As I indicated at the beginning of Part II, facts are (at least) true claimables. (The problem with declarativism is not its acknowledgment of this as a *necessary* condition on facts, but with its insouciant commitment to this being also a *sufficient* condition. We'll see in Section 10 what more might be demanded, at least for objective empirical facts.) Does this mean that there are no facts that cannot be stated, that is, expressed in some language or vocabulary? I think we adequately acknowledge the intuitive language-transcendence of fact by affirming that for any vocabulary, there are facts that cannot be stated in that vocabulary. I think of this claim as a commitment, should you specify a vocabulary, to being able to find some facts not statable in it. (I don't think, for instance, that one can express in the language of physics facts such as that the stock market dropped yesterday, or that the Republicans' unwillingness to allow a vote on the judicial nominee was a strategic political blunder.) But I don't know how to understand a claim that reverses the quantifiers and asserts that there are facts such that no vocabulary can state them. It might well be possible to give some sense to this sort of wide open quantification over all possible vocabularies, but it does not already come with one.

More deeply, though, the claim is that key concepts of the *semantic* metavocabulary in which modal realism is stated are *sense-dependent* on concepts drawn from the *pragmatic* metavocabulary for modality offered by modal expressivism. One cannot understand the concepts fact and law except in a context that includes the concepts asserting and inferring. For facts are essentially, and not just accidentally, something that can be asserted. If one does not know that it is at least sometimes true that facts can be stated, one does not know what facts are. And laws are essentially, and not just accidentally, somethings that support subjunctively and counterfactually robust inferences. If one does not understand that Newton's second law of motion implies that if a force *were* (had been) applied to this moving body, it would accelerate (have accelerated), one does not grasp "F=ma" as having the force of a law.[38]

---

38. In articles such as "Abstract Entities" and "Grammar and Existence: A Preface to Ontology," reprinted as Chapters 7 and 6 of Scharp and Brandom (eds.), *In the Space of Reasons,* Sellars develops what he calls a "metalinguistic" approach to ontological-categorial concepts such as fact and property, which is much better worked out than his

One concept is sense-dependent on another if one cannot grasp or understand the first without grasping or understanding the second. This sense-dependence relation must not be confused with that of reference-dependence of one concept on another, which holds when the first cannot be true of something unless the second is true of something. The concepts parent and child are both reciprocally sense-dependent and reciprocally reference-dependent. One cannot understand one in isolation from an understanding of the other, and nothing can be a parent unless something is a child (indeed, its child), and *vice versa*. But there can be sense-dependence relations without corresponding reference-dependence relations. This is true of response-dependent properties. Suppose we define something as *hedonically beautiful for humans* just in case a human observer would respond to its perceptible presence with a feeling of pleasure. One cannot understand this dispositional property without also understanding the concept of pleasure (and, indeed, of human). But the exhibition of this property by an object does not require that there actually be feelings of pleasure. We can make perfect sense of the claim that there were sunsets that were hedonically beautiful for humans before there were humans. For to say that is just to say that *if* there *had been* humans to perceive them, those sunsets *would have* produced feelings of pleasure. And that can be true in a world without humans or pleasure. Similarly, if we define a planet as *supraterrestrial* just in case it has a mass larger than that of the Earth, that concept is sense-dependent on that of the Earth, but we can use it to describe a possible world in which *all* planets are supraterrestrial, and the Earth does not exist.

To claim that the concepts fact and law were reference-dependent on the concepts of asserting and inferring would be to assert an objectionable and obviously false sort of language- or mind-dependence of crucial categorial features of the objective world. But to claim the corresponding sense-dependence claim is not in the same way objectionable. For it is compatible with the truth of the counterfactual that there would have been facts and laws even if there had never been asserters and inferrers—indeed that in our

---

corresponding views on modality. Here, too, I think his basically Carnapian concept of the metalinguistic is far too undifferentiated to do the work he needs it to do in order to express the insights by which he is motivated. I discuss his pragmatic expressive nominalism in Chapter 7.

world there were facts and laws before there were asserters and inferrers. The claim is just that one cannot understand what one is saying when one talks about an objective world characterized by facts and laws (which is to say just a determinate world) unless one understands facts as the kind of thing that can be stated and laws as the kind of thing that can support subjunctively and counterfactually robust reasoning. Modal expressivism helps explain what the claims of modal realism mean.

10. Modal realism asserts that modal vocabulary is used to form empirical descriptions of objective facts. Modal expressivism asserts that modal vocabulary plays a content-explicating expressive role that distinguishes it sharply from that of ordinary empirical descriptive vocabulary. Saying something about the broader sense in which modal vocabulary can nonetheless be understood as descriptive will further illuminate the complex complementary relations between what MR says about modal vocabulary in a semantic metavocabulary and what ME says about it in a pragmatic one. Here is a suggestion: A broader sense of "fact-stating" and "description" that is not yet so promiscuous as the declarativist candidate is defined by the dual requirements of *semantic government* of claimings by facts and *epistemic tracking* of facts by claimings.

By "semantic government" I mean that descriptive claims are subject to a distinctive kind of ought-to-be (related only in complicated ways to the ought-to-dos that Sellars contrasted them with). It ought to be the case that the content of a descriptive claiming stands in a special relation, which we might as well call "correspondence," to a modal fact, which it accordingly purports to state (and in case there is such a fact, succeeds in stating). In virtue of that semantic norm, claimings are answerable for their correctness (accord with that norm) to facts. The underlying thought here is that what one is talking *about* is what exercises a certain kind of *authority* over what one says; what one says is *responsible to* what one is talking about, in a way that is characteristic of this relation as *semantic*. What one is talking about provides a standard for the assessment of what one says.

What is the nature of the correspondence that the norm enjoins? The contents of possible claimings are articulated by relations of material consequence and incompatibility to the contents of other potential claimings. These notions are themselves specifiable in a *deontic normative* pragmatic metavocabulary: committing (or entitling) oneself to one claim can commit (or entitle) one to others, and can preclude entitlement to still others. The contents of facts and possible facts are also articulated by relations of material consequence and incompatibility to the contents of other possible facts. In this case, these notions are specifiable in an *alethic modal* semantic metavocabulary: the obtaining of one fact has the obtaining of others as a necessary (that is, subjunctively, including counterfactually, robust) consequence, makes others possible, and rules out still others as not possible. Normative semantic government of claimings by facts says that it ought to be the case that there is a fact whose content is articulated by objective modal relations of material consequence and incompatibility that line up with the subjective (in the sense of pertaining to knowing and acting discursive subjects) normative relations of material consequence and incompatibility that articulate the content of a claiming. If that norm is not satisfied, the claiming does not live up to the standard provided by the fact it purports to state.[39]

Where semantic government of claiming by facts is a (deontic) *normative* matter, epistemic tracking of facts by claimings is a(n) (alethic) *modal* one. It is a matter of the subjunctive and counterfactual robustness of the conceptual content correspondence between facts and claims. The tracking condition holds just insofar as the subjunctive conditional "If the fact were (or had been) different, the claiming would be (or would have been) correspondingly different" is true. Insofar as this condition holds, there is a *reliable* correspondence between the contents of facts and the contents of claimings. That is to say that the inference from a claim about the content of a claiming to the content of the corresponding fact is in general a good one. I have written elsewhere about the sense in which deontic normative and alethic modal vocabularies are two sides of one (intentional) coin. I cannot here pursue this significance of this particular application (to the complementary conditions of semantic governance and epistemic tracking) of that general (meta-) conceptual complementarity.[40]

---

39. The concept of propositional content as what is articulated by relations of material consequence and incompatibility is a development of the Fregean metaconceptual semantic dimension of *Sinn*, while the normative relation of aboutness between objective facts and subjective commitments is a development of his metaconceptual semantic dimension of *Bedeutung*.

40. For instance, in Chapter 6 of *Between Saying and Doing*.

11. I think it is a fundamental mistake to try to do all the work done by the concept of semantic government with that of epistemic tracking, as for instance Fodor and Dretske do. What goes missing is the fine structure of the crucial interaction between activities on the part of the claiming subject, expressed in a deontic normative pragmatic metavocabulary, and how it is with the objects and facts those claims are about, expressed in an alethic modal semantic metavocabulary, and how the two sides stand in both normative relations of semantic government and modal relations of epistemic tracking. It is precisely in these intricate relations that the complementary character of modal expressivism and modal realism becomes visible.

When the two requirements of semantic government and epistemic tracking are satisfied, it makes good sense to think of the claimings in question as fact-stating and descriptive. They purport to say how things are with what they are, in the normative sense of semantic government, *about.* The actual applications of the vocabulary in question, no less than their normative status as correct or not, are epistemically *responsive* to and *controlled* by the corresponding facts. The notions of correspondence, semantic government, and epistemic tracking do not invoke causal connection—only subjunctively robust reliable covariation. For this reason, they define a notion of description or fact-stating that applies equally well to mathematical vocabulary as to empirical.

This is also evidently true of modal vocabulary, supposing we grant the dual claims of modal realism and modal expressivism. For modal *expressivism* tells us that modal vocabulary makes explicit normatively significant relations of subjunctively robust material consequence and incompatibility among claimable (hence propositional) contents in virtue of which ordinary empirical descriptive vocabulary *describes* and does not merely *label, discriminate,* or *classify.* And modal *realism* tells us that there are modal facts, concerning the subjunctively robust relations of material consequence and incompatibility in virtue of which ordinary empirical descriptive properties and facts are determinate. Together, these two claims give a definite sense to the possibility of the correspondence of modal claimings with modal facts. If we can then say what it is for a norm of semantic governance to be instituted and the modal fact of epistemic tracking to be achieved, the descriptive, the fact-stating character of modal vocabulary according to ME and MR will have been made intelligible.

It is a consequence of the version of Kant-Sellars modal expressivism that I outlined in Part I that instituting normative semantic government of modal claims by modal facts, and of achieving modal epistemic tracking of modal facts by modal claims, must be an aspect of the process of instituting semantic government of ordinary empirical descriptive claims by the facts they state, and of achieving epistemic tracking of those facts by ordinary empirical descriptive claims. For the essence of that view is that what is expressed explicitly (that is, put in claimable, propositional form) by the use of modal vocabulary is already implicit in the norms governing the use of OED vocabulary.

Empiricism, in both its traditional and its twentieth-century logical forms, offered a three-stage layer-cake picture of empirical inquiry that is particularly clear in Carnap's version. The task of the first stage is semantic: to determine the empirical concepts to be used, to fix the meanings to be expressed by OED vocabulary. The task of the second stage is epistemic: to settle, on the basis of the meanings fixed at the first stage, the claims expressed using that vocabulary that are taken to be true. The task of the third stage is explanatory: to identify, on the basis of regularities exhibited by the claims made at the second stage, laws governing the facts stated at the second stage. The first stage is a matter of convenient conventions, the last two of the assessment of empirical evidence—fraught at the second stage by the potentially problematic transition from applying observational descriptive vocabulary to applying theoretical descriptive vocabulary, and at the second stage by the potentially problematic transition from observed regularity to conjectured law. Quine sees that separating the first two stages, which makes good sense when one's model is artificial languages, is not possible when one addresses natural languages. There is just one thing discursive practitioners do: use vocabulary to make claims. Doing that must be understood as at once fixing meanings and beliefs, language and theory. Like Hume, Quine doesn't think the third stage can be rationally warranted—though this empiricist conclusion sits ill with his avowed scientific naturalism. But modal expressivism is motivated by the same pragmatic considerations about the use of vocabularies that motivate Quine's recognition of the semantic and epistemic enterprises as aspects of one process of empirical inquiry. As Sellars puts the point (in a passage I quote at the end of Section 5): "although describing and explaining . . . are *distinguishable*, they are also, in an important sense, *inseparable* . . . the descriptive and explanatory resources of the language advance hand in hand."

Determining and applying descriptive concepts inevitably involves committing oneself as to the subjunctively robust inferential and incompatibility relations they stand in to one another. Rectifying concepts, determining facts, and establishing laws are all projects that must be pursued together. Empirical evidence bears on all of the semantic, epistemic, and explanatory tasks at once, or it bears on none of them. Of course, there is a lot more that needs to be said about how this actually works and should work. The multifarious ways in which commitments of one sort—semantic, doxastic, subjunctive—bear on and can be traded off for commitments of other sorts need to be investigated and explicated in detail. (I've sketched a story about the next level of gross structure in the first three chapters of *Reason in Philosophy*.) And I certainly would not claim that seeing how modal expressivism and modal realism complement and illuminate one another clears up at a stroke all the vexing problems in the epistemology of modality—even when pursued outside the confines of the straitjacket of empiricism. But all I need here is the general conclusion—which gives us confidence that there must be solutions to those problems.

If that is right, then modal claims (and the concepts that articulate them) exhibit semantic government by and epistemic tracking of facts no less than ordinary empirical descriptive ones do. Far from being incompatible with this fundamental modally realistic claim, modal expressivism is just what is needed to make it intelligible. By showing how the use of modal concepts and the use of ordinary empirical descriptive concepts are inextricably bound up with one another, modal expressivism also shows itself and modal realism as two sides of one coin.

Again

12. I have argued that modal realism and the right kind of modal expressivism belong together. The tendency to understand views of this kind as incompatible alternatives—to take the sense in which modal vocabulary plays, as Sellars put it, a "metalinguistic" expressive role relative to ordinary empirical descriptive vocabulary to rule out the possibility of its being also fact-stating and descriptive of something other than language use—is the result of failing to attend to the distinction between *pragmatic* and *semantic* metavocabularies. I think we don't know very much about the various ways in which what is said in these two sorts of metavocabulary are related for various vocabularies they might address. In *Between Saying and Doing*, I explore the expressive roles of various kinds of pragmatically mediated semantic relations between vocabularies, a genus that includes pragmatic metavocabularies, without saying much at all about the relations between what they make explicit and what is made explicit by traditional semantic metavocabularies of the Tarski-Carnap variety. (This was the only model Sellars had available, Procrustean though it made his efforts to formulate what I take to be his pragmatic expressivist insights.) One of my aspirations in the present chapter has been to begin the process of investigating those crucial relations by looking as a test-case at a vocabulary of particular philosophical interest and importance: alethic modal vocabulary. I hope the results will be of interest to those moved by expressivist intuitions concerning other vocabularies: some kinds of normative vocabulary, moral or aesthetic, for instance, or even (were we to follow Sellars in his metalinguistic nominalism about universals) ontological-categorial or metaphysical vocabularies.

I have finished my argument. But I want to close with a lagniappe, indicated in the final word of my title. Why claim, as that title does, that the result of this story is to put modal expressivism and modal realism together *again*? Why should the story be thought of as recounting a *reunion*? The answer I want to leave you with is this: It is because we've seen something very like this constellation of metaconceptual commitments before. I started my story with Kant, and that is where I want to end it. Claiming that one should be a *pragmatic* modal expressivist (an expressivist about what one is *doing* in applying modal vocabulary) but a *semantic* modal realist (a realist about what one is *saying* in applying modal vocabulary) is, I think, recognizably a development and a descendant, for this special but central case, of Kant's claim that one should be a *transcendental idealist*, but an *empirical realist*. That is what I mean by saying that the view I have been presenting puts modal expressivism and modal realism together *again*. Here, I think, is a way of developing Kant's ideas in the vicinity that is much more promising than the one Sellars pursues as a rereading of the phenomenal/noumenal distinction that I deplore in the second half of Chapter 1.

CHAPTER SIX

Sortals, Identity, and Modality: The Metaphysical Significance of the Modal Kant-Sellars Thesis

1. Sortals and Identity

Frege explicated the distinction between predicates, such as 'red' or 'heavy', which are characterized semantically by their associated circumstances and consequences of application, and sortalizing predicates or kind-terms, such as 'dog' or 'electron', which in addition have associated practices of identifying and individuating the things to which they apply. Sortals are expressions for which the question can arise whether or not the things they apply to are the *same* K: the same dog, the same electron (direction, shape, number)—perhaps in different circumstances (such as times) or differently specified. Quine calls sortal expressions "count nouns," because their associated criteria of identity and individuation make it possible to count them: to say (or ask) *how many* Ks there are in some collection.[1]

---

1. The two principal species of kind-terms are distinguished in that things to which sortals apply can be counted (a sense has been given to questions of the form "How many?") while things that fall under mass nouns can be measured (a sense has been given to questions of the form "How much?"). Mass nouns are sortalized by introducing units of measurement: one can count *liters* of water and *grams* of gold. Those quantity expressions give sense to questions such as "Is this the same *volume* or *mass* of water as that is of gold?" They are introduced by abstraction, but the equivalence relations that serve as abstractors are embedded in and defined in terms of much richer structures, generated by *asymmetric*, transitive (only the details of implementation depend on whether they are reflexive or irreflexive), *comparative* relations exhibiting distinctive kinds of higher-level symmetry. In the case of volume, mass, and utility (the measure of preference) these include additivity and the existence of a zero.

The process of introducing units of measurement for mass nouns that gives sense to questions such as "Is this the same volume of water as that?" should not be confused with

Philosophical confusions have resulted from the existence in natural languages of pseudosortals, such as 'object', 'thing', and 'item'. These expressions occupy the grammatical places held by genuine sortals, but do *not* have associated criteria of identity, which are semantically essential to real sortals. For this reason, they do not semantically support counting. There is no definite answer to the question "How many things are on my desk?" Are all the parts of things also things—even spatiotemporal parts of indivisible particles (if such there be)? Are shadows (and their parts) things? Sometimes these pseudosortals function as anaphoric prosortals: "There are books, and papers, and the remains of today's lunch on my desk, and all those things need to be cleared away." Sometimes they are just sortal placeholders, where the specific sortal they are to be taken to stand in for are to be gathered from the context: "What a nice skirt!" "Oh, that old thing?" But sometimes they stand for an attempt to quantify over all possible genuine sortals—as an otherwise uncontexted request to enumerate the things on the desk would be. Sortally unrestricted quantification (of the sort Frege is supposed to have introduced) runs the risk of having to be understood this way—though it is better to think of the domains of quantification as specified in a semantic metalanguage, using genuine sortals providing criteria of identity that do permit counting. (Of course, one can *stipulate* a meaning for 'object': by 'object' I shall mean fundamental physical particle, and all mereological sums of them. One must keep in mind, however, that one thereby runs the risk—as I'll argue below—of ruling out as objects the things falling under practically all other sortals.)

A question of long-standing interest is how we should understand the relations between the two central aspects of the use of sortal expressions:

---

the only superficially similar process of sortalizing predicate adjectives (though abstraction is involved in both). One can indeed introduce sortals that give sense to questions such as "Is this the same hue or shade of red as that?" when the latter is *not* based on the introduction of a space of measures (the color-sphere articulated by the three dimensions of hue, saturation, and intensity, each defined by its own sort of asymmetric comparison of more and less) but just on the basis of a (supposed) equivalence relation of a kind of indistinguishability. ('Supposed' because transitivity notoriously fails for indistinguishability of shade; so much the worse for the rough-and-ready notion of a shade of color.)

their criteria of application and their criteria of identity.² On one view, these can vary independently, in the sense that two sortals can have different criteria of application and the same criteria of identity, or the same criteria of application and different criteria of identity. Examples of the former case are not far to seek. Phase sortals, such as 'kitten', 'tadpole', and 'child' are applicable only to proper subsets of what 'cat', 'frog', and 'human' are applicable to. But they are individuated and counted the same way. Two different children are two different humans, and two different humans who are children are two different children. The other sort of case is more contentious and difficult to illustrate. A principal candidate example is 'passenger' and 'person riding in a vehicle' (or something similar—the details of the criteria of application are not the point here). Passengers are important to airlines, and they count them. US Airways says that in 2010 it flew 59,809,367 passengers. It did not fly that many different people. When I flew from Pittsburgh to San Francisco, I got counted as a different passenger than I did when I flew back. But it was only one person getting counted as two passengers in those two plane trips.

Impressed by examples such as these (and others that individuate down rather than up, such as 'surpersons' who are people, but such that two people with the same surname are the same surperson), Geach argued that identity itself must be understood as sortally relative.³ This view has been widely, and I think convincingly, objected to as mislocating the sortal-relativity.⁴ The idea is that the criteria of identity should be associated with the terms related by identity locutions, rather than those locutions. I agree that the most interesting issues concern the relations between the way identity claims interact with the constellation of criteria of identity, sortals semantically governed by them, and terms that fall under those sortals. I think that putting the

---

2. I will use the traditional vocabulary of "criteria," subject to the proviso that there is no implication that the criteria are explicit, that there must be statable principles in the vicinity. Talk of "criteria of identity" is talk about aspects of the practice of using count nouns.

3. P. T. Geach, "Identity," *Review of Metaphysics* 21 (1967): 3–12; reprinted in P. T. Geach, *Logic Matters* (Oxford: Blackwell Publishers, 1972). Also P. T. Geach, "Ontological Relativity and Relative Identity," in M. Munitz, ed., *Logic and Ontology* (New York: New York University Press, 1973).

4. For instance, J. Perry, "The Same F," *The Philosophical Review* 64 (1970): 181–200; A. Gupta, *The Logic of Common Nouns* (New Haven, CT: Yale University Press, 1980).

issue of the supposed sortal-relativity of identity at center stage has in many ways bent this discussion out of shape. It has in any case become clear that the need to relativize identity does not follow from the claim that prompted it. This is the claim that there can be individuals a and b that are Fs and are the *same* F, but are also Gs, and are *different* Gs. Here F and G might be 'person' and 'passenger' or 'surperson' and 'person'. It is this claim on which I want to focus. It is accepted by many (such as Gupta and Gibbard) who reject the conclusion Geach draws from it.[5] Can the same thing (I'll use the pseudosortal here so as not to prejudice important issues) in fact fall under two sortals used according to divergent criteria of identity?

Let us look at the question more closely. Geach's view can usefully be codified in the form of two claims:[6]

D) '$a = b$' is an incomplete expression. One should, in order to complete it, say the same *what* a and b are. A full identity statement is always of the form '$a =_F b$' (read: a is the same F as b').

R) It is possible for a to be the same F as b, while not being the same G as b.

(This would be put by Geach, in accordance with (D), as $a =_F b$ and Ga and Gb and $a \neq_G b$.) As just indicated, I take the upshot of the (extensive) literature in this area to be that (R) has emerged as the fundamental issue, with (D) taking its place as one optional diagnosis and analysis of how (R) could be true. The key issue here is that for (R) to be true, a and b must be terms that can fall under two sortals whose criteria of identity diverge. On this account, what we could call "strong cross-sortal identities" must be intelligible, and some of them must be true. The qualification 'strong' indicates that the sortals in question are associated with different criteria of identity.

---

5. Gupta, *The Logic of Common Nouns*; A. Gibbard, "Contingent Identity," *Journal of Philosophical Logic* 4(2) (1975): 187–221.

6. The names are due to D. Wiggins, *Identity and Spatio-Temporal Continuity* (Oxford: Blackwell Publishers, 1967); D. Wiggins, *Sameness and Substance* (Oxford: Blackwell Publishers, 1980). I follow Zemach's formulation here; see E. Zemach, "In Defense of Relative Identity," *Philosophical Studies* 26 (1974): 207–218.

The criteria of identity are what are used to count *F*s and *G*s. If the criteria of identity are the same, only weak cross-sortal identities are underwritten. Thus the inference:

1) All kittens are cats,
2) There are at least 10 million kittens in the U.S.,

therefore

3) There are at least 10 million cats in the U.S.,

is a good one. The difference between 'kitten' and 'cat' is one of criteria of application: everything 'kitten' applies to, 'cat' applies to, but not *vice versa*. But they have the same criteria of identity. If *a* and *b* are the same kitten (different kittens), then *a* and *b* are the same cat (different cats). And if *a* and *b* are the same cat (different cats), and they are kittens, then they are the same kitten (different kittens). Identities of the form

This kitten = This cat

where both expressions refer to *a* are *weak* cross-sortal identities. That is why the inference goes through.

4) All passengers are people,
5) US Airways flew at least 59 million passengers last year,

therefore

6) US Airways flew at least 59 million people last year,

is not a good one. As with 'kitten' and 'cat', the criteria of application of 'passenger' apply to only a subset of things the criteria of application of 'person' do. But if *a* and *b* are the same person and they are both passengers, it does not follow that they are the same passenger. Identities of the form

7) This passenger = This person

are *strong* cross-sortal identities. That is why the inference does not go through.

The principal difficulty with embracing (R) is that it stands in tension with the principle of the indiscernibility of identicals: the claim

LL) If $a = b$, then for all properties P, Pa iff Pb.[7]

Let us name the passenger who is Bob flying from Pittsburgh to San Francisco on that day "Procyon," and the passenger who is Bob flying back from San Francisco to Pittsburgh on the next day "Lotor." Then consider the property

P_1) ... would still have existed if Bob had never flown from Pittsburgh to San Francisco.

Bob has that property. Procyon does not (assuming "this passenger," used to fix the reference of the name, individuates at least as finely as "this person traveling on this itinerary").[8] Indeed, the property

P_2) ... = Lotor

is a property that, on the assumption of the intelligibility and possible truth of strong cross-sortal identities, Bob has and Procyon does not. These observations bring that assumption into conflict with the indiscernibility of identicals, (LL).

Are weak cross-sortal identities any better off? Supposing that kittens must be cats younger than one year, doesn't

P_3) ... would still exist after one year of life

---

7. The designation 'LL' reflects the fact that the indiscernibility of identicals is one-half—the more plausible half—of Leibniz's Law. The other half, the identity of indiscernibles, is plausible only in the context of strong auxiliary hypotheses concerning the expressive power of the language in which the properties are specified.

8. Not all such subjunctive or counterfactuals involving Procyon are false. Procyon *would* still have existed if Bob's flight from Pittsburgh to San Francisco had taken off ten minutes later than it actually did. Other issues, such as what to say in case that flight had been cancelled and Bob rebooked on another airline, are less clear—but matter only to airlines.

distinguish this cat, whom we have named Archie, from this kitten, whom we have named Paws? No. On the supposition that kitten-cat identities are only weakly cross-sortal, that is, that 'kitten' and 'cat' have the same criteria of identity and only different (nested) criteria of application, when I say "I hereby name this kitten (= this young cat) 'Paws'," I am naming the *cat*, who is now young. The fact that the reference-fixing designation quickly fails to be true of him does not alter the reference that was fixed—no more in this case than for any other name. (Other adjectivally restricted sortals, such as "red car," work the same way: the restriction applies to the criteria of application, while the criteria of identity go with the unrestricted sortal. If I painted this red car green it would be the same car, even though it would no longer be a red car.)

It will be helpful at this point to consider another sort of example, adapted from Gibbard.[9] Suppose a mold is made in the shape of a giant man, and in it plasticine clay is mixed up from calcium carbonate, petroleum jelly, and stearic acid. A lump of plasticine clay in the shape of a giant man results. At this point someone introduces the name 'Goliath' to refer to the resulting statue, and also introduces the name 'Lumpl' to refer to the lump of modeling clay. Some time later, both are incinerated and destroyed. We are to think of the two, the statue and the lump of clay, as having come into existence simultaneously, and going out of existence simultaneously. Should we say that they are not only spatiotemporally coincident, but identical: that Goliath = Lumpl? If so, that is a strong cross-sortal identity. For 'statue' and 'lump of clay' have quite different criteria of identity. That difference manifests itself in the subjunctive-dispositional properties that distinguish them. Lumpl, but not Goliath, has the property

P_4) ... would not have been destroyed had it been reshaped into a sphere.

Lumps can survive radical reshaping, but statues cannot.

Because by definition the sortals involved in strong cross-sortal identities are associated with different criteria of identity, the items identified will always be distinguished by their possession of different subjunctive-dispositional properties: those that express the different conditions under which

---

9. Gibbard, "Contingent Identity."

they would remain Ks, or would remain the same K. Another way of putting that point is that strong cross-sortal identities are always *contingent* identities. Even if Lumpl and Goliath are identical, they might not have been. For instance had Lumpl been reshaped into a sphere, it would not then have been identical to the statue Goliath. Assertions of strong cross-sortal identities violate the indiscernibility of identicals—but in a distinctive way. We could say that the lump of clay Lumpl and the statue Goliath, or the passenger Procyon and the person Bob, during their coincidence share all their *actual* properties, differing only in some of their *modal* properties.

Notice that Kripke rejects this possibility. If the terms involved in an identity claim are modally rigid designators, as he takes names to be (we could just stipulate that the names we have introduced in these examples are abbreviations of descriptions that have been modally rigidified by applying Kaplan's 'dthat' operator, and so pick out the same things in all worlds), then if the identity claim is true, it is necessarily true. Identity claims can be contingently true only if they are read *de dicto*: Barack Obama is the 44th U.S. President. He might not have been (that identity is only contingently true), in the sense that the *dictum* "Barack Obama is the 44th U.S. President" might not have been true. But read *de re*, we use the description "the 44th U.S. President" to pick out a person in *this* world, and then follow *him* through other worlds. In effect, my argument above was that, so long as they are read *de re*, cross-sortal identities involving terms falling under phase sortals (and indeed any members of the genus of adjectivally restricted sortals of which they are a species) and terms falling under the sortals of which they pick out phases are not merely contingently true. On Kripke's understanding, the use of names and demonstratives ("this very man") enforces the *de re* reading. Although he does not draw explicitly this conclusion, ruling out contingent *de re* identity has the consequence of ruling out the truth of *any* strong cross-sortal identity claims.

Who is right: Gibbard, who thinks that "Lumpl = Goliath" is true, or Kripke, who claims it cannot be? Gibbard constructs his example using proper names for the clay and the statue, rather than just descriptions, to show that Kripke is wrong at least in thinking that understanding proper names as modally rigid (so forcing *de re* readings of the identity claims) by itself settles the issue. We have put ourselves in a position to see that what is really at issue is the intelligibility and truth of strong cross-sortal *de re* identities. What matters is the sortals, not the modal rigidity of the expressions that fall under them. If true, those strong cross-sortal *de re* identities can be true only contingently. The intelligibility of such identities depends, in turn, on restricting the principle of the indiscernibility of identicals so that it does not apply to subjunctive-dispositional properties. For such properties will always distinguish the terms of strong cross-sortal identities.

2. Empirical Descriptive Vocabulary and Subjunctive-Dispositional Vocabulary

We have reached the crux of the issue. In order to be entitled to assert strong cross-sortal identities, one must distinguish between subjunctive-dispositional properties—those having to do with what *would* be the case *if*...—and some base of nonmodal properties. For one must exclude the former from the scope of the indiscernibility of identicals, arguing that that principle applies only to properties that do *not* depend on what *would* happen if.... The question I want to raise is whether such a distinction can be made out.

Of course, the idea of restricting the applicability of Leibniz's Law to a privileged subset of properties is an old one. The question of how to make sense of the possibility of the persistence of objects through change is a special case of understanding criteria of identity—where the index of variation is time, rather than possible world. Aristotle responds by distinguishing essential from accidental properties. In effect, he suggests that identicals need only be indiscernible with respect to essential properties. The dog barking now can be the same dog as the silent dog earlier, if whether it is barking or silent is not essential to its being the dog that it is.

Thought of in the most general terms, the question is whether there is, and whether there must be, a distinction between properties P for which the inference

LL1) For Ks a and b, if Pa and ~Pb, then a and b are not the same K,

does hold, and those for which it does *not*.[10] (LL1) follows from (LL). We can call the claim that there can be no properties for which (LL) does not hold "identity absolutism."

---

10. A different set of properties would support the inference from bs not having P to bs not being a K (some K or other) at all.

Notice that it does not follow from (LL1) *failing* to hold of some kind K and property P that possession of P is *accidental* to being the same K, in the sense that whether or not one possesses that property makes no difference to being the same K. For if, as we should, we take seriously the nonmonotonicity of the material inferences involved, it could be that although (LL1) is true for K and P_1, it is not true for K and the conjunctive property $P_1\&P_2$. That failure of (LL1) is compatible in turn with (LL1) holding for K and $P_1\&P_2\&P_3$, failing again for $P_1\&P_2\&P_3\&P_4$, and so on in a never-ending oscillating hierarchy. For this reason, the presence of a distinction for kind K between properties for which (LL1) holds and those for which it does not does not have the consequence that there are properties which are accidental to being the same K in the stronger sense. Making that inference is not taking seriously the nonmonotonicity of material inference.

For the temporal case, perdurantism (which sees objects as having temporal parts analogous to their spatial parts) and endurantism (which sees objects as fully present at all times at which they exist, and relativizes property-possession to times) in their original, classic forms as Lewis formulated them are contrasting ways of retaining the *un*restricted applicability of the indiscernibility of identicals (as, not surprisingly, is Lewis's own counterpart theory for the modal case).[11] Beyond that, issues of how to understand identity of physical objects through time raises issues over and above those raised by modally involved properties—though not, to be sure, independent of them. I will not here enter into the intricacies of these debates, nor try to say how the hard line I am arguing for in the modal case bears on the temporal case.

Indeed, I am not going to attempt to assess or adjudicate the comparative merits of the grand strategies of holding onto the indiscernibility of identicals in unrestricted form and restricting it somehow. On the one hand, treating (LL) as *defining* identity provides a particularly clear concept to work with, one that yields the right answers in a number of puzzle cases. On the other hand, *some* restrictions on (LL) seem evidently to be in order. Intentional properties, regarding what people believe or how their other intentional states (such as desires, hopes, and so on) can be specified, are cardinal examples. This

---

11. David Lewis, "Survival and Identity," in Amelie Rorty (ed.), *The Identities of Persons* (Berkeley: University of California Press, 1976), pp. 117–140. Reprinted with significant postscripts in Lewis's *Philosophical Papers*, vol. I (Oxford: Oxford University Press, 1983).

point is enforced by considering Church-style iterations of them. "No-one has ever doubted that everyone who believes that ⌜Pa⌝ believes that ⌜Qa⌝" is a context that will distinguish almost any lexically distinct substituends for P and Q. In effect, what such contexts do is enforce *de dicto* readings of the corresponding identities.[12] What I am arguing for is only that there are no contingently true *de re* identities. My reasons are quite different from Kripke's.

What I am going to argue for is what might be called "*modal* identity absolutism." This is the claim that we should understand the indiscernibility of identicals as including within its scope *modal* properties, both implicit and explicit. What I want to contest is the viability of any version of the non-absolutist strategy that relies on distinguishing modal, subjunctive, or dispositional properties as a special class for which Leibniz's Law does *not* hold. There is an important distinction between property-specifying (predicative) vocabulary that is *explicitly* modal and vocabulary that is not explicitly modal. By "explicitly modal" vocabulary I mean vocabulary such as modal operators ('possible', 'necessary', 'contingent', . . .), the use of subjunctive mood ('could', 'would', 'might', . . .), and dispositional terms ('fragile', 'rigid', 'irascible'), which would be explicated by appeal to subjunctives and modal vocabulary ("fragile things are those which would shatter if lightly struck," "irascible people are those who would become angry if provoked").[13] One key point I want to make is that even vocabulary that is *not* explicitly modal—in particular, ordinary empirical descriptive (OED) vocabulary such as 'mass', 'cat', 'copper', and 'red'—must be understood as *implicitly* modal. By "implicitly modal vocabulary" I mean vocabulary whose applicability entails the truth of some modal, subjunctive, or dispositional claims.

We can start by considering a particularly clear case. The concept of (Newtonian) mass essentially, and not just accidentally, is articulated by necessary connections to the concepts force and acceleration. Describing an object as having a nonzero mass commits one to the claim that (under suitable background conditions) it *would* accelerate if a nonzero force *were*

---

12. The detailed account of how *de dicto* and *de re* ascriptions of propositional attitude work that I offer in Chapter 8 of *Making It Explicit* (Cambridge, MA: Harvard University Press, 1994) provides the theoretical tools for explicating the connection between *de dicto* readings and propositional attitude ascribing locutions that this claim relies on.

13. I have argued in Chapter 4 that some important kinds of modal vocabulary can be introduced—its use specified—entirely in terms of the use of vocabulary that is not explicitly modal.

applied to it, and that if it *had* accelerated, a force *would* have been applied to it. To have a nonzero mass *is, inter alia,* to be disposed to accelerate if and only if a nonzero force is applied. Applying this bit of OED vocabulary to something in *this* world entails claims about what *would* happen in other worlds. If those subjunctive-dispositional claims are not true, neither is the claim about the possession of mass in this world.

In much the same way, describing a coin as *copper* commits one to claims about what *would* happen *were* one to heat it to 1085° C (it would melt), and what *would* happen *were* one to rub it with a sharp diamond (it would be scratched), and a myriad of other such subjunctive-dispositional claims. Nor is being implicitly modal or modally involved, in the sense of having subjunctive-dispositional necessary conditions, a special feature of scientific or theoretical concepts. Cat and red also have such consequences of application. To be a cat is essentially, and not just accidentally, to be something that *would* die if deprived of oxygen, food, or water for long enough, if struck by lightning, if crushed by having a large lump of clay dropped on it, and so on. Red things *would* reflect light at around 7000 angstroms *if* suitably illuminated.

This thought is a core insight of Kant's, and forms the basis of his response to Hume. As he might have put it, lawful connections are already implicit in the use of ordinary empirical descriptive concepts. That is why we cannot be in the predicament Hume thought we were in: understanding those concepts perfectly well, but having thereby no rational grip at all on what is made explicit by modal or dispositional concepts, no understanding of subjunctive (including counterfactual) inferences. Sellars codified the point in a slogan he used as the title of one of his essays: "Concepts as Involving Laws, and Inconceivable without Them." I call the claim that *every* empirical descriptive concept has subjunctive-dispositional consequences, which accordingly serve as necessary conditions of its correct applicability, the "Kant-Sellars thesis about modality." According to it, there are no empirical descriptive properties that are *modally insulated*, in the sense that they can apply in one possible world regardless of what is true in any other.

3. Modal Identity Absolutism and Its Consequences

The next claim I want to make is that the modal Kant-Sellars (KS) thesis is incompatible with restricting the applicability of Leibniz's Law to nonmodal, i.e. modally insulated, properties, in a sense that restricts the indiscernibility required for identity to properties that are *not* dispositional or subjunctively committive. The reason is straightforward: since all empirical descriptive predicates have subjunctive-dispositional consequences, indiscernibility with respect to empirical descriptive properties requires indiscernibility with respect to all the subjunctive-dispositional (SD) properties they entail.[14] We *have* to take SD properties into account when assessing the indiscernibility of two putatively identical things, because their applicability is a necessary condition of the applicability of ordinary empirical descriptive vocabulary. So if, as everyone surely must admit, identity requires indiscernibility with respect to OED vocabulary, then according to the modal KS thesis, it requires also indiscernibility with respect to SD vocabulary.[15]

If that is all right, then there can be no true strongly cross-sortal identities. For such identities by definition relate terms falling under sortals associated with *different* criteria of identity. The difference in criteria of identity ensures that the putatively identical items will have different subjunctive, counterfactual, and dispositional properties. For they will remain the *same* K (or indeed, a K at all), under different circumstances. Thus, if the clay *were* reshaped into a sphere, the statue Goliath, but not the lump of clay Lumpl, would be destroyed. If, as the modal Kant-Sellars thesis tells us, we cannot exclude such properties from the scope of Leibniz's Law in assessing identities, on the principle that it does not apply to subjunctive-dispositional properties, then we must conclude that in the actual world in which, by hypothesis, they coincide spatiotemporally, Goliath is not identical to Lumpl. If we call whatever intimate relation they *do* stand in "material

---

14. Is this perhaps an antecedently specifiable proper subset of subjunctive-dispositional properties generally? No. For any particular SD predicate, it is possible to construct a predicate that is nondispositional in the ordinary sense (since I am denying that there are any properties that are "nondispositional" in the sense of modally insulated) whose correct applicability entails the correct applicability of the given dispositional one.

15. As I said of this argument in Chapter 1, I think this is a strong argument. But it does not rule out in principle the possibility of partitioning modally involved predicates into two classes X and Y, insisting that only those from class X are referentially transparent (indiscernible with respect to identity, within the scope of the intersubstitution license made by identity claims), and then claiming further that some strongly cross-sortal identities come out true because the predicates/properties that modally distinguish the sortals include only those from class Y. All I can do is point out how demanding the criteria of adequacy are for such an attempted partition, downstream of the modal Kant-Sellars thesis.

constitution" of the statue by the clay, then we must conclude that (as the slogan has it) "Material constitution is not identity."

Nor can any surperson be a person. Geach emphasizes that the criteria of application of 'person' and 'surperson' are the same: surpersons *are* persons. Only the criteria of identity are different (Gupta agrees). So something, say, me, *is* both this person and this surperson. That is a strongly cross-sortal identity. Because of the difference in criteria of identity, the person and the surperson have different subjunctive properties. If I, Bob, a person, *were* to legally change my last name, I *would* still be the same person, but *would* no longer be the same surperson as my father. If I became single-named, hence not surnamed (as is a fashion among some celebrities), I would no longer be *any* surperson, never mind the same one. But I would still be a person, and the same one. So Bob the person has the property *would survive loss of surname,* which Bob the surperson does not have. The strongly cross-sortal identity is at most contingently true. Contingent identities are intelligibly true only if the scope of Leibniz's Law is restricted so as not to rule out discernibility of identicals by subjunctive-dispositional properties. But the modal Kant-Sellars thesis tells us that requires a discrimination that cannot be made, since even paradigmatically "nonmodal" properties are *implicitly* modal, in the sense their instantiation entails the instantiation of *explicitly* subjunctive properties.

The same reasoning underwrites the conclusion that no passenger is identical with any person. As counterintuitive as it might sound, passengers are not people (which fact may serve as an explanation, if not a backhanded justification, at least conceptually, for the way airlines treat their passengers). The passenger Procyon and the person could be at most contingently identical, since if Bob *had* missed the plane, he *would* not have been identical to *that* passenger, Procyon. But he would still have been identical with the person, Bob. Property (P1) above discriminates Bob from the passenger Procyon. The modal KS thesis prohibits us from excluding such properties from the scope of the indiscernibility of identicals, so the person and the passenger cannot be identical. I suppose that passengers are something like *roles* that persons can play: a distinctive sort of thing that can be true of them.

The modal Kant-Sellars thesis commits us to modal identity absolutism. This is the claim that the set of properties with respect to which identicals must be indiscernible must include explicitly modal (subjunctive, including counterfactual, and dispositional) properties if it includes ordinary empirical descriptive properties. That is because the modal KS thesis tells us that ordinary empirical descriptive vocabulary is *implicitly* modal, in the sense that it *entails* the truth of claims formulated in SD vocabulary. Modal identity absolutism in turn entails that the only identities that can be contingently true are identities read *de dicto*. (We can force the *de re* reading by using proper names, demonstratives, or other rigid designators, or by using rigidifying operators such as Kaplan's 'dthat'.) Because strongly cross-sortal identities (whose terms can, in all the controversial cases, be rigidified) by definition relate terms falling under sortals with different criteria of identity, they could only be true contingently, and are accordingly ruled out by modal identity absolutism.

This line of argument also has significant consequences for a certain kind of project in reconstructive metaphysics. A tempting strategy, adopted by Lewis, is to turn sortal placeholders such as 'object' into genuine individuating sortals by stipulating a class of base sortals and extending it mereologically. So one might take as the base sortals some collection of kinds of subatomic particles—perhaps with the idea that they play a privileged role in explanations in fundamental physics. One stipulates that all of these (everything that falls under those base sortals) count as objects. Then, in the recursion clause, one stipulates that the class of objects is to be the smallest set that comprises all these basic objects, and all of their mereological sums or fusions. These are then taken to be all the objects there are or can be. The base sortals specify how to identify and individuate the mereological ur-elements, and mereological theory then tells us how to identify and individuate their sums. This procedure provides a clear and definite sense to the term 'object'—we might call them "mereological objects" on that base—turning it into (replacing it with) a genuine individuating sortal with criteria of identity as well as criteria of application. It then becomes possible for the first time to be entitled to talk about possible worlds as though they were relational structures of the model-theoretic sort. For now it makes sense to think of them as having *domains:* the set of all objects in that world.

So far, so good. The argument that leads from the KS-thesis about modality, through Leibniz's Law, to a modal identity absolutism that denies the truth of any strongly cross-sortal identities entails that *whatever* the mereological base is (so long as it is a proper subset of the sortals in play in natural language), almost *no* identities between mereological objects and ordinary objects will turn out to be true. The domains of possible worlds construed according to this mereological strategy will not include *any* of the ordinary or scientific kinds of things we think of our world as comprising. Persons are not mereological sums of subatomic particles, nor are cats, coins, rocks, trees, clouds, molecules, genes, viruses, cells, most kinds of artifacts,. . . . For all these kinds of things have criteria of identity that are radically different from those of mereological sums of particles. They are accordingly subjects of quite different subjunctive-dispositional properties. Mereological sums are not altered by disruptions of spatiotemporal contiguity: the sum is the same mereological sum no matter *where* its parts are. That is not true of *any* of the kinds on the list of ordinary thing-kinds I offered above. Again, all of those ordinary and scientific kinds of things would retain their identity upon *some* substitutions of parts for similar parts. I would not be a different person had I had only one radish in last night's salad, instead of two. Corresponding claims hold for all kinds of living things, and for artifacts. Perhaps we should not say that something would have been the same molecule if one of its electrons had been swapped for a different one, but things of almost every kind that are made of molecules would survive substitution of one of its molecules for another of the same kind. Mereological sums do not.

One might think of fundamental ontology as a discipline that is constitutionally committed to biting bullets of this sort. One decides on a privileged vocabulary (for instance, a set of base sortals and the mereological apparatus for elaborating them), Ramsifies theories in any further target vocabulary, and looks for the "closest realizers" specifiable in that privileged vocabulary of the functional roles that result from the Ramsification. The modal identity absolutism that we have seen is a consequence of the modal Kant-Sellars thesis need have no quarrel with such a procedure. Its strictures extend only to forbidding confusing the relation between such realizers and the things falling under the target sortals that got Ramsified with *identity*. (The case is analogous to that of material constitution, the clay being a kind of realizer of the statue.) Ontological reduction to a privileged vocabulary construed in terms of identities relating items governed by sortals of the base and target vocabularies will almost always be strongly cross-sortal, hence ruled out by modal identity absolutism. I discussed this issue more fully in Chapter 1.

The modal Kant-Sellars thesis reveals a pragmatically mediated semantic dependence of predicates Quine taught us to think of as *extensional* on predicates he taught us to think of as *intensional*. For the claim is that *all* extensional empirical predicates have subjunctive-dispositional, hence intensional, consequences, which accordingly provide necessary conditions for the applicability of the extensional predicates. The underlying pragmatic dependence is that an essential aspect of *grasping, understanding*, or mastering the *use* of OED vocabulary is grasping, understanding, or mastering subjunctive and counterfactual reasoning in which that vocabulary occurs. To know what cats or copper are requires knowing at least something about how they *would* behave under various circumstances: what follows from being a cat or made of copper, when that claim is conjoined with various auxiliary hypotheses, independently of whether one takes those auxiliary hypotheses to be true.

This much is not news to proponents of intensional semantics. What is grasped or understood when one knows how to use a predicate must include at least its intension. ("At least" because the fact that *intentional* predicates *do* fail the indiscernibility of identicals shows that there is *more* to what is cognitively *grasped* in deploying vocabulary than just the *intension*.) But taking seriously the pragmatically mediated semantic dependencies between vocabularies asserted by the modal KS thesis does oblige us to distinguish between two concepts of extensional predicate that the tradition for which Quine speaks runs together. The first is the idea that a sentential context, a (possibly complex) predicate P is extensional just in case all that matters to its applicability is the identity of the object to which it is applied, regardless of *how* it is referred to. It is the requirement that

1) P is extensional$_1$ iff if Pt and $t=t'$, then Pt'.

This is just the condition that P falls within the scope of the indiscernibility of identicals. The other idea of extensionality is that predicates are extensional if their applicability depends only on what is true at a single index, paradigmatically a possible world, and not at all on what happens at other values of that index. So, the thought is we only need to look at *this* world to tell whether something is a cat or has a mass of 5 kilograms, but we need to look at other possible worlds to tell whether it is fragile or water-soluble.

EXT2) P is extensional$_2$ iff whether Pt is true at world w depends only on the facts at w. Differences in the facts at any other world w' are irrelevant to whether Pt is true at w.

This is the sense of 'extensional' that matters for the contrast with *intensional* predicates, whose applicability at any given index can depend on the whole *function* from indices to extensions.

Although Quine would not have countenanced the way I have articulated the second sense, he clearly thought that (EXT1) and (EXT2) amount to the same condition—that they are at least extensionally equivalent (in the sense of EXT1). For his reason for rejecting appeal to predicates that are *not* extensional$_2$ is that they are not extensional$_1$. He takes extensionality$_1$ ("referential transparency") to be the hallmark of comprehensibility.[16] The good thought that Leibniz's Law provides our best grip on the notion of identity is a good reason for such an attitude. We can see, however, that in the context of the modal Kant-Sellars thesis, subjunctive-dispositional vocabulary is extensional$_1$ without being for that reason extensional$_2$. The modal KS thesis shows that the idea, at the core of Quine's thought, of a purely extensional$_2$ language that is autonomous—that is, that could be a language game one played though one played no other—is an ultimately incoherent fantasy. It does not follow that the idea of an autonomous language that is extensional$_1$ is incoherent. Nor does the modal KS thesis in principle threaten the semantic strategy of defining intensions in terms of extensions, as functions from indices to extensions. One must just deploy this fundamental conceptual machinery of intensional semantics in the context of a full appreciation of the *pragmatic* dependence of the use of vocabulary that is extensional$_1$ on what is made explicit by the use of vocabulary that is *not* extensional$_2$.

One might, of course, consider these radical conclusions as a *reductio ad absurdum* of the line of argument that leads to them—so arguing by *modus tollens* rather than *modus ponens*. As far as I can see, to do so requires rejecting the modal Kant-Sellars thesis. That is the principal piece I have added to the puzzle about sortals and identity as classically conceived, to

---

16. "I find extensionality necessary, indeed, though not sufficient, for my full understanding of a theory." W. V. O. Quine, *From Stimulus to Science* (Cambridge, MA: Harvard University Press, 1995), p. 90.

yield the modal identity absolutism that in turn commits one to the potentially objectionably radical conclusions. But I take the KS thesis to codify a deep insight about how what is made explicit by alethic modal vocabulary is implicit in and fundamental to the use of any autonomous vocabulary whatsoever. Offering any empirical description, attributing any empirical property, involves commitments as to what *would* happen to what is so described under various circumstances: what would be true of it *if* various other claims *were* true. What distinguishes description from mere labeling is precisely that *circumstances* of appropriate application are paired with *consequences* of such application. Thus describing something places it in a space of implications, which inferentially articulate the content of the description. And those inferences always include subjunctive ones: inferences that involve collateral premises or auxiliary hypotheses not drawn exclusively from one's current commitments. One who understood *none* of the subjunctive implications one was committing oneself to by applying the terms 'mass' or 'cat' could not count as grasping the concepts they express. If that is right, though, one cannot consistently restrict the properties with respect to which identicals must be indiscernible to properties that are "nonmodal" in the sense of being modally insulated: their possession has no consequences for how things are in possible worlds other than the one in which they are exhibited. For there are no such properties. Perhaps we could introduce predicates stipulated to behave like this—and in that way, quite unlike those of our actual languages-in-use. Even so, there could be no autonomous language—one that could be used though no other was—whose use consisted *only* in applying predicates expressing such properties.

In Chapter 1 I argued that the scientific naturalism of the *scientia mensura*, which Sellars proposed in articulating a contemporary version of Kant's phenomena/noumena distinction, essentially depends on the truth of identities relating items referred to in the vocabulary of the manifest image and items referred to in the vocabulary of the scientific image. These will almost always have to be strongly cross-sortal identities. In this chapter I have argued from premises central to Sellars's own thought about the categorial status of alethic modal concepts—in particular from what I have been calling the "modal Kant-Sellars thesis"—that such cross-sortal identities are never true. If all that is right, then there is a fundamental tension between the two big Kantian ideas that I have argued structure Sellars's systematic thought: what he made of the Kantian idea of the categories, as concepts articulating essential features of the framework within which empirical description and explanation are possible, and what he made of the transcendental distinction between appearance and reality, in terms of the manifest and scientific images. If and insofar as these two lines of thought do collide, I have been urging that what Sellars made of the idea of the categories is the one to hold onto.

CHAPTER SEVEN

Sellars's Metalinguistic Expressivist Nominalism

1. Introduction

The five years from 1958 through 1962 were extraordinarily productive ones for Wilfrid Sellars. His monumental "Counterfactuals, Dispositions, and the Causal Modalities," appearing in 1958, was a suitable follow-up to *Empiricism and the Philosophy of Mind* (which had been delivered as three lectures at the University of London in 1956).[1] Sellars never further developed the expressivist approach to alethic modality that he sketched in that paper, apparently having taken the ideas there as far as he could.[2] In that same year, he delivered two lectures at Yale, under the title "Grammar and Existence: A Preface to Ontology," which announced an expressivist, nominalist project in ontology that he then pursued in two other equally remarkable and original essays: "Naming and Saying" and "Abstract Entities."[3] Jumblese, dot-quotes, and distributive singular terms, the conceptual tools he developed and deployed in those essays to respond to the challenges to his

---

1. "Counterfactuals, Dispositions, and the Causal Modalities," in Herbert Feigl, Michael Scriven, and Grover Maxwell (eds.), *Minnesota Studies in the Philosophy of Science*, vol. II: *Concepts, Theories, and the Mind-Body Problem* (Minneapolis: University of Minnesota Press, 1958), p. 225–308. Hereafter CDCM. "Empiricism and the Philosophy of Mind" is reprinted in Robert B. Brandom (ed.), *Empiricism and the Philosophy of Mind* (Harvard University Press, 1997). Hereafter *EPM*.

2. I assess how far he got and speculate about the difficulties that could have prevented further progress, in Chapter 5.

3. "Grammar and Existence: A Preface to Ontology" (1958; hereafter GE), "Naming and Saying" (1962; hereafter NS), and "Abstract Entities" (1963; hereafter AE) are all reprinted in Kevin Scharp and Robert Brandom (eds.), *In the Space of Reasons: Selected Essays of Wilfrid Sellars* (Harvard University Press, 2007).

approach to universals he had identified in GE, were to remain at the center of Sellars's philosophical enterprise for the rest of his life. Taken as a whole, these three essays provide an unusually detailed picture of the philosophical process through which Sellars progressed from an initial characterization of problems whose solutions he could not see clearly to the introduction of novel conceptual machinery that solved those problems to his durable satisfaction.

Sellars's point of departure is a view Carnap had put forward in *The Logical Syntax of Language:* to say that triangularity is a property is a way of saying in the material mode (the object language) what is said more perspicuously in the formal mode (in a certain kind of metalanguage) as "'triangular' is a monadic predicate."[4] This is the idea he is committed to making work in the three essays on nominalism. What Sellars calls "classifying contexts" are uses of ontological-categorial vocabulary, paradigmatically common nouns for ontological categories such as 'property' and 'kind' (and their genus, 'universal'), the property and kind names that fall under such common nouns ('triangularity', 'lionhood'), and the higher order relations those properties and kinds are taken to stand in to their instances (such as 'exemplification' in "Anything that is triangular exemplifies triangularity"). The Carnapian idea is that vocabulary of these sorts is covertly *metalinguistic.* Its use appears to tell us something about the world: what kinds (ontological categories) of things are in it. There are not only particulars, but also their properties and kinds, related to those particulars by the distinctive relation of exemplification. But actually the claim is that the information conveyed by the use of such ontological vocabulary concerns the syntactic form of language or thought, and is not about the world talked or thought about. "Lionhood is a kind" really means "'Lion' is a common noun (sortal expression)."

We have already seen this sort of metalinguistic expressivism as the key idea behind Sellars's treatment of modality, and I have claimed that it is at the center of what he made of Kant's conception of the pure concepts of the understanding more generally. The issue of how such an expressivism relates to a corresponding realism, which we saw in Chapter 5 as a central

---

4. Like Sellars, I will use "triangular" as short for " . . . is triangular," where confusion is not likely to result.

issue for the understanding of modality, arises here, too. In this chapter, I consider the sophisticated way in which Sellars extended this line of thought to vocabulary that expresses ontological categories. The paradigm for Sellars is terms that purport to pick out universals.

Adopting a metalinguistic species of nominalism about universals would have obvious attractions to those already of a nominalistic bent (perhaps due to a taste for desert landscapes). Is there any reason that those not already hagridden by nominalistic commitments should take it seriously? One potentially powerful argument is that one who knows how to use predicates such as " . . . is triangular" or common nouns such as "lion" already knows how to do everything one needs to know how to do to use abstract terms such as 'triangular' and 'lionhood', and categorizing vocabulary such as 'property' and 'kind'. Sellars says:

> [T]o know how to use singular terms ending in '-ity' is to know that they are formed from adjectives; while to know how to use the common noun 'quality' is (roughly) to know that its well-formed singular sentences are of the form '—is a quality' where the blank is appropriately filled by an abstract noun. (That the parallel points about '-keit' and 'Qualität' in German are genuine parallels is clear.)
>
> Thus, while my ability to use 'triangular' understandingly involves an ability to use sentences of the form '—is triangular' in reporting and describing matters of physical, extralinguistic fact, my ability to use 'triangularity' understandingly involves no new dimension of the reporting and describing of extralinguistic fact—no scrutiny of abstract entities—but constitutes, rather, my grasp of the adjectival role of 'triangular'.[5]

'Triangularity' and 'lionhood' are singular terms formed by nominalizing adjectives and sortal common nouns, and 'property', 'quality', and 'kind' are categorizing sortals under which those nominalized adjectives and common nouns fall. Of course this consideration is not immediately decisive, since we can imagine a Bergmannian language in which one first learned to respond

---

5. GE §XIV.

to triangular things by applying "... exemplifies triangularity," and only later, on that basis, learned to use "... is triangular." Nonetheless, it seems clear that one must begin by using expressions that are equivalent to predicates (adjectives): ground-level classifications. Even in the Bergmannian context, higher-order ontological classifiers such as 'property' will still be sortals that apply to nominalizations of these.

In GE, Sellars identifies two major objections that any metalinguistic nominalism about properties and kinds (universals) of this shape must face. The first is that ontologically categorizing statements such as "Triangularity is a property" do not mention linguistic expressions, while their proposed paraphrases, such as "'Triangular' is a monadic predicate" do. This difference becomes clear when we think about translating both the ontologically categorizing sentence and its explicitly syntactic paraphrase into another language. "'Triangular' ist ein Prädikat" and "'Dreieckig' ist ein Prädikat" are not equivalent. Which one is supposed to be the correct paraphrase of "Dreieckigkeit ist eine Eigenschaft," which translates "Triangularity is a property"? The difference between the material mode statement and its supposed paraphrase into the formal mode is even more striking when we consider counterfactuals involving them. Presumably, "Triangularity is a property" would still have been true even if the English language had never developed. Not so "'Triangular' is a predicate."[6] If the claim that "'Triangularity' is a property" is "covertly metalinguistic" or "quasi syntactic" in character is to be sustainable in the face of these facts, the qualifications "covertly" and "quasi-" will have to be explicated in a way that avoids these consequences.[7] This consideration is exactly parallel to the one we saw arise in Sellars's metalinguistic treatment of modality.

The second objection Sellars considers is, in effect, that metalinguistic nominalism would be at best a half-hearted nominalism. For it does not avoid ontological commitment to properties (or universals, more generally). Rather, it eliminates nonlinguistic properties and kinds for linguistic ones. In place of *triangularity* and *lionhood* we get *predicatehood* and *sortalhood*, the kinds to which belong everything that has the property of

---

6. Cf. Sellars's §XIV of GE.
7. "Quasi-syntactical" is the technical term Carnap uses in *The Logical Syntax of Language* for material mode expressions that should be given metalinguistic analyses.

being a predicate or *being a sortal*. It seems that metalinguistic nominalism cannot do without expression-kinds and properties of linguistic expressions. Unlike the previous objection, this one does not directly address the adequacy of a metalinguistic account of the expressive role of ontological classifying vocabulary. It just points out that such an account is only *locally* deflationary about property-talk and kind-talk, remaining committed to it as regards *linguistic* properties and kinds.

In the large, the project Sellars announces in "Grammar and Existence," motivates in "Naming and Saying," and completes in "Abstract Entities" is to refine Carnap's deflationary, expressivist idea that ontological category vocabulary is fundamentally metalinguistic, by developing it in a way that is immune to these two fundamental objections. In what follows, I describe how he does that and critically assess the result. In brief, his response to the first objection is to introduce the technical apparatus of dot quotation, formed according to what Sellars calls the "illustrating sign-design principle." His response to the second is to introduce further technical apparatus: the notion of distributive singular terms. This linguistic device plays a central role in drawing a distinction between what could be called "two grades of nominalistic involvement." Sellars distinguishes a broader notion of repeatability from a narrower notion of universality, under the slogan "the problem of 'the one and the many' is broader than the problem of universals."[8] He designs his metalinguistic nominalism so that the linguistic repeatables that replace worldly universals in his theory are not universals in the narrow sense.

The main critical claim I want to defend is in three parts. First, Sellars's subtle and sophisticated development of Carnap's metalinguistic nominalism in fact gives us a good account of the expressive role characteristic of the vocabulary of ontological categories, in particular of terms such as 'triangularity', 'lionhood', 'property', and 'kind'. Second, though, I want to claim that he misunderstands the significance of this penetrating analysis. What he offers is best understood as an account of what speakers are *doing* when they say things like "'Triangularity' is a property," namely, classifying expressions that play the same conceptual role as the English " . . . is

---

8. AE, p. 166.

triangular" and the German "... ist dreieckig" as adjectives. The nominalistic conclusion he wants to support, however, concerns not what one is *doing* in saying "'Triangularity' is a property," but what one is *saying* by doing that. His analysis is properly understood as conducted in a *pragmatic* metavocabulary, but the conclusions he draws must be formulated in a *semantic* metavocabulary. Lacking the concept of a pragmatic metavocabulary, Sellars is not in a position to separate these considerations. As a result, Sellars's analysis is *compatible* with semantic nominalism about universals, but does not provide an *argument* for it. For, as we saw was the case with modality, expressivism in pragmatics does not automatically preclude realism in semantics.

Third, I discuss the largely independent motivation for nominalism about universals that Sellars offers in "Naming and Saying." This is epitomized in his introduction of a third bit of original technical apparatus: the language Jumblese. This argument, too, turns on the transition from a fundamental pragmatic observation about the *use* of language—that *predicating* is a kind of doing that is in principle only intelligible in terms of *saying* (asserting) and *naming* (referring), which are accordingly more conceptually basic kinds of discursive doing—to controversial claims about semantics and ontology. Its essential reliance on inferences of these forms, from what one is *doing* to what one is *saying* by doing that, shows Sellars's *metalinguistic* semantic and ontological *nominalism* to be a particular kind of *pragmatist expressivism*.

2. Dot Quotes and the Objection from Language Relativity

The divergent behavior of "Triangularity is a property" and "'... is triangular' is an adjective," under translation and in various counterfactual circumstances, shows that ontologically categorizing vocabulary such as 'property' and property-terms such as 'triangularity' are not metalinguistic in the narrow sense (Tarski's) of being common nouns and singular terms falling under them that refer to the expressions of a particular object-language, such as English. This does not mean that they could not be understood to be metalinguistic in a broader sense. To specify such a sense, Sellars introduces the idea of a special kind of quotation: dot-quotation. Generically, like other forms of quotation, it is a mechanism for forming expressions from expressions. It does not, however, form *names* of expressions. Indeed, it does not form singular terms at all. I have the impression that many readers of Sellars think of dot-quoted expressions as being names of functional or conceptual roles: that •triangular• names the conceptual role played by 'triangular' in English.⁹ This is not right, and in the context of Sellars's version of nominalism about properties, it is absolutely essential to see why it is not right.

The principal features of expressions formed using dot-quotes are

1. All expressions formed by dot-quoting other expressions are common nouns (sortals), not singular terms. That is why their basic use is in conjunction with indefinite articles as in "'dreieckig' is a •triangular•" (compare: "Rex is a dog") or, equivalently, "'dreieckig's are •triangular•s" (compare: "Terriers are dogs").
2. The items falling under this kind of common noun are expression-types.
3. All the items falling under a particular common noun formed by dot-quoting an expression stand to the type of that expression in the equivalence relation . . . plays the same functional-conceptual role as ____.

So if *e* and *e'* are specifications of expression-types, *e'* is a •*e*• just in case *e'* plays the same conceptual role in *its* language that *e* plays in its language. Because . . . plays the same functional-conceptual role as ____ is an equivalence relation, one *could* treat it as an abstractor, and appeal to it to define an abstract singular term that *does* refer to the conceptual role shared by all the expression-types that stand in that relation to one another. (Perhaps one thinks of it as a name of the equivalence class defined by that relation—though that construal is certainly not obligatory.) But that is not what dot-quotes do. They would not be of much help to a program of working out a deflationary nominalist analysis of abstract entities such as properties if they did. They do serve a broadly *classificatory* function, producing a common noun that applies to all the expressions that share a conceptual role. But they do not do so by abstraction. This distinction, and the possibility it enforces of classifying without abstracting, is central to Sellars's response to the second objection to metalinguistic nominalism.

---

9. I blush to confess that I have spoken and even written carelessly in this way myself—but even Sellars himself is not always as careful on this point as he teaches us to be in AE.

Sellars is rather casual about the equivalence relation other expression-types must stand in to the type of the illustrating expression in order to fall under the common noun that results from dot-quoting it. He talks indifferently about "playing the same role," "serving the same function," "performing the same office," and "doing the same job." He is happy to call it a "functional" role, or a "conceptual" role. He says that what is at issue is the *prescriptive* relations it stands in to other expressions, not the descriptive ones, so he is clearly thinking about roles articulated in *normative* terms. He explicates this point by analogy to the role played by the pawn in chess. In a footnote, he indicates that he thinks these roles can be specified in terms of (norms governing) the language-entry, language-language, and language-exit transitions of a language.[10] I think Sellars's lack of specificity here should be seen as evidence that the relation . . . (in English) functions similarly to ____ (in German) should be seen as a placeholder, or parameter. Filling in the respects of similarity in some definite way gives rise to a correspondingly definite specification of the meaning of a particular dot-quoting locution. Dot-quoting is intended to be a *kind* of quotation, comprising as many species as there are respects of similarity of function. The elasticity of the notion of <u>prescriptive features of conceptual or functional role</u> should be regarded as a feature of the account, not an oversight in it.

The expression-token that appears between dot-quotes specifies the class of role-equivalent expression-types that fall under the sortal formed by the dot-quotes by *illustrating* it. The class in question is all the expression-types that are role-equivalent to the type of the quoted token. This is the "illustrating sign-design principle." This is a kind of use of the quoted expression that is more than a mere mention of it. For, unlike standard quotation, which does merely mention the quoted expression, one cannot *understand* something of the form •*e*• unless one understands the quoted expression *e*. For unless one grasps the conceptual role *e* plays in its home language, one does not know how to tell what other expression-types stand to it in the . . . plays the same functional-conceptual role as ____ relation, and so does not know what expression-types fall under the sortal •*e*•.

10. AE, pp. 176–179. The footnote in question is Note 13.

Expressions formed using dot-quotes are metalinguistic in a straightforward sense. They are common nouns that apply to expression-types. Sellars's idea for developing Carnap's metalinguistic analysis of what appear on the surface to be names of properties or universals, like 'triangularity' and 'lionhood', is to analyze them semantically in terms of this sort of common noun. Ontologically classifying contexts, such as "Triangularity is a property" and "Lionhood is a kind," he analyzes as "•... is triangular•s are adjectives" and "•lion•s are common nouns." *This* kind of metalinguistic statement is not subject to the first objection to Carnap's simpler version. Though they are statements in English (extended by adding some technical apparatus), they do not *refer* specifically to expressions of any particular language. Unlike ordinary quotation, but like "Triangularity is a property" and "Lionhood is a kind," they can be translated into other languages. The illustrating expressions, from which the dot-quotes are formed, can be translated right along with the rest of the sentences in which they are used. And just as it is true that even if there had never been English speakers, triangularity would still have been a property, it is true that even if there had never been English speakers, •... is triangular•s would still have been adjectives. (To deal with counterfactuals regarding the absence of language altogether, we must allow the expression-types that fall under common nouns formed by dot-quotation to include virtual ones, that is, expression-types in merely possible languages.) I conclude that the apparatus of dot-quotation permits Sellars to formulate a successor-theory to Carnap's that retains the motivating strategy of metalinguistic analysis, while successfully immunizing itself against the first objection.

3. Two Kinds of Repeatables, Two Grades of Abstract Involvement

Addressing the second principal objection to the claim that abstract entity talk is metalinguistic requires more than the crafting of a sophisticated extended sense of 'metalinguistic' (epitomized by the technical notion of dot-quotation), however.[11] It requires thinking hard about the nature and motivation

---

11. Sellars is happy to put his claim more baldly: "[A]bstract entities which are the subject of contemporary debate between platonist and anti-platonist philosophers—qualities, relations, classes, propositions, and the like—are linguistic entities"; AE §I, p. 163. In the next section, I'll give reasons why we should resist this formulation.

of nominalistic commitments concerning abstract entities. For understanding triangularity in terms of •triangular•s—as in the formulation "To say that triangularity is a property is to say that •triangular•s are monadic predicates"—is understanding the candidate abstract entity triangularity in terms of the linguistic expression-*type* •triangular•. And expression-types are themselves repeatables, under which various possible expression tokenings (in different actual and possible languages) can fall. So it would seem that being a •triangular• is a property that expressions (for instance, "dreieckig" in German) can have. In that case, nonlinguistic abstract entities, such as the property of triangularity (which triangular things have), are being analyzed in terms of linguistic abstract entities, such as the property of being a •triangular•. That suggests that metalinguistic nominalism about abstract entities is only a half-hearted nominalism, rejecting, it seems, only nonlinguistic abstract entities, but embracing linguistic ones. Such a view would in turn raise the question of the motivation for such a metalinguistic form of nominalism. Why should it be seen as a responsive answer to the considerations that motivate nominalistic commitments in the first place? Indeed, it obliges us to ask the questions: What do nominalists want? What are the rules of their game?

It cannot be that nominalism consists in insisting that all we do is refer to particulars using singular terms. Nominalists must allow that we also *say* things. Doing that is more than merely referring to things. Even in the simplest case, it is saying something *about* the particulars we refer to. It is classifying those particulars somehow. Classification involves some kind of repeatability on the part of the classifiers. Leo and Leona are both lions, and they are both tawny. Leo and Leona are classified together in that one can correctly say " . . . is a lion" and " . . . is tawny" of the two of them. (In the previous chapter we considered some crucial differences between *sortal* and non-sortal predication.) Sellars thinks of explaining what we are saying when we say that as a modern version of the classical "problem of the one and the many." The beginning of wisdom in the area, for Sellars, is to distinguish that problem from the problem of universals: the problem of saying what properties are. His analysis

> requires us to hold that not all *ones* over and against *manys* are universals (i.e. qualities, relations, sorts, kinds, or classes), and consequently

to conclude that the problem of "the one and the many" is in fact broader than the problem of universals.... [12]

That is, Sellars will distinguish a narrower class of abstract entities—what he calls "universals"—from a broader class. He offers a deflationary metalinguistic nominalist analysis only of the narrower class. I will call this the strategy of distinguishing two grades of involvement in abstraction.

Following Carnap, Sellars is an ontological nominalist because he is a semantic nominalist. (And I will argue further along that that semantic deflationism is rooted in conceptual dependencies at the level of pragmatics—that is, in deep features of the *use* of the expressions addressed.) Here is a crude initial statement of the line of thought. Nominalism, as its name suggests, begins with views about *names*—or more broadly, singular terms. What there is can be named. (That is the connection between ontology and semantics, for nominalists of the sort under discussion.) What appear to be property-names or kind-names are not genuine names. So there are no such things. Sellars takes it, though, that common nouns, sortal expressions, are part of the apparatus of naming. For singular terms require criteria of identity and individuation that are supplied by covering sortals. The sortals also supply basic criteria and consequences of application for those singular terms (distinguishing them from mere labels).[13] Those sortals are, accordingly, a kind of "one in many" with respect to the objects that are referents of singular terms they govern. By contrast to the narrower class of universals, this, Sellars thinks, is a kind of one in many that the nominalist cannot and should not do without. He says:

---

12. AE §I, p. 166.
13. Sellars discusses this distinction in CDCM §108:

> ... although describing and explaining (predicting, retrodicting, understanding) are *distinguishable,* they are also, in an important sense, *inseparable.* It is only because the expressions in terms of which we describe objects . . . locate these objects in a space of implications, that they describe at all, rather than merely label.

In addition to the treatment of it in earlier chapters of this book, I talk about it in Chapter 8 of *Reason in Philosophy* (Cambridge, MA: Harvard University Press, 2009).

[T]o refer to such a *one* we need a singular term other than the singular terms by which we refer to individual pawns, and yet which does not refer to a universal of which they are instances.[14]

If sense can be made of this kind of unity in diversity, then the way is open to understanding linguistic expression-types on this model, rather than on the model of universals and their instances or exemplifications. Doing so provides a way of responding to the second large objection to metalinguistic nominalism.

For a paradigm of a "one against a many" that is *not* a universal, not an abstract entity in the narrower, objectionable sense, he offers *distributive singular terms* (DSTs), such as "the lion" or "the pawn." We can use them to say such things as "The lion is tawny" and "The pawn cannot move backwards." These can be understood as paraphrases of "Lions are tawny" and "Pawns cannot move backwards." These latter are things one understands as part of understanding how to use the common nouns, which is already part of understanding the use of singular terms such as 'Leo'. Here is the strategy:

If, therefore, we can understand the relation of *the lion* (one) to *lions* (many) without construing *the lion* as a universal of which lions are instances; and if the looked-for singular term pertaining to pawns can be construed by analogy with "the lion"—indeed, as "the pawn"— then we would be in a position to understand how *the pawn* could be a one as against a many, without being a universal of which pawns are instances. This in turn would enable a distinction between a generic sense of "abstract entity" in which the lion and the pawn as well as triangularity (construed as the •triangular•) and that two plus two equals four (construed as the •two plus two equals four•) would be abstract entities as being ones over and against manys and a narrower sense of abstract entity in which qualities, relations, sorts, classes, propositions and the like are abstract entities, but of these only a proper subset, universals but not propositions, for example, would be *ones* as over and against *instances* or *members*. This subset would include the kind *lion*

---

14. AE §I, p. 166.

and the class of pawns, which must not be confused with *the lion* and *the pawn* as construed above.[15]

The contrast between two levels of involvement in abstraction is then the contrast between two sorts of nominalizations of common nouns such as "lion," "pawn," and "•triangular•." Nominalizing common nouns (deriving singular terms from them) in the form of DSTs such as "the lion" is perspicuous and nominalistically unobjectionable, while nominalizing them to form kind-terms, such as "lionhood" is not. I want to propose that one lesson that can be drawn from Sellars is that we can understand nominalism in terms of differential attitudes toward different kinds of nominalization. But we will have to work our way up to this point.

The capacity to use distributive singular terms can be algorithmically elaborated from the capacity to use the common nouns they are derived from, via the schema

$$\text{The K is F} \equiv \text{Ks are F}.$$

The right-hand side of this equivalence is not a conventional quantification. In the case of natural kind-terms, like "lion," it is something like essential properties that matter. The claim about Ks can be thought of as modified by something like Aristotle's "generally, or for the most part" operator. (The existence of a non-tawny lion would not falsify "The lion is tawny.")[16] The case we really care about, DSTs formed from common nouns formed by dot-quoting expressions, has special features, however. Sellars introduces them by analogy to "the pawn," rather than "the lion." The features that determine the truth of statements of the form F(the pawn) ("The pawn cannot castle"), he says, are *prescriptive* rather than *descriptive* features of pawns. He means that it is the normative features that define the role something must play in a game to be a pawn—what features of its behavior are obligatory or permissible for pawns—that determine the truth-value of statements in which the DST occurs essentially. Besides those properties, each pawn will have

---

15. AE §I, p. 167.
16. What I say here should be understood as only a crude gesture at a complex and important topic. For a more nuanced discussion, see Part One of Michael Thompson's pathbreaking *Life and Action* (Cambridge, MA: Harvard University Press, 2008).

matter-of-factual properties, such as being carved of wood, or being less than one inch tall, which are contingent features of some realizers, some items that play the role of pawn. Those do not support statements using the DST "the pawn." In this respect, "the pawn" is like "the •triangular•." It is norms governing the use of •triangular•s that determine what is true of the DST, too—even though "the pawn," unlike "the •triangular•" is not metalinguistic.

The equivalence schema shows that DSTs are just a special way of referring to Ks: to lions or to pawns. Not to one single K, but to all of them, distributively. That the reference is distributive means that it is not to the *group* of Ks, but, as it were, to Ks *as* Ks.[17] We can contrast this special mode of distributive reference with another bit of technical machinery that has been used by another kind of nominalist (Goodmanian nominalists) to do some of the same work Sellars wants DSTs to do: mereology. Mereological sums, too, are "ones in many." And they are different from universals. The part-whole relation they stand in to their mereological parts is not that of kind or property to *instance*. The difference is that mereological sums are a special kind of thing, over and above their parts. Singular terms referring to such sums are not special ways of referring to the parts, as DSTs are for particulars to which the common nouns from which they are formed apply. In this respect, mereological nominalism is *less nominalistic* than Sellarsian metalinguistic nominalism. For DSTs are not construed as singular terms referring to a different kind of entity from ordinary particulars. The mode of reference is different, specifically, distributive. But what is referred to is just what common nouns apply to. And that is the same particulars that singular terms refer to. There is no appeal to things of other ontological categories besides particulars. By contrast, mereological sums are formed from their parts by abstraction, as sets are. The difference between mereological sums and sets lies in the equivalence relation that is the abstractor, not in their

---

17. Sellars says remarkably little about just how he thinks plural statements such as "Lions are tawny," in terms of which statements formed using DSTs, such as "The lion is tawny," are to be understood. He might have only a slippery grip on the point that what is true of "the mayfly" can be quite different from what is true of most mayflies. Michael Thompson offers a sophisticated discussion of this point in *Life and Action*. Ruth Millikan's notion of Proper Function underwrites quite a different analysis of the same phenomenon.

abstractness.[18] Sellarsian nominalism must regard mereological sums, no less than sets, as ultimately metalinguistic in character.

The case Sellars really cares about, of course, is where the common nouns from which DSTs are formed are themselves the result of dot-quoting expressions of some type. An instance of the DST equivalence is

The •triangular• is a predicate ≡ •triangular•s are predicates.

And, given Sellars's analysis of property-names, we can extend this to

The •triangular• is a predicate ≡
•triangular•s are predicates ≡
triangularity is a property.

Unlike "the lion" and "the pawn," "the •triangular•" is a *metalinguistic* DST. It refers, distributively, to expression-types (in a variety of actual and possible languages). That is why this Sellarsian analysis is, like Carnap's less sophisticated account, a *metalinguistic* nominalism about what is expressed by property-names as a subset of ontological category vocabulary. Triangularity-talk is understood to be a misleading (because not explicitly metalinguistic) way of talking about the •triangular•, that is, •triangular•s, that is, expression-types that stand to "triangular" in some suitable (not for these purposes fully specified) relation of functional equivalence.[19] The equivalence relation is not, however, being appealed to as an abstractor that yields a singular term referring to an abstract object (perhaps identified with the equivalence class) that stands to the things it is abstracted from in a relation of exemplification. This is the difference between talking about the lion, or just lions—which is a way of referring to lions—as opposed to lionhood.

That is the difference between two kinds of ones-in-many, which is the basis of Sellars's response to the objection that metalinguistic nominalism

---

18. Cf. the discussion in Chapter 6.

19. I have suppressed niceties concerning Sellars's distinction, in AE, between "triangular" and ★triangular★ (the first being a quote-name of a word type, the second a quote-name of a sign-design type). Expressions formed by dot-quoting are officially common nouns applying to the latter, not the former.

about properties and kinds must just trade nonlinguistic universals for linguistic ones. The strategy of distinguishing two grades of involvement in abstraction does trade nonlinguistic universals (lionhood, triangularity) for linguistic ones-in-many (the •lion•, the •triangular•), but not for linguistic *universals*. The explanatory progress being made corresponds to crossing the line between two sorts of unity in diversity. Universals (properties, kinds) are eschewed entirely.

4. Nominalism and Nominalization, Functions and Objects

I said above that a metalinguistic nominalism that relies so heavily on this distinction between different kinds of repeatables—abstract entities in a strict or narrow sense where singular terms and covering common nouns are introduced by abstraction using equivalence relations on their instances and divided (distributive) modes of reference to particulars—raises questions about the motivation for nominalism of this sort. Nominalism can be thought of as a hygienic recommendation regarding the conditions under which it is appropriate to introduce names—or, more generally, singular terms. More particularly, I think it is useful to think of nominalism as a policy concerning *nominalization:* the introduction of new singular terms (and common nouns or sortal expressions governing them) by grammatically transforming other expressions.

Sellars is concerned to distinguish two ways of nominalizing common nouns. "Lion" can be nominalized by abstraction, to form the property-name "lionhood." Or it can be nominalized by forming the distributive singular term "the lion," which we can understand in terms of the *plural* "lions." The basic claim of this sort of nominalism is that nominalizations of the former sort are unperspicuous and misleading, requiring metalinguistic analysis in terms of operators that form common nouns applying to expression-types by dot-quoting expressions illustrating those types, and operators that form DSTs from those dot-quoted expressions. (Abstractive nominalizations are "quasi-syntactic," that is, material mode versions of statements perspicuously framed in the formal mode, as Carnap describes them in *The Logical Syntax of Language*. Sellars's corresponding term is "covertly metalinguistic.") Nominalizations of the latter sort are all right as they stand. Adjectives such as "... is triangular" and "... is red" take only nominalizations of the misleading abstractive sort: "triangularity" and "redness." Nominalism is a set of scruples about nominalization—a division of nominalization strategies into acceptable and unacceptable, or at least perspicuous and unperspicuous.

Although my focus here has been on predicate-nominalizations and properties, Sellars also thinks that declarative sentences have only nominalizations of the narrow sort, which purport to name abstract entities in the form of propositions. He proposes that these be analyzed metalinguistically, by equivalences of the form

"That snow is white is a proposition." ≡
"The •Snow is white• is a sentence." ≡
"•Snow is white•s are sentences."

So an extensional characterization of the split between nominalizations that unperspicuously invoke abstracta in the narrow sense (which are to be analyzed metalinguistically, using dot-quotes and DSTs), and nominalizations that invoke ones-in-many that are not covertly metalinguistic is this: kind-terms (sortals, common nouns) can go either way, depending on what sort of nominalization is at issue. Predicates (adjectives) and declarative sentences only take nominalizations that seem to refer to abstract entities in the narrow sense, and are to be understood by deflationary metalinguistic paraphrases. The only categories of expression-types that admit of nominalizations that are not to be construed as covertly metalinguistic are singular terms themselves (which are, as it were, their own nominalizations) and common nouns.[20] What is the motivation for this way of distinguishing the two grades of involvement in unperspicuous abstraction?

I said above that for the metalinguistic nominalist, the reason common nouns take nominalizations that are not covertly metalinguistic (such as "the lion" and "lions") is that they are already involved in the mechanism of singular reference to particulars—that is, broadly speaking, in naming. They also take unperspicuous, covertly metalinguistic nominalizations, purporting to name abstract entities in the narrow, objectionable, sense (such as "lionhood"), because besides incorporating criteria of identity and individuation (permitting plurals and so distributive reference) they

---

20. For a possible qualification, see the remarks about gerunds (present participles) at the end of Section 6.

are like predicates in incorporating criteria and consequences of application. This means common nouns come with associated predicate-adjectives ("... is a lion"), which admit nominalizations purportedly naming abstract entities in the narrow sense the metalinguistic nominalist is concerned to deflate. But the reason common nouns also take nonmetalinguistic nominalizations must be that they can be construed as mechanisms of reference to particulars, albeit in the distinctive mode of plural, divided, or distributive reference, not just that there can be no singular term reference in the absence of individuating sortals. For it is equally true that there can be no singular term reference ("naming") in the absence of assertion of declarative sentences ("saying") or (therefore) predicating. Yet nominalizations of expression-types of those grammatical categories admit only ontologically unperspicuous nominalizations.

At the end of "Abstract Entities" Sellars offers a further characterization of the difference between abstract entities in the narrow sense, invoked by unperspicuous nominalizations to be nominalistically paraphrased metalinguistically, and in the wider sense. It corresponds, he says, to the distinction between abstract entities which are not *objects*, but *functions*.[21] He explicitly mentions Frege in this connection (while denying that there is anything paradoxical about reference to functions). Kind-terms (which have both criteria of application and criteria of individuation and identity) admit both readings, while predicate adjectives (which have only criteria of application) initially support only the functional reading. (They do admit of nominalizations that refer to objects, as we see below, but these are doubly unperspicuous and covertly doubly metalinguistic.)

> The possibility that the word "kind" might have these two senses throws light on Russell's erstwhile distinction between classes as ones and classes as manys. Or, with an eye to Frege, we can say that in contexts such as ["The •the lion• is a DST," which reduces to "•the lion•s are DSTs"] kinds are *distributive objects,* whereas in ["The •lion• is a common noun," which in turn reduces to "•lion•s are common nouns"

---

21. AE §VII, pp. 188–189.

(Sellars's paraphrase of "Lionhood is a kind")]-like contexts they are concepts or functions.[22]

Again, he offers as examples:

Triangularity is a quality and not a (distributive) individual (i.e., The •triangular• is a predicate and not a DST).

Triangularity is a (distributive) individual and not a quality (i.e., The •the •triangular•• is a DST and not a predicate).[23]

Triangularity as a quality is a paradigm of a *function*, while *triangularity* as a distributive individual is a corresponding object. (Sellars marks the difference by using italics in the latter case.)[24] This sort of derivative nominalization corresponds to meta-metalinguistic DSTs.

While it is not immediately clear what Sellars means by saying that some of these nominalizations refer to functions rather than objects (and the invocation of Frege's views from "Concept and Object" and "Function and Concept"[25] threatens to explain *obscurum per obscurius*), it does seem that he is lining up abstract entities in the *narrow* sense with *functions*. Nominalizations that invoke functions are the unperspicuous ones (cf. "classes as ones"), by contrast to nominalizations that invoke objects, albeit distributively (cf. "classes as manys").

5. Saying, Naming, and Predicating

I think Sellars explains his reasons for drawing where he does the line between nominalizations of the two kinds—straightforward and covertly metalinguistic—and for the appeal to a distinction between objects and functions, in the third of the trio of essays I have been considering, "Naming and Saying." The proximal topic of this essay is the contrast between two

---

22. AE §V, p. 186.
23. AE §VII, p. 189.
24. AE §IV, pp. 183–184.
25. In Peter Geach and Max Black (trans.), *Translations from the Philosophical Writings of Gottlob Frege* (Oxford: Blackwell Publishers, 1966); originally published in 1952.

different approaches to universals: that of Gustav Bergmann (of the Vienna Circle) and one Sellars associates with Wittgenstein's *Tractatus*.²⁶ Of particular interest is that accounts of both sorts end by appealing to something *ineffable*—though the ineffability arises at characteristically different places in the two. Though himself coming down firmly on the Tractarian side of the dispute, as he understands it, Sellars diagnoses the objectionable ineffability as having a common aetiology in the two cases—as being rooted in the same failure of understanding.

In its crudest terms, the Bergmann-*Tractatus* debate is about how many ontological categories of things there are in the world, and how we should understand their relations. For Bergmann, there are two kinds of things, particulars and universals, and just one relation, *exemplification* of a universal by particulars, that they can stand in.²⁷ Saying that two particulars stand in some relation, for instance that Ludwig is subtler than Gustav, is producing names of the two kinds (names of particulars and names of a universal) in a way that conventionally conveys that they stand in the relation of exemplification. The disappointing addendum is that that relation is ineffable. Naming (nominalizing) it, for instance, 'exemplification', is at best of heuristic and not analytic value, since the relation between it and the particulars and universal it relates (e.g. Ludwig, Gustav, and the relation of being subtler than) would itself have to be understood as . . . exemplification. And then we are off to the races on a Bradleyan regress.

By contrast, according to the Tractarian view Sellars considers, there is only one kind of thing in the world: particulars. They stand in a variety of relations. Saying that two particulars stand in some relation, for instance that Ludwig is subtler than Gustav, is arranging names of the particulars

---

26. There are many fine things in this essay that I shall not discuss. Two subtleties worthy of at least passing mention are i) Sellars's sensitive and judicious treatment of the vexed interpretive question of exactly what stand the *Tractatus* takes on the intelligibility of multiple distinct *monadic* facts (since facts are "arrangements" of objects); and ii) the distinction between color and shape predicates in this context: "green" has both adjectival and substantival uses, which invites confusion (it can serve as its own adjective-nominalization—"Green is a color"—though it also takes "greenness"), whereas "triangular" nominalizes *only* as "triangularity."

27. Sellars: "[F]or Bergmann there is . . . only *one* relation, i.e. exemplification, and what are ordinarily said to be relations, for example *below*, would occur in the world as *relata*." NS, p. 109.

in a way that conventionally conveys the fact that the particulars stand in that relation. The disappointing addendum is that the relation (picturing) between statement (the fact that the names are arranged as they are in the saying) and the fact (that the particulars stand in the relation) is ineffable. It is not itself a fact that can be stated, as a relation obtaining between a names-fact and a particulars-fact, but something that can only be shown. Here what threatens is not so much a regress as circularity: the explicit statement of the semantic picturing relation between statements and facts could be understood only by someone who already implicitly grasps the relation between statements and facts, and so could not substitute for or ground such a grasp.

Here is Sellars's summary:

> To keep matters straight, it will be useful to introduce the term 'nexus' in such a way that to say of something that it is a nexus is to say that it is perspicuously represented in discourse by a configuration of expressions rather than by a separate expression. If we do this, we can contrast Bergmann and Wittgenstein as follows:
>> *Wittgenstein:* There are many nexus in the world. Simple relations of matter of fact are *nexus*. All objects or individuals which form a nexus are particulars, i.e. individuals of type 0. There is no relation or nexus of exemplification in the world.
>> *Bergmann:* There is only one nexus, exemplification. Every atomic state of affairs contains at least one . . . individual which is not a particular.
>
> If one so uses the term 'ineffable' that to eff something is to signify it by using a name, then Wittgenstein's view would be that what are ordinarily called relations are ineffable, for they are all nexus and are expressed (whether perspicuously or not) by configurations of names. For Bergmann, on the other hand, what are ordinarily called relations are effed; it is exemplification which is ineffable.[28]

Notice that Sellars here expresses the nominalism being opposed to Bergmannian ontological profligacy as a restriction on what can strictly be *named* (hence how nominalizations are to be understood: where

---

28. NS, p. 109.

straightforwardly and where in terms of metalinguistic paraphrase). An assumption taken to be common to all concerned is that what can be named and what is "in the world" coincide, and that anything else is strictly "ineffable." One might rather tie ineffability to what cannot be *said* (explicitly) but at most only shown or otherwise conveyed (implicitly). I'll return to this question.

Sellars sensibly takes the invocation of something ineffable as a symptom of analytic and explanatory failure. His diagnosis (repeated with emphasis in the concluding sections of both NS and AE) is that the surplus beyond what is named when we say something, what shows up on these mistaken accounts as ineffable, is not a *thing* but a *doing*.

> Thus the "relation" of exemplification which for Platonists binds the realm of becoming to the realm of being, and which for more moderate realists binds the "real" order to the "logical" or "conceptual" order, is an offshoot of the "relation" of truth, which analysis shows to be no relation at all, but a sign of something to be *done*.[29]

The supposedly ineffable alternatives, exemplification (Bergmannian platonism) and the relation between statements and facts (Tractarian nominalism) are both manifestations of what is invoked by truth-talk. And that, Sellars thinks, is best understood not in terms of a word-world relation but in terms of the propriety of a metalinguistic *inference*.

> What, then, does it mean to say
> That green a is a fact
> Clearly this is equivalent to saying
> That green a is true
> ...
>
> This, however, is not the most perspicuous way to represent matters, for while the equivalence obtains, indeed necessarily obtains, its truth depends on the principle of inference—and this is the crux—
>
> From 'that green a is true' (in our language) to infer 'green a' (in our language).

---

29. AE, p. 203. My italics.

And it is by virtue of the fact that we *draw* such inferences that meaning and truth talk gets its connection with the world. In this sense, the connection is *done* rather than *talked about*.

Viewed from this perspective, Wittgenstein's later conception of a language as a form of life is already foreshadowed by the ineffability thesis of the *Tractatus*. But to see this is to see that no ineffability is involved. For while to infer is neither to refer to that which can be referred to, nor to assert that which can be asserted, this does not mean that it is to fail to eff something which is, therefore, ineffable.[30]

A number of moves are being made here. First, the "two ineffables," exemplification and the relation between statements and facts, are both being traced back to what is expressed by statements using 'true'. "a *exemplifies* green" is a way of *stating* the *fact* that a is green. (Stating is the paradigmatic kind of saying.) Second, "A fact is a thought that is true."[31] (Keep in mind the "notorious 'ing'/'ed' ambiguity" here: he does *not* mean 'thought' in the sense of a thinking, an act, but in the sense of what is thought—or better, thinkable—a content.) Third, talk about truth is (as Frege also recognized) misleading talk about what one is *doing* in saying something in the sense of making a statement: the use of 'true' is to be understood in terms of the platitude that asserting is taking-true. Fourth, the way 'true' expresses what one is doing in asserting is also expressed in the propriety of the disquotational *inferences* codified in Tarskian T-sentences.

All of these moves are contentious. I am not concerned to defend them here. I am concerned to understand the original motivation and general rationale for connecting nominalizations the Sellarsian nominalist wants to treat as not referring to *things*, such as "triangularity," with discursive *doings*. For this, I want to suggest, is what becomes of the otherwise puzzling distinction, evidently intended to be coextensional, which we worried about at the end of the previous section, between referring to *objects*

---

30. NS, p. 125.
31. G. Frege, "The Thought," *Mind* 65(259) (1956): 289–311. For Sellars, "The crucial ineffability in the *Tractatus* concerns the relation between statements and facts. Is there such a relation? And is it ineffable? The answer seems to me to be the following. There is a meaning relation between statements and *facts*, but both terms are in the linguistic order." NS, p. 124.

and invoking *functions*. As we might break things down, in the first step, functions are what articulate functional roles. In the second step, functions, as Sellars is thinking of them, are things only in the sense of things *done:* doables. Nominalization of functions is what Sellars's nominalism invites us to forbid in perspicuous languages, and to give a deflationary treatment of the functioning of, in unperspicuous ones.

I think we can begin to understand the idea behind this line of thought if we look at the activities that give "Naming and Saying" its title, and how the relations between them are thought to be made more perspicuous by the third technical innovation (besides dot-quotes and DSTs) that Sellars uses to articulate his nominalism. This construction, introduced in that essay, is the language-form he calls "Jumblese."[32] We can sum up the line of thought in NS that I have been considering in the following slogan: Appeal to an ineffable semantic relation is a sign that one is trying to do in one's *semantic* theory what can only be done in the *pragmatic* theory, the theory of the *use* of the language. *Saying,* putting something forward *as* true, asserting—the central and paradigmatic use of declarative sentences—is a *doing,* not a semantic relation. So is *naming,* in the sense of referring (using an already established term, rather than naming in the sense of introducing such a term). Referring is the central and paradigmatic use of singular terms.

If the first lesson Sellars wants us to learn is that the result of trying to explain what one is *doing* in *saying* something (a pragmatic matter), in terms of the semantic relation between a name and what is named, is an appeal to an ultimately magical, ineffable version of that relation, then the second, nominalist, lesson is that even within the realm of semantics, the name/named model cannot be used to understand the use of predicates or sentences. In particular, predication, in the sense of the act of predicating (classifying something nameable) is a *derivative* speech act. It does not belong at the same level of analysis as the more fundamental acts of saying and naming. Predicating something (universal) of something (particular)

---

32. The name comes from Edward Lear's nonsense poem "The Jumblies," Sellars tells us, because "Far and few, far and few, are the lands where the Jumblies live." (He does not mention that "Their heads are green, and their hands are blue . . . ," though his topic is the significance of just such predications. Greenness and blueness are not mentioned on the inventory of things they took with them when they "went to sea in a Sieve.")

is just saying something *about* something. It is to be understood in terms of the relation between a kind of *doing*, asserting, which in the base case essentially involves the use of singular terms, and the semantic relation of referring, which holds between a name (singular term) and what is named (referred to).[33]

It is because the speech act of predicating is a derivative one that predicative expressions play a semantic role that is subordinate to that of singular terms and sentences.

> [T]he classical problem of universals rests in large part on the fact that, in such languages as English and German expressions referring to universals are constructed on an illustrating principle which highlights *a design which actually plays a subordinate role,* and consequently tempts us to cut up such sentences as
>
> Triangular (*a*)
>
> into two parts, one of which has to do with the universal rather than the particular, the other with the particular rather than the universal, and tempts us, therefore, to construe the statement as asserting a dyadic relation ("exemplification") to obtain between the particular and the universal.[34]

Jumblese is designed to make *syntactically* vivid the derivative *pragmatic* role of predication, which in turn underlies the deflationary, nominalist metalinguistic *semantic* analysis Sellars is recommending for *nominalizations* of predicative expressions, such as "triangularity." Jumblese has no predicative expressions. Its sentences consist entirely of names (singular terms). The names specify what one is talking *about* (referring to). What one is *saying* about what one is talking about is expressed by *styles of arrangement* of those names. So, in one version the claim that Wilfrid is subtler than Gustav might be expressed by juxtaposing them and writing the first name

---

33. Though he does not say so, I expect that Sellars learned from Kant the lesson that one cannot, as the pre-Kantian tradition tried to do, understand *saying* in terms of *predicating*. I explain how I take Kant to have learned this lesson, and the central role it plays in his thought, in Chapter 1 of *Reason in Philosophy*.

34. AE, p. 201.

in larger type than the second: Wilfrid **Gustav**. That Gustav was Austrian might be expressed by writing his name in a distinctive font: Gustav. Jumblese, we might want to say, overtly marks only naming and saying: what one is referring to, by the singular terms used, and what one is asserting about it, by the style in which the terms are written (including the relations between the singular terms). Predication is only implicit in what one is doing in saying something about something named.

A consequence of the absence of overt predicate-expressions is that there is nothing to nominalize into an analog of "triangularity." There is nothing to which to apply the "illustrating principle" that forms •triangular•s, which could tempt one to introduce the new common noun "property," enabling one to say, "Triangularity is a property," that is, •triangular•s are predicates (the •triangular• is an adjective). Of course, we *could* introduce nominalizations of predicate-adjectives even into (a dialect of) Jumblese, perhaps by using names of the styles the level-0 names are written in. Since it is the *fact that* "Gustav" is written in the Script-MT-Bold font that *says that* Gustav is Austrian, we could say that • . . . is Austrian•s are predicates (that is that being Austrian is a property) by saying that Script-MT-Bold is a predicate-indicating font—or, in a Jumblese metalanguage, by asserting "**Script-MT-Bold**" (where writing the font-name in the Berlin Sans FB font indicates that it is the nominalization of a predicate).[35] But while Jumblese *permits* such nominalizations, it does not *encourage* them. And it does not even *permit* the formation of those nominalizations according to an *illustrating* principle, which is what makes ontological-category talk such as "Triangularity is a property" *covertly* metalinguistic (Carnap's "quasi-syntactic"): a formal-mode statement masquerading in material mode. "**Script-MT-Bold**" is

---

35. In Section VIII of AE, Sellars considers how bound variables might work in Jumblese. (But do his readers care? The result of this expository choice is an *extremely* anticlimactic ending—one could not say conclusion—to the already long and technical essay.) Elsewhere in the same piece, he indulges himself in speculations about Jumblese metalanguages (*inter alia*, for Jumblese), and about the adventure that would consist in translating Bradley's *Appearance and Reality* into Jumblese. Oddly, he says nothing about the *spoken* version of Jumblese—the version in which, we are authoritatively informed, the Jumblies said, "How wise we are! Though the sky be dark and the voyage be long. . . ." One version of spoken Jumblese would be tonal: melodic. The effect would be reminiscent of Gregorian chants. A written Jumblese *pragmatic* metavocabulary for such spoken Jumblese would resemble musical notation (and *its* use, a Glasperlenspiel).

overtly metalinguistic, consisting, as it does, of a name of a style of writing, here, a font (itself, of course, written in a particular style).

6. From Semantic to Pragmatic Metalanguages: Assessing Metalinguistic Nominalism

In the earliest of the three essays I have been discussing, Sellars identifies two major objections to Carnap's metalinguistic nominalism about ontological category vocabulary, principally predicate-nominalizations (such as "triangularity") and their associated common nouns (such as "property"). First, statements such as "Triangularity is a property" do not mention any linguistic expressions, and so are not metalinguistic in the classical sense. Unlike Carnap's proposed paraphrase, "'Triangular' is a predicate," they would be true even if no-one had ever spoken English and do not change their reference or become unintelligible to monolinguals if translated into German. Second, it seems such an approach just trades nonlinguistic universals, such as "being triangular" for linguistic ones, such as "being a predicate." Sellars's response to the first objection is that it turns on too narrow and undifferentiated a conception of the metalinguistic. He offers a more capacious and nuanced one, reformulating Carnap's paraphrase using dot-quotation to form common nouns that functionally classify expression-types using the "illustrating sign-design principle." He responds to the second by conceding that classification under repeatables is not to be explained away, but insisting that we should distinguish the broader "problem of the one and the many" from the narrower "problem of universals." The formation of plurals from common nouns (including those formed by dot-quotation of illustrating expressions: "•triangular•s are predicate-adjectives") and their nominalization by forming distributive singular terms instead of kind-names ("the •triangular•" rather than "•triangular•ness"—in the nonmetalinguistic case, "the lion" rather than "lionhood") allow the metalinguistic nominalist to endorse a version of Carnap's paraphrase without commitment to linguistic (or any) universals in the narrow, objectionable sense.

I think these responses are wholly successful in producing a development of Carnap's idea that is immune to the objections that prompted them. The second move, however, raises the question of why we should resist reifying universals in the form of properties and kinds. Why should we insist on metalinguistic paraphrases of claims made using *these* nominalizations, and hence reject a straightforward referential semantics for these singular terms, which understands them as referring to abstract entities? Sellars's argument, as presented in "Naming and Saying," turns on the second-class ("derivative," "subordinate") character of *predicating* (and, more generally, classifying), relative to saying and naming. That is, the basis for metalinguistic nominalism about property and kind nominalizations in *semantics* is to be found in considerations proper to *pragmatics:* considerations concerning what we are *doing* when we use various expressions. I think we can and should resist this move.

Sketched with a very broad brush, I think the argument goes like this. Predicate-adjectives have a very different function and use than do singular terms. *Hence,* it is misleading to understand singular terms formed by nominalizing them as referring to a special kind of *thing:* abstract entities.[36] I don't think this is a good inference. It is true both that predicating is not naming, but must be understood in terms of the relations between naming and saying, and that one can only understand singular terms formed by nominalizing predicates in terms of the use of the underlying predicates. On this latter point, Sellars argues in effect that the capacity to use ontological category talk—predicate- and kind-nominalizations, such as "triangularity" and "lionhood," and the common nouns that govern their identity and individuation, such as "property"[37] and "kind"—is *pragmatically dependent* on the capacity to use the underlying predicate-adjectives and common nouns. In the terms I use in *Between Saying and Doing,* this is a PP-necessity claim.[38] Unless one has the capacity to use the nominalized terms, one cannot count

---

36. A corresponding argument goes through for common nouns, which are like predicate-adjectives in having classifying criteria of application, even though they are unlike predicate-adjectives in also having criteria of identity and individuation for the singular terms associated with them. Also, Sellars wants to adopt the same sort of metalinguistic paraphrase strategy for nominalizations of sentences ("that snow is white," together with the corresponding common nouns such as "proposition"). Again, the avowed motivation for this is that what one is *doing* in *saying* something is different from *referring* (though referring to particulars is in the base case included as one aspect of saying). Nonetheless, for simplicity, in this summary, I focus on the predicate-adjectives and their nominalizations.

37. And, though he doesn't say so, others such as "trope," understood as something like "unrepeatable instance of a property."

38. Robert Brandom, *Between Saying and Doing* (Oxford: Oxford University Press, 2008). Hereafter *BSD*.

as having the capacity to use their nominalizations. Further, his version of the Carnap metalinguistic paraphrase strategy shows us how the capacity to use predicate-adjectives (" . . . is triangular") can be *algorithmically elaborated* into the capacity to use the nominalizations ("triangularity").[39] This is a special kind of PP-sufficiency claim. I agree with all this and think that showing how to algorithmically elaborate the ability to use adjectives into the ability to use nominalized property-talk is a significant achievement. Further, I agree that the pragmatic dependence (PP-necessity) claim suffices to show that Bergmann is wrong to think of the nominalization-talk as *conceptually prior* to the use of the predicate-adjectives and ground-level common nouns. Bergmann is right that there is a *semantic* equivalence between saying that *a* exemplifies triangularity and saying that *a* is triangular. However, there is an underlying *pragmatic a*symmetry. One *could* learn how to use " . . . is triangular" (•triangular•s) first and only then, and elaborated solely on that basis, learn how to use " . . . exemplifies triangularity" and the property-talk that goes with it (as the common noun to this nominalization-by-abstraction). One could *not* learn it the other way around. In this sense, property-exemplification talk is not *pragmatically autonomous* from the use of predicate-adjectives, as Bergmann's priority claim commits him to its being. This sort of *pragmatically mediated conceptual dependence* is the same sort of priority claim that Sellars makes for "is"-talk over "seems"-talk, in *EPM*.[40] So far, so good.

---

39. Sellars suggests that the fact that some kind-terms mark *functions* rather than *objects* (discussed in Section 4 above) means that thinking of them as naming universals is committing something like the naturalistic fallacy. In this respect, he seems to be putting abstract-entity-talk in a box with normative vocabulary. Normative vocabulary, like modal vocabulary, he takes to play the expressive role, not of describing something ("in the world in the narrow sense"), but of explicating the *framework* within which alone describing is possible. (I discuss this Kantian move in Chapter 5.) These vocabularies are what in *BSD* I call "universally LX": elaborated from and explicative of every autonomous vocabulary. I have just been claiming that the use of ontological-category vocabulary (such as "property" and "proposition"—the common nouns that govern singular terms purporting to pick out abstract objects such as universals like triangularity) can indeed be elaborated from the use of ordinary predicates and declarative sentences. One very important question that I do not address in this chapter is whether (for Sellars, and in fact) such vocabulary is *also* explicative of essential features of the framework within which ordinary empirical descriptive vocabulary functions, and if so, of *which* features.

40. As discussed in Chapter 2 and 3 above.

More particularly, Sellars's claim is that what one is *doing* in saying that triangularity is a property is classifying •triangular•s as predicate-adjectives. That is a metalinguistic doing—of a distinctive kind, marked out by the use of the illustrating principle, to get a common noun, •triangular•, that applies to expression-types that stand to the displayed "triangular" in a parameterized functional-role equivalence relation. So it is fair to conclude that the *use* of ontological-categorial vocabulary involves a distinctive kind of metalinguistic expressive role. The question remains: what conclusions should one draw about the *semantics* of such expressions? Does playing that *pragmatic* metalinguistic expressive role *preclude* understanding the nominalizations ("triangularity," "lionhood"—or "being a lion") as *also* standing in referential ("naming") relations to *objects*? I do not see that it does. The fact that "good" essentially, and not just accidentally, has as part of its expressive role the possibility of being used to *commend* does not mean that it does not *also* describe in the sense of attributing a property. A corresponding point goes through for *modal* vocabulary.[41] From that fact that what one is *doing* in *saying* that triangularity is a property is classifying •triangular•s as predicate-adjectives, it does not follow that that is what one is *saying*. It certainly does not follow that that is *all* one is saying. Sellars's analysis leaves *room* for denying that "triangularity" refers to a property. It provides an alternative. But he has not shown that these are *exclusive* alternatives, that we must *choose between* them. The singular terms formed by nominalizing parts of speech other than singular terms are, we might agree, distinguished by having a metalinguistic expressive function. But that is not yet to say that they do not *also* refer to a distinctive kind of object: property-universals (and propositions, including the true ones: facts).

Traditional Tarskian metalanguages—the kind we normally think about in connection with "metalinguistic" claims—are *semantic* metalanguages. They contain the expressive resources to talk about aspects of discursive *content*. Accordingly, they let us discuss truth conditions, reference relations, inferential relations, and the like. Carnap also deploys *syntactic* metalanguages that let us talk about syntax, grammar, and lexical items (though Carnap himself uses "syntax" in an idiosyncratically wide sense in *The*

---

41. As I argue in Chapter 5, "Modal Expressivism and Modal Realism, Together Again."

Logical Syntax of Language). *Pragmatic* metalanguages have the expressive resources to talk about the *use* of language and the proprieties that govern it, for instance the activities of asserting, inferring, referring, predicating, and so on.[42] If I am right that the principal insight driving Sellars's metalinguistic nominalism is the idea that what one is *doing* in deploying concepts such as triangularity, lionhood, property, and kind is functionally classifying expressions using metalinguistic vocabulary of a distinctive kind (nominalizations formed according to the "illustrating sign-design principle"), that is an insight properly expressible in a *pragmatic* metalanguage. The conclusion he wants to draw, however, concerns the *semantics* proper for that class of nominalizations and covering common nouns. The inferential relations between claims couched in pragmatic metalanguages and claims couched in semantic metalanguages are quite complex and little understood, however.[43] The inference Sellars is committed to here would go through only in the context of one or another set of auxiliary hypotheses, many of which would be implausible, or at least controversial, none of which does he discuss.

Sellars makes this slide unaware (to be sure, in the good company of expressivists addressing other sorts of vocabulary) because he doesn't have available the distinction between semantic and pragmatic metalanguages. According to that diagnosis, his argument is vulnerable because it relies on too crude and expressively impoverished a concept of the metalinguistic. This is an ironic situation, because I am accusing Sellars of making a mistake (or suffering from a disability) of a piece with the ones he discerns in the opponents he discusses in these essays. As we have seen, the first principal objection to Carnap's metaphysical nominalism (and, indeed, his metalinguistic treatment of modality) that Sellars addresses he diagnoses as the result of appealing to insufficiently nuanced concepts of being metalinguistic. He responds by giving us more nuanced ones, which evade the objection. I am claiming that his notion of the metalinguistic is still too crude. Again, he diagnoses Bergmann and the *Tractatus* as running together *pragmatic* issues, of what one is *doing* in saying something or *predicating* something, with *semantic* issues. In particular,

---

42. Pragmatic metavocabularies are one of the topics discussed at length in *BSD*.

43. *BSD* introduces the topic and provides a wealth of examples of the sort of complex relations between meaning and use that can be discerned once we start to think systematically about their relations.

he claims that attempting to understand what one is *doing* in predicating or claiming by forcing it into the form of a semantic relation inevitably results in commitments to the ineffability of that relation. This is the same genus as the mistake I am claiming Sellars is making (both here and in the case of modality): running together *pragmatic* issues, of what one is *doing* in saying something, with *semantic* issues of what is *said* thereby.

This line of thought suggests that there are a number of different strands of broadly nominalistic thought in play. One genus is what might be called "nominalization nominalisms." These views make an invidious distinction between two classes of singular terms. *Genuine* singular terms are *referential*. They are to be understood semantically in terms of reference relations (the "name-bearer" relation), and successfully using them is referring to a referent. Genuine singular terms in this sense can fail to refer, but they, as we might say, *perspicuously purport* to refer to particulars. They are not *grammatically* precluded from being used to refer, and in any case are to be semantically assessed in terms of reference relations (or the lack thereof). By contrast (almost all) singular terms formed by nominalizing other parts of speech are grammatically misleading. These merely *ostensible* singular terms only grammatically, but *unperspicuously purport* to refer to particulars. On Sellars's development of Carnap's view, they are to be given *metalinguistic* readings. All singular terms have criteria of identity and individuation lodged in associated common nouns or sortals, which accordingly can also be divided into genuine and ostensible. This division generally corresponds to that between nouns that are not and those that are formed by nominalizing other parts of speech. The exception is that *some* nominalizations of common nouns or sortal expressions are sometimes counted as genuine (for instance, by Sellars and Kotarbinski).[44]

In these terms, I want to distinguish semantic and pragmatic species of the genus of nominalization nominalisms. The first kind of nominalization

---

44. It seems, for the same reason: otherwise the nominalization nominalist about the "problem of universals" has difficulty addressing the "problem of the one and the many." T. Kotarbinski, *Gnosiology. The Scientific Approach to the Theory of Knowledge*, trans. O. Wojtasiewicz (Oxford: Pergamon Press, 1966). This is a translation of Kotarbinski's *Elementy teorii poznania, logiki formalnej i metodologii nauk* (Lwow: Ossolineum, 1929). Kotarbinski distinguishes between "genuine" and "non-genuine" names, and between semantic and ontological nominalisms.

nominalism addresses the semantic *content* of the two classes comprising genuine and merely ostensible singular terms (the latter consisting of transcategorial nominalizations). Only genuine singular terms are to be understood in terms of their referential relations to particulars. The latter kind of nominalization nominalism addresses the pragmatic *use* of the two classes of terms and associated common nouns. The pragmatic nominalization nominalist understands the *use* of transcategorial nominalizations in metalinguistic terms of classifying linguistic expression-types. By contrast, the use of genuine singular terms is to be understood exclusively as *referring*, which is one essential feature of *saying* anything *about* particulars. I have claimed that the step from pragmatic to semantic nominalization nominalism is not straightforward. For one might distinguish transcategorial nominalizations from other singular terms by seeing their use as involving metalinguistic classification without thereby concluding that they do not *also* stand in referential relations to a distinctive kind of abstract entity. They just have this *extra* expressive function that *ordinary* singular terms do not have. Perhaps there is an illuminating and important relation between playing that distinctive expressive role and picking out the kind of object they do.[45]

In any case, when we discover that some kind of linguistic expression plays a distinctive expressive role (one not played by paradigmatically referring singular terms, for instance), we would seem methodologically to have two choices. We can think about that new expressive role in an *exclusionary* or in a *permissive* way. The exclusionary reading claims that the expressive role that has been discovered must exhaust what is available to determine semantic content. The contrasting permissive reading allows that playing that expressive role might be compatible with also playing other expressive roles (for instance, referring), and so not ruling out the corresponding semantics still being applicable. The fact that expressivists who want to adopt the exclusionary reading should argue for adopting this stance rather than the permissive one (as should those who want to adopt the less common permissive stance), of course, is not limited to the case of expressive nominalists.

---

45. I have in mind determining the equivalence relation that is the abstractor.

What I have called "nominalization nominalisms" concern the use and content of linguistic expressions. Nominalism is usually thought of as an *ontological* thesis, however. Sellars endorses such a view:

> It is also argued that exemplification is a 'quasi-semantical' relation, and that it (and universals) are "in the world" only in that broad sense in which the 'world' includes linguistic norms and roles viewed (thus in translating) from the standpoint of a fellow participant.[46]

I take it that being "in the world in the narrow sense" means being in the *nondiscursive* world: the world as it was before there discursive beings, or a counterfactual world in which there never were discursive beings. If this is indeed the narrow sense of "in the world" that contrasts with the broad sense invoked in this passage, then it seems to me that there is a tension between this claim and the response to one version of the first objection to naïve Carnapian metalinguistic expressivism about transcategorial nominalizations. This objection is that it cannot be right to understand sentences such as "Triangularity is a property" metalinguistically, because they would still have been true even if there had never been discursive beings. Sellars's response commits him to the claim that "•triangular•s are predicates" would still have been true even if there never had been discursive beings. Perhaps there are ways to vindicate this claim without being committed to •triangular•s being "in the world" in the narrow sense, but it is hard to see how. I suppose that he thinks that •triangular•s *are* "in the world in the narrow sense," but that that is compatible with his claim, since •triangular•s are not universals and are not exemplified by the expression-types they classify. (They are "ones in many," but not universals.) The presumptive presence of •triangular•s "in the world in the narrow sense" suggests that some work will need to be done to clarify and entitle oneself to appeal to this "narrow sense."

Be that as it may, what is "in the world in the narrow sense" is being taken to exclude universals because they are not, as we first might have thought, referred to by *genuine* singular terms, but only by *ostensible* ones. Nominalism

---

46. NS, p. 103.

in the ontological sense is the thesis that the world ("in the narrow sense") consists exclusively of *nameables:* things that could be referred to by *genuine* singular terms. This connection between *semantic* nominalism, which distinguishes genuine from merely ostensible ˢnamesˢ (singular terms), and *ontological* nominalism, which restricts the real to what is nameable by genuine ones, is explicit in Kotarbinski. It seems to be Sellars's picture as well.

Now I am not at all sure that ontological nominalism in this sense is in the end so much as intelligible. In Sellars's version of semantic nominalization nominalism, among the transcategorial nominalizations that are analyzed metalinguistically, and which accordingly show up as not genuine singular terms, are *sentence* nominalizations, and their associated common nouns such as "proposition" and "fact." ("That snow is white is a proposition" is analyzed as "•Snow is white•s are declarative sentences.") Although "Naming and Saying" defends a Tractarian view against Bergmann on *some* important points, Sellars parts company with the *Tractatus* in taking a reistic position according to which the world (narrowly conceived) is *not* everything that is the case, a world of facts, but is rather a world exclusively of particulars, nameables not statables. As far as I can see, Sellars is envisaging a world in which the "ones-in-many" needed to make sense of an *articulated* world are such as could be referred to by common nouns (sortals). That is the alternative to universals he seems to be working with. But to avoid commitment to universals, it seems that the criteria of identity and individuation associated with the (already, as it were, nominalized) common nouns must either do *all* the work, or must somehow immunize the criteria (and consequences) of application from supporting or making intelligible the contribution of the universals that threaten when predicate adjectives, which *only* have circumstances (and consequences) of application, but not criteria of identity and individuation, are nominalized. I don't pretend to know that this strategy cannot be made to work. But I also don't see that Sellars has given us many of the tools that would need to be deployed to make it work. Perhaps more fundamentally, I don't see that we have the makings of a story on the ontological or the semantic side of what corresponds on the pragmatic side to *saying* (claiming, believing) something. If the world is a collection of particulars—of course, collections are not "in the world in the narrow sense" either—what is one doing in *saying that* things are thus-and-so? How for Sellars are we to understand *either* the "thus-and-so" *or* the "saying that"? I am buffaloed.

Here is a potentially more tractable puzzle. I have interpreted the semantic side of Sellars's nominalism as what I have called a "nominalization nominalism," which distinguishes two classes of singular terms, genuine and merely ostensible. The merely ostensible ones are to be read metalinguistically, in the broad, nuanced sense of "metalinguistic" that applies to DSTs formed from dot-quoted expressions using the "illustrating sign-design principle." More specifically, I have claimed that all transcategorial nominalizations count for Sellars as merely ostensible singular terms according to this classification, and so, according to the ontological side of his nominalism, do not correspond to anything "in the world in the narrow sense." One kind of transcategorial nominalization, starting with a nonnominal part of speech and forming singular terms from it, is gerunds or present participles, such as "doing," "saying," "making," "breaking," "swimming," and "heating." These constructions form common nouns and singular terms from verbs. If my account of how the motivation of "Naming and Saying" shapes the account of "Abstract Entities" is correct—if being a transcategorial nominalization is sufficient for not being a genuine singular term for Sellars—then all singular terms formed from verbs must be merely ostensible, and correspond to nothing in the world construed narrowly. Sellars never discusses this case. Would he offer a broadly metalinguistic account of these terms and common nouns? If so, how would it go? Does his nominalism allow that the world "in the narrow sense" can include particular swimmings and heatings? These seem like particular events, rather than universals. A particular swimming falls under the common noun "swimming" as a particular dog falls under the one-in-many " . . . is a dog," rather than by way of exemplification. And the processes of Sellars's late ontology can be thought of just as extended events, and seem naturally to be picked out by gerunds and present participles. So it seems that either there is a tension in Sellars's nominalism on this point, or I have characterized his nominalization nominalism too broadly. But if that is so, how should we determine which nominalizations of verbs and adjectives are alright, forming genuine singular terms and common nouns, and which are not? The considerations of "Naming and Saying" do not seem to give us adequate guidance here.

I want to close with the observation that, putting aside the slide I have accused Sellars of making from pragmatic to semantic considerations (via an exclusionary expressivism), however well semantic nominalization nominalism *fits with* ontological nominalism, the semantic thesis is not in the right shape to provide an *argument* for the ontological one—as Sellars in effect claims that it is in the passage from NS I quoted above. Even if the semantic claim that transcategorial nominalizations are not genuine (referring) singular terms is accepted, that in no way entails that only what *can* be so referred to exists in the real world. Such an ontological stipulation is at most *compatible* with the semantic commitment. So I do not think that there is an argument from Sellars's metalinguistic pragmatic and semantic nominalization nominalism to his ontological nominalism.

Nor can I see that the scientific naturalism epitomized in Sellars's *scientia mensura* passage—"In the dimension of describing and explaining the world, science is the measure of all things, of what is that it is, and of what is not that it is not"—yields an argument for reistic ontological nominalism.[47] That is, it would not help to restrict what exists in "the world in a narrow sense" to what can be *described*. The descriptive language of science is just as much up for alternative interpretations, nominalistic and otherwise, as ordinary language. If all that is right, then we should see Sellars's commitment to a reistic ontological nominalism of the sort epitomized by Kotarbinski (before his pan-somatist turn) as rock-bottom, not derived from or supported by other commitments. His metalinguistic expressivism about transcategorial nominalizations should be understood as aimed at showing that one *need* not countenance universals and propositions to understand the use of the expressions that ostensibly refer to them.

I conclude that Sellars has introduced and deployed the metalinguistic machinery of dot-quotes, distributive singular terms, and Jumblese to offer a sophisticated account of a distinctive metalinguistic role that transcategorial nominalizations and their associated common nouns play. That account, though, operates primarily at the level of *pragmatics:* as part of a theory of the *use* of these expressions. He has *not* thereby put himself in a position to be entitled to draw nominalistic *semantic* or *ontological* conclusions from the identification of that distinctive expressive role. In the absence of a fuller analysis of this case, we should no more draw that conclusion from Sellars's expressivist analysis of the use of property-terms than we should from his expressivist account of the use of alethic modal vocabulary.

47. *EPM* §41.

Credits

Chapter 2, "The Centrality of Sellars's Two-Ply Account of Observation to the Arguments of *Empiricism and the Philosophy of Mind*," was published as Chapter 12 of my book *Tales of the Mighty Dead: Historical Essays in the Metaphysics of Intentionality* (Cambridge, MA: Harvard University Press, 2002).

Chapter 3, "Pragmatism, Inferentialism, and Modality in Sellars's Arguments against Empiricism," was first published in Willem de Vries (ed.), *Empiricism, Perceptual Knowledge, Normativity, and Realism* (Oxford: Oxford University Press, 2009), pp. 33–62; and is reprinted here with the permission of the publisher.

Chapter 4, "Modality and Normativity: From Hume and Quine to Kant and Sellars," was first published as Chapter 4 of my 2006 John Locke Lectures, *Between Saying and Doing: Towards an Analytic Pragmatism* (Oxford: Oxford University Press, 2008); and is reprinted here with the permission of the publisher.

Index

a priori, 39, 45, 54–55, 143, 150n5, 152, 174–175, 185, 199
ability, 52, 92–93, 99–100, 103, 105, 117, 122, 130, 135, 141, 143, 149, 155–156, 166n18, 172, 206, 238, 264; practice-or-ability, 26, 49, 50–51, 53–55, 93, 155–156, 159–160
absolutism. *See* identity
"Abstract Entities" (AE), ix, 18, 188n21, 208n38, 236, 236n3, 240–248, 250n19, 253–254, 257, 260–261, 271
abstract entity. *See under* entity
abstraction, 111, 216n1, 242, 246, 248–249, 251–252, 264
abstractor, 216n1, 242, 249–250, 268
access, 107, 152; cognitive, 114; privileged, 105, 186
adjective, 238, 241, 244, 251, 255n26, 261, 264, 271; predicate, 217, 239, 252–253, 261–265, 270
agency/agent, 13, 15, 167
Agrippan trilemma, 6
analysis, 5, 28, 29, 53, 56, 66, 83, 93, 108–109, 114, 122–123, 127–128, 138, 147, 160, 219, 240–242, 244–246, 249n17, 250–251, 257, 259–260, 265, 272; and definition, 122; meaning-use, 154–156, 168, 173 (*see also* meaning-use relations); and paraphrase, 122; and reduction, 122; and supervenience, 123; and translation, 122; and truth-making, 123
analytic philosophy, 1, 4–5, 9, 20, 32, 34, 97, 120; core programs of, 122–123
anaphora, 153, 217
application, of concepts, 102–104, 124, 150, 167, 186, 188, 193, 203, 206;

circumstances/consequences of, 41–42, 51, 55, 61, 67, 73–74, 84, 121, 131, 133, 140, 172, 181, 184n14, 191, 216, 227, 234, 246, 253, 270; criteria of, 74, 77–78, 84, 218, 220, 222, 229–230, 246, 253, 263n36, 270
Aristotle, 46–47, 69–70, 201–203, 224, 248
articulation, 13, 38, 45, 54, 63, 69, 74, 78, 83 84, 102, 112, 143, 145, 151, 167, 174–175, 179, 183, 185, 204–205, 210–211, 226, 243, 259, 270; by rules of reasoning, 31, 37; inferential, 42–43, 103–104, 113, 115, 125, 134–135, 144, 148, 153, 169n19, 170–171, 177, 182, 189, 192, 203, 234–235
artifact, 87, 101, 118, 231
assertion/assertibility, 51 52, 64n31, 79n43, 108–110, 136–139, 140n21, 168–172, 182, 207–210, 241, 253, 258, 260, 266; and taking-true, 258–259; force of, 168–172, 187–188, 190. *See also* declarative sentences
atomism: semantic, 7, 23, 37, 40, 148–149, 152; logical, 40n12
authority, 2, 44, 59, 61–63, 84–85, 88, 93, 113, 210
autonomous discursive practice (ADP), 48, 52, 55, 57–58, 94, 124, 126, 148, 157–160, 163, 168–169, 173
autonomy, 21–23, 83–84, 137, 157, 167–168, 233–234; of a language game/stratum of language, 104, 106, 109, 117, 124, 129, 233–234; of discursive practices, 6–7; pragmatic, 124–125, 134, 264; semantic, 7, 124–127, 131, 134, 148–149. *See also* autonomous discursive practice
auxiliary hypothesis. *See* nonmonotonicity

awareness, 104; conceptual, 39, 101, 111; perceptual, 111, 116–117; preconceptual, 101, 111, 115

Bauch, Bruno, 33
Begriffsschrift, 146, 175–177
behaviorism, 16, 60, 132
belief, 6–7, 102, 165, 170; and assertion, 112, 154, 170, 188; background, 106–108, 118, 126; box, 170; and content, 124; noninferential, 6, 104, 148; observational, 101; perceptual, 148; and theory, 213; and update, 165–166
Bergmann, Gustav, 238–239, 255–257, 264, 266, 270
Between Saying and Doing (*BSD*), ix, 13, 49n23, 55, 58n29, 94, 155, 159, 160n15, 166, 179n9, 189, 205n36, 206, 211n40, 215, 263–264, 266
British Idealism, 2, 34

Canberra planners, 80
capacity, 38, 50, 99–101, 103–104, 110–111, 114, 116–118, 120, 125, 157, 160, 177, 191–192, 248, 263–264
Carnap, Rudolf, 2, 4–5, 7, 24, 32–34, 36, 39–40, 43–44, 48–49, 52, 64, 83, 85, 92, 145, 186, 209, 213, 215, 237, 239n7, 240, 244, 246, 250–251, 261–262, 264–267, 269
categories, 2, 4, 24–29, 31, 35–40, 43, 46–48, 50, 52–58, 78, 87–90, 91n57, 94–97, 143, 150n4–5, 174–175, 185, 201–202, 234–235, 237–241, 249–250, 255, 261–263, 264n39, 265. *See also* framework
causation, 13, 37, 46, 84, 115, 121, 132, 143, 151–152, 154, 175–178, 182, 184–187, 194, 203–205, 212. *See also* law
ceteris paribus, 72, 83, 164, 192. *See also* nonmonotonicity
Churchland, Paul, 31
circumstances/consequences of application *See* application.
claimables, 50, 180, 191, 212–213; descriptive, 191; and facts, 195–196, 208. *See also* content
classification, 47, 163, 180, 239, 245, 262; functional, 28, 80, 262, 266; metalinguistic, 47–48, 268. *See also* label
classifying, 100, 141, 240, 242, 245, 259, 263, 265, 268–269; vs. describing, 180, 212 (*see also* labels); ontologically, 39, 237, 240, 244. *See also* predicating
cognition, 31, 39n9, 100–104, 111, 114, 120, 124, 148, 163, 232
Cohen, Hermann, 33
collateral premises. *See* nonmonotonicity
commitment, 2, 7, 14, 124, 152, 158, 167, 169, 171–172, 186–187, 211, 214; assertional, 112–113, 170–171, 190; attributing, 112–113; consequential, 170–171; dispositional, 151; doxastic, 102–103, 165, 190; inferential, 51, 135, 139, 141–142, 151, 161, 163, 181–182, 184n14, 191, 193–194, 206, 214; modal, 26–27, 134, 141, 149, 150n5, 195n26, 199; subjunctive, 68, 193, 206, 211n39, 214, 226–228, 234; undertaking, 103, 107, 112–113, 125, 167, 170, 204; withholding, 107–109, 126, 156
common noun, 237–238, 242–244, 253, 261, 264–265, 271. *See also* sortal
concept application. *See* application
concept, 4, 8, 12, 28, 33, 47, 64n31, 68, 101–102, 106, 118, 121, 140n21, 144, 147, 150–151, 153, 158, 184–186, 204, 208–209, 213, 246, 254, 257, 264; acquisition, 100, 111–113, 117; and content, 6–7, 23, 31, 44–45, 102–103, 120–121, 125, 146, 148, 152, 163, 177, 189, 192, 203, 205–206, 211; framework-explicitating/categorial, 2, 94, 174–175, 235; grasping/understanding, 42–43, 55, 102, 105, 113, 124, 141, 150, 193, 209, 227, 234; metaconceptual/metalinguistic, 8, 24, 31, 34, 37, 39–40, 48, 52–56, 146, 154, 173, 174, 211n39, 215; modal, 4, 24, 26–27, 37–38, 43, 45, 48, 50, 121, 127–128, 143, 147–148. 150n5, 167, 174–179, 188, 205, 214, 227, 234; normative, 4, 24; (non)descriptive, 3,4, 23–24, 35–40, 42–43, 45, 55, 57, 67, 78, 95–96, 133, 141–143, 174–175, 178–179, 181–183, 185–186, 189–190, 192–193, 198, 203, 206, 214, 227; (non)logical, 3, 36, 57, 95, 133, 176, 199, 205; nonpsychological conception of, 203–204; observational use of, 100, 104–105, 114–119, 123–126; ontological, 4, 24, 208n38; pure, 2, 24, 29, 31, 37–40, 45–46, 48, 52, 54, 63, 87, 94, 143, 150n5, 174, 185, 237 (*see also* categories); realism, 77n41, 204; rectifying, 214; thick moral, 119. *See also* application; LX

Index

"Concepts as Involving Laws, and Inconceivable Without Them", 45, 67, 141, 150, 178, 227
conceptual role, 7, 24, 48, 151, 179, 240, 242–243
concept-use, 4, 14, 23, 28, 37–39, 42, 48, 52, 54–55, 104–105, 114, 116, 118–119, 121, 124, 141–143, 150n4, 151, 161–162, 167, 174–175, 178–179, 184n14, 190, 195–198, 203–206, 214, 266
conditional, 51–53, 55, 72, 82, 128, 139, 154, 161, 167, 176–177, 191, 193, 207; fact, 35; counterfactual supporting/robust, 128, 130–131, 166, 193; modally qualified, 160, 182–184, 194; subjunctive/subjunctively robust, 3, 13, 26, 67, 71–73, 75, 77–80, 82–87, 211
consequence, 38, 41–43, 51–52, 55, 67–68, 70–72, 108–109, 115, 133, 154, 162–163, 170–172, 177, 180, 227–228, 232, 234; logical, 201; material, 198, 200–204, 206, 210–212. *See also under* application
content, 6, 21, 23, 37, 40, 42–43, 63, 74, 81–82, 85–86, 94, 102–104, 108, 110, 111, 120, 124, 129, 137–139, 145–146, 151–154, 161, 167, 171–172, 178, 184, 188, 190–191, 200, 205, 210–211, 258, 265, 268–269; conceptual, 6–7, 23, 31, 44–45, 56, 102–104, 121, 125, 146, 148, 150n4, 152, 163, 177, 180–182, 185–186, 189, 192, 199, 203, 205–206, 211 (*see also under* concept); inferentially articulated, 125–126, 170, 177, 234; propositional, 161, 169, 169n19, 211n39, 212
context, 23, 54, 58, 64n31, 65–66, 90, 124, 168, 207, 226, 253–254; classifying, 237, 244; contextual implication, 137n17, 138n18, 139, 187; extensional, 65–66; referentially opaque/transparent, 64; sentential, 64, 65, 232
converse. *See* property
conveying, 139, 154, 188, 237, 255–257
coreference, 62–66. *See also* identity
correspondence, 210–212
count noun. *See* sortal
counterfactual, 78, 130, 133, 142, 145–146, 148, 150, 190, 193–195, 198, 209, 211, 221n8, 228, 230, 239, 241, 244, 269; counterfactual-supporting, 127, 131, 130, 133, 145, 150, 183, 198; counterfactually robust inferences, 128, 131, 141–143, 151, 153, 159–160, 162–163, 166, 192, 205, 208, 211, 227; reasoning, 53, 210, 232. *See also* conditional
"Counterfactuals, Dispositions and the Causal Modalities" (CDCM), ix, 3n2, 23n12, 14, 36n6, 40n13, 57n27, 68n34, 95n60, 132, 134n10, 135n11–13, 136n14–15, 137n16–17, 138n18–19, 140n21, 142n23, 176n4, 178n6–7, 182n12, 184n15, 187–188, 194n25, 236, 246n13
covering law. *See* deductive-nomological model
criterion, 218n2; of adequacy, 29, 60, 77, 121, 127, 136, 144, 228n15; of application, 74, 77–78, 84, 218, 220, 222, 229–230, 246, 253, 263n36, 270; of identity and individuation, 27, 74–79, 83–84, 216–220, 222, 224, 228–231, 246, 252–253, 263n36, 267, 270
critique, 5, 83, 134, 137, 148, 152, 156, 171, 240; of empiricism, 22, 26, 29, 99, 120–124, 148–149, 156
Critique of Pure Reason, 2, 19, 32, 54, 175
cross-sortal identity. *See under* identity

de Saussure, Ferdinand, 179
declarative sentences, 36, 40, 58n29, 64n31, 93, 161, 169, 171–172, 180–181, 207, 252–253, 259, 264n39, 270. *See also* description
declarativism, 207–208, 210
deductive-nomological model, 194. *See also* law
defeasor/defeasibility, 84, 97–98, 164–166, 192–193. *See also* nonmonotonicity
Dennett, Daniel, 86
dependence, 7, 22–23, 48–49, 84, 129, 146, 198, 246, 264; pragmatic, 26, 58; 122, 124–125, 135, 156–157, 232–233, 263–264; sense/reference-dependence, 208–209
deployment, 16, 39, 43, 45, 58, 90, 93, 119, 124, 142, 153, 161–162, 233, 266; of vocabularies, 49–55, 90, 123, 125, 130, 134, 138, 141, 143–144, 152, 155–157, 159–160, 163, 166–168, 172–173, 191, 232
Derrida, Jacques, 179
describing, 4, 28, 35, 38, 41, 45, 68, 94, 97, 132–133, 136, 138, 141–143, 180–181, 183, 186–187, 191, 204, 206–207, 226–227, 234, 238, 264n39; and explaining, 15, 30–31, 40, 54, 57, 68n34, 79, 84, 96, 135, 140n21, 178–180, 194, 213, 246n13, 272

description, 23, 27, 36, 38, 40–42, 45, 56–59, 80, 84–85, 87–88, 94, 130, 134–135, 141–142, 166–167, 174, 178, 194–195, 198, 207, 212, 223; empirical, 2–4, 8, 22–24, 30, 35, 40, 46–47, 54, 80, 83, 94, 96, 143, 181, 210, 234–235; vs. label, 41–43, 68, 181–183, 234; scientific, 15, 80, 83
descriptivism (antidescriptivism), 3, 8, 15, 22, 24, 36, 57, 90, 91n57, 93–97, 133
descriptivist fallacy, 35
determinable, 69, 110, 111n8, 202–203. See also determinateness
determinateness/determinate negation, 68–70, 110, 111n8, 150, 167, 183, 199, 210; Hegelian, 14, 199–204; Spinoza, 199; Tractarian, 202. See also incompatibility
difference, mere vs. exclusive. See under distinctions
discourse/discursive, 3–4, 6, 8, 13–14, 25, 31, 35–36, 39, 46, 52, 54, 57, 88, 91–97, 110, 128, 132, 134–137, 139, 140n21, 146, 149, 163, 165, 172, 188, 206, 211, 213, 241, 256, 258, 265, 269; practice, 5, 13, 38, 48, 52, 55, 57–58, 91–94, 124, 126, 148, 155, 157–158, 160, 163, 168–169, 173
disjunctivism, 41
disposition, 41, 59, 71–73, 101, 107–110, 113, 115–116, 118, 126–127, 131, 133, 142, 145–146, 148, 150, 165n17, 169, 180, 209, 222, 224, 226–233; finkish, 71; manifestation of, 71, 73
dispositionalism, 71
distinctions: asserting/inferring, 168–169, 209; base/target vocabulary, 26, 83–84, 122–127, 130–131, 144; causes/reasons, 135; contingent/necessary identities 76, 223, 226, 229; criteria of application/identity, 74–78, 216–220, 222, 229–230, 253, 263n36; de re/de dicto, 76, 223–224, 226, 230; derivative/fundamental speech act, 171, 259–260; describing/labeling 23, 40–43, 53, 68, 119, 135, 178–183, 191, 212, 234, 246n13; description/evaluation, 207; description/explanation, 2–4, 38, 40, 57–58, 85–86, 135, 141, 178, 182–183, 195; descriptive/prescriptive, 58, 134, 140n21, 167, 187, 243, 248; determinable/determinate, 68–70, 110, 111n8, 202–204; doing/saying, 205–206, 215, 241, 263n36, 267; downstream/upstream,
41, 121, 171–172; empirical-descriptive/subjunctive-dispositional vocabulary, 224–227; endurantism/perdurantism, 225; epistemic tracking/semantic government, 210–214; exclusive/mere difference, 69–70, 200–202; explicitly/implicitly modal properties/concepts, 23, 26–27, 136, 152, 167, 178, 226–227, 229–230, 234; extensional/intensional predicates-properties, 64–65, 147, 176, 232–233; genuine/ostensible singular terms, 267–271; 'look'/'is'-talk, 83, 105–109, 125; meaning/use, 7–8, 23, 35n5, 41, 48–55, 89–94, 105, 122, 125–126, 142, 154–160, 167–173, 181, 189–191, 203, 206, 213, 259, 266n43; pragmatic/semantic/syntactic metavocabulary, 5, 43, 48–49, 58, 91, 189–190, 206, 208, 212, 215, 241, 265; modal expressivism/realism, 27–28, 174, 183, 194–195, 199, 205–215; alethic/causal/conceptual/deontic/logical/metaphysical modality, 5, 14, 35, 121, 132, 151–152, 154, 172–173, 178, 184–185, 198, 203, 211; opacity/transparency, 64, 77, 228n15, 233; pragmatic/semantic nominalization nominalism, 267–272; repeatability/universality, 240, 244–251, 269–270; sense/reference dependence, 208–209; sortally restricted/unrestricted quantification, 217; token/type, 6, 243, 245
distributive singular term (DST), 188, 236, 240, 247–254, 259, 262, 271–272
doing, 97, 134–136, 139–140, 143, 154, 156, 160n15, 173, 182, 188–190, 205, 257–261, 263, 266–267, 270; vs. saying, 205–206, 215, 241, 263n36, 267; metalinguistic, 265
dot-quotes, 80, 188, 236, 240–245, 247–254, 259, 261–262, 264–265, 269–272
Dretske, Fred, 212
DST. See distributive singular term
Dummett, Michael, 4, 10–11, 16, 60, 64n31, 181

elaboration, 26–27, 48, 55, 57–58, 90, 94–95, 122–123, 157, 159–160, 168, 173, 205n36, 231, 264n39; algorithmic, 50–52, 166n18, 169, 172, 248, 264; response substitution, 172. See also LX
elaborated from and explicative of. See LX
embedding, 139, 154, 207. See also Frege-Geach embedding test

Index

emergence/emergentism, 88
empiricism, 3, 5, 8, 16, 19, 23–24, 34, 36, 40n12, 57, 95, 100–101, 103, 111, 123, 132, 134, 142–144, 147–148, 152, 156–157, 179, 213–214; ambitions of, 120, 122, 143; critique of (*see under* critique); and foundationalism, 21–22, 148; instrumentalist, 130–131; logical, 6, 26, 33, 40, 120, 123, 128, 213; and naturalism, 133, 145, 147; phenomenalist, 26, 127–128, 130–131, 156; semantic presuppositions of, 43, 137, 142, 149; species of, 123–126, 133–134; traditional/classical, 34, 40, 99, 121, 128, 146, 151, 213
"Empiricism and the Philosophy of Mind" (EPM), vii, ix, 3, 6–7, 9, 11, 14–22, 24, 26, 30, 32n2, 33, 34, 60, 71, 73, 83, 99, 101, 103n4, 105–106, 113–114, 116, 120–127, 132, 134, 144, 148n3, 185, 236, 264, 272n47
endorsement, 55, 103, 107, 112–113, 115–116, 133, 142, 170–171, 189; of an inference, 72, 136, 140–141, 154, 161–162, 165–166, 182–183, 190–193, 205; of maxims, 167; practical, 138–139, 141; scope of, 110; withholding, 107–110, 126 (*see also under* commitment)
entailment, 102, 137–140, 166, 187, 228–229; physical, 138–139. *See also* consequence
entity, 47, 93, 106, 249; abstract, 14, 24, 27, 29, 46, 59, 238, 242, 244–247, 251–254, 263, 264n39, 268; theoretical, 16, 59, 60–61, 114, 130
entitlement, 2, 16, 102–104, 107, 112, 114, 142, 169, 171–172, 211, 224
environment, 82, 100, 113, 125, 129, 163, 180
epistemic tracking, 210–214
epistemology, 5–8, 21–22, 24, 31, 37–38, 61, 89–90, 95, 101, 106, 109, 120, 133, 145, 147, 149, 167, 184–185, 214
"Epistemology and the New Way of Words", 4n3–4, 7, 95n59
equivalence, 85–86, 130–131, 166, 190–191, 196, 207, 233, 239, 242, 248–250, 252, 257, 264; classes, 64, 200n33, 242–243, 250; relation, 116n1, 242–243, 249–251, 265, 268n45
error, 107–108, 110, 118
evidence, 6, 22–23, 91n43, 93, 102, 111–112, 124–125, 148, 169, 213–214

evidential role, 22–23
exclusive difference. *See under* distinctions
exemplification, 203, 237, 239, 247, 250, 255–258, 260, 264, 269, 271
experience, 7, 15, 21–23, 26, 34, 54, 56, 82–83, 111, 116, 120–121, 123, 127–129, 148–149, 151, 167, 179
explanation, 16–17, 37–38, 40, 45, 60, 67, 85–88, 92–93, 116, 133, 136, 141, 146, 178–179, 182–184, 194–195, 208, 210, 213–214, 230, 251, 254, 257, 259, 262; and description, 2–4, 15, 24, 27, 30–31, 35–36, 40, 42–43, 54, 56–58, 68n34, 79, 84–85, 87–88, 96, 135, 194–195, 213–214, 235, 246n13, 272; order of, 8, 105
explicitation/making explicit, 2, 4, 24, 26–27, 35, 37–38, 43, 45–46, 48, 50, 54–55, 58, 63, 66, 88, 90, 94, 96, 133, 143, 150–152, 158–159, 161, 163, 166–167, 172, 174, 177–178, 181–183, 185, 189, 191, 193–194, 205, 212, 215, 227, 233–234. *See also* LX
expression, 3, 7–8, 27, 36, 40–41, 44–50, 57, 63, 65, 68n34, 91n57, 93–96, 107, 126, 132, 134–135, 138–139, 140n21, 142, 151–152, 160, 178, 186–189, 207, 216–217, 219–220, 223, 239, 241–245, 248, 251, 256, 260–263, 265–266, 268, 271; of belief, 102, 104, 112, 188; nonlogical, 199; metalinguistic, 40, 57n28, 90, 189; modal, 134–136, 140n21, 142, 151, 182, 187, 189; sortal, 217, 237, 246, 251, 267; (quasi-)syntactical, 39, 48, 239n7; token, 243; types/kinds, 240, 242–245, 247, 250–253, 262, 265, 268–269; use of, 5, 7, 21, 23, 93, 119, 153–154, 180, 182, 186, 189, 196n30, 239, 246, 269, 272
expressive role, 2, 26–29, 35–39, 43, 45, 48, 50, 52–54, 57n28, 58n29, 72, 74–75, 88, 94, 96, 134–135, 152, 155, 158, 178, 183, 189–192, 205, 210, 215, 240, 268, 272; exclusionary vs. permissive view of, 268; nondescriptive, 4, 24, 94, 264n39; metalinguistic, 90, 186, 189, 214, 265; pragmatic, 27, 189. *See also* framework
expressivism, 28, 184, 188–189, 215, 236–237, 240, 266, 268, 271–272; modal, 27–28, 56, 174, 183, 186, 190, 194, 199, 205–208, 210, 212–215; metalinguistic, 186, 237, 269, 272; nominalist, 56, 236; pragmatic/pragmatist, 8, 28–29, 97, 190, 215, 241; semantic, 190

extension, 55, 64–66, 68, 128, 137, 145, 146n2, 147, 175–176, 232–233, 252, 258. *See also* distinctions: opacity/transparency
extensionalism, 64–66, 68, 70
externalism, semantic, 153, 185

fact, 16, 35–36, 130, 167, 180, 188, 195–196, 198, 203, 207–214, 233, 238, 255n26, 256–258, 261, 265, 270; conditional, 35; modal, 66, 196, 198–199, 203, 210, 212–213; and norm/normative, 13, 35, 115; perceptible/observable, 100, 133, 149; semantic, 35, 50
fact-stating, 35–36, 93, 207, 210, 212, 214, 258
fallacy: descriptivist, 35; of lost contrast, 71; naturalistic, 264; Platonic, 16, 59
"Fido"-Fido model, 179–180
Fodor, Jerry, 85, 212
force, 140n21, 187; assertoric, 171, 187; modal, 176, 184; Newtonian, 37–38, 67, 150, 174, 208, 226–227; pragmatic, 103, 154, 190
form: and content, 6, 38; logical, 43–44; propositional, 213; syntactic, 237, 252
formal mode/material mode, 64, 237, 239, 251, 261
foundationalism/foundations, 6–8, 21–22, 106, 108–109, 148.
"Foundations of a Metaphysics of Pure Process", 15n8
framework, 44–45, 183, 185, 206; and description/explanation, 2, 35, 45–46, 54, 88, 96, 143, 175, 183, 235, 264n39; framework-explication, 4–5, 35–36, 38, 43, 45, 174, 264n39; of Givenness, 22; metaconceptual, 174; metaphysical, 70; naturalist, 95; of physical objects, 129; of sense contents, 129. *See also* categories; LX
Frege, Gottlob, 33, 64n31, 90, 146n2, 153, 175–181, 183–184, 189–190, 193, 195, 201, 211n39, 216–217, 253–254, 258
Frege-Geach embedding test, 139
function, 24, 28, 38, 58, 65, 78, 80, 85, 96, 121, 129–131, 138, 151, 161, 178–179, 204, 217, 233, 242–243, 250, 259, 263; expressive, 100, 108, 164, 182, 265, 268; functional classification, 28, 47, 80, 262, 266; framework-explicating/categorial/explicative, 4, 25, 54, 57, 96; vs. object, 251–254, 258–259, 264n39; proper, 249n17

functional role, 6–7, 23, 81, 188, 231, 242–243, 259, 265
functionalism, 7, 14, 21, 83–84, 87–88, 121–122, 124–126

Galilei, Galileo, 37
Geach, Peter T., 218–219, 229
generality, 175–177, 184; of inferences, 183–184
generalization, 82, 85–86, 127–131, 133, 137, 145, 162, 194
gerrymandering, 41, 84
Gibbard, Allan, 219, 222–223
given, 6–7, 21–22, 33, 83, 110, 123; givenness, 22, 33, 83, 99. *See also* Myth of the Given
giving and asking for reasons, 100, 102–103, 113, 117–119, 168–169, 171
Goodman, Nelson, 34, 83, 249
grades of involvement, 240, 244, 246, 248, 251–252
"Grammar and Existence: A Preface to Ontology" (GE), ix, 18, 188n21, 208n38, 236–240
Grice, H. Paul, 90
Gupta, Anil, 10, 218n4, 219, 229

Hegel, Georg Wilhelm Friedrich, 29, 31–34, 70n37, 100, 200n32, 203–204; and idealism, 2, 5, 14; and negation/determinateness, 14, 199–204
Heidegger, Martin, 33, 58
Hume, David, 5, 19, 26, 32, 37–38, 40, 43, 97, 120, 128, 130, 132–134, 145, 149, 150n5, 166–167, 173, 184, 213, 227
Humean predicament, 38, 133, 142, 149, 152, 167, 173, 179, 227
hypotheticals, 38n8, 71, 161, 175, 177, 183

idealism, 2, 5, 14, 31, 34, 38, 40, 96, 100, 136n15, 215
identity, 15, 27, 62, 69–70, 74, 78–79, 87–88, 92, 96, 201, 216, 222, 225, 228–229, 231, 232–234, 263; (modal) absolutism, 224, 226–227, 229–231, 234; contingent, 223, 229, 230; and coreference, 62–63, 66; criteria of, 27, 74–77, 78n42, 79, 83–84, 216–220, 222, 224, 228–231, 246, 252–253, 263n36, 267, 270; cross-sortal, 27, 74–80, 98, 219–224, 228–230; *de re* vs. *de dicto*,

223–224, 226, 230, 234; and intersubstitution license, 63, 65; extensionalism about, 68, 70; and indiscernibility, 27, 63–64, 66, 74, 76–77, 80, 221, 223–226, 228–229, 232, 234; and modally insulated properties, 65; necessary, 76; relativity of, 218–219
idiom, 103n6, 106, 148–149, 160n15. *See also* vocabulary
illustrating sign-design principle, 240, 243, 262, 266, 271
image, manifest/scientific, 2, 15, 27, 57–59, 61–62, 70, 77–81, 83–85, 87, 96, 234
immediacy, 15, 39, 106, 111, 114. *See also* given
implication, 42, 45, 68, 128, 136, 182, 234; contextual, 137n17, 138n18, 139, 187; space of, 23, 40, 42, 68n34, 135, 141, 178, 181–182, 191, 234, 246n13. *See also* consequence; entailment; inference
implicit. *See* explicitation
incompatibility, 69, 102, 108–110, 161, 201, 203, 205–206, 214; material, 14, 166, 198, 200–205, 210–212. *See also under* distinctions
incorrigibility, 92–93, 105, 108–110, 117
indiscernability of identicals. *See under* identity
individuation, 69, 85, 88, 98–99, 155, 216, 218, 221, 230, 253, 263; criteria of, 27, 74–79, 83–84, 216, 246, 252–253, 263n36, 267, 270. *See also* criterion; sortal
ineffability, 255–259, 267
inference, 6–7, 16–17, 21, 23, 37, 40, 42–43, 58n29, 59–61, 74, 89, 98, 102–105, 107, 112–116, 118–119, 124–125, 130–131, 135–136, 138–144, 149, 153–154, 157, 161, 168–169, 172, 177–179, 181, 183, 186, 190–191, 193–194, 203, 208–211, 220–221, 224, 257–258, 265–266; and articulation, 42–43, 45, 103, 112, 125, 134–135, 153, 169n19, 170–172, 177, 179, 189, 234; license/ticket, 63, 151, 161, 182; inferential know-how, 113; material/materially good or bad, 43–45, 51–53, 141–142, 160–163, 165–166, 181–182, 191–193, 205, 225; nonmonotonic/defeasible, 72, 162–166, 192–194, 225; propriety of, 138, 190–191; inferential practices, 124; inferential role, 47, 121, 148, 153; rules of, 42–44, 154, 182, 189; semantic vs. pragmatic, 139, 154; subjunctively/counterfactually/modally robust, 45–46, 53, 131, 133, 141–143, 151, 160, 162–163, 177, 183–184, 193, 206, 208, 214, 227; substitution, 63, 65
"Inference and Meaning", 18, 44n15–16, 139, 153, 188n20
inferentialism, 14, 23, 40, 45, 72, 120–122, 124–126, 135–136, 140, 142, 181, 183, 184n14, 190
information, 79n43, 154, 199, 237
innatism, 112
inquiry, 2, 74, 79n43; empirical, 45, 186, 199, 203–204, 213
instrumentalism, 60–61, 130–131; vs. realism, 16, 59–61
intension. *See* extension
intentionality, 2–3, 8, 13, 16, 24, 35, 37, 55, 97, 146, 167, 211, 225, 232
intersubstitution licenses. *See under* identity; substitution
involvement. *See* grades of involvement

James, William, 33
judgment, 7, 37–39, 46–47, 102, 104, 124, 128, 150, 170, 175, 177, 180–181, 186, 204; analytic, 175; and action, 2, 14, 97, 167; empirical, 4, 38–39, 120, 150n4, 151; observational/perceptual, 59, 100, 103–104, 109; terminating/nonterminating, 81–82, 128. *See also* application; assertion; statement
Jumblese, 236, 241, 259–261, 272
justification, 37, 79n43, 115–116, 120, 133, 135–136, 149, 165, 167, 169, 171, 175, 178–179, 181–183; and circularity, 6; demand/responsibility for, 4, 110, 171; justificatory practices, 80; order of, 147; and regress, 6, 21; and space of reasons/normative space, 3, 22, 30, 97. *See also* entitlement; reasons; warrant

Kant, Immanuel, 1–5, 8, 13–15, 17, 19–20, 22–26, 29–35, 37–40, 42–48, 50–52, 54–56, 59, 62–63, 66–67, 78–79, 84–85, 87, 95–97, 103, 132n7, 140, 143, 145, 149–150, 167, 173–175, 178–179, 183–186, 189, 191, 194, 203, 215, 227, 234–235, 237, 260n33, 264n39; and idealism, 2, 31, 215; Kantian phase, 5, 19, 32, 97, 120

Kant-Sellars thesis: modal, 13, 25–27, 57, 67–68, 70, 74, 76–80, 88, 96–98, 143, 148–160, 163, 166, 172, 179, 213, 216, 227–230, 232–234; normative, 13, 26, 166–172
Kaplan, David, 147, 198, 223, 230
Kim, Jaegwon, 86
kind-term, 216, 248, 252–253, 264n39; natural, 248. *See also* sortal
knowing how, 26, 39, 42, 45, 50–51, 55, 102–103, 113, 141–143, 152, 157, 160n15, 172, 175, 179, 185, 191, 238
knowledge, 6, 40n12, 82, 103, 106, 110–111, 116, 124–125, 129, 147, 170, 174n1, 177, 186, 199, 204, 211, 232; characterizing an episode as, 3, 22, 30, 31; empirical, 4, 22, 33–34, 37, 40n12, 100–101, 109, 120; foundations of, 106; and normativity, 22; observational, 101, 103, 116; theoretical/inferential, 114
Kotarbiński, Tadeusz, 267, 270, 272
Kripke, Saul, 9–10, 19, 76, 147, 152, 184, 198–199, 203, 223, 226

label, 119, 180, 200n33, 246; vs. description, 23, 40–43, 53, 68, 135, 178–183, 191, 204, 212, 234, 246n13; predicate, 180. *See also* classification
language, 40, 43–44, 48–49, 58–59, 62, 77n41, 78, 81–83, 86–87, 89, 104, 124–125, 135, 138n18, 141, 145, 186, 192, 198, 203, 208, 221n7, 237–239, 241, 250, 257–260, 272; dependence, 209; empirically meaningful, 4, 7, 95n59, 96; extensional, 233; formal/artificial vs. natural, 65, 186, 213, 217, 231, 234; game, 52, 57, 103–106, 109, 117, 124, 126, 129, 148, 233; language-entry, 103, 112, 120, 243; language-exit, 243; language-language move, 103, 112, 243; learning a, 112; object, 140n21, 186–188, 237; and modals/norms, 3, 153–154, 173; perspicuous, 39, 259; philosophy/theory of, 4–5, 8–10, 36, 179; quantificational, 145; relativity, 241–245; resources of, 40, 43, 68n34, 135, 178, 194, 214; of thought, 23; transcendence, 208; use, 4, 7–8, 48, 58, 89–90, 93, 125, 129, 152, 154, 168, 186, 214, 241, 259, 266. *See also* metalanguage; metavocabulary; vocabulary
"Language, Rules, and Behavior", 46n17, 152n7, 182n10

law, 38, 45, 78, 85, 88, 130, 133, 138, 143, 145, 148–150, 162, 183, 194, 207–210, 213–214; lawful connections/relations/regularities, 37, 45, 174, 178, 185n16, 227; court, 72, 98, 192; of nature, 3, 132, 147, 153, 184–186, 195–196, 198, 203–204; statement/expression of, 37, 123, 132, 141–143, 167, 175
Leibniz's Law, 63, 80, 221n7, 224, 226–230, 233
Lewis, C. I., 2, 32–34, 81, 83, 128
Lewis, David, 9–10, 14, 17, 71n40, 77, 80, 147, 198, 225, 230
linguistic rationalism. *See* rationalism
logic, 5, 34, 43–44, 55, 72, 121–123, 128, 132, 134, 138, 146–147, 151–152, 163, 175–178, 184, 191–192, 198, 201, 203, 257
'looks': talk, 83, 100, 105–110, 125–126; vs. 'is', 83, 105–109, 125; generic, 110, 117
LX (*el*aborated from and e*x*plicative of), 27, 52–55, 58, 90, 94–95, 150n5, 159–160, 168, 173, 205n36, 264n39

Macbeth, Danielle, 146n2, 175n2
Making It Explicit, 64n31, 153, 226n12
manifest image. *See* image, scientific image
mass, 37–38, 45, 60, 66, 68–69, 143, 150, 174, 195, 201, 207, 209, 216n1, 226–227, 232, 234
mass noun, 216n1
master-idea, 24, 35, 39, 96, 99, 116, 121
material constitution, 74, 228–229, 231
material mode, 237, 239, 251, 261. *See also* formal mode/material mode
materialism, eliminative, 92
mathematics, 15, 33, 92, 118, 133, 138, 150, 163, 192, 196, 212
McDowell, John, 19, 22, 31, 34, 100n1, 118n10, 153
meaning, 7, 14, 16, 37, 49–50, 60, 102, 115, 122, 149, 181, 185–186, 195–196, 206, 213, 217, 237, 243, 257, 258n31; and analyticity, 6–7, 21; claims, 80; and inference, 148, 258; meaningful, 4, 7, 22, 89–91; and normativity, 22, 31; and practice/use, 92, 122, 126, 206, 213, 266; and rules, 43–45; theories of, 181
meaning-use analysis, 154, 156, 168, 173
meaning-use diagram (MUD), 49, 51, 53, 58n29, 155–160, 168
meaning-use relation (MUR), 155–160, 163, 168; PP-necessity, 156–159, 263–264;

PP-sufficiency, 51, 53, 158–160, 166n18, 168–169, 264; PV-necessity, 158–160, 168–169; PV-sufficiency, 49–51, 53, 155–160, 168–169; VP-sufficiency, 49–50, 53–54, 155–156, 158–160, 168; VV-relation, 155, 158; VV-necessity, 157
mediation, 200, 203
Mellor, Huw, 71
mereology, 78, 217, 230–231, 249–250
metalanguage, 39, 48, 66, 91n57, 140n21, 186, 237, 261; pragmatic, 8, 48, 89, 262, 266; semantic, 48, 147, 217, 262, 265–266; syntactic, 48, 265. *See also* metavocabulary
metalinguistic concepts/vocabulary, 2, 4–5, 39, 89–90, 140n21, 189, 197, 244, 249, 266; broadly, 24–26, 36, 39, 57–58, 188–189, 241; covertly, 36, 40, 43, 48–49, 237, 239, 251, 253–254, 261; and modality, 14, 29, 33, 43, 45, 57n28, 186–188, 191, 214, 237, 239, 266; and ontology, 8, 27, 29, 33, 47, 188–189, 208n38, 215, 236, 238–242, 244–247, 249–254, 257, 260, 262–272; and pragmatics, 29, 96–97, 265
metaphysics, 27–28, 35, 69–72, 77, 81, 92–93, 95, 109, 113, 132n7, 152, 215–216, 266; analytic, 97, 199; Humean, 97; metaphysical necessity, 152, 184, 198, 203; reconstructive, 230
metavocabulary: pragmatic, 5, 8, 49–50, 54, 91, 93–95, 97, 154–156, 189–190, 206, 208, 210–212, 215, 241, 261n35, 266n42; semantic, 58, 91, 147, 189–190, 206, 208, 210–212, 215, 241; (quasi)syntactic, 39, 43, 189. *See also* metalanguage
methodology, 4, 6, 16–17, 23, 59–61, 85, 109, 114, 122, 144, 268
Millikan, Ruth, 31, 249n17
modal expressivism. *See under* expressivism
modal identity absolutism. *See under* identity
Modal Kant-Sellars Thesis. *See under* Kant-Sellars thesis
modal operators, 65, 176–177, 183–184, 226
modal realism. *See under* realism
modal revolution, 145, 147, 152, 198
modal robustness, 127, 131, 133, 177, 198, 203. *See also under* conditional; counterfactual; inference
modality, 4–5, 10, 15, 18, 24, 26, 33, 37, 43, 46, 65–66, 70, 77, 88, 91n57, 106, 120–123, 127–128, 131–154, 157–161, 163, 166–168, 173–179, 181–199, 203–208, 210–216, 223–227, 229, 237–239, 241, 264n39, 265–267, 272; alethic, 3, 8, 13–14, 24, 26–29, 37–38, 40, 45, 48–49, 53, 55–57, 64, 94, 130, 132–133, 143, 145–146, 152, 154, 174–175, 179, 185, 189–190, 193, 199, 211, 215, 234, 236; causal, 121, 132, 178, 184, 187, 203; conceptual, 203; implicit/explicit, 23, 166, 226–227, 229–230; logical, 121, 132, 178, 203; metaphysical, 203; normative/deontological, 121, 132, 151, 178; physical, 184; modal property, 74–76. *See also under* expressivism; identity; realism
modally insulated/involved, 65–68, 70, 73–77, 225, 227, 228n14, 234
model-theoretic semantics, 65, 230
Montague, Richard Merritt, 147, 198
Moore, George E., 1, 34
move, 102–103, 113, 117, 167, 169–171; inferential, 112, 125; language-entry, 6, 103, 112; language-language, 103, 112
Mr. C (for Constant Conjunction), 137
Mr. E (for Entailment), 137–138, 142n23
Myth of Jones, 60–61
Myth of the Given, 5, 33, 111

name, 113, 180, 237, 241–242, 244, 246, 252, 255–257, 260–262, 267, 270; and bearer/named, 179–180, 259–260, 267; and nominalism, 246, 251; proper, 152, 223, 230; property-name, 246, 250–251; and reference, 221–223; surname, 218, 229
naming, 222, 241, 246, 252–255, 259, 261, 263, 264n39, 265
"Naming and Saying" (NS), ix, 18, 188n21, 236, 240–241, 254–259, 263, 269n46, 270–272
Natorp, Paul, 33
naturalism, 25, 31, 59, 62, 78, 88–89, 101, 123, 133, 145, 147, 234; Carnapian vs. Wittgensteinian, 92; expressive, 87; functionalist, 83; (non)descriptivist, 90, 93, 95; philosophical, 25; pragmatic, 87, 90–96; object vs. subject, 91–97; scientific, 2, 15, 24–25, 27, 31–32, 61–62, 79–81, 83–85, 87–88, 96–97, 133, 213, 272; semantic, 91, 93
Naturalism and Ontology, 6
necessitation, 46, 151, 175–177, 182, 185–186, 204. *See also* law

necessity, 33, 45, 65, 91n57, 119, 128, 132–134, 136–139, 141–145, 148–149, 150n4–5, 152–154, 161, 163, 169n19, 174–176, 182–184, 190, 193, 195, 199, 203, 211, 226, 257; causal, 154, 185; chemical, 198; conceptual, 152–153, 184–185; necessary condition/necessary for, 53, 67–68, 72–73, 75, 100–101, 126, 150, 169, 174n1, 202, 208, 227–228, 232, 233n16; and framework, 2, 35–36, 38, 43, 88; and Hume, 145, 167, 184; and identity, 76, 223; and Kant, 167, 184; logical, 184, 198; metaphysical, 152, 184, 198; natural, 176–178; rational, 176–177; practical, 167; and practices, 52–54, 58, 160n15, 168, 172. *See also* modality; rule; law

negation, 14, 161, 199–200, 203. *See also* incompatibility

neo-Kantianism, 2, 5, 31–34, 40, 62, 97

Neurath, Otto, 85, 123, 145n1

Newton, Isaac, 37, 59, 67, 150, 174, 196, 208, 226

Nexus, 256

Noether, Emmy, 196

nominalism, 14, 18, 24–25, 28–29, 46–47, 97, 179–181, 237–238, 240–242, 245–246, 248, 251–252, 256, 258–259, 266–269, 271–272; deflationary, 242, 246, 260; and expressivism, 27, 57, 208n38, 236, 268; Goodmanian, 249; half-hearted, 239, 245; and instrumentalism, 59; mereological, 249; metalinguistic, 27, 215, 238–242, 245–247, 249–252, 261–263; ontological/metaphysical, 241, 246, 266, 267n44, 270–272; Sellarsian, 250, 259, 271; semantic, 241, 246, 267n44, 270; Tractarian, 257. *See also* grades of involvement; nominalism; nominalization

nominalization nominalism, 267–272

nominalization, 238–239, 251–256, 258–261, 263–267, 270; by abstraction, 251, 264; of common nouns, 248, 251–252; by forming DSTs, 251, 262, 265; predicate-, 252–253, 261–263; sentence-, 252, 263n36, 270; sorts/kinds of, 248, 251–252, 254; transcategorial, 268–272. *See also* illustrating sign-design principle; nominalism; nominalization

nonmonotonicity, 72–73, 75, 77, 98, 163–166, 192, 225

Normative Kant-Sellars Thesis. *See under* Kant-Sellars thesis

normativity, 13, 15, 41, 79n43, 89–90, 91n57, 97, 103, 145, 167, 170–171, 211–213, 243, 248; and alethic modality, 14, 211; and authority, 62; normative concept, 5, 24, 167; normative fact, 35, 115; and practice, 13; and space of reasons/implications/justification, 3, 22–23, 31, 97; normative status, 2, 113, 169, 171–172, 212; normative vocabulary, 3–4, 8, 13, 16, 25–26, 28, 55, 58, 90, 94, 101n3, 115, 123, 146, 149, 154, 157, 159–160, 166–169, 172–173, 189, 210, 212, 215, 264n39. *See also under* Kant-Sellars thesis; vocabulary

norms, 186, 190–191, 213, 243, 249, 269; inferential, 116; social, 78; transposed language of, 153–154, 158, 173

"nothing-but-ism", 132, 143

noumena/phenomena distinction, 2, 15, 25, 30–32, 56, 59, 62, 78–81, 84–85, 87, 96–97, 215, 234

object, 35–36, 39–40, 47, 56, 68n34, 82–83, 93, 135, 144, 178, 181, 212, 217, 224–226, 230, 246, 253, 258, 265, 268; abstract, 92, 97, 147, 250, 254; Aristotelian conception of, 69–70, 202–204; vs. function, 251, 253–254, 265n39; and identity, 62–63, 70, 74–75, 77, 231–232; and incompatibility/difference, 14, 68–69, 201–202; mereological, 230–231; naturalism, 91–93, 95, 97; observable/empirical, 59–60, 114–115, 117–118, 128, 130; physical, 81, 83–84, 92, 129; and property, 27, 69–70, 91, 201–202, 209, 265; theoretical, 59–60, 114–115, 118; Tractarian conception of, 70, 255n26, 256. *See also* property

objectivity, 13–14, 23, 26, 38, 83, 91, 96, 123, 125–128, 130, 139, 144, 152, 195, 198–199, 202, 204–211

observability, 37, 59–61, 70, 73–74, 118–119, 123, 125, 130, 133, 149; and dispositional property, 73; methodological vs. ontological, 16, 60, 114–115. *See also* observation; theoretical entities

observation, 33, 42, 60, 73, 99–101, 103, 108–109, 114–119, 124–125, 130, 148, 157–158, 165n17; observational capacity, 99, 110, 114, 116; report, 58n29, 59, 104, 107, 113,

Index

115–118, 120, 124, 180–181; observationally used/observational vocabulary/term/concept, 16, 26, 53, 61, 100, 104–105, 114, 116–118, 123–126, 130–131, 149, 151, 163, 167, 213. *See also* observability
Ockham, William, 47
one-in-many, 246, 249–252, 269–271
ontological (in)egalitarianism, 61
ontology, 28–29, 31, 46, 59, 61–63, 70, 79, 92, 95, 105, 114, 147, 231, 236, 239, 241, 244, 246, 253, 256, 261, 263, 267n44, 269–272; ontological concepts/categories, 5, 24, 201, 208n38, 237–238, 240, 249, 255; of pure processes, 15, 79; ontological status, 16, 33, 60–61, 114; ontological vocabulary, 4, 8, 28, 35, 37, 39, 48, 53, 55–58, 188–189, 215, 237, 240–241, 250, 262, 264n39, 265
ordinary empirical descriptive (OED) vocabulary/concepts; 24, 26, 36–40, 43, 45, 51–55, 57, 66, 83–84, 90, 94–96, 143, 149, 167, 173–175, 178–179, 183, 189, 191–192, 194, 199, 205–207, 210, 212–214, 226–228, 230, 232, 264n39. *See also under* vocabulary
opacity. *See under* distinctions
organism, 72, 100–101
ought-to-be/ought-to-do, 210

parrot, 101–102, 112, 117, 125, 170
particulars, 35, 69, 110, 111n8, 147, 237, 245, 249, 251–253, 255–256, 259–260, 263n36, 267–268, 270–271
passenger, 75–76, 85, 218–221, 223, 229
perception, 7, 12, 40, 46, 68n34, 70n37, 82, 100, 102–104, 109, 116–117, 120, 123, 129, 135, 148, 170, 209
phenomena/noumena. *See* noumena/phenomena distinction
phenomenalism, 26, 81, 83–84, 96, 123, 125–132, 156
"Phenomenalism", 18, 23, 26, 81–83, 87, 127–129, 132, 134, 143–144
"Philosophy and the Scientific Image of Man", 18, 23, 57n26
physical, 81–84, 86, 92, 101, 129–130, 138–139, 164, 175–176, 184–185, 196, 217, 225, 238
physics/physicist, 70, 78, 85–87, 91–94, 115–116, 145, 164, 176, 184, 192, 195–197, 208, 230

picturing, 13, 15, 256
Platonic fallacy, 16, 59
Platonism, 244n11, 257
Pope, Alexander, 147
possibility, 6, 69, 86, 132–133, 143, 147–150, 152–153, 161, 163, 166, 174, 184–185, 190, 193, 196n30, 198–199, 203–204, 211–212, 226; of description/explanation, 2, 4, 8, 24, 35–38, 43, 45–46, 54, 96, 174–175, 235, 264n39; of knowledge, 33; possible situations, 68. *See also* modality
possible world, 65–66, 70, 147, 198–199, 209, 224, 227, 230–232, 234; semantics, 14, 65–66, 198–199
PP-necessity. *See under* meaning-use relation
PP-sufficiency. *See under* meaning-use relation
practice, 14, 92–93, 103, 105–106, 124, 126, 147, 216; and abilities, 26, 49–54, 93, 122, 155–160, 168, 206; and assertion, 168–169, 171; of describing and explaining, 36; discursive, 5, 13, 36, 38, 48, 52, 55, 57–58, 91–94, 124, 126, 148, 155, 157—158, 160, 163, 168–169, 173; of giving and asking of reasons, 168–169, 171–172; inferential, 124; justificatory, 80; of using (a certain) vocabulary/words, 49, 92, 108–110, 143, 206, 218n2. *See also* autonomous discursive practice, LX
practices-or-abilities, 49–51, 53–54, 93, 155–157, 159–160. *See also under* practice
pragmatically mediated. *See* meaning-use relations
pragmatics, 7, 93, 246; and expressivism, 241; pure, 7–8, 49, 89–90, 93–97; and semantics, 26, 241, 263, 272
pragmatism, 1, 5–10, 17, 21, 105, 109, 120, 122, 124–127, 131, 134–136, 140, 142, 144, 156, 173, 241
predicate, 39, 64–65, 81, 86, 88, 180, 216, 226, 232, 234, 238–240, 250, 252–254, 255n26, 259–265, 269–270; complex, 64n31; descriptive/ordinary, 51, 67, 71–72, 78, 86, 106, 181, 228; (non)extensional/modally insulated, 64–66, 68, 71, 77, 232–234; modal/subjunctive/dispositional, 64, 228n14–15; monadic, 237, 239, 245; sortal, 27, 74, 81, 216, 245

predicating, 241, 253–254, 259–260, 266; derivative pragmatic role of, 260–261, 263; and naming, 263; and saying, 266–267
premises, 6, 21, 59, 72, 102–104, 113, 116, 124, 137n17, 141, 142n23, 148, 161–165, 168, 169n19, 172, 176, 181, 192, 193n24, 194, 234. *See also* reasons
Price, Huw, 90–91, 197
property, 28, 49, 53, 70, 86, 119, 143, 150, 198, 208n38, 237, 239, 248–249; and disposition/dispositional, 71–73; determinate, 68–69, 200–203, 212; and identity, 27, 63–65, 69–70, 74–75, 77. 80, 221–225, 228–229, 234; and incompatibility, 14, 68–69, 200–203, 206; intensional/extensional, 64–65, 68; intrinsic, 77; monadic, 69n36, 201n34; modally involved, 68, 70, 74–76, 225; modally insulated, 65–66, 70, 73–74, 76–77, 227, 234; matter-of-factual, 249; mongrel categorical-hypothetical, 71; natural, 77; and nominalism, 47, 56, 239–242, 244–246, 250–252, 261–266, 269, 272; (non)modal, 27, 70, 74–76, 223–224, 226, 229, 234; and object, 23, 27, 70, 91, 127, 201–202; and ontological-categorizing vocabulary, 4, 8, 24, 35, 39, 188, 237–242, 264n39; phenomenal, 81, 105n7, 111n8; quantification over, 221; response-dependent, 209; semantic, 48; subjunctive/dispositional, 79–80, 209, 222, 224, 226, 228–231; theoretical, 16, 70
propositional attitude ascription, 207, 226n12
psychological entity, 60. *See also* theoretical entities
psychologism, 89–90
pure concepts (of the Understanding). *See* categories
Pure Pragmatics and Possible Worlds: The Early Essays of Wilfrid Sellars (*PPPW*), 4n3–4, 44n15–16, 46n17, 88n51, 95n59, 139n20, 141n21, 150n4, 151n7, 153n12, 154n13, 182n10, 188n20
pure pragmatics. *See under* pragmatics
Putnam, Hilary, 86
PV-sufficiency. *See under* meaning-use relation

quality, 46–47, 56, 238, 244n11, 245, 247, 254; perceptual, 46, 82, 109, 110, 129; primary, 123, 131, 144; secondary, 123, 126, 131–132
quantification, 81, 145, 175–176, 183, 193–194, 208, 217, 248
Quine, Willard Van Orman, 1, 5–7, 10, 16, 19, 21, 26, 34, 45, 64–66, 85, 130, 132–134, 145–149, 152–153, 179, 186, 213, 216, 232–233
quotation, 80, 188, 236, 240, 241–244, 248, 250–252, 258–259, 262, 271–272. *See also* dot-quotes

Ramsification, 80–81, 83–84, 87, 231
rationalism, 44, 100, 103–104, 111–112, 117, 132n7, 137, 139–140, 144, 187; linguistic, 171
Rawls, John, 2, 32
RDRD. *See* reliable differential responsive disposition
realism, 5, 38, 257; about theoretical entities, 60–61, 114n9; about universals, 28; conceptual, 77n41, 204; scientific, 16, 56, 59–61, 114n9; modal/MR, 27–28, 77n41, 174, 194–199, 202, 204–208, 210, 212, 214–215, 237, 241
"Realism and the New Way of Words" (RNWW), ix, 4n3, 88n51, 89, 90n54, 98n61
realizer, best/closest. *See* Ramsification
reasoning, 53, 72, 97, 135–136, 137n17, 142n23, 176, 210, 232; informal/formal, 72, 164; practical, 167; role in, 23, 103–104, 121, 124, 126, 151, 179; and rules, 37, 40, 137; theoretical, 166
reasons, 3, 31, 135–136; giving/providing/having, 6, 22–23, 97, 100, 102–103, 113, 117–119, 168–169, 171–172; inferential, 116; serving as/standing in need of, 102–103, 124, 135, 169, 171, 181; space of, 3, 22, 30, 103, 125. *See also* evidence, inference
Redding, Paul, 34n4
reference, 27–28, 47, 49, 59–66, 77, 79–80, 87, 92–93, 96–97, 186, 188–189, 220–222, 228n15, 232–234, 241–242, 244–247, 249–254, 258, 260, 262–263, 265, 267–270, 272
reference-dependence, 209. *See also* sense-dependence
referring, act of, 241, 245, 258–261, 263n36, 266–268
regress, 6, 21; Bradleyan, 255–256

regularity, 127–130, 145, 213; accidental/contingent, 162, 176; counterfactual-supporting, 130; matter-of-factual, 132, 167; lawlike, 176. *See also* law
reification, 106, 262
reliable differential responsive disposition (RDRD), 59, 73, 101, 103, 107, 112–113, 115–119, 126, 165n17, 180
repeatable, 111n8, 240, 244–245, 251, 262, 263n36. *See also* universals
report, 6, 93, 102, 108–110, 121, 126, 148–149, 165n17, 238; of appearance/seeming, 105–106, 110, 117; empirical, 26, 109; and disposition, 73; noninferential, 59, 99, 104, 107, 114–116, 123–124, 148, 163; observational, 58n29, 59, 101, 104, 107, 113, 115–120, 180–181
representation, 5–7, 13, 15, 21, 39, 56, 91–92, 106, 180, 256
response substitution. *See under* elaboration
responsibility, 2, 97, 109–110, 112–113, 165, 167, 170–171, 210
responsiveness, 42, 73, 100–102, 104, 107–112, 116, 141, 165n17, 191, 204, 212. *See also* reliable differential responsive disposition
Rickert, Heinrich, 33
rigid designator, 152, 223, 230
robustness. *See* conditional; counterfactual; inference; modal robustness
role, 7, 21, 38, 44, 80, 87, 120, 168, 172, 183, 229, 238, 248–249, 260, 269, 272; causal, 84; conceptual, 24, 48, 240, 242–243; descriptive, 27, 35, 57n28; evidential, 23; explanatory, 86, 230; expressive, 2–5, 24, 26–29, 35–39, 43, 45, 48, 50, 52–54, 58n29, 72, 74–75, 88, 90, 91n57, 94, 96, 134–135, 152, 155, 158, 178, 183, 186, 189–192, 205, 210, 214–215, 240, 264n39, 265, 268, 272; and framework-explication, 45; functional, 6–7, 23, 81, 109, 188, 231, 243, 259, 265; inferential, 47, 115, 121, 148, 153; normative, 22; observational, 126; in reasoning (*see under* reasoning)
Rorty, Richard, 3n1, 4, 6, 9–10, 17, 21, 25, 30–32, 56–57, 92, 97
Rosenberg, Jay, 31
Royce, Josiah, 5, 33
rule, 13, 52, 129, 133, 143, 149, 151, 167, 169–170, 176–177, 181, 186; inferential/for reasoning, 37, 40, 43–46, 137, 145, 182, 189; and law, 38; L-rules/P-rules, 40, 43–44; material/formal, 43–45; transformation, 44; of use/deployment, 39, 41, 43, 46, 55, 151–152, 154, 182, 186. *See also* law
Russell, Bertrand, 1, 34, 145, 146n2, 175, 253
Ryle, Gilbert, 16, 18, 60, 151, 161, 163, 166, 182–183, 193–194

sapience, 101, 124
saying, 154, 172, 190, 205, 215, 245, 253–261, 263–265, 268, 270–271; and conveying/contextually implying, 139, 154, 187–188; and doing, 50, 54, 122, 125–126, 136, 139–142, 155–156, 160n15, 173, 190, 206, 241, 159, 265–267, 270–271; and 'looks', 108. *See also* assertion/assertibility; metalinguistic concepts/vocabulary
Schlick, Moritz, 33, 145n1
science, 2, 15, 17, 25, 30–31, 33, 56–59, 61–63, 70, 72, 78–79, 87–89, 91, 93–96, 114n9, 133, 138, 145, 150, 164, 184, 192, 195, 198, 203, 205, 272; unity of, 85–86
Science and Metaphysics: Variations on Kantian Themes, 1, 19, 32, 56
Science, Perception, and Reality, 3n1, 18, 30n1, 103n6
scientia mensura, 15, 27, 31–32, 57–59, 61–62, 79–80, 84–85, 88, 91, 95–96, 234, 272
scientific image, 15, 27, 57–59, 61–62, 70, 77, 79–81, 83–84, 234–235
scientism, 95, 143
scorekeeping, 169, 172
Sellarians, left/right-wing, 25, 31, 56–57, 59, 94, 97
semantic government, 210–214
semantics, 7, 13, 16–17, 24, 31, 35, 41, 48, 58–61, 89, 93, 121–124, 127, 131, 133, 137, 143–149, 151–152, 167, 179–180, 185, 197–199, 205, 210–211, 213–218, 241, 244, 246, 256, 260, 263, 267–269, 272; semantic atomism, 7, 23, 37, 40, 42–43, 148–149, 152; semantic autonomy, 7, 124–127, 134, 148–149; semantic externalism, 153, 185; extensional/intensional, 66, 147, 232–233; semantic foundationalism, 22; semantic functionalism, 121, 124–126; semantic holism, 7–8; semantic inferentialism, 14, 23, 40, 45, 72, 120, 124–126, 184n14; model-theoretic, 10, 65;

semantics *(continued)*
   and possible worlds, 14, 65–66; and pragmatics, 8, 13, 26, 48–54, 58, 91, 131, 139, 153–154, 156–160, 173, 190, 232–233, 259–260, 262, 264–268, 270–272; semantic presupposition, 37–38, 149, 157–158; pure, 90, 95n59; representational, 91–92; semantic skepticism, 132–133, 184; semantic (meta)vocabulary, 3, 35, 37, 55, 101n3, 146, 189–190, 206, 208, 210, 212, 215, 217, 241
sensa, 15, 25
sense content, 81–82, 110, 129
sense impressions, 60, 114, 117, 121
sense-dependence, 208–209
sentience, 101, 117–118
Shannon, Claude, 199
sign-design, 13, 89, 168, 189, 250n19. *See also* illustrating sign-design principle
singular term, 64n31, 238, 242, 246–247, 249, 251, 253, 259–261, 263, 265, 268; distributive (*see* distributive singular term); genuine/ostensible, 267–272; and identity, 74, 246; and metalanguage, 39, 93, 241, 252; and object/particular/entity, 36, 245, 249–250, 252, 263 264n39; and universals, 49
skepticism, 35, 65, 124, 132; and Hume, 37–38, 128, 130, 184
"Some Reflections on Language Games", 18, 103
sortal, 47, 81, 86, 231, 237–240, 242–243, 245–246, 251–253, 270; and criteria of identity and individuation, 27, 74–77, 79, 83, 216, 218–219, 222, 228, 230, 267; and identity, 27, 74–80, 98, 216, 218–224, 228–231, 233–234; and manifest-image, 78, 84–85, 87; phase, 75, 85 218, 223; prosortal, 217; pseudosortal, 217, 219, 230
space of implications/reasons, 3, 22–23, 30, 40, 42, 68n34, 97, 103, 125, 135, 141, 178, 181, 191, 234, 246n13
speech-act, 171–172, 190; derivative, 259–260
Spinoza, Baruch, 199
Stalnaker, Robert, 147, 198
statement, 35, 134, 136n15, 138–140, 164, 174, 239, 248–249, 256–258, 260; hypothetical, 161, 183; and identity, 219; 'looks', 110; metalinguistic, 244, 251, 261–262; modal, 37, 132, 138–143, 185, 187

statue (and lump of clay), 74, 222–223, 228–229, 231
status, 4, 43, 45, 62, 116, 124, 145, 148, 174; categorial, 26, 57, 60, 88, 175, 234; normative, 2, 113, 169, 171–172, 212; ontological, 16, 33, 60–61, 114; social, 113
Strawson, Peter, 2, 23n3
subjunctively robust consequences, 38, 55, 67, 211. *See also under* conditional; counterfactual; inference; modal robustness
substitution, 64n31, 81, 107, 118, 153, 226, 231; intersubstitution license, 63–66, 74–75, 77, 228n15; response substitution, 172
sum, mereological, 78, 217, 230–231, 249–250. *See also* mereology
summa genera, 46–47
supervenience, 66, 88, 123, 199
syntax, 7, 39, 43, 48, 53, 89–90, 189, 237, 239, 251, 260–261, 265. *See also* pragmatics

Tarski, Alfred, 48, 186, 215, 241, 258, 265
tautology, 3, 36, 57, 95, 133
term, singular. *See* singular term
theoretical entities, 16, 59–61, 114, 130. *See also* entity
theory-ladenness, 104, 119
tie shop, 107, 116, 118, 126
time-slice, 75, 85
token, 6, 23, 104, 163, 243, 245
"Towards a Theory of the Categories" (TTC), ix, 24, 40n12, 46, 47n20–22
Tractatus Logico-Philosophicus, 17, 61, 70, 179, 201–202, 255, 257–258, 266, 270
transcategorial, 268–272
translation, 83, 122, 128, 130, 140n21, 239, 241, 244, 261n35, 262, 269
transparency. *See under* distinctions
transposed language of norms. *See under* norms
truth, 7, 71–72, 79n43, 143, 150, 209, 221, 223, 226, 230, 234, 248; truth-conditions, 128, 265; logical, 134; truth-maker, 91, 123, "relation" of, 257; truth-talk, 257–258; truth-value, 248
two-ply (two-factor/two-pronged/two-legged) account, 99–101, 103–105, 107, 109–110, 113–114, 132
type, 256; belief-, 6; expression-, 242–245, 247, 250–253, 262, 265, 268–269

understanding, 14, 39–40, 42, 44, 54, 68n34, 135, 163, 170, 178, 194, 232, 233n16, 238, 246n13, 247; and concept, 102, 124, 167, 193, 209

unity of apperception, 14

universals, 4, 14, 24, 27–28, 33, 35, 48–49, 56, 69, 97, 111n8, 188, 215, 237–241, 244–247, 249, 251, 255, 259–260, 262, 264n39, 265, 269–272; problem of; 240, 245–246, 260, 262, 267n44. *See also* one-in-many, nominalism

unobservables, 16, 61, 115

update (problem), 160, 165–266

use. *See* concept-use; deployment; distinctions; expression; language; meaning; meaning-use analysis; meaning-use relation; rule; vocabulary

van Fraassen, Baas, 16

Vienna Circle, 133, 145n1, 255

vocabulary, 35–36, 54, 56, 73, 85, 126, 172, 196n30, 208; arithmetic/mathematical, 92, 212; autonomous, 157, 167–168, 234, 264n39; base, 26, 83, 122–127, 130–131, 134, 137, 144–145, 206, 231; behavioral, 16, 60; conditional, 161, 193; culinary, 52, 151; (non)descriptive/empirical, 4, 24, 26–28, 36–37, 39–40, 43, 45, 48, 52–55, 58, 61–62, 66, 77, 79–81, 83–85, 87–88, 90, 91n57, 93–96, 134–136, 138, 141, 143–144, 152–153, 157–160, 163, 167, 173, 179, 183, 189, 191–192, 194, 199, 204–207, 210, 212–214, 224, 226–228, 230, 232, 264n39; dispositional, 142, 224, 228, 230, 233; epistemic, 3; index, 52; indexical/demonstrative, 55, 153; intentional, 3, 8, 16, 35, 55; (non)logical, 55, 123, 128, 146–147, 163, 176–177, 191, 198; mental, 16, 60; metalinguistic/metavocabulary, 4, 5, 8, 39, 43, 48–51, 54, 58, 91, 93–95, 97, 147, 154–156, 189–190, 206, 208, 210–212, 215, 241, 261n35, 266; modal, 3, 8, 13, 14, 26–28, 35, 40, 43, 48–49, 53, 55, 57–58, 64, 66, 91n57, 94, 122–123, 128, 130, 132–137, 139–143, 145–154, 157–161, 163, 166, 173, 178–179, 182–184, 186–191, 193–194, 196–198, 205–206, 210–215, 226, 234, 264n39, 265, 272; naturalistic, 91, 101; nautical, 52, 151, 196; normative/deontic, 3–4, 8, 13, 16, 25–26, 28, 55, 58, 90, 91n57, 94, 101n3, 115, 123, 146, 149, 154, 157, 159–160, 166–169, 172–173, 189, 215, 264n39; objective, 125, 127–128, 130; observational, 16, 123–125, 131, 151, 163, 167; ontological/metaphysical, 48, 53, 215, 237; ontologically categorizing, 4, 8, 28, 35, 37, 55–58, 188, 215, 237–238, 240–241, 250, 262, 264n39, 265; ordinary empirical descriptive (OED) (*see* ordinary empirical descriptive vocabulary/concepts); phenomenal(ist), 82–83, 123, 125, 127–129; physical, 196; primary quality, 131, 144; probabilistic, 123, 149; relations between, 48, 50–53, 122, 140n21, 155–156, 160, 168, 189, 215, 232; scientific, 78–81, 84, 86–87, 94–95, 234; secondary quality, 131; semantic, 3, 35, 55, 101n3, 146; target, 26, 83–84, 91–92, 122–123, 130–131, 144, 231; theological, 52; theoretical, 16, 61, 123, 130–131, 144, 149, 165n17; use/deployment of, 4, 126, 135, 142, 144, 154, 156–158, 163, 166, 168, 182, 189, 213, 232–233. *See also* discourse; idiom; language; LX

VP-sufficiency: *See* meaning-use relations

VV-necessity: *See* meaning-use relations

VV-relation: *See* meaning-use relations

warrant, 79n34, 171. *See also* evidence; justification; reasons

what is said vs. what is contextually implied. *See under* context; implication; saying

Wilson, Mark, 78n42, 86, 192n22

Wittgenstein, Ludwig, 16, 36, 60, 89, 92–93, 195, 256; hinge proposition, 36n7; late-Wittgensteinian, 5, 36, 258; *On Certainty*, 36n7; *Philosophical Investigations*, 179, 196n28; pragmatism, 5, 97. *See also Tractatus Logico-Philosophicus*

world, 13, 15, 47, 88, 136n15, 185, 203, 255–258, 269–272; and concept-users/humans, 196, 209–210; and describing, 3–4, 15, 30, 35–36, 38, 45, 57–58, 91, 95, 133–134, 140n21, 142, 186–187, 198–199, 205–206, 237, 264n39, 272; empirical, 100; of everyday experience, 56; lifeworld, 2, 58, 84; furniture of the, 92; nonlinguistic, 179; objective, 13, 38, 91, 96, 199, 202, 204, 206, 209–210; phenomenal/noumenal, 56, 87; possible (*see* possible world); story, 13; Tractarian, 202; world-theory, 84

www.ingramcontent.com/pod-product-compliance
Lightning Source LLC
Chambersburg PA
CBHW021829090426
42811CB00032B/2092/J